Landscape into Cityscape

Frederick Law Olmsted's Plans for a
Greater New York City

Frederick Law Olmsted (1822–1903), about 1860. (From *Forty Years of Landscape Architecture*, Vol. II: *Central Park, 1853–1895*, ed. Frederick Law Olmsted, Jr., and Theodora Kimball [New York, 1928]; courtesy of Stephen P. Gill and G. P. Putnam's Sons.)

Landscape into Cityscape

›››-›››-›››‹‹‹-‹‹‹-‹‹‹‹

FREDERICK LAW OLMSTED'S
PLANS FOR
A GREATER NEW YORK CITY

›››-›››-›››‹‹‹-‹‹‹-‹‹‹‹

Edited with an introductory essay
and notes by ALBERT FEIN

VNR VAN NOSTRAND REINHOLD COMPANY
NEW YORK   CINCINNATI   TORONTO   LONDON   MELBOURNE

First published in paperback in 1981
Copyright © 1967, 1981 by Albert Fein
Library of Congress Catalog Card Number
81-50480
ISBN 0-442-22539-3

Van Nostrand Reinhold Company
135 West 50th Street, New York, NY 10020

Van Nostrand Reinhold Ltd.
1410 Birchmount Road, Scarborough, Ontario
M1P 2E7

Van Nostrand Reinhold Australia Pty. Ltd.
17 Queen Street, Mitcham, Victoria 3132

Van Nostrand Reinhold Company Ltd.
Molly Millars Lane, Wokingham, Berkshire,
England RG11 2PY

Cloth edition published 1968 by
Cornell University Press

1 3 5 7 9 11 13 15 16 19 12 10 8 6 4 2

"The Olmstead Renaissance: A Search for
National Purpose" reprinted in *The Art of the
Olmsted Landscape*, The New York City
Landmarks Preservation Commission, 1981

CONTENTS

CONTENTS

Preface to the Paperback Edition:
THE OLMSTED RENAISSANCE:
A SEARCH FOR NATIONAL PURPOSE

Anyone concerned with recent American history may well ask why there has been such a continuous growth of interest in the life and work of Frederick Law Olmsted (1822–1903) over the past three decades. Since the 1950s he has emerged from relative obscurity to national prominence.[1] Once known best to historians of the antebellum South as a reporter of that region and to practitioners of land planning and design as the cofounder, with Calvert Vaux (1824–1895), of the profession of landscape architecture, he is now recognized as a major historical figure who was concerned with the emergence of a modern American society.

A reasonable explanation for this recognition has been the discovery that Olmsted's varied contributions as theorist, planner, designer, and administrator are relevant to the needs of the nation today. To a post-World War II generation that witnessed public programs of highway construction and urban renewal injurious to cities and to the larger landscape, he represented an alternative — albeit minority — tradition of governmental intervention. Increasingly, his planning is seen as providing recreational facilities essential for a democratic society, conservative of communities, and protective of natural resources. To those groups concerned with historic preservation there has come a new perception of the significance of his work as a public planner. As a result, Olmsted's career can be fairly compared in national importance with those of the three presidents whose contributions to public planning intersected with his own: Thomas Jefferson (1743–1826), Abraham Lincoln (1809–1865), and Theodore Roosevelt (1858–1919).

There are significant links between Olmsted's contribution to planning and the principles of stewardship advocated by Jefferson, Lincoln, and Roosevelt. All three defended the proposition that governmental intervention was necessary to protect social democracy.[2] During the pre–Civil War period, when Olmsted was establishing an international reputation as a critic of the antebellum South, he turned to Jefferson as a source for successful democratic planning. Olmsted's three massive volumes on that region, published between 1856 and 1860 and collectively known as *The Cotton Kingdom*, reveal a careful study of Jefferson's life and work—particularly *Notes on the State of Virginia*—with respect to such matters as social values, methodology, and evidence. He incorporated Jefferson's conclusions into his own explanation of the relative social and economic decline of the South since the founding days of the Republic. Just as a leading Southern politician was compelled in his defense of slavery to reject Jefferson's democratic principle that "all men are born free and equal," Olmsted believed that the region's decline was owing to a departure "from the principles of Democracy and the old Democratic party" once espoused by Jefferson.[3]

While he never completely rejected the Jeffersonian notion held by the South that " 'the best government . . . governs the least,' "[4] Olmsted came increasingly to believe in the need for greater governmental intervention in a complex urbanizing society. A truly civilized existence was impossible without a minimum amount of large-scale planning. He understood democracy to mean something more than the free marketplace of goods and ideas.

The central mission of America was social justice, created by "a democratic condition of society as well as of government." In the Jeffersonian tradition, Olmsted remained "convinced that the average progress in happiness and wealth, which has been made by the people of each State [in America], is in almost exact ratio to the degree in which the democratic principle has been radically carried out in their constitution, laws, and customs." For Olmsted, "The Great [American] Experiment" was meant to be "a form of government in which all men are declared to be equal; in which there are no privileged orders; no ruling class; in which the laboring class is dignified by being made, equally with the capitalist and the professional scholar, the recipient of governmental power."[5]

Olmsted's renaissance in the 1950s is related to the extent to which he adapted a Jeffersonian rural-born ideology to the requirements of the modern American city. Just as Jefferson believed in the need for public education in a rural America, so Olmsted stressed the importance of public recreation in an urban America. Americans who in the post-World War II period increasingly became absorbed in leisure-time activities were able to understand Olmsted's position that recreational facilities were not a luxury but a necessity. His own generation had developed a still useful reform consensus regarding the importance of play. They would not "derogate . . . from the dignity of work. . . . [One would] by a fixed law of nature . . . [let it] pass into play. This is its proper honor and joy."[6]

Recreation was understood to be a natural antidote to the nervous exhaustion of the nineteenth century, produced by the intensity of commerce and industry. Open spaces furthered recuperation by providing for *active and passive recreation;* as such, the creation of public parks was the response of a civilized government to the fundamental phenomenon of urbanization. As Olmsted explained, "civilization can only advance . . . by processes which admit of a division of life into two parts, one given to some service of general commerce—it may be that of a banker, lawyer, a carpenter or a cabman—the other occupied in such a manner as will relieve the effort of the . . . strains and restraints of the first."[7]

Olmsted and his partner Calvert Vaux were outspoken champions of passive recreation. Public parks afforded immediate release of tension through free, easily accessible, and safe spaces for walking, running, rowing, ice skating, and bicycling. More, spaces were also needed to provide the feeling that came with "being" in a different but attractive environment, one that permitted "the unbending of the faculties." And this was possible only when the imagination was occupied with "objects and reflections of a quite different character from those . . . associated with their bent condition. . . . what is found by townspeople in a park."[8]

The rediscovery of Olmsted is directly related to our appreciation of the public park's remarkable adaptability to varied patterns of recreational use. The history of Prospect Park—designed by Olmsted and Vaux in 1865–1866 for the then independent City of Brooklyn—like that of other open spaces, reflects its changing uses: picnicking in the Woods; croquet and tennis on the Long Meadow; rowboating, ice skating, miniature-yacht sailing on the large lake; swan boating on a smaller pond; carousel riding near the children's playground; bicycling on its drives and paths.

Olmsted and Vaux were also aware—as a result of their experience with Central Park—of the huge public demand for active sports. Although their original design for the Kings County Parade Ground—a separated but integral part of the plan for Prospect Park—sought to provide a space for military reviews, it was soon modified to allow for active types of recreation such as baseball and cricket. By 1874 the Parade Ground had become "the most desirable ground for field sports of all kinds at present open to the youth of either Brooklyn or New York."[9]

As the automobile became central to later American society, Olmsted and Vaux's comprehensive plan for Prospect Park was altered. What is surprising, however, is that the advance of modern technology did not completely obliterate the park's recreational purpose. When in 1926 traffic became heavy and the accident rate high, cars were routed one-way, easing the problem and permitting the park to fulfill the original intention of its designers. This system is still in use and directs traffic counterclockwise.[10]

By 1942, on warm, pleasant Sundays—when parks were most frequented—it was not unusual, according to one estimate, to have 80,000 automobiles on Prospect Park's drives, threatening pedestrians with noise and pollution and bicyclists with bodily harm. In 1936 several neighborhood bicyclists petitioned the city for some restricted bike paths in Prospect Park, claiming that the streets and drives had become dangerous. In 1973, at the height of the environmental movement, the city in response to citizen pressure closed most of the drives of Central and Prospect parks to automobiles during the summer months, restricting them to bicyclists, joggers, rollerskaters, and pedestrians.[11] The public park continued to offer safe recreation areas while at the same time encouraging an alternate means of transportation—the bicycle.

By the 1960s public parks had become testing grounds of the nation's capacity to maintain a democratic and harmonious urban society. Industry and a large white middle-class moved out of cities; the newcomers were the rural poor of the South, who were most often black. Historic urban parks could have become—like Detroit's Belle Isle in 1943, for which Olmsted provided a plan in 1882—battlegrounds of racial unrest. They did not, even in the riot-ridden decade of the sixties. The parks reflected all kinds of urban problems and tensions, but they were not the scene of major unrest. Nor were they abandoned. While victimized as much by lack of maintenance as by wanton acts of vandalism, historic urban parks have survived far better than much of the elaborate domestic architecture that once lined our cities' most fashionable avenues.[12]

There are many reasons for the survival of historic parks. They surely benefitted from the civil rights laws of the 1960s, which caused the reduction of racial tensions. Cities also received additional funding from new federal programs. It is reasonable to believe, too, that historic parks have survived because Americans of all races and ethnic backgrounds came to recognize their intrinsic importance in community life. During the proceedings for landmark designation of Eastern Parkway in Brooklyn — an Olmsted and Vaux plan still serving as a major local amenity — representatives of both black and white groups in the neighborhood supported the proposal. But the explanation of the social significance of Central Park recently offered by a columnist of the *New York Times* is equally applicable to other Olmsted parks across the country: "Thus this grand oasis . . . is, as it was at its 19th-century inception, an experiment in democracy. It has become one of the few settings where this experiment — not in quest of pluralistic perfection but of existing together in respect — any longer takes place."[13]

It is noteworthy that in pursuit of this goal Olmsted is one of the few 19th-century American planners with whom blacks and whites can identify. His reputation as a critic of slavery and as an abolitionist gave him credibility among black Americans. The noted black activist Malcolm X wrote that "books like the one by Frederick Olmstead [sic] opened my eyes to the horrors suffered when the slave was landed in the United States." It is apparent from simply visiting Olmsted's parks that they have become very important to black people living in older cities. The now classic *Report of the National Advisory Commission on Civil Disorders* emphasized the need for recreational facilities as a means of reducing urban tensions.[14]

For residents who remained and for the small but significant number of mostly white people who returned to live in the older sections of cities, Olmsted parks became more important than ever before. Many of the neighborhoods rehabilitated in the last two decades are anchored by older open spaces often planned by Olmsted in conjunction with Calvert Vaux or with his two sons, who joined him in the practice of landscape architecture. This is notably true in New York City, where neighborhoods surrounding Central, Prospect, and Fort Greene parks continue to be revitalized, as do those around Delaware Park in Buffalo and those near much of the Boston park system.

For Olmsted, public parks were designed to attract precisely this type of middle-class population. They were meant to become social magnets for stable, tax-paying, civic-minded property-owners. His open spaces were planned to strengthen family life for all social classes by offering recreational activities as alternatives to alcoholism, gambling, and prostitution. Opposing nineteenth-century laws prohibiting the sale of alcoholic beverages, Olmsted wrote that "amputation of a vicious habit does not remove vice from the system. Little good will be done . . . if the food of health is not provided." This view that public planning of recreational activities has an important social therapeutic dimension is captured in books such as Edward Higbee, *The Squeeze: Cities Without Space* (1960).[15]

Parks, in addition to providing alternative recreational activities, allowed for expressions of communal celebration basic to a civilized society. Throughout their history they have accommodated gatherings on holidays such as Arbor Day and Memorial Day, as well as musical and theatrical events. Increasingly, on a year-round basis, they have become extraordinary theaters of diversity and pleasure. At their optimum, these places reflect precisely those spontaneous releases of energy and civic participation Olmsted understood to be fundamental to urbane, democratic life.

Planning for communal purposes was neither inexpensive nor simple. It was costly even by today's standards, involving large capital outlay and meticulous social, technical, and administrative effort. However, there was among the social leadership of mid-19th-century America a near unanimity of opinion that governmental intervention in park planning was more than a social necessity; it was a moral imperative in a nation becoming increasingly secular in belief and cosmopolitan in population.[16] For them, the common good depended in part on the creation of common lands. As their spokesman, Olmsted wrote:

> Consider that the New York [Central] Park and the Brooklyn [Prospect] Park are the only places in those associated cities where, in this eighteen hundred and seventieth year after Christ, you will find a body of Christians coming together, all classes largely represented, with a common purpose, not at all intellectual, competitive with none, disposing to jealousy and spiritual pride toward none, each individual adding by his mere presence to the greater pleasure of all others, all helping to the greater happiness of each. You may thus often see vast numbers of persons brought closely together, poor and rich, young and old, Jew and Gentile.[17]

Olmsted's emergence as a significant national figure in the 1960s did not stem simply from his role as a theoretician, planner, and designer of urban open spaces. He was recognized as a pioneer in supporting the introduction of drainage and sewer systems in treating polluted land. Just as environmental legislation of the 1960s and 70s was based on the public's justifiable fear of the consequences of pollution, nineteenth-century park legislation was motivated by a pervasive concern with epidemic diseases (such as cholera) that periodically threatened urban centers. These frightful occurrences were believed to be caused by environmental contamination, for which principal antidotes were natural elements such as sunlight, fresh air, trees, and the installation of drainage and sewer systems. Olmsted was noted for his success in transforming unsanitary land areas, viewed as breeding places for pestilential diseases, in New York City and Boston into health restoring places — Central Park and the Back Bay Fens.[18]

His planning provided an alternative to pernicious land development in theories and practices relevant to the modern environmental condition. Olmsted stressed common-sense concepts as the separation of noxious land uses from residential districts; a comprehensive survey of an area's natural resources *before* deciding upon the best location for residences, highways, open spaces; and a transportation system linking city and suburb.[19]

Of particular timeliness were Olmsted's observations on suburbanization. He had a modern understanding of the critical importance of suburbs in the American landscape. To Olmsted, suburbanization required careful planning lest the process destroy the urban basis that nurtured it. Olmsted's theory of suburban growth as part of metropolitan development was best set forth in his classic address before the American Social Science Association in 1870, in his plan for the development of a campus community in Berkeley, California, and in the design of Riverside, Illinois.[20]

The generation of the 1960s understood how much Olmsted's planning relied on the contributions of others representing interrelated environmental disciplines. In many respects his most significant role was in coordinating the work of skilled professionals. This perception grew as historians showed increased interest in such topics as public health, social work, art, and architecture. As studies on these subjects were published, several of Olmsted's closest associates were being discovered. These included Dr. Elisha Harris, a founder of public-health theory and practice, who served with Olmsted during the Civil War as a member of the United States Sanitary Commission. Olmsted was Executive Secretary of this multipurpose medical planning and service agency during its formative period (1861–63). In 1870 Harris, Olmsted, and the noted American architect Henry Hobson Richardson coauthored a monumental planning report for Staten Island. Another associate, George Waring, Jr., a pioneer of modern sanitary engineering as well as the founder of a modern system of sanitary services, was the agricultural engineer for Central Park. Charles Loring Brace, a close friend from childhood, was a founder of the Children's Aid Society, which provided much-needed social services for children. Many of the Society's buildings were designed by Calvert Vaux. The social significance of Olmsted's design efforts has been redefined as part of American art history, as has his contribution to the architecture of his close friend, H. H. Richardson.[21]

There was a consistent effort in all of Olmsted's work to accept the given site and to modify it only minimally. A fundamental principle of the profession of landscape architecture became the attainment of a natural aesthetic. "If men design and work harmoniously with nature," Olmsted wrote, "the results will have the charm of nature." Soil, rock, and climate had to be respected. During the 1960s this idea was given prominence by two American landscape architects: Phillip Lewis, Jr., of the University of Wisconsin and Ian McHarg of the University of Pennsylvania, whose book *Design with Nature* (1969) articulated this concept for a new generation of land planners and designers.[22]

The search for a natural aesthetic, however, did not mean that Olmsted viewed his work only in "American" terms. Aware that the forces reshaping the American landscape were affecting every industrial nation, he studied parks in England and on the continent. His investigations disclosed a worldwide and diverse park movement in Austria, Belgium, France, Germany, Italy, Poland, Portugal, Russia, Spain, and, of course, England. He believed that much could be learned from each nation's particular approach to park design and management, and he made visits to gather detailed information on these subjects.[23]

The same conscientiousness that he brought to his study of parks and park-related problems is evident in his use of plant materials. When confronted in 1886 with the challenge of planning a campus for Leland Stanford in California's warm and arid climate, he realized that the introduction of materials used in the East and of the support systems that sustained them would be useless, so he sought information and models in the Mediterranean countries of southern Europe.[24]

Despite his scientific approach to horticulture, there was some criticism of his use of foreign plant material, and in 1888 he was compelled to defend his approach against an editorial that appeared in *Garden and Forest*, a magazine he had founded that year with the noted dendrologist Charles Sprague Sargent. The editorial criticized the introduction of "foreign" plants in Brooklyn's Prospect Park. The criticism was not based on functional or even stylistic grounds; rather, it was cultural, approximating in social attitudes the negative feelings being displayed by nativist groups organizing against "new" immigrants. The editorial argued:

> It is not that their [imported] flowers are too showy or conspicuous for such positions. The flowers of some native shrubs like the Elder, the flowering Dogwood, and the Viburnums are as showy as those of any garden shrubs. The reason is rather that we have become accustomed to see certain plants adapted by nature to fill certain positions in combination with certain other plants in a given region; and that all attempts to force nature, so to speak, by bringing in alien elements from remote continents and climates, must inevitably produce inharmonious results.[25]

Olmsted's response was clear and emphatic. He wrote:

> The large majority of foreign trees that have been introduced with us during the last fifty years, and which have promised well for a time, have been found unable to permanently endure the alternate extremes of our climate, but that there are many perfectly suited with it we have abundant evidence. Does the White Willow flourish better or grow older or larger in any of the meadows of its native land than in ours? Was it not under this tree that the most American of our poets sang of the family of trees, "Surely there are times when they consent to own me of their kin, and condescend to me and call me cousin," forgetting that, if so, it was the case of "a certain condescension of foreigners"? . . . But on this point of the adaptability of many foreign trees to flourish in American climes, only think of Peaches, Pears and Apples.[26]

Ecological integrity was central to Olmsted's plans.

By the 1960s Olmsted's contribution to a tradition of conservation also could be better understood. Although much more remains to be known about this aspect of his career, it is evident that his support for governmental intervention to preserve Yosemite Valley in California, the land around Niagara Falls, and the forests of the Adirondacks in New York State, as well as his forestry planning for George Vanderbilt's private estate, Biltmore, in Asheville, North Carolina, was done out of concern for natural-resource planning on a regional scale.[27]

Olmsted first visited Yosemite in 1863, when he moved to California after resigning as Executive Secretary of the United States Sanitary Commission. An active participant in the Civil War, he came to know and admire Lincoln for his dedication to saving the Union as well as for the emancipation of the slaves. He respected Lincoln's willingness to use governmental power to further a Jeffersonian concept of democracy by protecting resources like Yosemite for the general public. Lincoln had signed into law on June 30, 1864, the legislation designating the California site as a public preserve for all future generations. "At that moment," one authority has written, "the national parks were born."[28]

A year later Olmsted authored the official report "The Yosemite Valley and the Mariposa Big Trees," noting that without such intervention the area surely would have become "the monopoly by privileged classes," as scenic sites tended to become among "the aristocracy of Europe." For the same reason, Olmsted declared, that "rivers should be guarded against private appropriation . . . , portions of natural scenery [had to] be guarded and cared for by government." The rationale for conservation included "the value of the district in its present condition as a museum of natural science and the danger, indeed the certainty, that without care many of the species of plants now flourishing upon it will be lost and many interesting objects . . . defaced or obscured if not destroyed." Yosemite, Olmsted noted, "yet remains to be considered as a field of study for science and art."[29]

In 1866 Olmsted prepared a general plan for "the national agricultural colleges" meant to be a guide to the development of land-grant colleges established on federal land set aside under the Morrill Act signed by Lincoln in 1862. A Jeffersonian principle underlay the report: a democratic government, Olmsted wrote in defense of public higher education, must ensure that a maximum number of its citizens "reads similar books, wears similar clothing, has similar amusements, and dwells in a similar house, with similar furniture" to that possessed by the more privileged.[30]

It would be naive to believe that Olmsted's point of view ever was fully adopted. While his principles of planning were effected in selected campuses, urban parks, some regional forest preserves, and the national park system, these were not the primary places where Americans lived and worked. His completed projects were benchmarks of quality, but they were not characteristic of the larger development of the American landscape. A fundamental problem was that as the complexities of modern industrial life grew, the power and effectiveness of government to intervene diminished. The last third of Olmsted's life was marked by the rise nationally of a belief, translated into governmental policy, in laissez-faire economics and its cultural equivalent, Social Darwinism — the "survival of the fittest." In the struggle for private profit the public sector had few protectors.

Olmsted's was a lonely voice in the 1870s, warning the nation of its most conspicuous failure—the planning and management of the American city. He wrote:

Let what the country needs of the government of its great cities be compared at intervals of five years with what it finds them able to perform, and on the whole the gap will always be found ominously wider. If we must continue to let it widen, the occurrence of a grand catastrophe is plainly only a question of time. And it will be a catastrophe not merely for the republic but for civilization; for our great cities stretch their hands to all the world, and all the peoples of the world are provided through them.[31]

It was not until the beginning of the 20th century, as part of the Progressive Movement in politics, that a president—Theodore Roosevelt—sought to effectively control in the public interest the large-scale economic forces that were transforming an agrarian society into an industrial-urban nation. Roosevelt's efforts to shape such a governmental structure reflected Olmsted's work during the second half of the 19th century. Born and educated in New York City, Roosevelt was a member of a social class of older American families that regularly supported Olmsted's varied efforts to maintain Central Park, preserve Niagara Falls as an international public site, and protect the Adirondacks. Roosevelt's father had been a dedicated supporter of Charles Loring Brace's Children's Aid Society. In 1882, as a young assemblyman from New York City, Roosevelt read Olmsted's pamphlet *Spoils of the Park*, which treated in grim detail the political obstacles to the management of Central Park and—implicitly—to the planning needed by the nation's most important city. Referring to the administration of New York City's Department of Parks—typical of many urban agencies—Olmsted wrote: " 'This disorganized body has been masquerading before the public, a headless trunk, without policy, without order, without self-defined purpose.' "[32]

Roosevelt's response to the pamphlet embodied a set of attitudes toward government that later would characterize his governorship of New York State and his stewardship of the nation. He offered to promote more effective leadership by appointing a Board of Commissioners dedicated to the public welfare who were also familiar with the needs of park management and planning. As governor, Roosevelt, like Olmsted, actively supported the preservation of the Palisades from commercial development; as President, he was the first occupant of that office to champion the national conservation of forests, minerals, and water power, and to enlarge the national parks.[33]

Although Olmsted never held elective office and functioned for most of the post—Civil War period as a private practitioner, he espoused positions similar to those of Roosevelt, particularly the use of the powers of the presidency to curb selfish private interests.[34] Both men spoke and acted out of a perception of national need. As it happened, the full impact of the failure to provide effective national planning would not be felt until the 1960s. When during this critical decade there developed almost simultaneously national reform movements concerned with civil rights, urban needs, and environmental quality, Olmsted was recognized as one of the few Americans—perhaps the only one—whose career addressed all three issues in ways meaningful to the second half of the 20th century. What gives Olmsted's renaissance a special dimension is that so many

xvii

of his original creations, although badly in need of maintenance and repair, were still mostly intact and vital to the communities surrounding them. They continued to provide millions of Americans and visitors with an emotional release analogous to experiences with music, art, or architecture. In the rediscovery of these places Olmsted's name was quickly identified and spread by those involved with historic preservation.

Although historic preservation has been concerned with structures more than with spaces, the 1960s saw the founding in New York City, where Olmsted began his public work, of the Friends of Central and Prospect Parks. These were the first of many such organizations throughout the United States, recently formed into the National Association of Olmsted Parks. In response to popular demand from park groups, organizations such as the American Society of Landscape Architects, and many individuals, Congress authorized the National Park Service to purchase the office and home Olmsted established in 1883 at 99 Warren Street in Brookline, Massachusetts, as an historic site, thus honoring the man and his work. Governmental ownership and management protects *in situ* the invaluable collection of visual documents housed there, making possible the continued preservation, restoration, and adaptive uses of many historic landscapes.

About the same time that the Friends of Central and Prospect Parks was being formed, the City of New York under the leadership of Mayor John V. Lindsay and Parks Commissioner Thomas Hoving supported the establishment of a new administrative position for these parks—curator—thereby recognizing the special needs of these historic areas. The position has been continued and expanded under the title "administrator." It also should be noted that John Lindsay was recognized as a national spokesman for a much-troubled urban America concerned with the root causes of civic unrest. He served as co-chairman of the National Advisory Commision on Civil Disorders. In this climate of opinion the public park was perceived more clearly as an integral part of the whole urban fabric as it originally was designed.

The creation of the position of park curator/administrator institutionalized the application of history in ways that could only enhance Olmsted's reputation. It is appropriate that this should have occurred, since Olmsted was deeply interested in the role of history in the shaping of society.[35] Each of his parks was the embodiment of natural history; the care given to planning a site was mandated by an awareness that design always meant intervening with the accumulated physical development of thousands of years of growth. Also, some of his parks were planned to memorialize specific historic events: the "Battle Pass" in Prospect Park was the site of an important engagement during the American Revolution; a monument in Brooklyn's Fort Greene Park holds the remains of American prisoners of war who died on prison ships during the Revolution.[36]

In his publications—books, articles, and reports—Olmsted paid careful attention to setting his work within an historic context. He consistently noted that his planning was a response to needs brought on by industrialization and urbanization. Describing his design as "modern,"

Olmsted traced its sources to the theories and accomplishments of those who preceded him—notably the English school of landscape design and his American predecessor, the landscape theorist and designer Andrew Jackson Downing.[37]

While history *does not* repeat itself, similar needs or types of causes can lead to similar events. The growth of "Friends" of Olmsted parks, and the introduction of unified management of some of his parks, resembles developments of more than a century ago. The movement that led to the creation of public parks in the nineteenth century, as with the development of many other reforms, originated outside the political process and reflected a broad range of professional and popular concerns. A similar cross-section of interest is evident in support for his parks today.

Olmsted also understood that preservation depended upon public opinion. He helped found the magazine *Garden and Forest* to further such an understanding. The "Friends" of his parks today, for identical reasons, sponsor tours, lectures, and publications. A hopeful note for the future is the fact that in Central Park and Prospect Park another 19th-century social invention has been reconstituted to educate the public— Park Rangers. These young men and women parallel Olmsted's "Park Keepers" and function as educators as well as supervisors of park land. In addition, Prospect Park and other parks house environmental centers offering school children lessons on scientific and aesthetic subjects.

The creation of the position of park curator/administrator is another example of similar needs leading to parallel solutions. The park was designed as a set of interrelated systems dependent upon a unified administration to oversee all aspects of maintenance and use. It is sometimes forgotten that Olmsted was better known during the early years of his career as an administrator than as a designer or planner. His selection as Executive Secretary of the United States Sanitary Commission during the early years of the Civil War was a result of his success in directing the construction of Central Park in an efficient, nonpolitical way. He and Calvert Vaux served as Superintendents of Prospect Park from 1866 to 1873. Neither Central Park nor Prospect Park could have been completed or adequately maintained during its early period without such a unity of management. It is now more fully understood that they cannot be maintained or restored without similar coordination.

Olmsted's renaissance, therefore, derives from the continuing relevance of his work and the ideas on which his efforts were based. In this sense, the public park may be understood as a paradigm for a nation concerned with the future of its highly complex, postindustrial, and metropolitan civilization. The open spaces Olmsted planned and designed in cooperation with others represent a high standard of governmental intervention in response to needs that were and are simultaneously social, environmental, cultural, and administrative. As such, he has gained, during a period of American history when such integrated planning is again perceived as critical, a permanency comparable to that of the three presidents whose careers touched his own. He—like Jefferson, Lincoln, and Roosevelt—is remembered for espousing a strong democratic government responsive to civilized needs.

FOOTNOTES

1. The most complete bibliography of books and articles concerning Frederick Law Olmsted and his work is found in Elizabeth Stevenson, *Park Maker: A Life of Frederick Law Olmsted* (New York, 1977), pp. 457–61; more than fifty percent of the items listed have been published since 1950. For a sense of this scholarly movement, see Victor A. Kramer and Dana F. White, "Introduction: Yankee Visitor," in White and Kramer, eds., *Olmsted South: Old South Critic/New South Planner* (Westport, Conn., 1979), pp. xxxi–xxxvi.

2. For a moving and synoptic view of Olmsted's meaning of democracy, see Laura W. Roper, *FLO: A Biography of Frederick Law Olmsted* (Baltimore, 1973), pp. xiii–xv; for an analysis of Olmsted's meaning of democracy, see Albert Fein, *Frederick Law Olmsted and the American Environmental Tradition* (New York, 1972), *passim;* for specific references to Olmsted's view of governmental responsibility, see Frederick Law Olmsted to Charles L. Brace and Charles L. Elliott, 1 Dec. 1853, Olmsted Papers, Manuscript Division, Library of Congress, hereafter cited as Olmsted Papers; Frederick Law Olmsted, *A Journey in the Back Country in the Winter of 1853–54* (New York, 1907 [1860]), II, 219–220; Frederick Law Olmsted, *A Journey in the Seaboard Slave States, with Remarks on Their Economy* (New York, 1856), p. 214. This principle of governmental responsibility runs through each of his major planning reports, contained in two anthologies: Albert Fein, ed., *Landscape into Cityscape: Frederick Law Olmsted's Plans for a Greater New York City* (New York, 1981); S. B. Sutton, ed., *Civilizing American Cities: A Selection of Frederick Law Olmsted's Writings on City Landscapes* (Cambridge, Mass., 1971).

3. Olmsted, *Seaboard Slave States*, pp. 165–215, 257–70, 489, 492; Olmsted, *Back Country*, II, 272–73.

4. Frederick Law Olmsted, *Walk and Talks of an American Farmer in England* (New York, 1852), Part II, p. 105.

5. Olmsted to Brace and Elliott, 1 Dec. 1853; Olmsted, *Seaboard*, p. 214.

6. For a discussion of increased recreation in the post-World War II period, see Robert Lee, *Religion and Leisure in America: A Study in Four Dimensions* (Nashville, 1964), pp. 17–68; Paul F. Douglass *et al.*, eds., "Recreation in the Age of Automation," *The Annals of the American Academy of Political and Social Science*, 313 (Philadelphia, 1957), *passim;* Charles E. Silberman, "The Money Left Over for the Good Life," in The Editors of Fortune, *America in the Sixties: The Economy and the Society* (New York, 1960), chapter 12. For an excellent analysis of the changing attitudes to leisure and recreation as a response to industrialization and urbanization in the nineteenth century, see Daniel T. Rodgers, *The Work Ethic in Industrial America 1850–1920* (Chicago, 1978), chapter 4; and Gunther Barth, *City People: The Rise of Modern City Culture in Nineteenth-Century America* (New York, 1980), *passim.* The quote is from Horace Bushnell, "Work and Play," in *Work and Play; or Literary Varieties* (New York, 1864), p. 18. Bushnell was the nation's principal nineteenth-century theoretician of Protestantism and Olmsted's mentor and friend.

7. Frederick Law Olmsted, "Of the Villagizing Tendency," [ca. 1886], Olmsted Papers.

8. Frederick Law Olmsted and Calvert Vaux, *Preliminary Report to the Commissioners for Laying Out a Park in Brooklyn* (Brooklyn, 1866), in Fein, ed., *Landscape into Cityscape*, pp. 100–101.

9. James S. T. Stranahan *et al.*, to the Mayor and Common Council of the City of Brooklyn, *Fourteenth Annual Report of the Brooklyn Park Commissioners for the Year 1873* (Brooklyn, 1874), p. 9.

10. *Annual Report of the Department of Parks, Borough of Brooklyn*, 1926–27, p. 10–11.

11. *Brooklyn Daily Eagle*, 4 Jan. 1942; p. 8; *Brooklyn Daily Eagle*, 27 Sept. 1936, p. 9; *New York Times*, 30 May 1973, p. 1.

12. For reference to racial violence in Belle Isle Park, see *Report of the National Advisory Commission on Civil Disorders* (New York, 1968), pp. 87, 224. For a discussion of the condition of historic urban parks, see August Heckscher, *Open Spaces: The Life of American Cities* (New York, 1977), *passim*.

13. For a discussion of the significance of Eastern Parkway see "Miracle on Eastern Parkway," *New York Times*, 20 May 1978. Sydney H. Schanberg, "Softball and Democracy," *New York Times*, 9 June 1981. For a similar evaluation of Belle Isle/Park, see Heckscher, *Open Spaces*, pp. 177–79.

14. *The Autobiography of Malcolm X* (New York, 1964), p. 175. Based on surveys of cities that had experienced major civil unrest, the *Report of the National Commission on Civil Disorders* listed "poor recreational facilities and programs" as being of equal importance with inadequate education as grievances of the "second level of intensity" after those of the "first level," which included police practices, unemployment and underemployment, and inadequate housing — pp. 7–8, 144–45, 148, 155–56, 196, 198.

15. Edward Higbee, *The Squeeze: Cities Without Space* (New York, 1960), *passim*. Another book that deals with the social aspects of parks is Ben Whitaker and Kenneth Browne, *Parks for People* (New York, 1973), *passim*; Olmsted, *Seaboard*, p. 627.

16. This theme is more fully developed in Albert Fein, "The American City: The Ideal and the Real," in Edgar Kaufmann, Jr., ed., *The Rise of an American Architecture* (New York, 1970), pp. 51–111; and in Fein, *Frederick Law Olmsted and the American Environmental Tradition*, *passim*.

17. Olmsted, *Public Parks and the Enlargement of Towns*, p. 18.

18. The same group of reformers who supported the legislation enabling the creation of Central Park fought for passage of New York City's landmark Metropolitan Health Bill of 1866. For an analysis of the development of a scientific approach to public health in the nineteenth-century American city, see Charles E. Rosenberg, *The Cholera Years: The United States in 1832, 1849, and 1866* (Chicago, 1962), *passim*. A fuller discussion of this group of reformers can be found in Albert Fein, "Centennial New York, 1876," in Milton M. Klein, ed., *New York: The Centennial Years 1676–1976* (New York, 1976), pp. 75–120. A brief description of the Central Park site as "a pestilential spot" is to be found in Henry Hope Reed and Sophia Duckworth, *Central Park: A History and a Guide* (New York, 1967), pp. 19–20; further discussion of the public health aspects of Olmsted's planning can be found in Fein, *Frederick Law Olmsted and the American Environmental Tradition*, pp. 28–29. For Olmsted's plans for the Fens and the Muddy River, see Walter Muir Whitehill, *Boston: A Topographical History* (Cambridge, Mass., 1959), pp. 180–81.

19. For Olmsted's views on the importance of separating land uses, see Olmsted, *Walks and Talks*, Part I, p. 82, and Olmsted and Calvert Vaux, *Report of the Landscape Architects and Superintendents to the President of the Board of Commissioners of Prospect Park*, Brooklyn (1868), in Fein, ed., *Landscape into Cityscape*, pp. 153–56. For an example of comprehensive planning, see Olmsted *et al.*, *Report to the Staten Island Improvement Commission of a Preliminary Scheme of Improvements* (1871), *Landscape into Cityscape*, pp. 173–300. It is interesting to note that at least one observer has found Olmsted's plans for Staten Island still relevant—see William H. Whyte, *The Last Landscape* (New York, 1968), p. 199. For Olmsted's views on a railroad system, see Frederick Law Olmsted and J. James R. Croes, Document No. 75 of the Board of the Department of Public Parks: *Report of the Landscape Architect and the Civil and Topographical Engineer, Accompanying a Plan for Local Steam Transit Routes in the Twenty-third and Twenty-fourth Wards* (1877), *Landscape into Cityscape*, *passim*.

20. Frederick Law Olmsted, *Public Parks and the Enlargement of Towns*; Olmsted, Vaux & Company, *Report upon a Projected Improvement of the Estate of the College*

of California at Berkeley, near Oakland (San Francisco, 1866); Olmsted, Vaux and Company, *Preliminary Report upon the Proposed Suburban Village at Riverside, near Chicago* (New York, 1868); Frederick Law Olmsted, *Public Parks and the Enlargement of Towns;* sections of all of the above are reprinted in Sutton, ed., *Civilizing American Cities.*

21. For a discussion of the contributions of Dr. Elisha Harris, see Rosenberg, *The Cholera Years*, pp. 187 – 88; the *Report to the Staten Island Improvement Commission* is reprinted in Fein, ed., *Landscape into Cityscape*, pp. 173 – 300. For an analysis of George E. Waring's contributions to the development of a modern system of "sanitation," see Richard Skolnick, "George E. Waring, Jr.: A Model for Reformers," *New-York Historical Society Quarterly* 47 (July 1963): 257 – 87; for an evaluation of Waring's contributions to sanitary engineering and waste disposal, see Martin V. Melosi, *Pragmatic Environmentalist: Sanitary Engineer George E. Waring, Jr.* (Washington, D.C., 1977). For good descriptions of Brace's work, see Jeremy P. Felt, *Hostages of Fortune: Child Labor Reform in New York State* (Syracuse, New York, 1965), chapter I, and Joseph M. Harris, *Children in Urban Society: Juvenile Delinquency in Nineteenth Century America* (New York, 1971), *passim.* For a partial listing of Vaux's work for the Children's Aid Society, see John David Sigle, "Bibliography of the Life and Works of Calvert Vaux," in *The American Association of Architectural Bibliographers Papers*, V (Charlottesville, Virginia, 1968), p. 92. Calvert Vaux deserves much greater treatment than he has yet received as an architect, a landscape architect, and member of New York City's artistic and literary community. Such a work was in progress by a gifted young architectural historian, Dennis Steadman Francis. Tragically, Mr. Francis died last year, cutting short what, in my judgment, based on my conversations and correspondence with him, would have been an important contribution to American environmental history. For Olmsted as an "artist," see Neil Harris, *The Artist in American Society: The Formative Years 1790 – 1860* (New York, 1966), pp. 215 – 16. For Olmsted's contributions to Richardson's development as an architect, see James F. O'Gorman, "The Making of a 'Richardson Building,' 1874 – 1886," in *Selected Drawings, H. H. Richardson and His Office: A Centennial of His Move to Boston 1874* (Harvard College Library, 1974), p. 30.

22. Frederick Law Olmsted, "Parks: A Glance Back and Forth," [n.d.].Olmsted Papers. For a discussion of Lewis and McHarg, see Whyte, *The Last Landscape*, Chapter 11.

23. As an example of places visited in 1850, see Olmsted, *Walks and Talks*, passim, and of places visited in 1878, see Roper, *FLO*, pp. 361 – 62; for a description of parks in different countries, see Frederick Law Olmsted, "Public Parks," *Garden* X (25 March 1876): 294 – 99.

24. Fein, *Frederick Law Olmsted and the American Environmental Tradition*, pp. 61 – 63.

25. [William A. Stiles], "Editorial," *Garden and Forest: A Journal of Horticulture, Landscape Art and Forestry* I (1 August 1888): 266; for an excellent analysis of the social and intellectual components of this nativism, see John Higham, *Strangers in the Land* (New York, 1962).

26. Frederick Law Olmsted, "Foreign Plants and American Scenery," *Garden and Forest* I (24 October 1888): 418.

27. For a seminal discussion of Olmsted as a conservationist, see Hans Huth, *Nature and the American: Three Centuries of Changing Attitudes* (Berkeley, Cal., 1957 [1972 ed.]), pp. 147 – 50, 171 – 73, 200. A book which can be described as symbolizing the search for a national planning policy is Stewart L. Udall, *Quiet Crisis* (New York, 1963). In chapters II, X, and XII Mr. Udall, who was Secretary of the Interior in President John F. Kennedy's administration, deals successively with Jefferson, Roosevelt, and Olmsted. An excellent historical analysis of the whole nature movement as related to urbanization is Peter J.

Schmitt, *Back to Nature: The Arcadian Myth in Urban America* (New York, 1969). Detail and analysis of Olmsted's involvement in specific conservation efforts can be found in Roper, *FLO;* Stevenson, *Park Maker;* and Fein, *Frederick Law Olmsted;* a suggestive essay on the regional significance of Olmsted's planning for George Vanderbilt in North Carolina is Frederick Gutheim's "Olmsted at Biltmore," in White and Kramer, eds., *Olmsted South,* pp. 239–46; the subject, however, deserves more systematic treatment than it has yet received.

28. For Olmsted's views of Lincoln, see Roper, *FLO,* pp. 167, 169, 176, 204. For a brief history of Yosemite, see Joseph L. Sax, *America's National Parks: Their Principles, Purposes and Prospects* (A National History Special Supplement, October 1976), pp. 59–62; the quote is from Sax, p. 59.

29. Frederick Law Olmsted, "The Yosemite Valley and the Mariposa Big Trees: A Preliminary Report (1865)," reprinted with an introductory note by Laura W. Roper, *Landscape Architecture* 43 (October 1952), pp. 12–25; this report was "lost" until Laura Roper discovered and published it; the quotations cited are found on pp. 21–22, 24.

30. Frederick Law Olmsted, *A Few Things to Be Thought of Before Proceeding to Plan Buildings for the National Agricultural Colleges* (New York, 1866), p. 10.

31. Frederick Law Olmsted, "The Beginning of Central Park: A Fragment of Autobiography (ca. 1877)," in Fein, ed., *Landscape into Cityscape,* p. 54.

32. For various interpretations on Theodore Roosevelt's contributions to a strong presidency, see Herbert Agar, *The United States, the Presidents, the Parties and the Constitution* (London, 1950), pp. 628–56; Sidney Fine, *Laissez-Faire and the General Welfare State: a Study of Conflict in American Thought 1865–1901* (Ann Arbor, 1956), pp. 373–400; Robert H. Wiebe, *Businessmen and Reform: a Study of the Progressive Movement* (Cambridge, Mass., 1962), chapter III; regarding the support Olmsted received in his preservation efforts, see Roper, *FLO, passim;* for a brief discussion of Roosevelt's father, see Edmund Morris, *The Rise of Theodore Roosevelt* (New York, 1979), p. 34; "Spoils of the Park," in Fein, ed., *Landscape into Cityscape,* p. 392.

33. Theodore Roosevelt to Frederick Law Olmsted, 19 March 1882, Olmsted Papers; Albert Fein, *Wave Hill, Riverdale, and New York City: Legacy of a Hudson River Estate* (Bronx, New York, 1979), pp. 19–24; George E. Mowry, *The Era of Theodore Roosevelt and the Birth of Modern America 1900–1912* (New York, 1962 [c. 1958]), pp. 214–16; Charles R. Lingley, *Since the Civil War* (New York, 1926), pp. 493–500.

34. For an evaluation of Theodore Roosevelt's use of the presidency to expand federal authority, see Arthur S. Link, *American Epoch: A History of the United States Since the 1890's* (New York, 1958), pp. 94–95.

35. The theme of Olmsted's interest in history is further developed in Albert Fein, "History and the Rediscovery of Frederick Law Olmsted," Foreword to White and Kramer, eds., *Olmsted South,* pp. xi–xxviii.

36. For a discussion of the "battle pass" site in Prospect Park, see Clay Lancaster, *Prospect Park Handbook* (New York, 1972), pp. 22–23; for a brief history of Fort Greene Monument, see Gerard R. Wolfe, *New York: A Guide to the Metropolis* (New York, 1975), pp. 384–88. As Wolfe makes clear, the present monument was designed by Stanford White and dedicated in 1908, but it is on the site designated by Olmsted and Vaux in 1868.

37. See, for example, Frederick Law Olmsted, *A Consideration of the Justifying Value of a Public Park* (Boston, 1881).

INTRODUCTION

Landscape into Cityscape

→»→»→»《《《《《《

A Changing World

A democracy born in the countryside—proclaimed by Americans as superior to the aristocracies of Europe—was having its system of government tested in the rapidly emerging cities of the nineteenth century. "Our country has entered upon a stage of progress," Frederick Law Olmsted wrote about 1877, "in which its welfare is to depend on the convenience, safety, order and economy of life in its great cities. It . . . cannot gain in virtue, wisdom, comfort, except as they also advance."[1] The city, he predicted, would shape the modes of thought and basic values of all future Americans. American civilization, in fact, would depend mainly upon the influence of its cities—and unless they were enlightening and uplifting they would not be truly democratic.

Olmsted's knowledge of history and the statistics of social trends, as well as his extensive travel throughout western Europe, led him to conclude by the end of the Civil War that the outstanding feature of Western civilization was the "strong tendency of people to flock together in great towns."[2] He was certain that this process of urbanization was permanently altering the social structure of all Western nations. The growth of London, for example, had been so rapid that from the early part of the century until his own time its population had in-

---

[1] Frederick Law Olmsted, "The Beginning of Central Park: A Fragment of Autobiography," *American Scenic and Historic Preservation Society, Nineteenth Annual Report* (1914), p. 52. See Document I.

[2] Frederick Law Olmsted and Calvert Vaux, *Preliminary Report upon the Proposed Suburban Village at Riverside, near Chicago* (New York, 1868), p. 4.

creased tenfold. Glasgow's rate of growth was six times that of Scotland; the population of Paris increased to account for half the growth of France; Berlin was growing twice as rapidly as all of Prussia; and even rural Russia, he noted, was witnessing a flight by the peasantry from the country into the large towns.[3]

The physical environment shaped by the rapid growth in commerce, manufacturing, and industry by 1865 appeared likely to inhibit social progress. In addition to opportunities for employment, city-dwellers required satisfactory homes and educational and recreational facilities in a physical environment conducive to social harmony. Olmsted was determined that cities such as New York use their economic power to become humanizing centers of cultural and intellectual activity. The city, he wrote, must come to epitomize social democracy's "higher" standards of wealth, represented by learning, science, and art. He consequently devoted himself to the landscape development of such social institutions as parks, colleges, and museums. To ensure that these facilities would be used and supported by a substantial element of the population, he planned them as integral parts of communities; the commercial and social activities of the city were to be physically separated. And these institutions would constitute the harmonizing elements of an organic, democratic metropolis.

Frederick Law Olmsted pioneered the professional development of landscape architecture and city planning in the United States. His interest in these fields grew out of his appreciation of the urban experience as well as out of his concern with the social problems challenging American democracy in the nineteenth century. He considered the displacement of rural America by the commercial and industrial city to be the most fundamental change confronting the nation during his lifetime. Born in the small New England town of Hartford, Connecticut, in 1822, he grew to believe that the unique democratic and cultural advantages of the post–Civil War city could best be conserved and extended by joining them to the social values

[3] Frederick Law Olmsted, *Public Parks and the Enlargement of Towns* (Cambridge, 1870), p. 4.

of the rural scene he had known as a child. For Olmsted, the ideal urban environment was to be a synthesis of landscape and cityscape.

Memories of Childhood

While Olmsted accepted as inevitable the fact that the city grew at the expense of the countryside, he was pained to see it replacing the village as the dominant way of life. In the village community, he would recall, families, however self-contained, were responsive to the needs of others. They were independent and contented; therefore, neighborliness and kindness came naturally. So Olmsted believed. He wanted to preserve this atmosphere of community which had so much personal meaning for him. His mother died while he was a very young child, leaving him with "but a tradition of memory rather than the faintest recollection of her."[4] His step-mother was a humorless, fervent Congregationalist more interested in God than in her adopted children. His father, a prosperous merchant, was anxious to do all that he could to help his children. He gave his two sons every opportunity to prepare for professions, encouraged their education, took them on outings, financed their travels, and even supported Frederick in various business ventures, each of which proved to be financially disastrous.

But the elder Olmsted seemed to his son to have felt socially uncomfortable even among the immediate family. In the company of close friends, Frederick recalled, his father "would sit silent and even answer questions unfrankly and with evident discomfort."[5] As a result, Frederick and his brother turned to each other for emotional sustenance. Frederick, who was older, assumed the role of father, as it were, to his younger brother John, who became his closest companion.[6]

After his father remarried, Frederick was repeatedly sent

[4] Frederick Law Olmsted, "Passages in the Life of an Unpractical Man," in *Forty Years of Landscape Architecture*, ed. Frederick Law Olmsted, Jr., and Theodora Kimball (New York, 1922), I, 46.

[5] *Ibid.*, p. 45.

[6] After his brother's death in 1857, Olmsted married the widow.

3

away from home. There were six separations between the age of six and early adolescence. Olmsted rationalized them by explaining that his father had felt unable to supervise his education adequately since the elder Olmsted's had consisted of "a superstitious faith in preaching and didactic instruction." Out of an expressed wish to "do right by the boy," Olmsted's father had transferred the responsibility for his son to rural clergymen.[7]

The "schools" to which the boy was sent, in which the ministers acted as "fathers by deputy," exemplified some of the worst aspects of early nineteenth-century rural life. Olmsted was exposed to an atmosphere of fundamentalist and anti-intellectual thought and to precisely the kind of religious training which the father had wished to avoid. The emotional experience was one which Olmsted would neither forget nor forgive, and it left him with hostile feelings toward all aspects of formal religion. Even well along in middle-life, he admitted how angry he remained at the thought that "the most outrageous falsehood—false assumptions of matters of fact—entered into this engineering and with much that was of the character of imposture and cruel cowardly tyranny toward a child."[8]

The warmth and friendship of community life became substitutes for parental care. "Every house, every room, every barn and stable, every shop, every road and highway, every field, orchard and garden was not only open to me but I was everywhere welcome," he later recalled.[9] Between school sessions he made his way to the homes of the large Olmsted family in the rural environs of Hartford. "There were," he wrote, "no less than ten households of grandparents, grand-uncles and uncles in which, . . . I was as welcome and intimate and as much at home as if I had been born to them."[10]

[7] Olmsted, *Forty Years of Landscape Architecture*, I, 47.

[8] Frederick Law Olmsted to Frederick J. Kingsbury, April 20, 1871, Olmsted Papers, Manuscript Division, Library of Congress. Cited hereafter as Olmsted Papers.

[9] Olmsted, *Forty Years of Landscape Architecture*, I, 49-50.

[10] *Ibid.*, p. 55.

As an adult, aware of his own emotional needs and grateful for the personal security that had been afforded him in childhood, Olmsted endeavored to transfer the social tone of the countryside to the impersonal city.

The sheer physical beauty of New England remained a life-long source of pleasure and the ideal for which he strived in his later work. He was particularly fond of the Connecticut Valley and its confluents, the White Hills, and the New England coast from the Kennebeck to the Naugatuck. His happiest memories, he recalled, were the walks and rides he had there with his father and step-mother in the woods and fields.[11]

Learning and Growing

Olmsted had no professional education to sustain his deep attachment to nature. There were no schools of landscape architecture or of city planning in America in the 1840's. Knowledge of the land had to come from practical experience rather than through an academic course of study. Compelled to leave Yale College in 1837 due to an eye ailment, Olmsted undertook the study of civil engineering as apprentice to a qualified professional in Andover, Massachusetts. Here he learned the science and art of surveying and its application in country and city.

In 1844, following two unhappy experiences—one as a clerk in a New York City dry goods store and another as an apprentice seaman—Olmsted began a serious study of scientific farming. First at his Uncle David Brooks's farm at Cheshire, Connecticut, and then under the expert tutelage of George Geddes, a prize-winning farmer living near Syracuse, New York, Olmsted, who was still in his early twenties, learned the techniques of agriculture, horticulture, and botany. Encouraged by Frederick's interest and success, the elder Olmsted bought his son a farm at Sachem's Head, Connecticut, and when this failed, another on Staten Island. The young man proceeded to turn the Staten Island homestead into a model of scientific farming and management as well as a beau-

[11] *Ibid.*, p. 46.

5

tifully landscaped country seat—but not into a financial success.

During this time, Olmsted had deepened his knowledge and appreciation of the problems of the land by attending lectures at Yale on geology and scientific agriculture (given by such authorities as Professors Benjamin Silliman and John T. Norton) and by experimenting in the university laboratories. In addition, he was reading widely on the subject as well as in other fields which stressed the general theme of nature.[12]

Olmsted found many ideas in his independent studies of English and American literature. From the work of such English landscape theorists as Uvedale Price[13] and William Gilpin[14] he drew both an esthetic theory and a set of techniques for the development of a natural, romantic landscape. He derived inspiration from the cultural "flowering of New England," notably the essays and poetry of contemporaries such as Ralph Waldo Emerson, James Russell Lowell, and William

[12] For biographical details see *ibid.*, pp. 4–5, and Dr. Charles McLaughlin's unpublished doctoral dissertation, "Selected Letters of Frederick Law Olmsted" (Harvard University, 1960), pp. 8–10.

[13] Sir Uvedale Price (1747–1829), in his book "An Essay on the Picturesque," argued for a landscape art which was natural and picturesque, as opposed to the formal landscaping then in vogue. This essay, which first appeared in 1796, was reissued very successfully in an Edinburgh edition of 1842. This was the version which Olmsted read (see Charlotte Fell-Smith, "Uvedale Price," *Dictionary of National Biography* [London, 1949–1950], XVI, 341–342).

[14] William Gilpin (1724–1804) was an English curate and educational reformer who also promoted the establishment of a new poorhouse. He is best known, however, for his work in landscape theory. Professor Hans Huth considers his essay "Upon Prints," published in 1768, to have "established the principle that a scene or picture has beauty if it conforms with the rules of painting." Gilpin's writings, Huth believes, "made it possible for the spectator to make precise definitions of all that was to be perceived in nature." Huth also demonstrates the influence which Gilpin had on American writers and painters during the first half of the nineteenth century (see George Simonds Boulger, "William Gilpin," *Dictionary of National Biography*, VII, 1262–1263; Hans Huth, *Nature and the American: Three Centuries of Changing Attitudes* [Berkeley, 1957], pp. 11–12).

6

Cullen Bryant. The theme of nature was the dominant synthesizing idea in the cultural and intellectual life of New England while he was maturing.[15] Yet his closest identification with nature derived from memories of childhood.

Although Olmsted did not accept the extreme Transcendentalist view as developed by such rural New Englanders as Thoreau and Emerson, he believed, as they did, in the moral value of nature.[16] "I have been reading Sartor Resartus," he

[15] The treatment of nature has at least two sides to it. The dominant and optimistic theme is perhaps best expressed by Van Wyck Brooks, *The Flowering of New England, 1815–1865* (New York, 1936), p. 527. He describes that period as one in which "there is a springtime feeling in the air, a joyous sense of awakening, a free creativeness, an unconscious pride, expressed in the founding of institutions . . . the mind begins to shape into myths and stories the dreams of the pre-urban countryside." Another idea evidenced in the literature of the period was that this preurban world was fast disappearing and that all of its values were being challenged by technology. This theme has recently been developed by Leo Marx, *The Machine in the Garden: Technology and the Pastoral Ideal in America* (New York, 1964), *passim*. Both sides may be found in Olmsted's thinking and practice.

[16] If New England Transcendentalism may be said to have had one beginning point, it was the publication in 1836 of Ralph Waldo Emerson's little book, *Nature*. "Those who read it," wrote Octavius Brooks Frothingham, the contemporary historian of the movement, "recognized signs of a new era, . . . and many who did not read it felt . . . the change it had introduced" (*Transcendentalism in New England* [New York, 1880 ed.], p. 122). Olmsted read it. In addition, Emerson's elder brother was Olmsted's neighbor on Staten Island. Judge William Emerson and Ralph Waldo were very close. Ralph Rusk, Emerson's biographer, has noted that "even in the matter of religious opinion" the men "had never been far apart" (*The Life of Ralph Waldo Emerson* [New York, 1949], p. 439). Olmsted and the Judge, who was an expert on German literature, had frequent and long conversations, particularly on religion. "I wrote you hastily from New York yesterday," Olmsted noted to his father. "Returning from there in company with Judge Emerson, I accepted an invitation to dine with him, and then on account of the storm to spend the night. An exceedingly agreeable visit" (Olmsted to John Olmsted, Feb. 29, 1850, Olmsted Papers).

While there is no evidence that Olmsted ever met Thoreau, they moved in the same circles and their paths crossed on at least two occasions. The first time was in 1843, when Emerson gave Thoreau a letter of introduction to his brother William. Thoreau, trying to

wrote his father in 1846, "—it took me about three weeks, but I was intensly [sic] interested before I finished—and now if any body wants to set me down for an insane cloud dwelling Transcendentalist, because I like Carlisle [sic], I hope they'l [sic] gratify themselfes [sic]."[17] Actually, he had sufficient self-awareness to recognize his need for contact with tangible things. He was too sensitive to social problems and too forceful a personality by now to accept a system of thought which removed him from intimacy with the world about him. Religion and philosophy were important elements in reform, but change, he felt, had to take place in the realm of the concrete as well as the abstract. Nature had not become for him a substitute for Community or God (as it had for Thoreau), but rather a medium through which both public and private needs could be served.

Olmsted read widely in the "radical" religious literature of his time, especially the writings of the fiery Unitarian minister Theodore Parker, whom Olmsted knew; and the sermons and pamphlets of Horace Bushnell, the important Hartford Congregational minister and theologian. These readings, added to his childhood experience with religious instruction, com-

---

break into the New York literary market, stayed on Staten Island for six months. In this period he met many of the people who were later to be part of Olmsted's social group (see Henry Seidel Canby, *Thoreau* [Cambridge, 1939], p. 143). Later, in October, 1856, Thoreau spent several weeks at Eagleswood, New Jersey, a quasi-Utopian community where many of Olmsted's friends lived. Interestingly enough, Thoreau was invited to survey the land for purposes of planning it as well as to give lectures (see Benjamin P. Thomas, *Theodore Weld, Crusader for Freedom* [New Brunswick, 1950], p. 233). Also, it seems likely that Olmsted would have read *Walden,* published in 1854, three years before he began work on Central Park.

[17] Olmsted to John Olmsted, Aug. 12, 1846, Olmsted Papers. Emerson first visited Thomas Carlyle in England in 1832. A life-long friendship and correspondence began. *Sartor Resartus,* published in 1838, told of Carlyle's spiritual transformation—how he came to value spiritual over material things—and was also a criticism of contemporary England with its aristocratic waste and lower class poverty. Carlyle's was one of the most important English influences on the American Transcendental and reform movements.

pelled him to reject any form of orthodoxy which tended to emphasize differences between people. Organized religion, as he had experienced and understood it, could only forestall the development of a truly Christian and democratic society. "I am at war," he wrote, "with all sectarianism—and party trammels. The tyranny of priests and churches is as great a curse to the country and the world as negro Slavery. I very much doubt if I shall join or array myself under any Communion that is not open to any 'follower of Jesus Christ.' "[18]

Democracy, expressed through nature and social institutions, had become for him a substitute for the mysteries and revelations of formal religion. A true feeling for democratic values, he insisted, could not be transmitted by churches "whose authority is not dependent on the untrammelled and honest judgment of free[,] intelligent minds."[19] This hostility toward established religion, assimilated into a broadened nineteenth-century concept of democracy, contributed to Olmsted's enthusiasm as a reformer. Nature with its power to conserve the virtues of the past was his instrument for improving the world.

As a "radical" Christian, he saw Christ as the spirit of God in the secular world—a man of good works—a committed upper-middle-class and democratic reformer. To an atheist Olmsted described Christ as "a man who, in all his actions for thirty years, you cannot suppose to have been governed by any motives inconsistent with justice, magnanimity, and benevolence. . . . You cannot find that he ever said, or thought, or did a single mean, unmanly, ungentlemanly thing. A man who avoided kingly honors; who did not labor for riches; who neither sought nor avoided the luxuries of life; who endured to be forsaken of his friends; who put up with contempt, reproach, and ridicule; who was always going about doing good, without either ostentation or secrecy."[20] Like

---

[18] Olmsted to John Olmsted, Aug. 12, 1846, Olmsted Papers.

[19] Frederick Law Olmsted, *Walks and Talks of an American Farmer in England* (New York, 1852), Part I, p. 31.

[20] *Ibid.*, Part I, pp. 240–241.

other Protestant reformers of similar age and social background, Olmsted had shaped for himself an image of Christ and Christian purpose which conformed to his own personal and social beliefs.

Importance of Community

Possessing these values, Olmsted was inevitably attracted to the communitarian movement which flourished among New Englanders in pre-Civil War America. The movement sought to create model communities[21] away from the growing commercial cities. He found most appealing the North American Phalanx community at Red Bank, New Jersey, established according to the philosophy of the French Utopian Socialist, Fourier.[22] Olmsted described the communitarians warmly as "hard-working, earnest, unselfish livers in the faith of a higher life for man on earth as well as 'above.'" The sense of community was so extraordinary, he observed, that "a man who spent a large part of his time in smoking and reading newspapers and talking and recreative employments only would feel ashamed of himself, [and] would . . . consider it a priv-

[21] For an analysis of the relationship of the communitarian movement to American social and intellectual development, see A. E. Bestor, Jr., *Backwoods Utopias* (Philadelphia, 1950), Ch. I. It is Professor Bestor's point that these communitarians were not escapists, but reformers in the American tradition, attempting to change society peacefully by the successful establishment of "model communities." In addition, the two principal founders of the movement, Charles Fourier and Robert Owen, looked to the creation of a new physical structure which would abolish all differences between town and country; "Fourier's ideal was an agrarian-handicraft economy, Owen's a combination of agriculture and factory manufacture" (see Edward S. Mason, "Fourier and Fourierism," *Encyclopaedia of the Social Sciences* [New York, 1931], VI, 403). Hence, the movement, although technically a failure, had considerable influence on Olmsted, and through him on the professions of landscape architecture and city planning.

[22] Francois Marie Charles Fourier (1772–1837) was a leading French Utopian Socialist who had a substantial following in America. The community at Red Bank was the best known of the Fourierist-inspired colonies in America and the most successful.

lege [sic] to be allowed to black boots and sweep and milk for a part of the time." Furthermore, he noted the success of these model communities in assimilating many religious groups. Though the majority of the group at Red Bank seemed committed to the mystical philosophy of Swedenborg, there was no one dominant religion. There were represented "persons of all the great nominally Christian Churches from Catholics to Unitarians, or rationalists."[23]

Such harmony was impressive in a period when Americans were intensely divided with regard to religious doctrine. Harmony extended to all aspects of life in the community. The Associationists, as they were called, seemed unconcerned with money and acted *"naturally* simply and unaffectedly" with each other and strangers. Life there seemed to be more in keeping with Christian principles than among "any equal number of persons" living together. In a spiritual sense, the Phalanx was a true community.

But Olmsted found lacking at Red Bank those many civilizing influences which he thought necessary for a truly democratic society. As in many such settlements, the economic situation was too precarious to permit the development of more than the crudest cultural and educational institutions. "They want an *educational Series* very much," Olmsted noted. "They have no fit teacher— . . . there is no proper nursery deptment [sic] . . . and not the children alone, are growing without any proper discipline of mind." He did not consider any of the Associationists to be very intelligent, refined, or highminded. As he put it, "they are not any of them *first class* people or if so they have forgotten some of their 5th Avenue notions." The inhabitants of Red Bank seemed to have given

[23] Olmsted to Charles Loring Brace, July 26, 1852, Olmsted Papers. Emanuel Swedenborg (1688–1772) was a Swedish scholar-philosopher whose ideas on religion led to the founding of a new church. He was popularized by American intellectuals before the Civil War—particularly Henry James, Sr., and Ralph Waldo Emerson, who considered him to be one of the great men of history. "Swedenborg," wrote Emerson, "has rendered a double service to mankind, which is now only beginning to be known. . . . He observed and published the laws of nature" (*Representative Men* [Boston, 1850], p. 145).

up the struggle for those other factors which made life meaningful and attractive. There were many conveniences they could easily have acquired, but none about which they cared sufficiently. The Community, he concluded sadly, was isolated from, and too little concerned about, the "world *outside*."[24]

Thus, while he considered Red Bank superior to the best of New England's villages, Olmsted was already too much the social reformer to be satisfied with this rather primitive community. Although by 1852 he regarded himself as *"more of a* Fourierist than before," and thought the Phalanx Community a desirable model for a large part of rural America, he did not consider it adequate for the nation's growing cities.[25]

Rejection of Rural Life

Olmsted's ambivalent reactions to the Community reflected a profound change in his own life-purpose. Until the 1850's he was convinced of the social merits and importance of farming as a profession. "Rural pursuits," he lectured his brother during this period, ". . . tend to elevate and enlarge the ideas, for all the proudest aims of Science are involved in them; they require a constant application of the principals [*sic*] and objects of the Chemist, Naturallist [*sic*], Geologist, Mechanic, etc. More than all of *them* it cultivates or should, the taste and sentiment, and there is no more occasion for anything vulgar or offensive in it's [*sic*] operations, than in their's [*sic*]. . . . I believe that our farmers are, and have cause to be, the most contented men in the world."[26] In fact, until nearly the age of thirty he had regarded agriculture as an

[24] Olmsted to Brace, July 26, 1852, Olmsted Papers. By "educational series" Olmsted meant a series of lectures on a learned topic—the lyceum method—a popular form of nineteenth-century culture and entertainment.

[25] The Federal Census of 1850, state censuses such as that of New York for 1855, increased immigration, and novels such as James Fenimore Cooper's *Home As Found*, affirmed what the eye could see—that American cities were growing very rapidly.

[26] Olmsted to John Hull Olmsted, June 23, 1845, Olmsted Papers.

ideal occupation for any intelligent young man seeking a socially useful and personally satisfying profession. His book, *Walks and Talks of an American Farmer in England*, first published in 1852, was written "especially for farmers and farmers' families."[27] And the signature "Yeoman" followed his description of the Seaboard Slave States, published a year later as a series in the *Times*. Like Jefferson, whom he admired, or the American philosopher of the agrarian way of life, John Taylor of Caroline, Olmsted considered the small independent farm the nucleus of democracy.[28]

By the time of his visit to Red Bank in 1852, however, he had begun to doubt the suitability of agricultural communities as social units. The tour of England (which also included Scotland, Ireland, Belgium, France, and Germany) begun in the spring of 1850 marks the starting point of this change in orientation. The change is evident in the quantity of material and space given over to urban matters—in spite of the dedication of the book to farmers. Also, there is at least as much emotional involvement in the discussion of cities—Liverpool, for example—as there is in his treatment of agricultural matters. Olmsted saw cities emerging as the future environment of the nation and recognized the need for democratic

---

[27] Olmsted, *Walks and Talks*, Part I, p. 1.

[28] Throughout the volumes on the South, Olmsted cited Jefferson as an example of the South that was. He quoted from Jefferson's writings to prove that the South once represented an antislavery, libertarian, and democratic point of view. "As the present policy so madly pursued has departed from the principles of Democracy and the old Democratic party, so that the words of Jefferson would now hang a man anywhere at the South, I do not much doubt that when reaction comes, the principles on which Jefferson desired to deal with slavery will be found . . . safe and profitable" (see Olmsted, *A Journey in the Back Country in the Winter of 1853–54* [New York, 1907], II, 272; originally issued in 1860). See also Olmsted, *Back Country*, I, 127; Olmsted, *A Journey in the Seaboard Slave States, with Remarks on Their Economy* (New York, 1856), 117–118, 260, 489, 492.

For an estimate of the importance of Taylor's philosophy in pre-Civil War America, see Roy F. Nichol's introduction to John Taylor's *An Inquiry into the Principles and Policy of the Government of the United States* (New Haven, 1950), p. 38.

systems of social planning and control which were rational and humane, and centralized in the hands of technical experts.[29]

By the end of the Civil War the prospective gentleman farmer had become the urban reformer, severely critical of North and South alike for failing to fashion a plan for the countryside worthy of a democratic society. He noted that roadsides were being defaced by "raw banks of earth, mud-puddles, heaps of rubbish and slatternly fences,"[30] and that there was much that was "draggling, smirching, fouling."[31] The deterioration of such facilities and objects of pride as public squares, burial grounds, buildings, and fountains symbolized to him the failure of the countryside to function democratically. In a truly democratic community, Olmsted declared, these would no more go unattended "than house floors would fail to be systematically swept, or body-linen to be systematically cleansed."[32] Rural communities, he found, even those of New England, had ceased to be intellectually and culturally productive. He described New England social gatherings as awkward and dull, and found her schools, meeting-halls, libraries, and other public institutions inadequate. He noted one lady's remarks: "If I were offered a deed of the best farm that I ever saw, on condition of going back to the country to live, I would not take it. I would rather face starvation in town."[33]

[29] Liverpool was of particular importance in Olmsted's development—so much so that he devotes more than four chapters in *Walks and Talks* to it and its newly planned suburb of Birkenhead. Birkenhead was the second city in England (London was the first) to undertake an extensive program of park development in an effort to improve its social and physical condition (on the development of the Liverpool and the Birkenhead parks see George F. Chadwick, *The Works of Sir Joseph Paxton (1803–1865)* (London, 1961), Ch. III.)

[30] Olmsted, *A Few Things to Be Thought of before Proceeding to Plan Buildings for the National Agricultural Colleges* (New York, 1866), p. 13.

[31] Olmsted, *Public Parks*, p. 6.

[32] Olmsted, *Agricultural Colleges*, p. 13.

[33] Olmsted, *Public Parks*, p. 5.

Olmsted Visits the South

The turning point in Olmsted's attitude toward the agrarian way of life was clearly his journeys through the South in the years 1853–1857. The Civil War, which occurred one year after the publication of the third volume of his account of the ante-bellum South, reinforced this experience. Ironically, the purpose of the trips was to help prevent the war by presenting an objective picture of Southern life and manners. Henry Raymond, the New York *Daily Times* editor who commissioned the project, believed this could be done by offsetting the extreme image of the South and slavery drawn by Northern abolitionists such as William Lloyd Garrison.

Raymond, who had recently founded the *Times*—partly as a reaction against the extreme social and economic views of Horace Greeley and his paper, the New York *Tribune*—was looking for just such a man as Olmsted. Olmsted's book on England had just been published. It had been well received by the press as a fair and interesting depiction of English social life. In it Olmsted had noted with disdain that America's foreign image was being drawn by evangelizing abolitionists. Of the English view of slavery, he wrote, "they are usually greatly misinformed, and view it only as an unmitigated and wholly inexcusable wrong, injustice, and barbarous tyranny for which all Americans are equally responsible, and all equally condemnable, and with regard to which all are to be held responsible, and everlastingly to be scolded at (except a few martyrs, called abolitionists, that obtain a precarious livelihood through their contributions)."[34] In addition, Olmsted and Raymond, both supporters of the Free Soil Whigs, shared similar political views opposing the extension of slavery into the territories. It was logical, then, for the editor to select Olmsted as the man for an objective Northern study of the South.

[34] Olmsted, *Walks and Talks*, Part I, p. 221; Olmsted, *The Slave States*, ed. with an introduction by Harvey Wish (New York, 1959), p. 11.

Olmsted began his trips regarding slavery as "an unfortunate circumstance." He felt that the people of the South themselves were blameless and that immediate abolition was impracticable. It was his intention to foster a conciliatory spirit in
the North by making an "objective" study of the "condition
and habits of the people of the South."[35] Such objectivity,
however, was clearly not possible for a Northern reformer
committed emotionally and ideologically to social democracy.
He began the trip already doubtful of the social value of
agriculture in the North and convinced that the country had
been divided into two competing civilizations: an aristocratic,
fundamentally agrarian society based on slave labor, and a
democratic, essentially commercial—and urban—order dependent on free labor.

In addition, during the time Olmsted was traveling through
the South sectional tensions were heightened by the reopening
of the question of slavery in the territories of Kansas and
Nebraska,[36] and by the caning of the abolitionist Senator from
Massachusetts, Charles Sumner, by the South Carolinian member of the House of Representatives, Preston Brooks.[37] These
events and the sectional response to them symbolized for Olmsted the irreconcilability of the two ways of life.

Essentially, then, Olmsted's "diaries," originally planned
as objective descriptions of the ante-bellum South, were in

[35] Olmsted, *Back Country*, I, iv–v.

[36] Olmsted had become a direct participant in "Bleeding Kansas"
by raising funds to purchase weapons for the New England Emigrant
Aid Society (see Olmsted, *The Slave States*, p. 14). Hence, Olmsted's
introduction to T. H. Gladstone, *The Englishman in Kansas; Or, Squatter
Life and Border Warfare* (New York, 1857), although culled from
his other books on the South, has a more belligerent tone to it. He
writes: "When our army is used as a reserve force for bands of robbers,
while they murder the sons, and ravish the daughters, and devastate
the property of our dearest friends and neighbors, and all in the service
of slavery, is it not reasonable to believe that there is greater danger
of our forgetting the evils which the people of the South suffer from
slavery than of our overlooking the advantages which they claim to
enjoy from it?" (p. xliii).

[37] Gladstone, *The Englishman in Kansas*, pp. xviii–xix; see also Olmsted, *Back Country*, II, 226.

reality efforts to prove that the Northern way of life was superior to the Southern and more in keeping with the historic destiny of the nation. Of course, the books contain much invaluable information and brilliant reporting which can be considered objective. But the unifying thread of all the volumes, otherwise organized only by regions of the South, is Olmsted's refutation of such leading defenders of Southern agrarian aristocracy as Chancellor William Harper and James D. B. De Bow, both of South Carolina—a rejoinder which is more apparent in each succesive publication.

Olmsted understood before embarking on his journeys that both Harper's logic and De Bow's statistics were as much an attack on urban-commercial democracy as a defense of Southern aristocracy. And in his reaction to these critics he tended to be defensive about the North rather than objective about the South. In the South he found the principle of government for democratic social ends "everywhere ridiculed and rejected, in public as well as in private, in the forum as well as the newspapers."[38] He attributed the considerably lower standard of living to a feudal-like economy and rigid class structure, which was completely antithetical to his concept of social progress. "A ruling or a subject class in a community," he wrote, "is in itself a very great hindrance . . . to its acquisition of wealth—moral, aesthetic, and mental, as well as material wealth."[39] He returned North after only the first trip "more than ever a democrat."[40]

But he tried to present a balanced view. Wherever possible he commented on some area of scenic beauty or on the charm of a city such as New Orleans, or on the manners and character of particular members of the Southern upper class whom he met and liked. At Austin, Texas, he admired the calm, judicious manner in which the state legislature functioned, and found there "many cultivated, agreeable and talented persons," notwithstanding great differences of opinion with

[38] Olmsted, *Seaboard*, p. 491.
[39] *Ibid.*, pp. 490–491.
[40] *Ibid.*, p. x.

them.[41] Such observations, however, were rare. The few favorable things he found in the South were associated with nature. Most notable among these were the views at Harper's Ferry, where "the Potomac hurries madly along high cliffs,"[42] the public gardens on the bluffs of Natchez before which stretched the grandeur of the Mississippi "lost in the vast obscurity of the Great West,"[43] and the green grasslands of Kentucky spreading "for hundreds of miles before you an immense natural park, planted, seeded to sward, drained, and kept up by invisible hands for the delight and service of man."[44]

The emotional tone of Olmsted's reporting was intensified when he described the physical brutality of "slave-management." "It was the first time I had ever seen a woman flogged," he wrote. "I had seen a man cudgeled and beaten, in the heat of passion, before, but never flogged with a hundredth part of the severity used in this case." The reason, explained the otherwise pleasant overseer, was that " 'She meant to cheat me out of a day's work—and she has done it, too.' "[45] This conduct, combined with the use of such "instruments of social control" as "nigger dogs" to hunt down escaped slaves, helped to convince Olmsted that slavery was as dehumanizing an institution for whites as it was a brutalizing one for Negroes. It was antithetical to civilized, Christian, democratic progress. Commenting on the particularly violent reaction of one East Tennessee editor to the public burning of a slave—the editor (also a "preacher") had wanted him tortured in public as well—Olmsted noted that such savage behavior was conditioned by the social system. "To follow the usual customs of civilization elsewhere would not be felt safe. To be faithful to the precepts of Christ would not be felt safe. To act in a spirit of cruel, inconsiderate, illegal, violent, and pitiless ven-

[41] Olmsted, *A Journey Through Texas; Or a Saddle-Trip on the Southwestern Frontier; with a Statistical Appendix* (New York, 1857), pp. 112–113.

[42] *Ibid.*, p. 2.

[43] Olmsted, *Back Country*, I, 32.

[44] Olmsted, *Texas*, pp. 10–11.

[45] Olmsted, *Back Country*, I, 89.

geance, must be permitted, must be countenanced, must be defended by the most conservative, as a 'means of absolute, necessary self-defence.' "[46]

By the end of the third trip he was more than ever convinced of the failure of the Southern way of life as a social system, of its incompatibility with the democratic patterns of the nation, and of its basically immoral standards of conduct. He warned the South that this was not his view alone, nor that of irresponsible men, but the opinion prevalent among the most distinguished leaders in all walks of Northern life, including "the first gentlemen, the purest patriots, and the soundest thinkers in the land."[47]

He now considered himself one of the vast majority of Northerners who were "abolitionists." As a member of the intellectual leadership which still wished to avoid a Civil War, he did not define an abolitionist as one who advocated the immediate eradication of the "dreadful institution." "I do not see," he wrote, "that a mere setting free of the blacks, if it could be accomplished, would surely remedy these evils. An extraction of the bullet does not at once remedy the injury of a gun-shot wound; it sometimes aggravates it."[48] Like Lincoln, whom he supported, Olmsted conceded the necessity for permitting slavery to remain as it was for the time being. "The laws and forces sustaining it," he reluctantly granted, "where it has been long established, may have become a temporary necessity, as poisons are to the life of some unfortunate invalids. Judge you of that. But laws intended to extend its field of improvidence are unjust, cruel, and oppressive. Revolutionary resistance to them by all men whose interest it is to have industry honestly paid, can only be wrong while likely to be unsuccessful."[49]

[46] *Ibid.*, II, 230–232. The editor, a Methodist preacher, wrote: "We unhesitatingly affirm that the punishment was unequal to the crime. Had we been there we should have taken a part, and even suggested the pinching of pieces out of him with red-hot pincers—the cutting off of a limb at a time, and then burning them all in a heap."

[47] Olmsted, *Texas*, p. xxvii.

[48] Olmsted, *Back Country*, I, vi.

[49] Olmsted, *Texas*, p. xv.

Southern Critics of the North

As for his commitment to the social improvement of the Northern city, it was more emphatic than ever. In all his readings in preparation for these studies of the South, as well as in conversations with Southern leaders, he found that a key point in defense of their civilization was the vulgarity inherent in commercial activities and in the cities which contained them. Southern defenders such as Harper and De Bow contended that the commercial city was foreign and contrary to an Anglo-Saxon tradition rooted in an agrarian past. Cities, they pointed out, contained large numbers of poor immigrants morally degraded by the very nature of urban life. Southerners claimed that "licentiousness at the North is far more captivating, irresistible, and ruinous than at the South."[50] There was a higher rate of drunkenness, prostitution, venereal diseases, and crime, among other indexes of social discontent, than in the South, with its predominantly agrarian society based on a well-controlled and highly disciplined labor force of slaves. Every society must have its "mud-sill" consisting of poor workers. How much better, more civilized, and more economical (urban land taxes were high) it was to have them controlled rather than free.

More ominous, for the future of the North as well as for the nation, was the Southern prophecy that commercialism nourished its own "seeds . . . of disaster." Southerners saw the germs of social revolution (which characterized most of Europe during the nineteenth century) in Northern "demands for 'Land Limitation,' in the anti-rent troubles, in strikes of workmen, in the distress of emigrants at the eddies of their current, in diseased philanthropy, in radical democracy, and

[50] Olmsted, *Seaboard*, pp. 600–601. Chancellor W. Harper, "Article IV, Memoir on Slavery," *De Bow's Review*, IX (1850), 487–488: "Nothing is so rarely heard of as an atrocious crime committed by a slave. . . . Compare all the evils resulting from this, with the enormous amount of vice, crime and depravity, which in an European, or one of our Northern cities, disgusts the moral feelings, and render life and property insecure."

in the progress of socialistic ideas in general." The very basis
of Northern life, they claimed, was antithetical to true civilization. Commercial progress had been made "under the high
pressure of unlimited competition," but as time went on,
Southerners predicted, "as the population grows denser, there
will be terrific explosions, disasters and ruin," while the South
"will ride quietly and safely at the anchor of Slavery."[51]

Olmsted did not deny most of the specific points, for they
were based on reports which were considered to be impartial
and accurate.[52] Few Southerners he knew could "on any subject whatever . . . get through a book, or even a business
or friendly letter, to be sent North, without . . . asserting
that Northern laborers might well envy the condition of the
slaves."[53] Although he sought to refute these attacks by proving—often with evidence provided by Southern statisticians
such as De Bow—that no Northern workingman was as badly
fed, clad, or housed as the most fortunate slave, this did not
really satisfy him. Fundamentally, he agreed that the commercial North had failed to create a civilization worthy of a democratic nation. But he rejected the idea that commercial cities
with their dense populations need remain as they were—that
they could never be appropriate instruments for achieving
social democracy.

He insisted that his experiences in the South proved that
a purely agrarian economy built on the isolated farm or plantation could never meet the increasingly complex demands of
a modern people. "There are improvements, and communities
loosely and gradually cohering in various parts of the South,"
he wrote, "but so slowly, so feebly, so irregularly, that men's
minds and habits are knit firm quite independently of this
class of social influences." By contrast, "the child born . . . on
the Northern frontier," he noted, "in most cases, before it

[51] Olmsted, *Seaboard*, pp. 183–184.
[52] Public institutions such as poorhouses, hospitals, prisons, and insane
asylums usually issued regular reports to the governmental body which
controlled their charters and/or to the appointed body of officials
responsible for their administration.
[53] Olmsted, *Seaboard*, p. 701.

21

is ten years old, will be living in a well organized and tolerably well provided community; schools, churches, libraries, lecture and concert halls, daily mails and printing presses, shops and machines in variety, having arrived within at least a day's journey of it, being always within an influencing distance of it."[54]

Olmsted Describes the South

Olmsted ascribed much of the primitive behavior and barbarism of the South to the dominance of a frontierlike society rather than to slavery alone. "There are," he wrote, "only six towns, having a town-like character, in the Slave States— New Orleans, Mobile, Louisville, St. Louis, Charleston, and Richmond." The others, like Savannah, he described as "simply overgrown villages in appearance, and in convenience."[55] As for Richmond, the future Confederate capital, and the only Southern town which Olmsted believed comparable to Northern urban centers such as New York, Boston, and Philadelphia, it proved false the impression given by Southern statesmen and journalists that Southern cities "were comparatively free from a low and licentious population." Olmsted wrote on his first trip, that "from what I have seen . . . I should be now led to think that there was at least as much vice, and of what we call rowdyism, in Richmond, as in any Northern town of its size"—this despite the absence of foreign commerce and a large immigrant population.[56] Yet, in a friendly debate with

[54] Olmsted, *Back Country*, II, 192–193.
[55] *Ibid.*, pp. 34–35.
[56] Olmsted, *Seaboard*, p. 52. Olmsted revisited Richmond on his third trip and declared his first impression to have been somewhat mistaken. Richmond, he admitted, "somewhat surprised me by its substance, show and gardens, and I was inclined to think that in coming to it directly from New York and Philadelphia, I had been led to rather underrate its quality at my first visit." He complimented the city on "having a history, and something prepared for a future a well," and on owning Thomas Crawford's monument of Washington, which he considered to be "the highest attainment of American plastic art, and would be a glory to any town or country. . . ." But, he quickly added, the statue was more a monument to the past than to the future of the

a Southern acquaintance he had to admit to a comparable degree of "rowdyism, ruffianism, [and] want of high honorable sentiment and chivalry of the common farming and laboring people of the N[orth]."[57]

A complete commitment to democratic values was the answer to the social ills of the North—not slavery, as the South claimed. A belief in democracy, Olmsted explained, was essential if men were to find rational and humane solutions to social problems inherent in urban life and aggravated by the force of profit-making. The profit motive seemed to him almost as destructive to the North as the economics of slavery was to the South. "They actually let nothing come in competition with *business* [in the North]," he wrote. "They will not pay their respect to God, until they have free leave from Mammon."[58] The corrupting influence of laissez-faire capitalism was, however, national—not sectional. Under the plantation system humans were sold and exploited as were goods and workers in the North. If economics was to be the principal motivation in America, he asked, "What does the success of our Democratic Nationality amount to—and what is to become of us?"[59]

In the South there seemed to be an almost total neglect of community services related to the general welfare of the public. The South no more accepted this aspect of social democracy for its white population than it did for its Negro slaves. In the important port city of Norfolk he found "all

section. He concluded therefore much as he had begun. "Compared with Northern towns of the same population," he wrote, "there is much that is quaint, provincial, and excessively slovenly, especially in whatever connects directly with the country." Furthermore, as a metropolis, it symbolized the problem of Virginians, "a people who have been dragged along in the grand march of the rest of the world, but who have had, for a long time and yet have, a disposition within themselves only to step backward" (see Olmsted, *Back Country*, II, 34–36).

[57] Olmsted to Charles Loring Brace and Charles L. Elliott, Dec. 1, 1853, Olmsted Papers.
[58] Olmsted to Charles Loring Brace, Nov. 12, 1850, *ibid.*
[59] Olmsted to Brace and Elliott, Dec. 1, 1853, *ibid.*

the immoral and disagreeable characteristics of a large seaport, with very few of the advantages that we should expect to find as relief to them. No lyceum or public libraries, no public gardens, no galleries of art . . . no 'home' for its seamen; no public resorts of healthful and refining amusement, no place better than a filthy, tobacco-impregnated bar-room or a licentious dance-cellar, so far as I have been able to learn, for the stranger of high or low degree to pass the hours unoccupied by business."[60] The cultural condition of the rural South was even worse. "From the banks of the Mississippi to the banks of the James," Olmsted wrote, he almost never saw "a thermometer, or a book of Shakespeare, or a piano-forte or sheet of music; or the light of a . . . reading-lamp, or an engraving, or a copy of any kind, of a work of art, of the slightest merit."[61]

The Southern way of life, he concluded, was based on a concept of social democracy antithetical to his own and to that of other Northern reformers. If a Southerner belonged to the Democratic Party, it was with the purpose of having complete freedom to do whatever was in the best interest of a very small and often self-styled aristocratic class. "It seemed to me," he wrote during his trip through the South, "that what had made these Southern Gentlemen Democrats was the perception that mere Democracy as they understand it—(no checks or laws upon the country more than can be helped) was the best system for their class. It gave capital every advantage in the pursuit of wealth and money gave wisdom and power."[62]

Olmsted understood democracy to mean something more than the mere exercise of the political process. Politics ought not to be so much a means of protecting the interests of the rich and powerful, as a way of helping the majority to advance. Its real goal was social justice, brought into being by "a democratic condition of society as well as of government."[63]

[60] Olmsted, *Seaboard*, p. 136.
[61] Olmsted, *Back Country*, II, 171.
[62] Olmsted to Brace and Elliott, Dec. 1, 1853, Olmsted Papers.
[63] *Ibid.*

In effect, Olmsted rejected the theory of laissez-faire, which held that the most desirable form of government was that which governed least. Notwithstanding the admission that Northern civilization was "one-sided, irregular, and awkward," he found greater reason for optimism there than on Southern plantations. He hoped that Northern leadership would apply itself in the future less to "matters of pure business, and . . . more to religion and politics and the good government of our individual bodies and minds, with their various appetites, impulses, functions, and longings"[64]—an objective not attained anywhere in the world of his day. He concluded from his trips that he must become "either an Aristocrat or more of a Democrat than I have been—a Socialist Democrat."[65] And he was now more dedicated than ever to finding a physical solution for the social problems of the much-criticized Northern city.

Even before the completion of his third volume on the ante-bellum South, Olmsted was hard at work in 1858 superintending his first important urban project in New York City—the construction of Central Park—which he designed together with Calvert Vaux, a noted architect. This project, aside from its intrinsic social and esthetic values, was meant in part to demonstrate the cultural capacity of a free urban society. He was mindful of Chancellor Harper's oft-quoted remark that history proved that only slave societies were capable of creating architectural structures of lasting greatness. "Let it be remembered," wrote Harper, "that all the great and enduring monuments of human art and industry—the wonders of Egypt—the ever-lasting works of Rome—were created by the labor of slaves."[66] For Olmsted the Park would

[64] Olmsted, *Seaboard*, p. 627.

[65] Olmsted to Brace and Elliott, Dec. 1, 1853, Olmsted Papers.

[66] Chancellor William Harper, *Memoir on Slavery* (Charleston, 1838), p. 53. Harper's *Memoir on Slavery* was reissued many times before the Civil War. Olmsted read it in James D. B. De Bow, *The Industrial Resources, etc., of the Southern and Western States* (New Orleans, 1853), Vol. II, and replied: "But the Egyptians and the Romans enjoyed the advantage of an unimpeded importation of slaves, when engaged in these works. . . . [Only] a *dense* slave population . . . made

be an enduring symbol of democratic achievement. It was, he wrote to Parke Godwin, a fellow New York City reformer, "a democratic development of the highest significance and on the success of which, in my opinion, much of the progress of art and esthetic culture in this country is dependent."[67]

The Civil War and Reconstruction

By 1860, shortly after the election of Lincoln, Olmsted had reluctantly given up any hope of averting war. "We intend to have two republics," he wrote to Charles Loring Brace, an old friend and the founder of the Children's Aid Society in New York City, "peaceably if we can, fighting, if we must, don't we? But my mind is made up for a fight. The sooner we get used to the idea, the better, I think."[68] And when the war came, Olmsted accepted in 1861 the key position of Secretary General of the United States Sanitary Commission (which later became the American Red Cross). He undertook his war work out of the same conscious motivation which had influenced his urban activity: it was an opportunity to defend his theory of democratic nationalism. "I want to exterminate the slave holders or rather slaveholding and the State of Society founded on it," he explained to the Reverend Henry Whitney Bellows, the dynamic, reform-minded New York Unitarian minister and moving spirit of the Commission.[69] A nation conceived historically as a democracy could not continue to exist part slave and part free. Furthermore, he believed that the war would eradicate any doubts among Northerners as to the ultimate national purpose. In a sense it had become

them possible; and if the South is to rival them it must reopen the African slave trade, or put a check upon the dispersion of its laborers, which is thus shown to be as much a measure of safety as of glory" (*Back Country*, II, 152–153).

[67] Olmsted to Parke Godwin, Aug. 1, 1858, Bryant-Godwin Papers, Manuscript Division, New York Public Library.

[68] Olmsted to Brace, Dec. 9, 1860, Olmsted Papers.

[69] Olmsted to Henry W. Bellows, Oct. 3, 1862, Bellows Papers, Massachusetts Historical Society. Hereafter cited as Bellows Papers.

for him as for other Northerners a national—not sectional—catharsis of all that was evil, immoral, and undemocratic.

Few men knew better than Olmsted the toll taken by the war in terms of human suffering. As working head of the Sanitary Commission, he had the duties of establishing field hospitals and supervising the care of the wounded and the dying. In the bloody Peninsular Campaign—at the battle of Fair Oaks—Olmsted helped to evacuate three thousand men with "the stench of rotting flesh . . . rising on the summer air."[70] He devoted himself to the Union cause with zeal and determination in the face of the most difficult circumstances of faulty administration imaginable. Under such stress, he broke down emotionally and physically in 1863 and accepted an offer to manage mining estates in California. The war, however, had made him more determined than ever—particularly after all the bloodshed and the loss of lives—to prove the viability of democratic institutions.

The war just could not have been fought in vain. He would not accept the rumor being circulated in California that it had caused a decline in the moral behavior of the North. The informant alleged that "it is scarcely possible to exaggerate the increased prevalence of intemperance, profanity and other vice throughout the population of the free states since the war began." Olmsted reacted strongly, declaring "I cant[sic] but think he is mistaken, and is riding a hobby and doing harm with it."[71] He had seen how Northern cities had rallied

[70] William Q. Maxwell, *Lincoln's Fifth Wheel, the Political History of the U.S. Sanitary Commission* (New York, 1956), p. 155. George Templeton Strong, a noted New Yorker and Treasurer of the Commission, commented in his diary about the fearsome quality of the battle: "Nothing new. Letter from Olmsted this afternoon at No. 498, ten pages long, giving a fearful, sickening account . . . of carloads of wounded men dumped on swampy river shores without food, medicine, or attendance; of men with fractured thighs lying neglected and forgotten forty-eight hours in two inches of water, struggling to raise themselves so as to pick the maggots from their rotting wounds and fainting after the effort, and yet keeping a good heart through it" (*Diary of the Civil War, 1860–65, George Templeton Strong*, ed. Allan Nevins [New York, 1962], p. 230).

[71] Olmsted to Bellows, March 4, 1865, Bellows Papers.

to the support of the Sanitary Commission. Without such commitment it could never have succeeded in helping the Northern soldier, thereby becoming known as "Lincoln's Fifth Wheel."

Now was the time to strike for raising the cultural tone of Northern cities, and through them that of the nation. He urged the establishment of an "association of book-buyers, centre[d] in New York—corresponding clubs every where—sub centres of distribution at Boston, Albany, Buffalo, Cleveland, Chicago, St. Louis, San Francisco."[72] He joined a small group planning for the publication of the weekly newspaper, the *Nation*, in New York City. It was unfortunate, he wrote to Bellows, that the newspaper was not already in existence. "Never was there so favorable a season for planting good seed, especially in New York. There is a tide in the affairs of men. There are tides and there is [a] tide up now, higher and stronger than ever before."[73] Thus, the city, in less than a decade, had supplanted the countryside as the object of Olmsted's interest and attention.

By this time, the countryside, which was Olmsted's ideal, had all but disappeared. Machines were replacing men, and world markets were destroying the independence of farming communities. The most spectacular innovation was the construction of the federally subsidized Union Pacific Railroad, its completion signifying a revolutionary change in agrarian society. It had led, Olmsted wrote, to "the greater dispersion of our food-producers, [and] has tended most of all to render them . . . independent of all . . . neighborhood agencies of demand and supply, manufacture and exchange, and to educate them and their children in familiarity with and dependence on the conveniences and habits of towns-people."[74] Clearly, the farm was no longer the nucleus of American society. Children born there, he noted, were "eager to leave . . . and to abandon rural occupations."[75]

[72] Olmsted to Bellows, Jan. 18, 1865, *ibid.*
[73] Olmsted to Bellows, July 28, 1863, *ibid.*
[74] Olmsted, *Public Parks*, p. 5.
[75] Olmsted, *Agricultural Colleges*, p. 12.

Country people demanded more and more manufactured goods—particularly luxury items. Olmsted pointed to the daily arrival in the cities of women who would "run in to do a little shopping, intending to return by supper time to farms perhaps a hundred miles away." And if the country could not always go the city, what did it matter, for the city had invaded the countryside with advertisements and catalogs. "Push out over the prairie," he wrote, "and make your way to the house of any long-settled and prosperous farmer, and the intimacy of his family with the town will constantly appear, in dress, furniture, viands, in all the conversation. If there is a piano, they will be expecting a man from town to tune it. If the baby has outgrown its shoes, the measure is to be sent to town. If a tooth is troublesome, an appointment is to be arranged by telegraph with the dentist."[76]

Industrialization had narrowed the economic basis of rural life, making it more dependent on the city and aggravating the already apparent decline in wealth, population, and influence. On his travels throughout the nation in the 1860's and 70's, Olmsted saw what seemed to him to be the disappearance of an older way of life—"the meeting-house closed, the church dilapidated; the famous old taverns, stores, shops, mills, and offices dropping to pieces and vacant, or perhaps with a mere corner occupied by day laborers; but a third as many children as formerly . . . in the school-houses, and of these less than half of American-born parents."[77]

No one event adequately explains Olmsted's shift of interest from the farm to the city. In addition to this changing pattern of the American landscape, which concerned him very personally, there were several other factors: his failure to establish a financially successful experimental farm on Staten Island in the late 1840's, which caused him to seek other means of earning a living; his respect for Andrew Jackson Downing, editor of the influential magazine, the *Horticulturist*, who in the 1840's began to emphasize the need for public parks, among other social institutions, in the growing city; his close friend-

[76] Olmsted, *Public Parks*, pp. 1-2.
[77] *Ibid.*, pp. 2-3.

ship with Charles Loring Brace, whose passionate concern with urban problems culminated in the founding of New York City's Children's Aid Society in 1853; and his publishing venture as co-owner of *Putnam's Monthly Magazine*, which (although a financial disaster) placed him in steady contact with the literature on urban affairs. As Putnam's representative in London in 1856 he saw evidence of the influence which a great metropolis could exercise on a nation and an empire. Finally, the death in 1857 of his brother John, who had accompanied him on his walking trip through England and on one of his trips through the South, seemed to mark the end of one phase of his life. The world he had known as a child, and some of the people for whom he had cared most of all, seemed to be passing, and so he turned his attention to some of the problems of the urban scene which had replaced that world. The city would now be called upon to compensate for the failure of the countryside as well as to struggle with conditions of urban life. The challenge, he understood, would be a great one, but the city could benefit by borrowing from the best aspects of rural life.

A Social Theory

The countryside had been the cradle of democracy and in his generation the source of social action which he considered vital to the national interest. New England, despite its many inadequacies, had in the nineteenth century provided the nation with pioneers and institutions of reform in keeping with its democratic heritage. Now, Olmsted held, it was the responsibility of government to provide for all its urban citizens the social and cultural advantages heretofore enjoyed in the countryside only by the privileged few. A democratic government must see to it that a maximum number of its citizens "reads similar books, wears similar clothing, has similar amusements, and dwells in a similar house, with similar furniture" to that possessed by the more privileged.[78] It was this social purpose which had to guide city planning.

[78] Olmsted, *Agricultural Colleges*, p. 10.

Olmsted hoped to achieve reform peacefully and harmoniously by attracting to the city an elite leadership. A social group similar to the New England rural gentry of his childhood, he maintained, would be committed to this meaning of democracy. They would be leaders who displayed "that form of conscientiousness that attends the honorable possession of honorable advantages"—men and women who by circumstance of family background, education, experience, and ability were equipped and willing to contribute to the improvement of the community and the nation. Social reform movements had failed to take hold in post–Civil War America, he would write, because society was still "piloted by people who have no ambition to wear the badge of a gentry."[79]

Olmsted recalled the conclusion reached by Chancellor Harper and other Southerners that democracies were doomed to collapse into anarchy for want of distinguished leadership. "Who shall estimate the value to Athens, of Solon, Aristides, Themistocles, Cymon or Pericles?" Harper asked. "If society have not leaders qualified as I have said, they will lead them blindly to their loss and ruin."[80] Olmsted admitted this failure of political leadership in the North, for he had had sufficient experience with local government to recognize how venal state and urban legislatures could be. "The New York Aldermen,"

[79] Olmsted, autobiographical scrap, n.d., Olmsted Papers. Olmsted's description of the ideal reformer parallels the description of the self-image held by the typical end-of-century progressive reformer given by Professor Richard Hofstadter: "Their ideal leader was a well-to-do, well-educated, high-minded citizen, rich enough to be free from motives of what they often called 'crass materialism,' whose family roots were deep not only in American history but in his local community. Such a person, they thought, would be just the sort to put the national interest, as well as the interests of civic improvement, above personal motives or political opportunism" (*The Age of Reform, from Bryan to F. D. R.* [New York, 1955], p. 140). It is also the view of Professor George Mowry, who has written in his examination of California progressivism that it "was an expression of an older America" ("The Urban Gentry on the Defensive," *The Progressive Era, Liberal Renaissance or Liberal Failure?*, ed. Arthur Mann [New York, 1963], p. 37).
[80] Chancellor William Harper, "Memoir on Slavery," p. 495.

he wrote to the Reverend Bellows during the Civil War, "need to be fought quite as much as Lee and Typhoid."[81] But his answer to the South and his basis of hope for the future was that leadership depended less on what was "required in politics than in other departments of service to the public."[82] What if "some of our senators [are] blackguards," he asked.[83] Had not the North channelled its leadership into more productive occupations of business, science, and the arts? It was this leadership, Olmsted held, which accounted for social progress, and which would eventually bring about an improved political system.

Faults of the City

The city in the mid-nineteenth century, however, could not attract such a group. In his explanation of this failure, Olmsted accepted the criticism of Southerners regarding the poor health, immorality, and barbarism of the commercial and industrial city. High density, he wrote, was the city's most distinct liability, and he likened the consequences to the hazards of a city without sewers. Medical authorities and social statisticians pointed out the threat to health and life. He noted the widely published health statistics of English cities compiled by the Registrar-General's Office in London: Londoners had an average life expectancy of twenty-six years, with an average population of 50,000 to the square mile; Liverpool, with a higher density of 140,000 to the square mile, showed a life expectancy of only seventeen years.[84]

An international "sanitary movement," commencing with the official publication by the British government of Sir Edwin Chadwick's "Health of Towns Report" in 1842, influenced Americans who, like Olmsted, were interested in improving

[81] Olmsted to Bellows, Oct. 3, 1862, Bellows Papers.

[82] Olmsted, *Back Country*, II, 252.

[83] *Ibid.*, p. 255.

[84] Frederick Law Olmsted and Calvert Vaux to the Brooklyn Park Commissioners, Jan. 1, 1868, in the *Eighth Annual Report of the Brooklyn Park Commissioners* (Brooklyn, 1868), p. 148. See Document IV below.

the city.[85] The Report demonstrated by means of statistical evidence that the physical dangers of urban concentration could be offset by such agricultural techniques as land drainage and sewers and by such "natural antidotes" as light and air. "We are able to reach the conviction," Olmsted wrote, "beyond all reasonable doubt, that at least the larger share of the immunity from the visits of the plague and other forms of pestilence, and from sweeping fires, and the larger part of the improved general health and increased length of life which civilized towns have lately enjoyed is due . . . to the gradual adoption of a custom of laying them out with much larger spaces open to the sun-light and fresh air."[86]

The new techniques, however effective in new cities and in extensions of the old, would not suffice for the original urban core, now almost exclusively dominated by commercial, manufacturing, and industrial buildings. Important urban centers such as Paris, London, Glasgow, and Liverpool had markedly failed to improve their central business districts despite large expenditures "for securing more space in and about the dwellings of that part of their population" forced to live there.[87] The nature of commerce and industry—the pace, competitiveness, and filth—could not be contained, and hindered the development of stable homes and harmonious communities. Olmsted was emphatic that "a high state of health, or a sound

[85] Chadwick, for example, influenced the thinking and the methodology of Lemuel Shattuck, author of a now classic mid-nineteenth-century study of the sanitary conditions of Massachusetts. A recent commentator on this study has noted that "it was undoubtedly from Chadwick that Lemuel Shattuck drew much of his inspiration" Lemuel Shattuck, et al., *Report of the Sanitary Commission of Massachusetts, 1850*, with a foreword by Charles-Edward Amory Winslow [Cambridge, 1948], p. vi.

[86] Olmsted and Vaux to the Brooklyn Park Commissioners, Jan. 1, 1868, p. 43. For a discussion of the "Myths About Fresh Air" current in Olmsted's time, see George R. Collins and Christiane Crasemann Collins, *Camillo Sitte and the Birth of Modern City Planning* (New York, 1965), pp. 192–194.

[87] Olmsted et al., *Report to the Staten Island Improvement Commission of a Preliminary Scheme of Improvements* (New York, 1871), p. 184n. See Document V below.

moral condition can never be acquired by children or preserved by adults under the requirements of success which
modern town life tends to impose."[88]

There were other aspects of urban life which troubled
him as much as they did any Southern critic. Among these
were the anonymity and absence of communal feeling, and
the replacement of land ownership by the social nexus of capital. As early as 1845, in fact, he had been bothered by the
requirement of the commercial world that one cater to the
"customer's humor and not his own."[89] Smiles, social manners,
and personality seemed to have become objects of exchange.
Urban living made it difficult to establish stable, trusting relationships; people tended "to regard others in a hard if not
always hardening way." In a stroll through "the denser part
of a town," he noted, "to merely avoid collision with those
we meet and pass upon the sidewalks, we have constantly
to watch, to foresee, and to guard against their movements."
In this respect, the city was the antithesis of the country village he had known as a child and of life in the Red Bank
community. It produced men who were apprehensive, hard,
and selfish because it provided no opportunity for people to
"experience . . . anything in common."[90]

A particularly alarming product of the urban environment
was the rising rate of social illness. It seemed to him that
in addition to crime, alcoholism, prostitution, venereal diseases,
and fires by incendiaries, there was an increase in mental disorders. Olmsted commented upon the many different cases
of "nervous feebleness or irritability" and noted "various functional derangements" which characterized urban life. New-
comers from the countryside especially complained of "the
effect on their nerves and minds of the street contact."[91] One
of Olmsted's principal planning goals, therefore, was to create

[88] *Ibid.*, p. 199.
[89] Olmsted to John Hull Olmsted, June 23, 1845, Olmsted Papers.
[90] Olmsted, *Public Parks*, p. 11. For a contemporary and particularly sensitive description of the impact of the city on the rural migrant
see Oscar Handlin, *The Uprooted* (Boston, 1951), especially Chs. III,
IX, and X.
[91] Olmsted, *Public Parks*, p. 11; see also Olmsted and Vaux, *Riverside*,
p. 6.

an environment which afforded tranquilizing recreation and which would be conducive to "a temperate, good-natured, and healthy state of mind."[92]

Ironically, it was those most responsible for the growth and economic well-being of the city who tended to abandon it. Statistical evidence accumulated by the 1850's and 60's demonstrated to Olmsted that "the sharp country boy . . . [who had become] the keen city man"[93]—the businessman and merchant—did not tend to live in the city's commercial center. Cities seemed incapable of retaining "the classes most advanced in civilization"—its real social leaders. And if they could not retain the wealthy, what hope was there for the rest of the city.[94] Those who remained, he lamented, were a group "which, by its avocations and its poverty, is practically precluded from moving [out of the heart of the city]."[95]

Importance of the City

The desertion of the city was for Olmsted an historical tragedy. For him, as for others of his generation, the city symbolized mankind's historic social progress. "The words urban, civilized and civil," he wrote, "once implied no more than that those to whom they were applied dwelt with other men in cities." But through centuries of progress, these terms had come to mean "manners differing from those of pagans."[96] Though he understood that urban growth was principally the product of changes in the economic system of the Western world, he pointed to other historic relationships, such as "the enlargement of popular freedom, the spread of knowledge by books, [and] the abatement of religious persecutions."[97] He

---

[92] Olmsted, *Public Parks*, p. 11; see also Olmsted and Vaux to the Brooklyn Park Commissioners, Jan. 1, 1868, p. 150.

[93] Olmsted and Vaux to the Brooklyn Park Commissioners, Jan. 1, 1868, p. 160.

[94] Olmsted *et al.*, *Staten Island*, p. 184.

[95] *Ibid.*, p. 184n.

[96] Olmsted, Scrap of Proposed History of Civilization, n.d., Olmsted Papers.

[97] Olmsted and Vaux to the Brooklyn Park Commissioners, Jan. 1, 1868, p. 138.

valued the "intimate connection . . . evident between the growth of towns and the dying out of slavery and feudal customs, of priestcraft and government by divine right, the multiplication of books, newspapers, schools, and other means of popular education and the adoption of improved methods of communication, transportation, and of various labor-saving inventions."[98]

Olmsted fully appreciated the relationship of social progress to economic growth and technological development. The phenomenal growth of the American city during his own lifetime, he explained, was due in large measure to the nation's sustained revolution in "communication, transportation and exchange." The laying of the first continental railroad and the discovery of the electric telegraph were but indications of urban change and the start of a "new chapter of commercial and social progress."[99] Never before in the history of man had it been possible to provide adequately for the economic and social needs of so many people. Facilities and products for the improvement of life were available, he observed, which the most aristocratic families could not have enjoyed even as late as 1800.[100] No nation could deliberately neglect its cities for none would want "to give up schools or newspapers, railroads or telegraphs, to restore feudal rights or advance rates of postage." He noted proudly that "king-craft and priest-craft . . . [were] nowhere gaining any solid ground."[101]

A Physical Plan: The Suburb

Olmsted's plan for a physical framework which would attract and maintain the leadership necessary to preserve these

[98] Olmsted, *Public Parks*, p. 4. For a recent analysis of the historical significance of the city which parallels Olmsted's, see James M. Fitch, "In Defense of the City," *Columbia University Forum*, III (Fall, 1960), 4–10.

[99] Olmsted and Vaux to the Brooklyn Park Commissioners, Jan. 1, 1868, p. 146; see Hofstadter, *op. cit.*, pp. 51 and 57.

[100] Olmsted, *Riverside*, pp. 4–5.

[101] Olmsted, *Public Parks*, p. 4.

gains was intended as well to contain the destructive influence of the commercial sections of the city. This was feasible, he felt, since "commerce does not require the same conditions to be maintained in all parts of a town."[102] It was undoubtedly Olmsted's rural background which led him to emphasize the introduction of "natural" elements in reforming the urban environment. But it would be inaccurate to characterize his point of view as either rural or antiurban. Rather, he hoped to fuse the best qualities of both country and city into a new physical and social unit: the suburb. As he expressed it, "No broad question of country life in comparison with city life is involved; it is confessedly a question of delicate adjustment."[103] This "adjustment" could best be achieved in governmentally designed communities distinct from, but connected to, the older commercial city, creating a new form for the metropolis.

These suburbs were not intended to be (as are suburbs now in existence) far removed from the heart of the city. The idea—recurrent in present-day urban planning literature—was to develop communities within easy reach of the city-center, inhabited by "urban villagers."[104] Olmsted believed that the many varieties of the light carriage (which had come into use in the nineteenth century) and the steam-railway would facilitate rapid and easy transportation between home and work. The city he looked forward to was an organic one in which its many parts, like the various rooms of a house, would have separate functions. This contrasted sharply with the American city of the time, in which sections tended to serve all purposes.

[102] *Ibid.*, p. 15.

[103] Olmsted and Vaux to the Brooklyn Park Commissioners, Jan. 1, 1868, p. 160.

[104] The theme of the "urban villager" is found in the work of such critics as Paul and Percival Goodman, *Communitas* (New York, 1947); Lewis Mumford, *The City in History* (New York, 1961); Jane Jacobs, *The Death and Life of Great American Cities* (New York, 1961); and Herbert J. Gans, *The Urban Villagers* (New York, 1962). Although all four have different approaches to the subject, each accepts almost as axiomatic that a satisfying urban life can only be had in small communities within the metropolis.

There was, he felt, no technical reason why the suburb should not combine the best features of city and country. The cultural advantages of urban life, he realized, would be lost even to "people living in houses a quarter or a half a mile apart." But the city need not be synonymous with "an unhealthy density of population." In fact, "the advantages of civilization" were perhaps best realized in "suburban neighborhoods where each family abode stands fifty or a hundred feet or more apart from all others, and at some distance from the public road."[105] Good roads and walks, adequate sewerage, a pure water supply, gas to light the dark streets, and low-cost, rapid, and comfortable transportation to urban centers could, he believed, "give any farming land in a healthy and attractive situation the value of town lots."[106] He had seen such suburban communities in his travels in England, and by the mid-1860's was actively engaged in constructing them.

Olmsted's opinion carried considerable weight. During the 1860's and 70's he had achieved the distinction of being America's foremost landscape architect and city planner. This reputation was based in part on the amazing technical achievements displayed in the design and construction of Central Park; a "master-plan" for the development of Brooklyn, then New York City's most important suburb; and a design in 1870 for Riverside, Illinois, a model suburb six miles outside of Chicago. Equally important, however, was the fact that his plans were based on a consistent social theory explained in most of the written reports accompanying the designs. His reputation as a social scientist equalled his fame as a landscape architect. His published reports on the South had been favorably compared to Arthur Young's classic discussion of France on the eve of the French Revolution. As administrator of the Sanitary Commission, he had presented very cogent reasons for the Northern defeat at Bull Run, pointing to the relationship between poor equipment, lack of training, and a failure of morale. A later Report to the Secretary of War contained a complete analysis of the organization of the Commission

[105] Olmsted, *Public Parks*, p. 9.
[106] *Ibid.*, p. 10.

and recommendations for its improvement which "won applause at home and admiration abroad."[107] In fact, his importance and fame as a landscape architect and city planner rested as much on his social thought as on his technical and administrative ability. His theory of urban design was generally acceptable to the political decision-makers of his day and understood by the informed public as well.

There was a direct continuity between his concept of urban growth and his administrative experience during the Civil War. During the war he had been a proponent of centralization of authority in the interest of efficient management of governmental operations. Local autonomy, he observed, could defeat a national democratic enterprise. Similarly, he had constantly urged that cities be granted increased administrative power in order to permit their logical expansion into neighboring territories already within their economic and social spheres of influence. Olmsted noted that political boundaries (arbitrarily established by state legislatures) were not a true measure of the influence of a city, which always affects an area greater than itself. He urged, for example, that the political boundaries of New York City—until 1874 confined to Manhattan Island—be extended to include that greater metropolis which was already in existence by the 1850's: upper Manhattan, Westchester, Brooklyn, and Staten Island. But such a huge territory, he maintained, could only be administered and controlled by concentrating decision-making power in a nonpartisan, technically expert elite. He was, therefore, a constant advocate of commission-type government. His dream, unfulfilled, was the establishment of a governmental agency endowed with comprehensive powers to plan for the growth and development of the entire urban region.

The immediate purpose of such an agency would be to guarantee that the portion of the metropolis not yet settled and developed would be planned as attractive suburbs. The opportunity was immediate and feasible. Those who fled the commercial parts of the city were settling precisely in these contiguous areas. It was, he argued, an axiom of urban behavior

[107] Maxwell, *op. cit.*, p. 114.

39

that large movements of population occurred as urban density rose and social amenities declined. But he regarded such population movement as an integral and inevitable part of the urban process—not as a rejection of the city. It was, he wrote, "a higher rise of the same flood, . . . end of which must be, not a sacrifice of urban conveniences, but their combination with the special charms and substantial advantages of rural conditions of life." The permanence of the suburb could be predicted on the basis that it was part of a world-wide movement "clearly perceptible, and almost equally so in Paris, London, Vienna, Berlin, New York, Boston and Philadelphia."[108]

Olmsted's commitment to the development of the suburban metropolis and his belief in the need for centralizing administrative and political power coincided with that of Andrew Haswell Green, the Democratic politician most influential in effecting the final union of the Greater City of New York in 1898.[109] Green, a powerful figure in city and state politics for most of the second half of the nineteenth century, had devoted much of his career to the accomplishment of this political and administrative end. He supported Olmsted so long as their planning and political objectives coincided. But he became a formidable antagonist when it seemed that Olmsted's plans—based as they were primarily on social considerations— would retard the physical amalgamation of the City, or when, in the 1870's, Olmsted's highly professional and centralized

[108] Olmsted, *Riverside,* pp. 5–7.

[109] The membership of the Commission of Inquiry established by state law (May 8, 1890) reads like a roll-call of the last of the old reformers who had pushed for consolidation since the late 1850's. Although Olmsted was not a member of the Commission because he was no longer a resident of the state, his influence was reflected through the presence of former associates. Andrew Haswell Green was President; James Stranahan of Brooklyn, with whom Olmsted had worked so well on Prospect Park (see preface to Part II, Brooklyn), was Vice-President; John Bogart, State Engineer, had been chief of construction of Central Park; George W. Curtis had been Olmsted's partner in the publication of *Putnam's Monthly Magazine* in the 1850's; and Calvert Vaux, his partner on so many projects, was a member (see John Foord, *The Life and Public Services of Andrew Haswell Green* [New York, 1913], pp. 186–187).

concept of administration interfered with Green's practical political purposes or those of his close associate and law partner, a presidential aspirant, Samuel J. Tilden. But during most of Olmsted's early work in New York City (in the late fifties and sixties), despite frequent and bitter clashes of personality and differences of opinion regarding the administration of Central Park, Green and Olmsted were an effective team. Both saw in the creation of the park an important step toward the design of a new and more efficient metropolis.

Once it had been reasonable to assume that the larger a city grew the greater would be its problems—so great as to make it unlivable. As a city increased in area and population, urban critics had charged, the more it "would be exposed to epidemic diseases, [and] the feebler, more sickly, and shorter . . . [the] lives [of its people] would be; the greater would be the danger of sweeping conflagrations; the larger the proportion of mendicants and criminals, and the more formidable, desperate and dangerous the mobs."[110]

But these assumptions, Olmsted believed, had been proved false. Cities, he wrote, had, in fact, increased in population until "there are many in Europe . . . several times larger than the largest of the Middle Ages, and in the largest the amount of disease is not more than half as great as it formerly was; the chance of living to old age is much more than twice as great; epidemics are less frequent, less malignant and more controllable; sweeping fires are less common, less devastating and are much sooner got under [control]; ruffians are much better held in check; mobs are less frequently formed, are less dangerous, and, when they arise, are suppressed more quickly and with less bloodshed; there is a smaller proportion of the population given over to vice and crime and a vastly larger proportion of well-educated, orderly, industrious and well-to-do citizens."[111]

Olmsted had become a nineteenth-century urban man. He welcomed—no longer feared—the large city, believing that

[110] Olmsted and Vaux to the Brooklyn Park Commissioners, Jan. 1, 1868, p. 145.
[111] Ibid.

41

the economic, social, and technical forces which had fostered it could now be applied toward its mastery and improvement. The future seemed promising, although the challenge was formidable. The nineteenth-century city, throughout the Western world, had been split functionally in two—the commercial and the residential—by the very same economic forces which had fostered its growth and prosperity at the cost of the countryside. The social advantages of both environments, however, could now be combined in a new synthesis: the suburb. Olmsted described suburbs as "the most attractive, the most refined and the most soundly wholesome forms of domestic life, and the best application of the arts of civilization to which mankind has yet attained."[112] Furthermore, the suburb offered planners a means by which to restore cities to some sort of structural unity and civilized purpose. The integration of the ordered landscape into the rapidly grown cityscape was the most logical solution for the problems of the nineteenth-century American city that the nation's most eminent landscape architect and city planner, born and reared in the countryside, could devise.

The purpose of this anthology is to present a body of documents, accompanied by an explanatory essay, to enable those interested in the contemporary city to learn first-hand what the principal theorist and planner of the modern American city, Frederick Law Olmsted, hoped to achieve by his work in New York. As such, it is designed primarily as a book of readings, and should raise many more questions than it can possibly answer. If, however, it leaves the reader with the feeling that Olmsted's plans for New York City were meant to remedy the social problems of his time, as he saw them, then it will have accomplished the goal set for it by the editor.

[112] Olmsted, *Riverside*, p. 7.

A NOTE ON THE DOCUMENTS

→⟫-⟫-⟫⟪-⟪-⟪

In the short space of twenty-four years Frederick Law Olmsted and his partner, Calvert Vaux (see Illustration I),[1] designed much of the man-made landscape which is now a permanent part of New York City. They began with their plan for Central Park, adopted in 1858, and completed most of their work by 1882, when Olmsted published his pamphlet, *Spoils of the Park*. During most of this time New York City meant Manhattan Island only, since Brooklyn was a separate city, the Bronx part of Westchester County, and Queens and Richmond separate counties. Olmsted, usually in cooperation with Vaux, prepared plans for each area, with a comprehensive design in mind—for the Greater City of New York, they realized, was already a sociological fact.

Of the twelve documents reprinted here nine are reports to governmental bodies regarding public works for some part

---

[1] Calvert Vaux was—at least in one way—a historically tragic figure. Trained as an architect in England, where he was born and educated, Vaux was brought to this country by Andrew Jackson Downing, the important American horticulturist and propagandist for naturalism in architectural and landscape design. Vaux designed part or all of such notable New York City buildings as the Jefferson Market Court, the Metropolitan Museum of Art, and the American Museum of Natural History; nevertheless, he believed that his real contribution to the urban scene was in the field of landscape architecture. He, like Olmsted, considered spaces to be more significant than solids in planning cities. However, Olmsted's varied contributions to American civilization, his national reputation as a gifted administrator, and his direct involvement in the political turmoils of the Park and in politics generally made him more prominent as a public figure. Furthermore, by the 1880's, Vaux's influence as an architect had diminished. Notwithstanding his important role in the artistic and literary worlds of New York City, Vaux died a bitter man, believing that he had somehow been cheated of a full share of the credit due him as codesigner of New York City's vital open spaces.

of the larger city. These are II, III, IV, V, VII, VIII, IX, X, and XII. Responsibility for their enactment rested elsewhere. There were, of course, other reports with plans for parks and projects designed by Olmsted (with Vaux or someone else) during this same period which are not included in this volume. These consisted mainly of plans for neighborhood parks in Manhattan and Brooklyn. To the best of my knowledge none of the nine reports have been reissued since their original date of publication, except for Document II, "Greensward," which was reprinted privately by the authors in 1868. It appears as well in Volume II of *Forty Years of Landscape Architecture*, edited by Frederick Law Olmsted, Jr., and Theodora Kimball (New York, 1928). An extract of Document II is found in *City and Country in America*, edited by David R. Weimer (New York, 1962). Document XI was published privately in 1882 and included in *Forty Years*.

The two other documents in this volume, I and VI, were not published during Olmsted's lifetime. Document I was edited by Frederick Law Olmsted, Jr., and printed in *Landscape Architecture*, Volume II (July, 1912). It then appeared in a *Report of the American Scenic and Historical Preservation Society* (1914), altered stylistically, and this is the version given here. Also, a portion of it was included in *Forty Years*, Volume II. Document VI, referred to in this volume as "Report on Rockaway Point," was in the form of a manuscript letter to the developers of that area, and has been edited here. The original is in the Olmsted Papers at the Library of Congress.

The sideheads in Document II and the Contents entries in Document VI have been included in the texts as subheads; this operation has occasionally required additional paragraphing of Olmsted's text. All the footnotes but one which appear in the body of the documents are Olmsted's.

PART ONE

⫸⫸⫸⫸⫸⫸⫸⫸⫸⫸⫸⫸⫷⫷⫷⫷⫷⫷⫷⫷⫷⫷

MANHATTAN

Document I, a small piece of autobiography written in the 1870's, contains Olmsted's astute analysis of how he—"an unpractical man," an idealist—came to be appointed in 1857 Superintendent in charge of construction of Central Park, New York City's most important architectural work. Olmsted recreates some of the political turmoil of New York City in the 1850's—the world of Fernando Wood versus Reform Democrats, Democrats versus Republicans, and the City opposed to the State in a time of shifting political structure. As the City's most expensive undertaking at the time, and one which employed an army of workers, the Park was also ripe for political patronage. Politics, in fact, presented a constant source of conflict and frustration.

In political terms Olmsted was "unpractical," for his motivation was in part what he considered to be the needs of his time and the spirit of his age. This incomplete autobiography reveals the extent to which Olmsted saw himself as an instrument of social change during "[a] period in which the work of the railroad and of universal suffrage began; in which what is called the temperance reformation and the abolition of slavery have occurred,"[1] and in which the city began to replace the countryside. Like other contemporary New Englanders, such as historians George Bancroft and Henry Adams, Olmsted had an almost religious respect for the meaning of history. This was quite understandable since their ancestors, the early settlers of New England, had revered the Bible not only as a source of personal enlightenment, but as the history of the world's creation and the unfolding of the Lord's purpose. Politics counted for little by contrast with what he saw as the larger purpose of reform.

[1] Frederick Law Olmsted, "The Beginning of Central Park: A Fragment of Autobiography," *American Scenic and Historic Preservation Society, Nineteenth Annual Report* (1914), p. 51. See Document I below.

47

Document II points up another side of Olmsted, also historically conditioned, which was his dedication to art as a social force capable of affecting the feelings and manners of people in significant ways. One of the reasons why he never completed his autobiography was that he concentrated during the last years on refining and clarifying his esthetic goals and techniques. "Where shall I find the definition of art which I want to correct me," he asked his friend and neighbor, Charles Eliot Norton, the noted art critic and intimate of John Ruskin, "a definition which will include landscape modification and accentuation? Is it absurdly incomplete to say as I do that the prime object of a work of art is to affect the emotions?"[2]

Document II, the plan for Central Park by Olmsted and Vaux, appropriately titled "Greensward" (see Illustration III), is an early example of his theory of landscape architecture translated into an art form. The plan was one of thirty-three designs submitted in 1858 in open competition. Among the entries were those of many of the country's most noted landscape planners. Olmsted and Vaux won the contest and a prize of $2,000. While the general objectives of the plan were not unlike those of the others submitted, its merits were in the degree of imagination and technical skill which the designers applied to the problem at hand. This essay is as much a social document as, for example, Olmsted's description of the South, published almost simultaneously. And it could be understood by the judges, or any intelligent reader of the time, for it used one of the special languages of the day, the dialect of nature. The essay shows how concerned the designers were with the future needs of the city.

[2] Olmsted to Charles E. Norton, Oct. 19, 1881, Norton Papers, Houghton Library. Hereafter cited as Norton Papers.

DOCUMENT I

>>>->>>->>>-<<<-<<<-<<<

FREDERICK LAW OLMSTED

The Beginning of Central Park: A Fragment of Autobiography (ca. 1877)[1]

>>>->>>->>>-<<<-<<<-<<<

Introductory Note by His Son, Frederick Law Olmsted [Jr.]

Among the papers left by my father were two fragments of an autobiography upon which he had made a beginning. Both are so interesting and so brief as to intensify our regret that he did not find time to complete such a book as he had in mind. Of the two fragments, only that which follows, is, as an isolated article, sufficiently related to professional subjects to be appropriate for a technical periodical.

It tells how my father was led to become superintendent of the inchoate Central Park; which in time led to his joining with his friend, Mr. Vaux, in preparing a plan for the development of the park, and thus brought him into the practice of an art which he did so much to establish upon a sound professional basis in this country. It does not tell of his preceding experience as a practical farmer, of how he was broadened by much travel and by observation, thought and writing directed both to social and economic subjects and to beauty in landscape, all of which led him to realize, as this fragment

[1] This fragment of the autobiography of the elder Mr. Olmsted is here reproduced by the courtesy of his son. It first appeared in the magazine Landscape Architecture in July, 1912. If forms an interesting chapter in addition to the history of Central Park by Edward Hagaman Hall which appeared in the Sixteenth Annual Report of the American Scenic and Historic Preservation Society. (1911.)

tells, the enormous influence for good in a great city of a park rightly managed, and also prepared .him to direct that management effectively. The episode is told, however, primarily from the broader point of view of the earnest, clear-sighted American citizen, anxious as to the political conditions and tendencies of his country, suffering from no illusions as to the proximate inefficiency, waste and corruption of our governmental agencies, but with unshaken confidence in the principle of democratic rule as the only safe basis for ultimate human progress. It was mainly his realization that real and permanent improvement is to be obtained only through the tedious process of bringing the people to face and understand the base uncolored truth about public affairs which led him to begin these autobiographic notes as well as to prepare that remarkable contribution to the study of the practical politics of his time entitled "Spoils of the Park," published in 1882. The following prefatory note and probably the fragment of autobiography must have been written during the late seventies.

FREDERICK LAW OLMSTED [JR.]

Brookline, Mass., July 5, 1912

Passages in the Life of an Unpractical Man

➤➤➤-➤➤➤-➤➤➤-❮❮❮-❮❮❮-❮❮❮

Preface

Since my journeys in the Slave States, twenty years ago, I have been making excursions in another field of much general interest and with regard to which the public seems embarrassed. It has been on my mind of late that I should publish some account of my observations therein. I have found, however, whenever I have begun to consider what material I had available for the purpose, that much of the knowledge that I had gained had come to me by multitudinous details of which no adequate report could be given; much more through personal communications, a fair report of which would be constantly headed off by private rights.

The only way in which the significance and weight of much that has come under my view could be made known to a stranger, therefore, would be by showing how the life of the narrator was affected by it. But the value of a narrative prepared with this purpose would depend so much on other circumstances of personal history that, to accomplish its purpose, it would need to be almost an autobiography.

These considerations would have brought the project to an end had I not been led, about the same time, to recall certain passages in my early life, in the review of which some light seemed to be cast not only on my own failure in practical ability, but on the apparent embarrassment of the public in respect to certain evils of comparatively recent origin, which are constantly growing and becoming more and more portentous.

This reflection finally gave shape to the present book.

In it I offer a small contribution of individual experience toward the history of the latter half of the first century of the American republic—the period in which the work of the railroad and of universal suffrage began; in which what is called the temperance reformation and the abolition of slavery have occurred; in which millions of people have been concentrated at New York, Philadelphia, Boston, Baltimore, Cincinnati, Chicago, St. Louis, and San Francisco, while rural neighborhoods in New England, Virginia, the Carolinas, and Georgia have been rapidly losing population, and still more rapidly losing various forms of wealth and worth.

Fragment Relating to Central Park

The agitation for a public park in New York began with an article published by Mr. Downing in 1848. This was followed, from time to time, by other papers, until his lamentable death four years afterward.

Mr. Downing's writings on the subject were much copied and favorably noticed by the leading newspapers, and, shortly before he died, the Common Council of New York, at the instigation of Mayor A. C. Kingsland, took action which led to an act of the State Legislature providing for a park on a tract of 150 acres of land situated on the East River. The following year a small politician, jealous of the advantages which another might gain by the success of this scheme, undertook to "head it off" by an alternate project. The idea striking him that a plausible argument could be made for a larger park more centrally situated, in a moment he adopted for his purpose the site afterwards accepted as that of the Central Park, neither knowing nor caring whether the ground was at all suitable in other respects than its geographical centrality.

The land was not fully acquired until 1856, and the Legislature having as yet made no provision for its government in the latter part of that year, Fernando Wood, then Mayor, near the end of his second term, obtained an act of the Common Council under which he with his Street Commissioner, Joseph S. Taylor, took charge of it. They appointed a Chief Engineer and a large corps of assistants, and expenditures were made and liabilities incurred on account of the park, as was alleged by their opponents, to the amount of $60,000, as the result of which all that could afterward be found of value to the City was an inaccurate topographical map of the ground.

It is often said that the failure of republican government in application to cities must be conceded, but of those Americans who make this concession few consider how much it involves.

Our country has entered upon a stage of progress in which its welfare is to depend on the convenience, safety, order and economy of life in its great cities. It cannot prosper independently of them; cannot gain in virtue, wisdom, comfort, except as they also advance.

On farms and in small towns, each household brings in its water, trims and fills its lamps, cultivates its garden, guards itself against fires, thieves and smallpox, keeps its drains open and removes its offal, breaks roads through the snow and takes care of its sick and destitute neighbors, all within itself. Every office of government may utterly fail without any unusual inconvenience being felt for months.

A man may come from this state of affairs to live in a large town, and may continue for years to profess as an article of religious faith that that is the best government which governs least, but it will be a faith that does not rest upon a recognition of the facts of life.

When, in large towns, desirable public ends seem likely to be more economically attained by the employment of a small organized force to do that which must otherwise be done by a much larger one working individually, there is a strong disinclination to such individual effort. The law in New York requires each householder to remove the snow from the gutters in front of his house within a certain period after it falls. The Corporation Attorney states that the neglect of this duty is so nearly universal that it would be absurd to attempt to enforce the penalty. The inconvenience and positive suffering experienced in consequence is frightful, and for this inconvenience and suffering the City government is blamed. There is no doubt that, if the business could be honestly and skilfully managed under government, the work could be done at a small percentage of the cost that would be required to have it done by householders.

Thus, and in various ways, as towns grow larger, the larger relatively to their size is likely to be the business which is required to be done under their government, and the more is their prosperity, and with their prosperity that of the whole country and of the world, to be dependent on the manner in which the business of this government is done.

In certain respect improvements are making. Special ability is enlisted and scientific means of securing fidelity and discipline are employed. Through the extraordinary exertions and expenditure of experts in insurance, for example, such means have been adopted with the Fire Department of New York. There can be no doubt, through the simple savings of capital which in all probability would have been lost but for the use of such means in this one particular, the population even of Kansas and Colorado is notably greater than it would otherwise be, or that that population has cheaper and better houses, roads, books, newspapers, clothes, food, teachers, doctors, and clergymen than it would otherwise have had.

And yet, in just this direction of steadiness, fidelity and discipline of service, our City governments are on the whole apparently losing ground. Let what the country needs of the government of its great cities be compared at intervals of five years with what it finds them able to perform, and on the whole the gap will always be found ominously wider.

If we must continue to let it widen, the occurrence of a grand catastrophe is plainly only a question of time. And it will be a catastrophe not merely for the republic but for civilization; for our great cities stretch their hands to all the world, and all the peoples of the world are provided through them.

There is a power which ordinarily lies ineffective back of all the political voices of our cities. At times it is stirred with shame, disgust and indignation; organizes itself and makes a loud demand for reform.

The politicians out of office take advantage of the opportunity, not only to secure the removal of those who have been in office, but to make them as they go forth serve the purpose of scapegoats. A few changes of form and method are made, and the citizens are reconciled to a system under which the old vices are cherished only more warmly than before.

One of these storms was rising at the period of which I have spoken, and Fernando Wood was to be the chief scapegoat by whose outgoing the indignation and wrath of the people were appeased.

Wood being a Democrat, the Republicans who held the majority of the State Legislature took advantage of the momentary popular disgust with him and his associates to take the regulation of certain parts of the City business from the elected government of the City, and to give it to a series

54

of professedly nonpartisan Commissions. One of these, composed of nine members, part Republicans, part Wood Democrats, part "reform" Democrats, part nondescript, was appointed to supersede Wood and Taylor in the special government of the Central Park. It had to go to the Common Council of the City for its supplies, and a majority of the members of the Common Council, siding with the Mayor, were disposed not to honor its requisitions. Eventually they would be obliged to do so unless indeed a decision of court could be obtained, as they professed to expect, declaring the act of the Legislature unconstitutional. But supplies could be delayed and, when yielded, given in driblets, and various difficulties and obstructions could be put in the way of the Commission.

Two considerable influences were working in favor of the Commission: first, a desire with many that some progress should be made in turning to use the property in the land appropriated to the park which had cost the City five million dollars; second, the desire of the laboring population to obtain the employment which the construction of the park was expected to give. This latter influence was strongest in those parts of the City where Wood and his supporters in the Common Council had hitherto obtained the most votes, and on their popularity in which they depended for re-election.

To counteract it, the act of the Legislature was denounced as a tyrannical usurpation of power, by which the Black Republicans and Abolitionists were to put themselves in office and plunder the City against the will of the local majority.

But these denunciations had to be uttered in the face of the fact that the Commission were to receive no pay; that they had elected a Democrat as their President, another Democrat as their Treasurer, and had reappointed Wood's whole engineer corps. They had gone so far in this respect that a clamor was beginning to rise from the Republican side that the Commission was wholly given over to the Democrats.

At this period in its history one of the Commissioners came to spend a Sunday at a seaside inn where I had been finishing the manuscript of my Journey in the Back Country. Sitting next [to] him at the tea table he told me what I have just re-

55

cited of the history of the Commission, and added that they were now taking on a force of laborers. Having no money as yet at their command, each of the men employed was required to sign an agreement releasing the Commissioners from personal liability on account of the wages he might earn, and, in lieu of wages, due bills against the City were to be issued, which would be payable when the Common Council should make the appropriation, in favor of which an additional element of popular interest would thus be established. He added that at their next meeting they intended to elect a Superintendent, and it was thought necessary that he should be a Republican. There were several candidates, but no Republican had appeared with whom he was much pleased, and he asked if I knew of a suitable man. I inquired what would be the duties of the Superintendent?

"He would be the executive officer of the engineer with respect to the labor force, and would have charge of the police and see that the proper regulations were enforced in regard to the public use of the park."

"Must he be a politician?"

"No, a Republican but not a politician; much better he should not be a practical politician. The Republicans can do little without the co-operation of the reform Democrats, and are ready to compromise on the understanding that the park shall be managed independently of politics."

"I am delighted to hear it," I said. "There's no limit to the good influence a park rightly managed would have in New York, and that seems to be the first necessity of good management."

"I wish we had you on the Commission, but, as we have not, why not take the superintendency yourself? Come now."

Till he asked the question, the possibility of my doing so had never occurred to me, though he probably suspected I was thinking of it. I at once answered, however, smiling:

"I take it? I'm not sure that I wouldn't if it were offered me. Nothing interested me in London like the parks, and yet I thought a great deal more might be made of them."

"Well, it will not be offered you; that's not the way we

do business; but if you'll go to work I believe you may get it. I wish that you would!"

"You are serious?"

"Yes; but there's no time to lose."

"What is to be done?"

"Go to New York and file an application; see the Commissioners and get your friends to back you."

"I'll take the boat to-night and think it out as I go. If no serious objection occurs to me before morning, I'll do it."

Accordingly, the next day I was looking for my friends in New York. At that season they were much scattered, but one I found who took up the matter warmly, and my application was in a few days fortified by a number of weighty signatures. I shall presently refer to the fact that among them was that of Washington Irving.

The President of the Commission being out of town on my arrival in New York, I first called on the Vice-President, bearing a letter to him from my friend in New Haven.

The Vice-President, who was a Republican, repeated that it was desirable that the Superintendent should not be a Democrat, yet that he should be as little objectionable as possible to the Democrats. He seemed to think that my prospects in this respect were good. He offered to introduce me to one of the Democratic Commissioners who was a very practical man, and also to the engineer, whom again he described as a very practical man; if their judgment should be favorable, I might count on his support.

The practical Democratic Commissioner having ascertained that I had had no experience in practical politics, even no personal acquaintance with the Republican leaders in the City, that my backing would be from unpractical men, and that I responded warmly to virtuous sentiments with regard to corruption in both parties, after a long conversation, gave me to understand that I might hope that, if the Republicans brought me forward, he should be less inclined to oppose me than a possible Republican who had been deep in the mire and who disapproved of the practice of virtue in politics.

The engineer I found at a house on the park about which

57

was a crowd of laboring men, each bearing a letter addressed to him. On the ground that my letter was from a Commissioner, I was allowed to precede those who had stood waiting outside the door before me. The room in which the engineer sat at a desk was crowded with applicants for employment, whose letters were collected in batches by men wearing a golden star on the breast of a very dirty and seedy jacket, and handed to the engineer. These letters were chiefly from members of the Common Council. As each was opened and its writer's name recognized, the bearer was either abruptly told that there was no work for him at present, or his name was taken and looked for on a list furnished by the writer of his letter, in which it appeared that a limited number had been named whom he wished to have preferred among all those to whom he gave letters. If found there, the applicant was, without further examination, given a ticket and told to call again on a given day.

At the first opportunity I presented my letter and card. Reading a few lines, the engineer glanced at me, dropped the letter and went on with his canvass of the laborers. I stood among them half an hour, and then, pointing to my card, asked if I might hope to find him less engaged later in the day. As he seemed to assent, I walked out a little way, looking at the ground for the park. I returned and withdrew again three times before I found the enlisting business ended. As I came in the last time the engineer was about leaving. I walked with him and took a seat by his side in the street car running to the City.

I then had an opportunity to state on what grounds I had ventured to think that he would find me useful as an assistant in his work. He replied that he would rather have a practical man. I did not learn why I could not be regarded as a possibly practical man, but it was only too evident that the gate of hope was closed to me in that direction.

Calling, by appointment, on the Vice-President the next day I was not surprised to find that doubts had been growing over night in his mind, as to whether the office of Superintendent should not be filled by a practical man.

Some time after my election, which occurred at the first subsequent meeting of the Park Board, another of the Commissioners told me that this objection would have defeated me had it not been for the autograph of Washington Irving on my papers. That turned the balance.

But one member in a full board of nine stood out in the final vote; it was Mr. Thomas C. Field[s]; and he never forgave me for it.

It is hardly necessary to say that even after my election I did not quite feel myself out of the woods. Had it been concluded that it was, after all, just as well not to have a practical man? Or had they been convinced that, after all, I was a practical man?

These gentlemen, most of whom had themselves made large fortunes in business, would hardly defer to Washington Irving on such a point. No, I owed my election to something else than their estimate of my value as a practical man, and to what I did not understand.

When I next came to the office on the park, my first experience was repeated until I said to the engineer: "I was instructed to report to you for orders, sir." Upon this, he called to one of the starred men: "Tell Hawkin to come here." Then to me: "I have given my orders to Mr. Hawkin; he is what I call a practical man, and I will tell him to show you what you have to do."

Mr. Hawkin, a cautious closemouthed, sensible-looking gentlemen, wearing no coat, and with trousers tucked in the legs of a heavy and dirty pair of boots, here opened the door and said, "Want me?"

"Yes; this is Mr. Olmsted, the new Superintendent; take him round the park and show him what work is going on, and tell the foremen they will take their orders from him after this."

"Now?"

The engineer looked at me.

"I am quite ready, sir."

"Yes, now."

In truth, as I had intended this to be rather a call of ceremony or preliminary report to my superior officer, I was not quite so well prepared as I could have wished to be for what followed.

Striking across the hill into what is now the Ramble, we came first upon a number of men with billhooks and forks collecting and burning brushwood. Under a tree near by a man sat smoking. He rose as we approached.

"Smith; this is Mr. Olmsted, your new Superintendent; you'll take orders from him after this."

All the men within hearing dropped their tools and looked at me. Smith said, "Oh! that's the man, is it? Expect we shall be pushed up, now." He laughed, and the men grinned.

"What is Smith doing?" I asked.

"He's grubbing 'round here, and burning up what he can get together," and Mr. Hawkin moved on.

"See you again, I suppose," said Smith, still laughing.

"Yes, sir; good-day, for the present."

And this process was repeated with little variation, as we passed from gang to gang to the number of perhaps fifteen, there being at this time about 500 men at work. As they were nearly all Democrats, and all appointed by a Democrat, and a Democrat who had himself been appointed first by Wood, and as they were mostly introduced to him by Democratic members of the Common Council, the presumption that the Commission was to be managed exclusively in the interests of the Republicans and as a means of defeating Wood was considerably weakened.

As I stood in the office I had not been able to observe that the slightest consideration was given to the apparent strength or activity of the laborers. Each man undoubtedly supposed that he owed the fact of his preference over others, often much abler than himself to do a good day's work, to the fact that a member of the Common Council had asked his appointment. He also knew that the request of his patron was made, not because of his supposed special fitness to serve the City on the park, but because of service that he was expected to render at primary meetings and otherwise with a view to the approaching election. He knew, too, that he was for an indefinite period to receive no pay for his work, but only a promise to pay which he must turn to account by selling it at a discount.

Under all the circumstances it was plain enough that when Foreman Smith pleasantly remarked that he supposed that they would be pushed up now, and the men laughed with him at the suggestion, it was because the idea that I might expect a day's work from them for each day's duebill was thought a good joke.

Neither Foreman Smith nor any other that day said anything aloud to me about my not being a practical man, but I saw it in their eyes and their smile, and felt it deeply. In fact, for other reasons I could have wished, long before our round was finished, that I had worn a pair of high-legged boots and left my coat behind me, for it was a sultry afternoon in the height of dog days, and my conductor exhibited his practical ability by leading me through the midst of a number of vile sloughs in the black and unctuous slime of which I sometimes sank nearly half-leg deep.

He said but one word to me during the afternoon beyond what his commission strictly required. As I stopped for an instant to kick the mire off my legs against a stump, as we came out of the last bog, he turned and remarked:

"Suppose you are used to this sort of business."

I believe that he was some years my junior, and it is probable that I had been through fifty miles of swamp to his one. There was not one operation in progress in the park in which I had not considerable personal experience, and he spoke with apparent gravity; nevertheless I felt very deeply that he was laughing in his sleeve, and that I was still a very young man. So I avoided a direct reply by saying that I had not been aware that the park was such a very nasty place. In fact, the low grounds were steeped in the overflow and mush of pigsties, slaughter houses, and bone-boiling works, and the stench was sickening.

For several days there continued to be something that stimulated good humor in my appearance, and in the inquiries and suggestions which I made as I walked from gang to gang, feeling my way to an intelligent command of the business. It was as if we were all engaged in playing a practical joke. The most striking illustration of this good fellowship that I remember occurred, I think, on the third day, when a foreman who was reading a newspaper as I came suddenly upon him, exclaimed, "Hello, Fred; get round pretty often, don't you?"

Having no power to discharge or secure the discharge of a man, I found it was better to give every offender the benefit of the largest possible assumption of ignorance, forgetfulness and accident, and urge him to give more attention to his duties and use more care.

DOCUMENT II

Frederick Law Olmsted and Calvert Vaux

Description of a Plan for the Improvement of the Central Park: "Greensward" (1858 [1868 reprint])

>>>->>>->>><<<-<<<-<<<

"Meantime, with cheap land, and the pacific disposition of the people, everything invites to the arts of agriculture, of gardening, and domestic architecture. Public gardens on the scale of such plantations in Europe and Asia, are now unknown to us. There is no feature of the old countries that strikes an American with more agreeable surprise than the beautiful gardens of Europe; such as the Boboli, in Florence, the Villa Borghese, in Rome, the Villa d'Este, in Tivoli, the gardens at Munich, and at Frankfort on the Maine: works easily imitated here, and which might well make the land dear to the citizen, and inflame patriotism."—*Emerson,* 1844

Note, 1868

The following Description was prepared in 1858 to accompany the first study of our design for the Central Park, the appended woodcut being printed with the Report.

A few notes are added in this edition, together with a map showing to what extent the intention of the plan has, thus far, been realized and in what manner the study has been elaborated.

O. & V.

Report

Topographical Suggestions

A general survey of the ground allotted to the park, taken with a view to arrive at the leading characteristics which present themselves as all-important to be considered in adapting the actual situation to its purposes, shows us, in the first place, that it is very distinctly divided into two tolerably equal portions, which, for convenience sake, may be called the upper and lower parks.

THE UPPER PARK

The horizon lines of the upper park are bold and sweeping and the slopes have great breadth in almost every aspect in which they may be contemplated. As this character is the highest ideal that can be aimed at for a park under any circumstances, and as it is in most decided contrast to the confined and formal lines of the city, it is desirable to interfere with it, by cross-roads and other constructions, as little as possible. Formal planting and architectural effects, unless on a very grand scale, must be avoided; and as nearly all the ground between the Reservoir and 106th Street (west of the Boston road) is seen in connection, from any point within itself, a unity of character should be studiously preserved in all the gardening details.

THE LOWER PARK

The lower park is far more heterogeneous in its character and will require a much more varied treatment. The most important feature in its landscape is the long rocky and wooded hill-side lying immediately south of the Reservoir. Inasmuch as beyond this point there do not appear to be any leading natural characteristics of similar consequence in the scenery, it will be important to draw as much attention as possible to this hill-side, to afford facilities for rest and leisurely contemplation upon the rising ground opposite, and to render

64

the lateral boundaries of the park in its vicinity as inconspicuous as possible. The central and western portion of the lower park is an irregular table-land; the eastern is composed of a series of graceful undulations, suggesting lawn or gardenesque treatment. In the extreme south we find some flat alluvial meadow; but the general character of the ground is rugged and there are several bold, rocky bluffs, that help to give individuality to this part of the composition.

Such being the general suggestions that our survey has afforded, it becomes necessary to consider how the requirements of the Commissioners, as given in their instructions, may be met with the least sacrifice of the characteristic excellencies of the ground.

Preliminary Considerations

Up to this time, in planning public works for the city of New York, in no instance has adequate allowance been made for its increasing population and business; not even in the case of the Croton Aqueduct, otherwise so well considered. The City-Hall, the best architectural work in the State, and built to last for centuries, does not at this time afford facilities for one-third the business for which it was intended. The present Post-Office, expensively fitted up some ten years ago, no longer answers its purpose, and a new one of twice its capacity is imperatively demanded. The Custom-House, expressly designed for permanence and constructed to that end at enormous expense less than twenty years ago, is not half large enough to accommodate the present commerce of the city.

The explanation of this apparently bad calculation is mainly given with the fact that, at every census since that of 1800, the city's rate of increase has been found to be overrunning the rate previously established.

A wise forecast of the future gave the proposed park the name of Central. Our present chief magistrate, who can himself remember market-gardens below Canal street, and a post-

and-rail fence on the north side of City-Hall park, warned his coadjutors, in his inaugural message, to expect a great and rapid movement of population toward the parts of the island adjoining the Central Park. A year hence, five city railroads will bring passengers as far up as the park, if not beyond it. Recent movements to transfer the steamboat-landings and railroad stations, although as yet unsuccessful, indicate changes we are soon to expect.

The 17,000 lots withdrawn from use for building purposes in the park itself, will greatly accelerate the occupation of the adjoining land. Only twenty years ago, Union Square was "out of town;" twenty years hence, the town will have enclosed the Central Park. Let us consider, therefore, what will at that time be satisfactory, for it is then that the design will have to be really judged.

No longer an open suburb, our ground will have around it a continuous high wall of brick, stone, and marble. The adjoining shores will be lined with commercial docks and warehouses; steamboat and ferry landings, railroad stations, hotels, theatres, factories, will be on all sides of it and above it; all which our park must be made to fit.

The demolition of Columbia College, and the removal of the cloistral elms which so long enshadowed it; the pertinacious demand for a division of Trinity churchyard; the numerous instances in which our old graveyards have actually been broken up; the indirect concession of the most important space in the City-Hall park for the purposes of a thoroughfare and the further contraction it is now likely to suffer; together with the constant enormous expenditure of the city and sacrifices of the citizens, in the straightening and widening of streets, are all familiar facts, that teach us a lesson of the most pressing importance in our present duty. To its application we give the first place in our planning.

The Transverse Roads

Our instructions call for four transverse roads. Each of these will be the sole line of communication between one side of the town and the other, for a distance equal to that between Chambers street and Canal street. If we suppose but one crossing of Broadway to be possible in this interval, we shall realize what these transverse roads are destined to become. Inevitably they will be crowded thoroughfares, having nothing in common with the park proper, but every thing at variance with those agreeable sentiments which we should wish the park to inspire. It will not be possible to enforce the ordinary police regulations of public parks upon them. They must be constantly open to all the legitimate traffic of the city, to coal carts and butchers' carts, dust carts and dung carts; engine companies will use them, those on one side the park rushing their machines across it with frantic zeal at every alarm from the other; ladies and invalids will need special police escort for crossing them, as they do in lower Broadway: eight times in a single circuit of the park will they oblige a pleasure drive or stroll to encounter a turbid stream of coarse traffic, constantly moving at right angles to the line of the park movement.

The transverse roads will also have to be kept open, while the park proper will be useless for any good purpose, after dusk, for experience has shown that even in London, with its admirable police arrangements, the public cannot be secured safe transit through large open spaces of ground after nightfall.

FOREIGN EXAMPLES

These public thoroughfares will then require to be well lighted at the sides and, to restrain marauders pursued by the police from escaping into the obscurity of the park, strong fences or walls, six or eight feet high, will be necessary. A public road thus guarded passes through the Regent's Park of London, at the Zoological Gardens. It has the objection that the fence, with its necessary gates at every crossing of the park drives, roads or paths, is not only a great inconvenience but a disagreeable object in the landscape.

To avoid a similar disfigurement an important passage across the garden of the Tuileries is closed by gates at night, forcing all who would otherwise use it to go a long distance to the right or left.

The form and position of the Central Park are peculiar in respect to this difficulty, and such that precedent in dealing with it is rather to be sought in the long and narrow Boulevards of some of the old Continental cities of Europe, than in the broad parks with which, from its area in acres, we are most naturally led to compare it. The Boulevards referred to are, however, generally used only as walks, not as drives or places of ceremony. In frequent instances, in order not to interrupt their alleys, the streets crossing them are made in the form of causeways and carried over on high arches. This, of course, destroys all landscape effect, since it puts an abrupt limit to the view. Some expedient is needed for the Central Park by which the convenience of the arrangement may be retained, while the objection is as far as possible avoided.

THE PRESENT DESIGN

In the plan herewith offered to the Commission, each of the transverse roads is intended to be sunk so far below the general surface that the park drives may, at every necessary point of intersection, be carried entirely over it, without any obvious elevation or divergence from their most attractive routes. The banks on each side will be walled up to the height of about seven feet, thus forming the protective barrier required by police considerations, and a little judicious planting on the tops or slopes of the banks above these walls will, in most cases, entirely conceal both the roads and the vehicles moving in them, from the view of those walking or driving in the park.[1]

If the position which has just been taken with regard to the necessity for permanently open transverse thoroughfares is found to be correct, it follows necessarily that the 700 acres allowed to the new park must, in the first instance, be subdi-

---

[1] Note, 1868.—In execution, the four traffic roads have been carried through the Park in the manner suggested.

vided definitely, although it is to be hoped to some extent invisibly, into five separate and distinct sections, only connected here and there by roads crossing them; and if the plan of making these thoroughfares by sunken roads is approved, they will, as it appears to us, from the nature of the ground, have to be laid down somewhat on the lines indicated on the plan. If so, the problem to be solved is narrowed in its dimensions, and the efforts of the designer can be no longer directed to an arrangement that shall agreeably use up the space of 700 acres allotted, but to making some plan that shall have unity of effect as a whole, and yet avoid collision in its detailed features with the intersecting lines thus suggested. It is on this basis that the present plan has, in the first instance, been founded. If the sunken transverse roads were omitted, the design would not be less complete in character; but it is, on the other hand, so laid out that the transverse thoroughfares do not interfere materially with its general or detailed effect.

SURFACE TRANSVERSE ROADS

After having planned the park drives agreeably to these views, we observed that three additional moderately direct, transverse roads had occurred. These will afford facilities for crossing the park to all vehicles of classes which it will be proper to admit upon them, such as hackney coaches and all private carriages; and thus seven transverse roads will be really provided to be used during daylight. Four roads will probably be amply adequate for the night traffic needing to cross the park; but it might be questioned if this number would be sufficient during the day.

The Exterior

As it is not proposed that the park proper shall be lighted at night, it is well worth while to consider if the advantages which it offers as an interesting promenade may not yet in some way be obtained at night.

FIFTH AVENUE

The ordinance that regulates the width of Fifth avenue, provides for an open space of fifteen feet on each side, exclusive of that required for the sidewalks and the roadway; consequently, a space of thirty feet in width is already prepared for on this side of the park for its whole length.

EIGHTH AVENUE RAILROAD

On the Eighth avenue a similar arrangement may probably be effected, and as there would be no occasion to back up carts against the park side of the avenue, it is feasible to carry the railway tracks close to the edge of the walk, thus leaving a clear space for carriages on the opposite or building side and making the access to the park side more clean and convenient.[2]

FIFTY-NINTH AND ONE HUNDRED AND SIXTH STREETS

On the southern boundary it is not desirable to reduce the already moderate width of the carriage way. It is, on the other hand, a question whether, as the streets and the park both, in reality, are the property of one owner—the City—this street should not be treated in a similar manner. It will, from its position, be in time rather crowded with traffic, and will, therefore, have some claim to be widened on this ground alone. As a question of beauty of arrangement for the park itself, however, it is conceived that if by this management a more stately character than could otherwise be obtained would be secured to the outer boundaries of the park, it would be cheaply purchased at the sacrifice of a few feet at the south end, off its present length of two and a half miles. In riding along any of the avenues, the eye cannot

[2] Note, 1868.—The sidewalks have been treated in execution as proposed, but the suggestion in regard to the railroad has not yet been carried out. In the Brooklyn Park however the intended arrangement has been fully realized.

fail to be struck with the great difference in dignity of effect, between such streets as Fourteenth and Twenty-Third, and those intermediate, and it would be a matter of regret that a source of effect so easily obtained, should be lost in connection with the grand approaches to the park, because it does not happen that its boundaries at present coincide with the wide streets laid out on the working plan upon which the city is being constructed. If, moreover, the advantage of the evening promenade is allowed to be of importance, we should be sorry to dispense with this section of it, which would be the only portion having a direct communication from the Sixth and Seventh avenues.

TREATMENT OF BOUNDARY LINES

For the purpose of concealing the houses on the opposite side of the street, from the park, and to insure an umbrageous horizon line, it is proposed, as will be seen in the plan, to plant a line of trees all around the outer edge of the park, between the sidewalk and the roadway.[3] On approaching the Fifth and Eighth avenue entrances, this line of trees along Fifty-Ninth street will come prominently into view, and have a handsome effect, if the street is widened; but if Fifty-Ninth street is allowed to remain as a narrow street, it is feared that it will be difficult to prevent this boundary line of the park from having a contracted and somewhat mean appearance. Hence, we have thought it proper in our plan to assume the advantage and practicability of this arrangement to be conceded; but, if this should not be the case, it will be readily perceived that it forms no essential part of our design.[4]

On the space originally provided for a sidewalk on the park side of the streets and avenues, there will, in any case, be room for such a line of trees as we have proposed. The

[3] Note, 1868.—This feature of the design has been partially carried into execution and is in progress from year to year, as the street and avenue grades become settled.

[4] Note, 1868.—In execution, 59th street has been treated as here recommended.

71

continuous exterior mall should by no means be given up, even though it cannot be made in all parts as wide as we have proposed. At many points, and frequently for quite long distances, it will form an elevated terrace, commanding extensive views over the park, of the most interesting character, and a mere parapet-wall three or four feet high, will, in such cases, be all-sufficient for the safety of promenaders and the protection of the park from interlopers.

Fifth Avenue Entrance

The finest approach from the city is certain to be along the Fifth avenue, and it has been thought necessary to view with special care the angle of the park first reached from this direction, because it will be generally felt that immediate entrance should be had at this point.[5]

The grade of the avenue has been established so high that considerable filling-in would be required to avoid a rapid descent, but directly this single difficulty is overcome, the ground beyond has great advantages for the purpose of a dignified entrance to the park. A massive rock that will be found in connection with this requisite made-ground, offers a sufficiently large natural object to occupy the attention, and will at once reduce the artificial feature to a position of minor importance. If, next, we stand upon that portion of the rock which (a little north of the large cherry-tree) is at grade-height, we find that there is another rocky hillock within a short distance, in the direction a visitor to the park would most naturally pursue—that is to say, towards the centre of the park. This can be easily reached by slightly raising the intermediate ground; by then sweeping to the right, the natural conformation of the surface offers an easy ascent (by the existing cart-way over Sixty-Third street) to a plateau (two rods west of the powder-house), directly connected with the

[5] Note, 1868.—We submitted a plan for a much needed amplification in this approach during the earlier stages of the work, but the suggestion has not yet been acted on.

extensive table-land which occupies the centre of the lower half of the park.

From this plateau (now occupied mainly by the nursery) a view is had of nearly all the park up to the Reservoir, in a northerly direction; and on looking to the south and west, we perceive that there are natural approaches from these directions, which suggest that we have arrived at a suitable point of concentration for all approaches which may be made from the lower part of the city to the interior of the park.

The Avenue

Vista Rock, the most prominent point in the landscape of the lower park, here first comes distinctly into view, and fortunately in a direction diagonal to the boundary lines, from which it is desirable to withdraw attention in every possible way. We therefore accept this line of view as affording an all-sufficient motive to our further procedure. Although averse on general principles to a symmetrical arrangement of trees, we consider it an essential feature of a metropolitan park, that it should contain a grand promenade, level, spacious, and thoroughly shaded. This result can in no other way be so completely arrived at, as by an avenue, which in itself even, exclusive of its adaptability for this purpose, contains so many elements of grandeur and magnificence, that it should be recognized as an essential feature in the arrangement of any large park. The objection to which it is liable is that it divides the landscape into two parts, and it is therefore desirable to decide at what point this necessity can be submitted to with the least sacrifice to the general effect. The whole topographical character of the park is so varied, so suggestive of natural treatment, so picturesque, so individual in its characteristics, that it would be contrary to common sense to make the avenue its leading feature, or to occupy any great extent of ground for this special purpose. It must be subservient to the general design, if that general design is to be in accordance with the present configuration of the ground, and we have therefore thought that it should, so far as possible, be complete in itself, and not become a portion of any of the leading drives. There is no dignity of effect to be produced by driving through an avenue a quarter of a mile long, unless it leads to, and becomes an accessory of, some grand architectural structure, which itself, and not the avenue, is the ultimatum of interest. An avenue for driving in should be two or three miles long, or it will be petite and disappointing. We have therefore thought it most desirable to identify the idea of the avenue with the promenade, for which purpose a quarter of a mile is not insufficient, and we can find no better place for such a grand mall, or open air hall of reception, as we desire to have, than the ground before us.[6]

THE PROMENADE

In giving it this prominent position, we look at it in the light of an artificial structure on a scale of magnitude commensurate with the size of the park, and intend in our design that it should occupy the same position of relative importance in the general arrangement of the plan that a mansion should occupy in a park prepared for private occupation. The importance that is justly connected with the idea of the residence of the owner in even the most extensive private grounds, finds no parallel in a public park, however small, and we feel that the interest of the visitor, who, in the best sense is the true owner in the latter case, should concentrate on features of natural, in preference to artificial, beauty. Many elegant buildings may be appropriately erected for desirable purposes in a public park, but we conceive that all such architectural structures should be confessedly subservient to the main idea, and that nothing artificial should be obtruded on the view as an ultimatum of interest. The idea of the park itself should always be uppermost in the mind of the beholder. Holding this general principle to be of considerable importance, we have preferred to place the avenue where it can be terminated appropriately at one end with a landscape attraction of con-

[6] Note, 1868.—In execution, this avenue has been planted with elms, as suggested later in the report, and is now called "The Mall."

siderable extent, and to relieve the south entrance with only so much architectural treatment as may give the idea that due regard has been paid to the adornment of this principal promenade, without interfering with its real character.

This avenue may be considered the central feature in our plan for laying out the lower park, and the other details of arrangement are more or less designed in connection with it.

Parade Ground

To the west is the parade ground, containing about 25 acres, that may, at a moderate expense, be levelled and made suitable for its purpose;[7] and also some eight or ten acres of broken ground, that will be more or less available for military exercises. Such a broad open plane of well-kept grass would be a refreshing and agreeable feature in the general design, and would bear to be of much greater extent than is here shown, if the lot were of a different shape; but under the circumstances, 25 acres seems as much as can well be spared for the purpose. A military entrance from Eighth avenue is proposed to be made at Sixty-Ninth street, which has been already, at considerable expense, cut through the rock at this point, and offers a suggestion for a picturesque approach, with a portcullis gate, and with the main park drive carried over it at a higher level.

Playground

The natural southern boundary of the table-land occupied by the parade ground is a rapid slope that occurs about in the line of Sixty-Sixth street; in this slope it is proposed to sink one of the transverse roads; and on a level plane below it, stretching to the south, a playground about ten acres in extent is located, as indicated on the plan. We have thought

[7] Note, 1868.—A Parade ground was demanded by the schedule of instructions furnished to competitors. In execution this open space under the name of "The Green" has been retained as a prominent feature of the design, but has not been and is not intended to be used for military exercises.

it very desirable to have a cricket ground of this size near the southern boundary of the park, and not far from the Sixth and Eighth avenue railroads, which offer the most rapid means of access from the lower part of the city.[8]

In this playground sites are suggested for two buildings of moderate dimensions: one for visitors to view the games, which would be appropriately located on a large rock that overlooks the ground; and the other for the players, at the entrance from the transverse road, by which an exit could be obtained from the playground after the other gates were closed.[9] Only one mass of rock of any considerable magnitude would require to be blasted out for the purpose of adapting this ground to its intended purpose; its position is indicated on the plan by a red cross, and the object of its removal will be seen on examination. This part of the design is illustrated in study No. 2. The ground at the south-west corner of the park it is proposed to fill in sufficiently to make, on the plan indicated, an agreeable Eighth avenue entrance.

The Lower Lake

To the south-east of the promenade, and between the Fifth and Sixth avenue entrances, it is proposed to form a lake of irregular shape, and with an area of 8 or 9 acres. This arrangement has been suggested by the present nature of the ground, which is low and somewhat swampy. It is conceived that, by introducing such an ornamental sheet of water into the composition at this point, the picturesque effect of the bold bluffs that will run down to its edge and overhang it, must be much increased;[10] and that by means of such a natural boundary, this rocky section of the park will be rendered more retired and attractive as a pleasant walk or lounge. The

---

[8] The playground has been arranged as here recommended.

[9] Note, 1868.—The foundation for this building was laid during the last season.

[10] Note, 1868.—An improvement of the soil and of the skylines of this rocky section, contemplated at the time the plan was made, was last year carried into execution, by means of earth filling on the more prominent summit levels.

proposed effect of this part of the design, as it will appear from the Fifth avenue entrance, is indicated on study No. I.[11]

The Arsenal

To the south-east of the promenade will be found that portion of the park in which the present Arsenal is situated. This ground is undulating and agreeable in its character, and will offer pleasant opportunities for shady walks. The Arsenal itself, although at present a very unattractive structure, and only tolerably built, contains a great deal of room in a form that adapts it very well to the purposes of a museum. It is proposed, therefore, to improve its external appearance so far as may be necessary, without changing its shape or usefulness, or going to any great expense; and as it occurs rather near the Fifth avenue entrance, and is, therefore, likely to occupy too considerable a share of attention if left exposed to view from the south, it is intended, as early as possible, to plant in its vicinity forest-trees, calculated to become handsome specimens of large size, and that will, after a few years, prevent the museum from attracting an undue share of attention in the general landscape.

Music-Hall

To the east of the promenade, there will be a half-mile stretch of lawn and trees extending from the vicinity of Fifty-Ninth street to Seventy-Second street, and this will be the dress ground of the park; and in a prominent position on this ground, and immediately connected with the grand mall, the site for a music-hall, called for in our instructions, has been set apart; and we have suggested that a palm-house and large

[11] Note, 1868.—The original requirements of the Commission in regard to boundary and expense necessitated, in the first study, a cramped and unsatisfactory arrangement of the entrances on Fifty-ninth street. We have since made studies for the amplification of each of the principal approaches, and the necessary legislation in regard to the entrance at 8th Avenue and 59th street having been obtained at the instance of the property owners in the neighborhood, this improvement is shown on the map of the Park, dated 1868.

conservatory should be added to this music-hall whenever it is built.[12]

This site is recommended because it is conspicuous without being obtrusive, and is easy of access from the promenade and from one of the leading avenue entrances; while, to the north, it commands from its terraces and verandas the finest views that are to be obtained in the lower part of the park. It also overlooks the site which we have selected as most appropriate for the flower-garden called for in our instructions; and this we consider a decided advantage, as the most attractive view of a flower-garden is from some point above it, that will enable the visitor to take in at a glance a general idea of the effect aimed at.

The Flower Garden

The garden is located in low ground to the north-east of the promenade, and close upon the line of Fifth avenue, the grade of which opposite the centre of the garden is about twenty feet above the present level of the ground; this, for the reasons above stated, we consider a desideratum, and have suggested that over the arcade or veranda that we propose should be built against the east wall of the park in connection with the garden, a structure should be erected, with an entrance on a level with the avenue, so as to give an opportunity for a view of the garden, both from this level and from another story above it. This idea is not, of course, necessary to the design, and the sketch submitted is merely a suggestion to show what may be done at some future time.[13]

[12] Note, 1868.—This site is now occupied by a building which we designed for a Ladies' Restaurant, sites on a somewhat larger scale being reserved for a music-hall and conservatory, which yet remain to be erected.

[13] Note, 1868.—While the construction of the park was in progress Messrs Parsons & Co., who held a contract granted by the Commissioners, employed us to develop this general idea in the form of a two-story glass building, of which the upper section is the conservatory proper and the lower portion is proposed to be used for the exhibition and sale of flowers, but the design has not yet been executed.

The plan of the flower-garden itself is geometrical; and it is surrounded by an irregular and less formal plantation of shrubs, that will serve to connect it with the park proper. In the centre it is proposed to construct a large basin for a fountain, with a high jet; other smaller jets are prepared for, as indicated; and, in connection with the north wall, which will be somewhat below the surface of the ground beyond, it is proposed to arrange some such wall fountain as the celebrated one of Trevi. The water for this fountain will, in the present case, be supplied from the skating pond and also from the Reservoir, and will fall into a semi-circular marble basin, with a paved floor. Such a fountain is out of place unless it can be furnished with an ample supply of water; but, in the position assigned to it on our plan, there will be no difficulty in procuring all the water that can be required for the purpose; and it seems desirable, therefore, to take advantage of the opportunity offered, for the effect of a sculptured fountain of this sort is quite distinct from that produced by a jet d'eau.

A colored plan of this part of the design is illustrated to an enlarged scale on study No. 11.

To the north-west of the promenade is a slope, offering an appropriate site for a summer-house, that in such a situation should have some architectural pretension; and further to the west, near Eighth avenue, is a stretch of table-land, terminated by an abrupt rocky descent, that suggests itself as well suited for a Casino or refreshment house.[14]

From the upper end of the promenade the rocky hill-side to the north, surmounted by Vista Rock at its highest point, comes in full view; and on this rock it will be generally conceded a tower should be erected—but by no means a large one, or the whole scale of the view will be destroyed.[15] To

[14] Note, 1868.—This ground still remains unimproved, it being the intention to develop the idea referred to in the report, although the plans for the structure are not yet finally decided on.

[15] Note, 1868.—The foundations for this work were commenced last

the north and north-west of the promenade, a tract of low ground is proposed to be converted into the skating pond called for in our instructions; and the picturesque scenery between Vista Rock and the promenade will thus be heightened in effect, when seen from the south side of this lake, of about 14 acres. A terrace approach, as shown on the plan, and on study No. 3, is proposed, from the avenue to the water.[16] This feature, although by no means absolutely necessary, would add much to the general effect, and could be introduced at any future time, if it is preferred at present to treat the ground occupied by it in a less artificial style.

Immediately in the vicinity of Vista Rock is the south wall of the present reservoir. This wall occupies the whole of the middle of the park, and is a blank, uninteresting object, that can in no way be made particularly attractive. We have therefore, thought it necessary to bear this in mind in arranging the general plan, and have given a direction to the lines of drive leading this way from the lower part of the park, that will enable them to avoid the wall of the reservoir altogether.[17] The necessity for doing this has induced us to commence diverting the lines of drive at the south end of the grand promenade, which seems to offer a sufficient reason for so doing, and to lead them afterwards on their northerly course in such a way that they may pass naturally to the east and west of the reservoir. If any drive proceeded in the direction of the line of avenue, and at once crossed the ground proposed to be occupied by the lake, the reservoir would inevitably become the terminal feature of the lower part of

---

season on a rocky promontory which formed a part of the Croton reservoir inclosure when it was expected to be bounded by street lines, but which has lately been added to the park territory, in accordance with our suggestion.

[16] Note, 1868.—The architectural treatment of the terrace approach has been developed in detail during the progress of the work, but much of the intended effect still remains to be realized.

[17] Note, 1868.—In execution, the lines have been carried out as here indicated, and as the trees grow up the old square reservoir is less and less thought of as an obstruction in the composition.

the park, and this would be disagreeable. The skating pond will offer a sufficiently natural barrier to this direct mode of proceeding, and will furnish a reason for locating the promenade in its proposed position, and also for terminating it where suggested; and by carrying a road along the edge of the water, an opportunity will be given to lengthen out the drive commanding the principal views in this vicinity; the lake will also help to give a retired and agreeable character to the hillside beyond, which is well adapted for pic-nic parties and pleasant strolls. Even if the reservoir did not occur in its present position, the conformation of the ground is such that the roads would naturally take, to a considerable extent, the direction indicated, leaving the centre of the park undivided by a drive.

The management of the ground between the skating pond and Vista Rock[18] appears to be indicated by its form and the character of its present growth. It is well sheltered, and large masses of rock occur at intervals. The soil is moist, and altogether remarkably well adapted to what is called in Europe an American garden, that is, a ground for the special cultivation of hardy plants of the natural order Ericacæi, consisting of rhododendrons, andromedas, azaleas, kalmias, rhodoras, &c.[19] The present growth, consisting of sweet-gum, spicebush, tuliptree, sassafras, red-maple, black-oak, azalea, and andromeda, &c., is exceedingly intricate and interesting. The ground is at present too much encumbered with stone, and with various indifferent plants.[20] By clearing these away, and carefully leaving what is valuable; by making suitable paths, planting abundantly, as above suggested, and introducing fastigiate shrubs and evergreens occasionally, to prevent a monotony of bushes, the place may be made very charming. Where the hill-side approaches the lake, sufficient openings are proposed to be left for occasional glimpses, or more open views, of the water;

[18] Note, 1868.—The ground here referred to is now called "The Ramble."

[19] Note, 1868.—This suggestion has been partially realized but yet remains to be fully developed.

[20] Note, 1868.—Many of these which we have marked for removal, have hitherto, for various reasons, been allowed to remain.

and glades of fine turf are intended to occur at favorable intervals, so as to offer pleasant spots for rest and recreation.

Playground

To the east and south-east of the present reservoir, the general conformation of the surface continues to be of the same easy, undulating character as that to the east of the promenade, and can be treated in a similar manner. The whole space is intended to be occupied with stretches of well-kept turf, with fine groups and single trees, so planted that they may appear to advantage, and not crowd each other. That portion which is immediately east of the reservoir is set apart for one of the playgrounds;[21] and in the strip of land between the main drive and the reservoir wall, a reserved garden is provided for, with gardener's house attached; this will be needed in connection with the flower-garden already described.

Winter Drive

On the west side of the reservoir the ground is of an irregular character, which continues past the old and new reservoirs to the upper end of the site. The spaces remaining for park use will, however, be so much contracted by the reservoir walls and embankments, that extended landscape effects are out of the question. It is intended, therefore, as the soil and situation are adapted to the purpose, to arrange in this locality a winter drive about a mile and a half in length, and to plant somewhat thickly with evergreens, introducing deciduous trees and shrubs occasionally, to relieve the monotony of effect that otherwise might occur. Large open glades of grass are introduced among these plantations of evergreens, as the effect aimed at is not so much that of a drive through a thick forest,

[21] Note, 1868.—This tract of ground is now recommended as the site for the formal flower garden in connection with a group of architectural structures that will include music-hall, art galleries, horticultural and other museums, and refreshment rooms on a liberal scale; the intention of allowing military exercises on the park having been abandoned, and the Green serving the purpose of the playground above proposed.

crowded with tall spindling trees, as through a richly wooded country, in which the single trees and copses have had plenty of space for developing their distinctive characteristics to advantage.[22]

Berceau Walks

Immediately south and west of the present reservoir, terraces have been already formed, and these can readily be converted into continuous arbors, or berceau walks. Access will thus be provided to all the gates of the reservoir, and the wall will itself be planted out. The effect of these closely shaded walks will also, it is conceived, offer an agreeable contrast to the views obtainable from Vista Rock, in the immediate vicinity.[23]

Police Station

In the northern section of this locality, and in connection with one of the transverse roads, will be found the house of the Superintendent, the office of the Commission, the police station, and other necessary buildings, such as stables, &c. The site is not far from the one at present occupied by the police, and is thought to be well suited for its purpose. By making a private entrance along the wall of the reservoir, the whole establishment can be immediately connected, by means of the transverse road, with the city streets, and at the same time be central and elevated without being unpleasantly prominent. It is proposed, as will be seen on the plan, to make short connections from the park roads to the transverse thoroughfare north of the present reservoir, so as to admit of visitors shortening the drive in this way if preferred.

Reservoir Ride

The new reservoir, with its high banks, will take up a great deal of room in the park, and although it will offer a large sheet of water to the view, it will be at too high

[22] Note, 1868.—These plantations have been made as designed.
[23] Note, 1868.—The idea of the berceau walk has been carried out in execution on the south side of the reservoir.

a level to become a landscape attraction from the ordinary drives and walks. It is suggested, therefore, that all round it a ride shall be constructed, and carefully prepared for this purpose only; and although this feature may be somewhat costly in the first instance, it is conceived that the result would be worth the outlay, for the sake of its advantages as a ride over a mile and a half in length, commanding the view of the reservoir, and uninterfered with by the regular drives, although in connection with them at different points.[24]

On the east of the new reservoir, the park is diminished to a mere passage-way for connection, and it will be difficult to obtain an agreeable effect in this part of the design, unless some architectural character is given to it. It is not recommended, however, to attempt any such effect immediately, or out of the funds of the Commission, but to accept the high bank of the reservoir as a barrier to the west, for a few years; because it is thought that as soon as this part of the city is built up to any considerable extent, it will not be difficult to obtain an enriched architectural effect, appropriate to the purpose, without expense to the Commission. An arcade, 100 feet deep, could be substantially built, and the drive could be carried above this arcade on a level with the reservoir, and overlooking Fifth avenue, the remainder of the ground being filled in; and it is thought that as this arcade may be lighted from the rear, and will face a fashionable thoroughfare, it will offer, at no distant period, very valuable lots for stores, or other purposes; and as it is a third of a mile in extent, it may be a source of revenue, in rent, to the park fund, instead of a burden on it.[25]

Tower on Bogardus Hill

The north-westerly portion of the park, above the new reservoir, is planned very simply, in accordance with what

[24] Note, 1868.—In execution the design of this separate bridle road has been much amplified.

[25] Note, 1868.—In execution the simpler plan above suggested was adopted, and the arrangement will probably remain intact for a number of years.

we conceive to be the suggestion of the ground. The evergreen drive is continued nearly to the foot of Bogardus Hill, and then somewhat changing its character, turns to the east. At this point a branch road crosses a brook, that is made to expand into a pool a little below the bridge; and this road then winds gradually to the top of the hill, which offers an available site for some monument of public importance, that may also be used as an observatory tower. If as is not improbable, the transatlantic telegraph is brought to a favorable issue, while the park is in an early stage of construction, many reasons could, we think, be urged for commemorating the event by some such monument as the one suggested on the plan, and in study No. 9. The picturesque effect of a spring of clear water, that already exists in this vicinity, may be heightened, as suggested in study No. 10.

The central portion of the upper section of the park is left as open as possible, and can be levelled so far as may be required for the purposes of the playgrounds indicated on the plan, and on study No. 7. At present, it is hardly thought that it would be necessary to make the Sixth avenue entrance to the north; but its position is indicated.[26]

The Arboretum

The north-east section of the upper park is shown as an arboretum of American trees, so that every one who wishes to do so may become acquainted with the trees and shrubs that will flourish in the open air in the northern and middle sections of our country.

[26] Note, 1868.—The postponement of operations in this quarter was recommended because we found that the 106th street boundary of the park required a revision, which could not, with propriety, be urged when the competition plan was made. The northern limit of the park was, subsequently to the date of this report, extended from 106th to 110th sts., and so much of the original plan as applied to the ground to the northward of that here described, was afterwards modified in order to connect satisfactorily with our design for laying out the additional territory which was approved by the commission in April, 1863.

This arboretum is not intended to be formally arranged, but to be so planned that it may present all the most beautiful features of lawn and wood-land landscape, and at the same time preserve the natural order of families, so far as may be practicable. The botanical student will thus be able to find any tree or shrub without difficulty. We have selected this tract, of about 40 acres, in the upper angle of the site, so as to interfere with the more special requirements of the park as little as possible. The spot chosen is in some measure separated from the rest of the grounds, by a ridge of land between Fifth and Sixth avenues, and includes the buildings on Mount St. Vincent. The wooden structures would be removed, and the brick chapel converted into a museum and library of botany, similar to that at Kew, but with more specific regard to landscape and decorative gardening. In the park itself there will be numerous specimens of all the trees, native or foreign, that are likely to thrive; but it is proposed to limit this particular collection to American trees, because the space necessary for a complete arboretum would occupy several hundred acres, and also because it will afford an opportunity to show the great advantage that America possesses in this respect. No other extra-tropical country could furnish one quarter the material for such a collection. In the whole of Great Britain, for example, there are less than twenty trees, native to the island, that grow to be over 30 feet in height; while in America we have from five to six times that number. There are, indeed, already over forty species of the largest native trees standing in the park, which is nearly equivalent to the number to be found in all Europe.

It is proposed to plant from one to three examples of each species of tree on open lawn, and with sufficient space about each to allow it to attain its fullest size with unrestricted expanse of branches; the effect of each tree is also to be exhibited in masses, so as to illustrate its qualities for grouping. Space is provided to admit of at least three specimens of every native which is known to flourish in the United States north of North Carolina; also for several specimens of every shrub; these latter, however, except in particular instances, are not expected to be planted singly, but in thickets, and as underwood to the coppice masses; as may best accord with their natural habits, and be most agreeable to the eye. Further details of this part of the design will be found in the explanatory guide to the arboretum, submitted with the plan, in which the proposed arrangement of all the trees is set forth in order.

The leading features of the plan have now, it is thought, been referred to. It has not been considered necessary to especially particularize the different trees proposed to be used in the various parts of the park. For the purposes of the avenue, the American elm naturally suggests itself at once as the tree to be used; and it is to be hoped that the fine effect this produces, when planted in regular lines, may in a few years be realized in the Central Park.

There is no other part of the plan in which the planting calls for particular mention, except to the south of the skating pond; an opportunity is there offered for an exhibition of semi-tropical trees, and it is intended to treat that portion of the park in the manner suggested in the study. A list of the trees to be used is appended to the explanation of the arboretum.

The plan does not show any brooks, except a small one in connection with the pool at the foot of Bogardus Hill, which can always be kept full by the waste of water from the New Reservoir. Mere rivulets are uninteresting, and we have preferred to collect the ornamental water in large sheets, and to carry off through underground drains the water that at present runs through the park in shallow brooks.

As a general rule, we propose to run footpaths close to the carriage roads, which are intended to be 60 feet wide, allowing a space of four feet of turf as a barrier between the drive and the path. Other more private footpaths are introduced, but it is hardly thought that any plan would be popular in New York, that did not allow of a continuous promenade along the line of the drives, so that pedestrians may have ample opportunity to look at the equipages and their inmates.

It will be perceived that no long straight drive has been provided on the plan; this feature has been studiously avoided, because it would offer opportunities for trotting matches. The popular idea of the park is a beautiful open space, in which quiet drives, rides, and strolls may be had. This cannot be preserved if a race-course, or a road that can readily be used as a race-course, is made one of its leading attractions.

PART TWO

BROOKLYN

O LMSTED had mixed feelings about the possibilities of planning New York City. On the one hand, the large quantity of undeveloped land gave him reason to be optimistic; the area was sparsely settled even as late as 1870.[1] He doubted, however, whether he would have the freedom to plan as he thought best. Because of his struggles with the political machinery of the city, he was reluctant to return from California after the war to his position as Landscape Architect and Superintendent of Central Park. In a letter to Vaux, he wrote of "how I abhor the squabbles with the Commission and politicians. . . . I feel them deeper every year. . . . My whole life is really embittered with it very much, and I think I shall feel it more as I grow older."[2]

After much hesitation he did return to the city and to his job at the Park, partly because Vaux had been commissioned in 1865 to do a preliminary study for a large park (see Illustration VI) in Brooklyn, New York's most important suburb. The possibility of achieving a comprehensive metropolitan design was now more promising, especially since Vaux reported that the Brooklyn Park Commission and its guiding spirit, James Stranahan, were in complete agreement with Olmsted's views concerning the future of the metropolis; that is, Stranahan felt as strongly as Olmsted that Brooklyn was an integral part of the Greater City of New York (see Illustration V). Eventually (in 1890), he joined hands with Andrew Haswell Green to help turn this belief into a legislative reality.[3] He wished to see Brooklyn become the sort of suburb which would attract the city's social leadership. While he granted that Manhattan would always be the city's commercial center,

[1] Seymour J. Mandelbaum, *Boss Tweed's New York* (New York, 1965), pp. x–xi (map).

[2] Olmsted to Calvert Vaux, March 12, 1865, Vaux Papers, Manuscript Division, New York Public Library. Hereafter cited as Vaux Papers.

[3] Stranahan was Vice-President of the Commission established to prepare plans for the incorporation of the Greater City of New York; Green was President of the Commission (see Introduction, p. 40n).

there was no reason, Stranahan felt, why Brooklyn should not become the residential center of the metropolis. Hence, he was willing to give Olmsted and Vaux complete control over the planning of the park and much of what was then Brooklyn. Olmsted responded warmly. "I like what you say of the spirit and ways of the . . . Commission," he wrote to Vaux, "and particularly admire your way of putting your business at the start upon a good foundation with them."[4]

Document III, the preliminary report for Prospect Park, is perhaps the most concise and best-written explanation ever presented by the designers regarding their concept of the relationship of social purpose to technique and esthetics. It demonstrates how very little in the Park's plan belongs to chance. Also, it reveals the planners' optimism and grand design for the New York metropolis. If all of his and Vaux's suggestions were adopted on both sides of the East River and if the much-talked-about bridges were constructed, Olmsted wrote, "the whole . . . would form a grand municipal promenade, hardly surpassed in the world either for extent or continuity of interest."[5]

Olmsted was very happy with his work in Brooklyn. He always considered it one of his most creative experiences. "My enthusiasm and liking for the work is increasing to an inconvenient degree," he wrote Charles Eliot Norton, "so that it elbows all other interests out of my mind."[6] In this mood he was moved to present in 1868 an analysis of the history of cities and of how he had related his work to the past. His approach to urban history, predictable from his writings, was based on a concern for the condition of the common man. "Men of literary taste or clerical habits," he once noted, "are always apt to overlook the working-classes, and to confine the records they make of their own times, in a great degree, to the habits and fortunes of their own associates, or to those

[4] Olmsted to Vaux, Aug. 1, 1865, Vaux Papers.
[5] Frederick Law Olmsted and Calvert Vaux, *Preliminary Report to the Commissioners for Laying Out a Park in Brooklyn* (Brooklyn, 1866), p. 127. See Document III below.
[6] Olmsted to Norton, July 15, 1866, Norton Papers.

of people of superior rank. . . . The dumb masses have often been so lost in this shadow of egotism, that, in later days, it has been impossible to discern the very real influence their character and condition has had on the fortune and fate of nations."[7] He focused on the same theme in his study of urban history as he had on his walking tour of England and on his trips through the South: the effects of the physical environment on the daily life of the average person.

This fascinating discussion of the history of cities is found in Document IV.

[7] Olmsted, *A Journey in the Seaboard Slave States, with Remarks on Their Economy* (New York, 1856), pp. 214–215.

DOCUMENT III

➤➤➤➤➤➤➤《《《《《《

FREDERICK LAW OLMSTED AND CALVERT VAUX

Preliminary Report to the Commissioners for Laying Out a Park in Brooklyn, New York: Being a Consideration of, Circumstances of Site and Other Conditions Affecting the Design of Public Pleasure Grounds (1866)

➤➤➤➤➤➤➤《《《《《《

Report

To the Board of Commissioners:

GENTLEMEN: We have been instructed to lay before you at this time such plans, accompanied by information and advice, as would aid you in a final review of the boundaries of the park proposed to be formed under your government. The study herewith submitted has been prepared for this purpose, and though not designed to be full or accurate in all details, is intended to be complete in those respects which are essential to an understanding of the advantages to be gained by such changes of the boundaries as we would recommend to be secured, before a plan of construction is definitively settled upon.

We proceed to show what these changes are, and why they are considered desirable.

In selecting a site for a park, it is evidently important that such natural advantages should be secured as are found

95

in well grown woods, an agreeable variety of surface and fair prospects both of distant and local scope. It is true, that a site may be deficient in any of these characteristics, and yet, with time enough and money enough, be convertible by well directed labor, into a park of varied and attractive scenery. If, however, such conditions as are most desirable to be added, should have been already provided by nature in the immediate vicinity of a site, it would be felt, on the one hand, to be an extravagance to repeat them by artificial means upon it; while, on the other, the disadvantage of its being without them would be greater, because more obvious. Moreover, there are two possible misfortunes of a site, which in no period of time, and by no expenditure of labor, can ever be remedied. These are, inadequate dimensions, and an inconvenient shape.

Our first duty has been to examine the site to which you have asked our attention, with reference to the several conditions we have thus indicated; that is to say, with reference to—

1. Convenience of its shape.
2. Amplitude of its dimensions.
3. Its topographical conditions, and the surrounding circumstances, in relation to which the value of its topographical conditions must in part be estimated.

The fact which first claims attention is the complete bisection of the site by a broad and conspicuous thoroughfare, (Flatbush avenue,) much used for ordinary and indispensable public travel, between Brooklyn and an important suburb that connects it with a large district of agricultural country. It is obvious that this division must seriously interfere with the impressions of amplitude and continuous extent, that the general dimensions of the ground assigned for a park would otherwise convey. To establish convenient communication between the two parts would involve a considerable outlay in bridge construction, which would not be called for if the public highway skirted the ground instead of traversing it. A thoroughfare crossing the park might be a useful and even necessary adjunct, if it were so situated that it served to connect two districts of the city that were likely in future to be closely built up, and that would otherwise be widely separated. Such, however, is not the case in the present instance, and a glance at the map of Brooklyn is sufficient to show that the line of travel, accommodated by the park section of Flatbush avenue, could be diverted, without much inconvenience, to Warren street and Washington avenue. If cross roads for business purposes are required at all, it is in a direction nearly at right angles to Flatbush avenue. The city, however, is so laid out, that no real necessity is apparent for any merely traffic-roads across the property.

Proceeding to consider the two main divisions of the site separately, the Reservoir is found to encroach so seriously on the smaller section east of Flatbush avenue, that it is in effect subdivided again into two portions of very insignificant dimensions for park purposes. The formation of the ground is, moreover, of a character that would make its improvement very expensive, and when the best possible had been done, it would always present a cramped, contracted and unsatisfactory appearance. For these reasons, we think it our duty to advise, that so much of the site as lies east of Flatbush avenue should be abandoned for park purposes.

The great reduction which we have thus suggested in the dimensions of the park site, as originally provided, would oblige you either to be content with a much smaller park than has hitherto been contemplated, or to determine on an extension of its original boundaries in some other direction.

As the number and value of the health and pleasure giving circumstances possible in any park must of course be limited by its size, the question of size may be thought to depend on the restrictions fixed in regard to the number of these circumstances; and it may perhaps be thought that a large park has advantages over a small one only in the greater number and the greater variety, of the pleasures which it offers. But it would be a serious mistake to entertain any such idea, as will be evident to any one who will ask himself: Is there any pleasure which all persons find at all times in every park, and if so, what does that pleasure depend upon?

The answer unquestionably must be, that there is such a pleasure, common, constant and universal to all town parks, and that it results from the feeling of relief experienced by those entering them, on escaping from the cramped, confined and controlling circumstances of the streets of the town; in other words, *a sense of enlarged freedom* is to all, at all times, the most certain and the most valuable gratification afforded by a park. The scenery which favors this gratification is, therefore, more desirable to be secured than any other, and the various topographical conditions and circumstances of a site thus, in reality, become important very much in the proportion by which they give the means of increasing the general impression of undefined limit. The degree of this impression, which will be found in any particular park, must unquestionably depend very much upon the manner in which it is laid out; that is to say, on the manner in which the original topographical conditions are turned to account by the designers; but as no degree of art can make the back yard of a town house seem unlimited, and as no art at all is required to make a prairie of some hundred square miles seem unlimited to a man set down in the midst of it, it is obvious that a certain distance between the points of resort within the park, and its exterior limits, is necessary in order to allow the fence or wall that would otherwise definitely establish the position of the boundary to be obscured by planting, if nothing more; and that therefore, until all other necessary requirements are provided for, it will not be entirely practicable to determine where the boundary lines of the park may be established, with a true economy of space.

We have first then to determine what accommodations are desirable to be secured within the park, and next how these shall be situated with reference to one another, and to exterior topographical circumstances. Our conclusions will depend first upon our understanding of the purposes which any town park should be designed to fulfill, that is to say, of the general principles to be observed, and secondly upon our estimate of the number and the special character of the people who are to use the particular park in question.

With regard to the latter point, we need only remark that we regard Brooklyn as an integral part of what to-day is the metropolis of the nation, and in the future will be the centre of exchanges for the world, and the park in Brooklyn, as part of a system of grounds, of which the Central Park is a single feature, designed for the recreation of the whole people of the metropolis and their customers and guests from all parts of the world for centuries to come. With regard, however, to the purposes which town parks in general should be intended and prepared to fulfil, this being a matter upon which little has ever been said or written, and upon which very different ideas prevail, and inasmuch as a clear understanding upon it must be had before a fair judgment can be formed of any plan for a town park, we propose to indicate the views which we have adopted, and out of which our plan has grown.

Purposes of a Park

The word park has different significations, but that in which we are now interested has grown out of its application centuries ago, simply to hunting grounds; the choicest lands for hunting grounds being those in which the beasts of the chase were most happy, and consequently most abundant, sites were chosen for them, in which it was easy for animals to turn from rich herbage to clear water, from warm sunlight to cool shade; that is to say, by preference, ranges of well-watered dale-land, broken by open groves and dotted with spreading trees; undulating in surface, but not rugged. Gay parties of pleasure occasionally met in these parks, and when these meetings occurred the enjoyment otherwise obtained in them was found to be increased. Hence, instead of mere hunting lodges and hovels for game keepers, extensive buildings and other accommodations, having frequently a festive character, were after a time provided within their enclosures. Then it was found that people took pleasure in them without regard to the attractions of the chase, or of conversation, and this pleasure was perceived to be, in some degree, related to their scenery, and in some degree to the peculiar manner of associa-

99

tion which occurred in them; and this was also found to be independent of intellectual gifts, tranquilizing and restorative to the powers most tasked in ordinary social duties, and stimulating only in a healthy and recreative way to the imagination. Hence, after a time, parks began to be regarded and to be maintained with reference, more than any thing else, to the convenient accommodation of numbers of people, desirous of moving for recreation among scenes that should be gratifying to their taste or imagination.

In the present century, not only have the old parks been thus maintained, but many new parks have been formed with these purposes exclusively in view, especially within and adjoining considerable towns, and it is upon our knowledge of these latter that our simplest conception of a town park is founded. It is from experience in these that all our ideas of parks must spring.

This experience shows that the great advantage which a town finds in a park, lies in the addition to the health, strength and morality which comes from it to its people, an advantage which is not only in itself very great and positive but which as certainly results in an increase of material wealth as good harvests or active commerce. And the reason is obvious: all wealth is the result of labor, and every man's individual wealth is, on the whole, increased by the labor of every other in the community, supposing it to be wisely and honestly applied; but as there cannot be the slightest use of the will, of choice between two actions or two words, nor the slightest exercise of skill of any kind, without the expenditure of force, it follows that, without recuperation and recreation of force, the power of each individual to labor wisely and honestly is soon lost, and that, without the recuperation of force, the power of each individual to add to the wealth of the community is, as a necessary consequence, also soon lost.

But to this process of recuperation a condition is necessary, known since the days of Æsop, as the unbending of the faculties which have been tasked, and this *unbending* of the faculties we find is impossible, except by the occupation of the imagination with objects and reflections of a quite different character from those which are associated with their bent condition. To secure such a diversion of the imagination, the best possible stimulus is found to be the presentation of a class of objects to the perceptive organs, which shall be as agreeable as possible to the taste, and at the same time entirely different from the objects connected with those occupations by which the faculties have been tasked. And this is what is found by townspeople in a park.

If now we ask further, what the qualities of a park are which fit it to meet this requirement? we find two circumstances, common to all parks in distinction from other places in towns, namely, scenery offering the most agreeable contrast to that of the rest of the town; and opportunity for people to come together for the single purpose of enjoyment, unembarrassed by the limitations with which they are surrounded at home, or in the pursuit of their daily avocations, or of such amusements as are elsewhere offered.

It may be observed, that these two purposes are not quite compatible one with the other; for that scenery which would afford the most marked contrast with the streets of a town, would be of a kind characterized in nature by the absence, or, at least, the marked subordination of human influences. Yet, in a park, the largest provision is required for the human presence. Men must come together, and must be seen coming together, in carriages, on horseback and on foot, and the concourse of animated life which will thus be formed, must in itself be made, if possible, an attractive and diverting spectacle.

How can these opposing requirements be harmonized?

Perfectly harmonized they cannot be, and, because they cannot be, success in realizing either must be limited. Yet, by a careful adjustment of parts, and by accommodating the means necessary to the effecting of one purpose to those necessary to the effecting of the other, both may be accomplished in a degree which experience shows is satisfactory.

In the endeavor to accommodate the requirements of the one purpose to those of the other, a perfect compromise at all points is not essential. On the contrary, it is desirable that each should be carried out at certain points in high degree and if the natural topography of the site chosen is varied, it will not be difficult to select points suitable for doing this.

It is, however, necessary, to a satisfactory result that what is wholly incompatible with one purpose and at the same time not absolutely necessary to the other should be everywhere rigidly avoided and excluded. For instance, a railroad station, a manufactory with chimnies and steam engines, advertising displays, wagons for commercial traffic, fast driving, gambling booths, a market place, though all of these may be seen in some town parks, are clearly there by mistake and want of proper consideration.[1] We may add that whatever the numbers to be accommodated, it is incompatible with the rural character required in a park, that anything like the embarrassing turmoil, confusion and discordant din, common to the crowded streets of the town should be necessarily encountered within it, while it is equally evident that no regard for scenery should be allowed to prevent the assemblage and movement of great crowds within the park—of crowds much greater than will occur anywhere else in the town.

To admit of this, and at the same time maintain anything of a rural, natural, tranquilizing and poetic character in the scenery, the driving room, riding room, walking room, sitting room, skating, sailing and playing room, must be not only liberally designed, but must be studied and adapted to all the natural circumstances of the site with the greatest care.

[1] There will always be a temptation to make use of the ground of a park for other public purposes than those to which it is primarily devoted, and, if this is not guarded against at the outset, there is great danger that after a time the purposes for which a park is especially designed will be subordinated, and all that has been done to meet them sacrificed to purposes which, with proper forethought and economy, would be equally well met on other sites. A park is a center about which public buildings are most appropriately placed, but if there is to be an obvious relation between the buildings and the scenery of the park, both should be parts of the same design. If no such relation is required, the buildings should not be seen from within the park. This subject is further discussed under the head of "Museums and other Edifices." [1866.]

How the Objects of a Park Are to Be Pursued

To illustrate the practical application of these views, we will take one of the many classes of arrangements for the accommodation of the movements of the public through a park: The drive, or carriage way, and consider what is required in it.

A drive must be so prepared that those using it shall be called upon for the least possible exercise of judgment as to the course to be pursued, the least possible anxiety or exercise of skill in regard to collisions or interruptions with reference to objects animate or inanimate, and that they shall, as far as possible, be free from the disturbance of noise and jar.

To secure these negative qualities, the course of the road must be simple; abrupt turns must be avoided, steep grades that would task the horses or suggest that idea must not be encountered. The possibility of the road becoming miry must be securely guarded against; its surface must also be smooth and be composed of compact material.

These being the first and essential engineering considerations, it is necessary, secondly, that they should be secured in a manner which shall be compatible with the presentation of that which is agreeable to the eye in the surrounding circumstances; that is to say, the drive must either run through beautiful scenery already existing or to be formed, and for this purpose it may be desirable at any point to deviate from the line which an engineer would be bound to choose as that which would best meet the first class of requirements. It must also be remembered that although the drive can hardly be expected in itself to add to the beauty of the scenery, it must always be more or less in view as part of it, and it should therefore be artistically designed so as to interfere as little as possible with the views, and to present at all points agreeable and harmonious lines to the eye. Moreover, as it is desirable that at some point in the course of a drive through every park, there should be an opportunity for those in carriages to see others and be seen by others, some portion of the ground, which by development of natural suggestions cannot be readily made very attractive to the eye, should be chosen for that purpose. And here it will be proper that the application of art to inanimate nature, as in architectural objects, and by festive decorations of the outlines of the drive itself, should distinctly invite attention, and aid to produce a general suggestion of sympathy with human gaiety and playfulness.

It is unnecessary to show here how the same general principles need to be regarded in planning the rides, the walks, the seats, the playing grounds, the skating fields, the places of refreshment, and in whatever other accommodations are proposed to be occupied by those who use the park. We would only remind you that no park has yet been made for the people of a large civilized town which has not been much more used than its designers had anticipated; and that all danger of damage, misuse and wasteful destruction of public property practically amounts to nothing, except as it results from insufficient extent of the means of communication and of rest within the park, or from an appearance of slovenliness, or want of completeness and finish in its arrangements for gratifying the eye, which adjoin these accommodations.

The Artistic Element in the Design of a Park

The general principles in regard to scenery, which have governed us in our study, remain to be indicated; and inasmuch as some misapprehension in our judgment generally prevails concerning the province of art in the formation of scenery, and especially of scenery in the natural style, we propose to briefly express our views upon that subject.

A mere imitation of nature, however successful, is not art, and the purpose to imitate nature, or to produce an effect which shall seem to be natural and interesting, is not sufficient for the duty before us.

A scene in nature is made up of various parts; each part has its individual character and its possible ideal. It is unlikely that accident should bring together the best possible ideals of each separate part, merely considering them as isolated facts, and it is still more unlikely that accident should group a number of these possible ideals in such a way that not only one or two but that all should be harmoniously related one to the other. It is evident, however, that an attempt to accomplish this artificially is not impossible, and that a proper study of the circumstances relating to the perfect development of each particular detail will at least enable the designer to reckon surely on a certain success of a high character in that detail, and a comprehensive bringing together of the results of his study in regard to the harmonious relations of one, two or more details may enable him to discover the law of harmonious relation between multitudinous details; and if he can discover it, there is nothing to prevent him from putting it into practice. The result would be a work of art, and the combination of the art thus defined, with the art of architecture in the production of landscape compositions, is what we denominate landscape architecture.

The first process in the application of this art upon any given site, is the formation of a judgment upon the capabilities and the limitations of that site, with reference to the artistic purpose. It is obviously impossible, for instance, to produce in the vicinity of Brooklyn such scenery as will affect the mind as it is affected by the Alps or the Sierras, on the one hand, or by the luxuriant vegetation of a tropical swamp on the other.

Moreover, there are certain kinds of scenery which experience shows to be most satisfactory within a town park, which require an extensive aggregation of their elements. It will be readily seen, for instance, that if all the wood, water and turf, within a certain area of ground, were distributed in patches, strips and pools, however extensive as a whole, and however varied in detail it might seem to those who should thoroughly explore all its parts, there would be no part which would not seem confined, there could be no large open single scene, and no such impression or effect on the mind would be produced as there would be, if all the water were collected in one lake, all the trees in one grove, all the strips of grass in one broad meadow. Such aggregations, and consequently the degree of the impression intended to be produced by them, must be limited by consideration for two other purposes: the purpose of variety of interest, and the purpose to make all the scenery available to the satisfaction of the public by ways of communication. Other limitations upon the artistic purpose, again, are imposed by conditions of soil and exposure, by rocks and springs. How far each of these can be overcome, as by blasting, draining, grading, screening, manuring and other processes, must be in every case a special study, and the artistic purposes of the plan must be affected in every part and particular by the conclusions arrived at.

In the case before us, it is obvious that we should attempt nothing which is incompatible with, or inappropriate to, comparatively slight variations of surface, and a climate of considerable rigor. On the other hand, there are no protruding ledges of rock, no swamps difficult of drainage, and there is no especial bleakness, or danger to trees from violent winds, to be apprehended. It is under similar conditions to these that we find in nature that class of scenery, already referred to, as the original and typical scenery of parks or hunting grounds, and which is termed pastoral. It consists of combinations of trees, standing singly or in groups, and casting their shadows over broad stretches of turf, or repeating their beauty by reflection upon the calm surface of pools, and the predominant associations are in the highest degree tranquilizing and grateful, as expressed by the Hebrew poet: "He maketh me to lie down in green pastures; He leadeth me beside the still waters." We know of no other landscape effects that can be commanded, within the limitations fixed by the conditions of this site, which experience shows to be more desirable in a town park than these. This being the case, no other should be sought for or retained, if, by discarding them, we can the better secure these. Only so far then as we can, without sacrificing any thing that will contribute to the highest practicable ideal of pastoral scenery, should we endeavor to secure any degree of those other ideals, of which the best types are found under widely dissimilar circumstances.

Although we cannot have wild mountain gorges, for instance, on the park, we may have rugged ravines shaded with trees, and made picturesque with shrubs, the forms and arrangement of which remind us of mountain scenery. We may perhaps even secure some slight approach to the mystery, variety and luxuriance of tropical scenery, by an assemblage of certain forms of vegetation, gay with flowers, and intricate and mazy with vines and creepers, ferns, rushes and broad-leaved plants. But all we can do in these directions must be confessedly imperfect, and suggestive rather than satisfying to the imagination. It must, therefore, be made incidental and strictly subordinate to our first purpose.

Having formed these general plans, we find, in further studying the site, its most important circumstance to be the fact, that a large body of trees already exist upon it, not too old to be improved, yet already old enough to be of considerable importance in a landscape. These trees are in two principal divisions, between which a space of two or three hundred feet in width is found, of undulating ground, not wholly ungraceful, and now mainly covered with a ragged turf. A few trees stand out singly upon this space. It is more nearly level, and less occupied by trees, than any other portion of the site. There is no rock in place upon it, nor would it be at all impracticable to reduce its few abrupt and graceless hillocks, and fill up its gravel pits and muck holes. If we imagine this to be done, and then look at it in connection with the surrounding groves, it is obvious that all that is required to form here a fair example of pastoral scenery is, first, an improvement of the turf, and, secondly, greater space, so that the observer may not see all the boundaries of free sunlight before him at a glance. The former requirement is certainly within our power, all that is needed to secure it being the drainage, deep tillage and enrichment of the soil, and the substitution of finer grasses for the present coarse grasses and weeds. Something may be done also with regard to the second, by cutting in upon the borders of the woods, where the ground lies in gentle slopes, leaving only the finer trees to stand out singly, or in small groups, upon the turf to be formed upon the new ground thus obtained. Were this done, however, the open space would still be comparatively an unimportant one in relation to the whole park. The observer would take it all in at a glance, and if this were all he felt that he could look for, the result would be tantalizing rather than satisfactory.

As a very important suggestion springs from this observation, we shall be pardoned for referring to a portion of the Central Park, New York, where somewhat similar conditions formerly existed, and where our views have been adopted and realized. Entering by the turn to the right, at the Merchant's Gate, in a few moments the visitor's eye falls upon the open space called the Cricket Ground, where originally was a small swamp, enlarged at great expense in the construction of the park, in order to meet a similar artistic purpose to that above explained, by the removal of several large ledges of rock, and now occupied by an unbroken meadow, which extends before the observer to a distance of nearly a thousand feet. Here is a suggestion of freedom and repose, which must in itself be refreshing and tranquilizing to the visitor coming from the confinement and bustle of crowded streets. But this is not all. The observer, resting for a moment to enjoy the scene, which he is induced to do by the arrangement of the planting, cannot but hope for still greater space than is obvious before him, and this hope is encouraged, first, by the fact that, though bodies of rock and foliage to the right and left obstruct his direct vision, no limit is seen to the extension of the meadow in a lateral direction; while beyond the low shrubs, which form an undefined border to it in front, there are no trees or other impediments to vision for a distance of half a mile or more, and the only distinct object is the wooded knoll of Vista Rock, nearly a mile away, upon the summit of which it is an important point in the design, not yet realized, to erect a slight artificial structure, for the purpose of catching the eye, and the better holding it in this direction. The imagination of the visitor is thus led instinctively to form the idea that a broad expanse is opening before him, and the more surely to accomplish this, a glimpse of a slope of turf beyond the border of shrubs in the middle distance has been secured. As the visitor proceeds, this idea is strengthened, and the hope which springs from it in a considerable degree satisfied, if not actually realized, first by a view of those parts of the Cricket Ground which lie to the right and left of his previous field of vision, afterwards by the broad expanse of turf on either side and before him, which comes into view as he emerges from the plantations at or near the marble archway.

The carrying out of this most important purpose in the scenery of the Central Park, owing to the rocky and heterogeneous character of the original surface, involved much more labor and a larger expenditure than any other landscape feature of that undertaking.

For the same reason that induced us to recommend that expenditure to the Commissioners of the Central Park, we feel dissatisfied with the limits of the space we are now regarding. It is evident at a glance, however, that if we do not restrict ourselves to the artificial boundary formerly fixed upon for the park, this space may readily be more than doubled in extent without encroaching upon any considerable natural elevation, and at a very moderate expense. Thus our second requirement would be met.

In addition to the special artistic advantage which the acquisition of this ground would secure, there are two other very important considerations in favor of obtaining it: First, such an addition is almost indispensable to a proper provision of playing grounds, there being no space of moderately level ground, not occupied by groves of trees of much value, sufficient for this purpose, upon the territory now controlled by your Commission; second, its acquisition will enable us to make a very great improvement upon any general plan of drives, rides and walks, which would otherwise be practicable, and in these and other ways, to which we shall hereafter allude, it will greatly lessen the danger of overcrowding the park.

Next to groves and greensward, a sheet of water is the most important element in the character of the scenery which we desire to realize. We find no place suited to the formation of such a feature of sufficient extent within the limits of the site now held by your Commission. At a short distance beyond them, there is, however, a broad plain, overlooked on the park side by the highest ground in the vicinity, from the top of which there is a prospect to the southward, which includes a large sweep of the ocean, the Highlands of Navesink, Sandy Hook, and all the outer harbor of New York. The formation of a lake on the low ground referred to, in such a manner that this elevation would be reflected upon its surface, would add such an unquestionable advantage to the landscape attractions of the park, that we should feel obliged to take the same course with reference to it as we have done in regard to the previously proposed extension of the limits of the site, even if no other considerations favored it. The great value of a park lake in this climate, however, for skating, and the attractiveness of the spectacle which crowds of skaters afford to others, added to its value for the recreation of rowing, afford additional inducements of no small consequence in favor of this course. With the further addition, which we therefore advise, it will be practicable to form a sheet of water having more than twice the accommodation for skaters of that in the Central Park. The Central Park Lake, though many objected to it originally as larger than necessary for any artistic purpose, while it occupied space which might be otherwise used to advantage, is already found much too small for the comfortable accommodation of those who are prepared to use it, and many turn from it, in consequence, to those small ponds where the payment of an admission fee secures greater space to individual skaters. If this is now the case, the need of very much larger skating space will be a very pressing one in the future, as population increases. We cannot doubt that a sheet of ice in Brooklyn, equally near to the present centre of population of the metropolis, and more than twice as large as that in the Central Park, would soon attract a larger number of persons than have ever yet resorted to the latter. This number has on several occasions been above one hundred thousand in a day and five hundred thousand in a week. If we consider that the opportunity afforded for this recreation would be worth in the acquisition of health and vigor to the whole body of citizens an amount equal to a dime for each visitor, it will be evident that the whole cost of purchasing the land in view, and of constructing the lake, might be defrayed by the use which would be made of it in a single season.

Supposing the more hilly land to be covered by plantations, and a green-sward to be formed upon the open ground which we have described, and the low plain to be mainly occupied by a lake, we have the three grand elements of pastural landscape for which we were seeking. What remains consists of limited strips of surface, generally stony and somewhat rough, and may be left to be treated incidentally, as before explained. To the important features of the greensward, the wood, the lake and the hill, the roads and walks must be accommodated in such a way as to give the visitor the best advantage, consistent with ease and comfort, for enjoying whatever charm they may be made to possess. Before referring particularly to the system of communications, however, it will be best to speak of certain other detached arrangements.

Places of Congregation and Rest

Besides the green, our study provides three places, each adapted to the assemblage of large numbers of people, and for their remaining together for some time at rest.

The first of these we designate the Look-out. The circumstances which make a special arrangement for the accommodation of an assemblage at this point desirable are, 1st, the view which is obtained here, and nowhere else in the park, of the outer harbor, the distant mountain ranges of New Jersey and the ocean offing; 2d, the peculiar advantages which the elevation offers for the enjoyment in hot weather of the sea breeze; 3d, the interest of the local scenery, which it is our intention should be quite different from that of any other part of the park; and 4th, The bird's eye view which will be presented of military evolutions, if the projected parade-ground should be formed south of the park.

We propose to form here a terraced platform, one hundred feet in length, with seats and awnings, connected by a broad terrace walk and staircase with an oval court for carriages,

111

three hundred feet long and one hundred and fifty wide. On the west side of the platform, provision is made for a small low building, designed for the special accommodation of women and children, and at which they may obtain some simple refreshment. This building is also intended to serve the purpose of shutting off the view westwardly from the lookout platform, as this would otherwise detract from the effect obtained in other directions.

All the principal walks of the park tend to lead the visitor from whatever entrance he starts, to finally reach the lookout, though he may visit every other part of the park, and yet avoid this if he prefers. From the lookout, broad walks lead across the park to the east end of the lake, where, at a point commanding the largest water view, together with a rich open meadow landscape, backed by the highest elevation of the park, pinnacled with evergreens, arrangements for open-air concerts are proposed. The orchestra will be situated upon an island in a bay of the lake, so that it can be seen from three sides. On the main land, within a distance of two hundred and twenty-five yards of this island—at which distance the music of a well appointed band can be perfectly appreciated—standing room is provided for horses and carriages in a circular space about five hundred feet in diameter and, in an oval space at a higher elevation, three hundred feet long and one hundred and seventy-five feet wide, while directly in front, at a distance varying from one hundred to five hundred feet, a space is provided, to be occupied by shaded seats, sufficient for over ten thousand people. Provision is made for the rapid dispersion of the audience, however large it may be, on foot, in carriages, and on horseback; also for checking the movement of carriages within the circular space, during the performance of music.

Midway between the lookout concourse and the music concourse, and with approaches for footmen and carriages from both, a series of terraces and arcades is provided, within which there will be room for a large restaurant. These look out upon the lake, and the floor of the lower arcade will be nearly on a level with the surface of the lake, so that it can be readily entered from the ice in winter or from boats in summer. The upper terrace is five hundred feet in length by sixty feet in width, and the remaining floor space of the structure one hundred and seventy-five by two hundred feet. The arcades are intended to be the principal architectural feature of the park.

Sylvan Features

There are four sylvan features of considerable importance in the plan. First, upon the green, the meadow, and the slopes of the upper lake, a display of the finest American forest trees, standing singly and in open groups, so as to admit of the amplest development of individuals, which will be further encouraged by the best attainable conditions of soil and situation.

Second, in the central portions of the park, an open grove of forest trees, in which visitors may ramble in the shade without impediment of underwood, and without danger of doing harm to anything through carelessness or any ordinary selfish impulse.

Third, a collection, arranged in the natural way, of the more delicate shrubs and trees, especially evergreens, both coniferous and of the class denominated in England American plants, such as Rhododendrons, Kalmias, Azalias and Andromedas: these would be situated on the interior slopes of the Lookout and the Friend's Hill, and in the valley between them, where, from the peculiar circumstances of exposure and protection they will be likely to thrive.

Fourth, picturesque groups of evergreens and deciduous trees and shrubs on the shore of the lake.

Play Grounds and Greensward

A portion of the green, nearest the Flatbush railroad and the refectory, and where the surrounding road and walks are at the greatest distance from the centre, is proposed to be fitted to be used for a ball playing ground, by the children of the public schools and others.

We should advise that the whole of the green, upon special occasions at least, if not at all times, should be open to all persons on foot, as a common. If the ground is properly prepared, there is no danger that the beauty of the turf would be seriously impaired, except perhaps immediately after heavy rains, at which time it would seldom occur that the park would be greatly crowded with visitors. If this is done, and the interior groves also thrown open to pedestrians, through their whole extent between the bridle road and the green, we consider that the danger that the walks and resting places would be overcrowded so as to force or sorely tempt visitors to go upon ground where they would really injure the elements of the scenery, or create disturbance, embarrassment and waste, would be very small.

Zoological Ground

The tract of broken ground, near the Ninth avenue, now partly occupied by gardens and residences, the features of which are quite varied, but rather diminutive for desirable park effects, we propose should be held in reserve for zoological collections, and, as it may properly be placed under the control of a special corporation for this purpose, we refrain at this time from suggesting in what manner it should be laid out. This subject will be recurred to.

Grazing Ground for Deer

The narrow sheltered strip of meadow, on the opposite side of the park, we propose to enclose with a sufficient iron paling and make use of as a pasture ground for deer, antelopes, gazelles, and such other grazing animals as can be satisfactorily herded together in summer upon it.

Water Works and Drainage

In regard to the water needed for the lake, we are informed that sufficient may be spared from the general supply already brought to the city by the Nassau Water Works. We recommend, however, that arrangements be had in view, not only for securing an independent supply, but also for keeping up a constant circulation, by pumping the water from the lake to the spring on the west side of the Friend's Hill, so that it may always be flowing from that point in a natural stream. The pump for this purpose would be worked by steam, in connection with the kitchen of the refectory. The stream furnished by the spring is intended to take first the character of a series of pools, overhung on the one side by the trees upon the north side of the Friend's Hill, and margined on the other by banks of turf. It would then assume more of the usual character of a small mountain stream, taking a very irregular course, with numerous small rapids, shoots and eddies, among rocks and ferns, until it emerged from the shadow of the wood upon a grassy slope; thence it would flow more quietly until, after falling over a body of rock, in connection with a foot bridge on the side of the park opposite that on which it started, it would assume the appearance of a small river with high and shaded banks and at length, passing the refectory and music concourse in two reaches, empty into the eastern bay of the lake. Here, on the north shore would be a low flat meadow with a few large trees and small thickets of bushes overhanging the water. In the coves would be beds of pond lillies and other aquatic plants, and, on the shores near them, flags, cat-tails, bulrushes and the like. This arrangement would give opportunity for every variety of water scenery which is practicable within the space of the park, with any moderate supply of water.

The natural outlet for the surplus water of the park would be in a southerly direction, and a plan of drainage may be adopted that will be more simple and less expensive than would usually be practicable upon a site of this extent, having such a considerable variety of surface.

Drives, Rides and Walks

The more important features of scenery and of local accommodations for various purposes, having been thus pointed out, we now turn to the several ways of communication by which they are connected and related one to another.

The drive, commencing with a width of sixty (60) feet, at the centre of the north or principal entrance to the park, is carried in a southerly direction for some little distance, but diverges slightly to the east, so as to accommodate itself to some high ground in the neighborhood. It there branches to the southeast and southwest, and becomes a part of the circuit drive, which is proposed to be of an average width of forty (40) feet. The arrangement of the lines and curves, at the junction, is such that carriages coming into the park will continue to proceed for a few hundred feet in a southeasterly direction, after reaching the circuit drive, and will thus be fairly started on the road that it is intended they should follow, for, although the formation of the ground naturally suggests this treatment of the lines, we should, under any circumstances, have made an effort to arrange the plan in some such way as is indicated in the design, because the southeasterly branch leads more directly into the heart of the park. It commands, moreover, from a point very near the entrance, a view in the direction of the length of what is now an unplanted stretch of ground, but which is treated in the design as open lawn or meadow, dotted with trees, it being the intention to reduce the height of a low, narrow ridge that crosses this piece of ground, so that its real extent may be fairly seen from the drive.

Continuing on the course already indicated, the road soon curves to the right, and ascends to a point from which it is proposed to obtain an extensive view, in a westerly direction, over the great green of the park. From this point, the road descends into the wooded defile where an old wayside inn now stands, marking the ground held by the Continental forces in an engagement during the battle of Long Island, at which point it will be practicable in perfecting the plan of the park to provide for some architectural memento of that important struggle.

Passing through the defile, a view is obtained over a pretty glade of turf to the left, intended to be used as a grazing ground for deer, and bounded on the opposite side by the thick coppice-wood which already effectually conceals the Flatbush avenue. Keeping to the right of the deer paddock, the drive continues to pass through the woods, but presently divides into two somewhat narrower branches, by which means full advantage is taken of the already existing opportunities for shade, and the standing trees are less interfered with than would otherwise be necessary, and then, reuniting, continues to run in a southerly direction, till it approaches the proposed Franklin avenue boundary line. At this point it divides again, and one branch enlarges almost directly into the open space previously described as the music concourse. The other branch or main line of drive, after passing the two entrances to the concourse, is carried round the head of the lake, and along the shore in a westerly direction, till it approaches the proposed Coney Island road boundary. It then curves to the northward, still following the shore of the lake, until it reaches the west side of the lookout hill. Although there is nothing interesting in the natural scenery of this stretch, the bank of the lake will be made so artificially, and there will be very agreeable views across the water, the north shore being the most picturesque part of the park. This is intended to be used more particularly as the promenade or common course of the park. The drive is consequently laid out of unusual width, and the bridle road, together with a broad walk, is carried in close connection with it.

The western foot of the look-out hill is one of the most important points on the whole line of drive. It is very desirable that the road should retain its circuit character, and continue on in a northerly direction when the hill is reached, as the whole lake has by this time been seen, the social or gregarious disposition is supposed to have been satisfied, and a considerable change is therefore needed in the landscape effect. The way in which we propose that this shall be managed will be readily understood by an examination of the plan; and, although the contour lines of the strip of ground proposed to be added in this immediate neighborhood will need to be somewhat modified, the object in view is really so essential to the development of the whole design, that its successful accomplishment will justify any reasonable expenditure that it may be necessary to incur for the sake of securing it. The main drive continues, therefore, in a westerly direction, leaving the Friends' Hill to the northward, and afterwards opening directly upon and keeping in view the most purely rural, and at the same time the most expanded and extended, view within the park. On approaching the Ninth avenue boundary, it curves to the east round the green, enters the western woods, divides again into two branches, and, after reuniting, passes on for some distance, still in the midst of groves, until, after passing along the side of the meadow stretch that was viewed in the direction of its length, at the commencement of the drive, it reaches the starting point near the main entrance.

In addition to the circuit drive thus described, a cross-road is introduced about the middle of the park, from which will be obtained a fine open out-look towards the country beyond the southern boundary. A loop from this interior road leads to the refectory and across a bridge, over an arm of the lake, to a carriage concourse of smaller size than the one already described, which it is proposed to construct on somewhat elevated ground, overlooking the lake and the music stand. A branch from this cross-road is proposed to lead up the slopes on the side of the look-out hill, to the open area on the upper level, which will command a view of the ocean. The connections with the various entrances are proposed to be made as shown on the plan, and the whole length of drive thus provided for is about five miles and a half.

The bridle road is so laid out on the plan, that by increasing the size of some archways needed for other purposes, it may, if desired, be kept distinct from the carriage road and the footpaths through the whole length of its circuit. It follows generally the line of the main road, sometimes in immediate connection with it, and sometimes passing along at a considerable distance from it. The whole length of the bridle road laid out on the plan is about four miles.

The drive and the bridle road being thus arranged for, the system of walks proposed by the plan next requires attention. It is very important to the comfort of pedestrians, that they should be able to proceed into the park from the entrances that will be chiefly used, without having to cross over the circuit drive or bridle road, and that, when once fairly in among the trees and grass stretches, they should be able to ramble over the whole extent of the property with as much apparent freedom as if the whole park had been intended solely for their enjoyment.

There are two points in the design which may be said to be central points, so far as the walk system is concerned: the summit level of the look-out hill overlooking the ocean, and the large open air hall of reception shown on the plan, near the principal carriage concourse already described. All the leading lines will be found to tend in these directions, and the intermediate walks are designed to give variety and intricacy, without interfering with this general intention of the design. From the main entrance two walks are proposed to start. One passes near the north-eastern boundary, and leads to the reservoir bridge over Flatbush avenue; it then continues in a southerly direction, skirting the deer paddock, and terminates at the music concourse. A branch of this walk passes under the carriage road, near the main entrance, and opens directly on to the meadow stretch which forms the northern division of the great green. The walk passes around this meadow, and crossing the green commands a full view of its whole extent; then through the woods into a ravine by the side of the brook and by an arched passage under the carriage road to the lawn-like open ground north of the look-out hill; then again through the woods till it meets the line, already described, which leads to the music concourse.

The second walk that starts from the main entrance passes in a rather more westerly direction. It has the same general tendency as the walks above mentioned, and leads both to the look-out and to the music concourse.

A walk extends all around the lake and around the green, and a system of walks is introduced to connect the music concourse and the look-out with the refectory; but it is not necessary to describe all these walks in detail.

From the principal entrance at the junction of Flatbush and Ninth avenues, from the entrance at the corner of Fifteenth street and Ninth avenue, from the foot entrance at the junction of Sixteenth street and the Coney Island road, and from the entrance from Flatbush avenue, near the Willink property, it is proposed to have walks, leading to the principal points of interest, that will not be interfered with by the carriage road. From the other two entrances, surface cross-walks are proposed, as it would be difficult, on account of the embankment that will be necessary to retain the waters of the lake, to adopt the plan used elsewhere.

Boundary Arrangements

Outside the exterior drives and walks, such extent of ground only is wanted as is necessary to enable us, by planting and otherwise, to shut out of view that which would be inharmonious with and counteractive to our design. This extent we find in all cases, without carrying the boundary beyond the nearest street line, as laid down on the city map, and except at the two points where the ground, which might otherwise seem to be more than is required to enable us to plant out the boundary, is occupied by the zoological grounds and the deer paddock before described, it will be found that the amount of ground taken into the park, beyond what is absolutely necessary for this purpose, is nowhere equal to the depth of an ordinary lot. Practically there will not be a foot of ground within the boundary the use of which will not add to the interest of the park and its value to the citizens. At one point, the boundary is kept a long distance within the nearest street line. This is where the orchards and villa gardens, on the east of the drive, near the music concourse, admit of a narrower margin than would otherwise answer. The fronts of these valuable grounds near the park are not likely to be built upon before its border trees will have become well grown, nor until a street has been opened along the boundary line. Any buildings then likely to be erected here will consequently be placed at such a distance as not to be conspicuous from the park, while the arrangement enables the city to avoid the purchase of any land having special value from its association with highly improved residences.

By adopting the line of Franklin Avenue for the boundary on the south, about half the space between an observer standing on Look-out Hill and the horizon, will seem to be occupied by the lake and the park. This effect will of course be merely an optical one, but a visit to the site will show at once that it will be all-sufficient to divert the attention of the visitor from the land occupied for agricultural purposes, and will serve to render the sea view more attractive. This advantage will be considerably increased, if the ground immediately beyond Franklin avenue should be appropriated for a parade ground, or any other public purpose which will prevent it from being occupied by tall buildings. A nearer boundary than Franklin avenue would probably fail to realize the effect desired in this particular.

It is proposed to widen Vanderbilt avenue to one hundred feet, as far as the limits of the property at present owned by the Commissioners; also to widen Ninth avenue to one hundred feet, as far as the limits of the park are proposed to extend; also to widen Fifteenth street, the Coney Island road and Franklin avenue, as shown on the plan, wherever they connect with the proposed boundary lines. In all these cases, the additional width is proposed to be added on the side of the road next to the park, leaving the lines on the opposite of the road as already laid down on the city map.

On the additional ground thus obtained, it is proposed to construct a thirty-feet sidewalk, shaded by a double row of trees, so that an ample gas-lighted and umbrageous promenade will be offered to the public in the immediate vicinity of the park, after the gates are closed at night. The comparatively close planting of these avenue trees will moreover help to shut out the houses that will be built on the opposite side of the street from the view of the visitors who may be in the interior of the park.

Arrangement of Exterior Streets

In conclusion, we wish to offer a few suggestions with regard to the management of some parts of the ground outside of the park boundaries.

Although, for the reasons given at the beginning of this report, we think it desirable that the section of the site as originally established, lying east of Flatbush avenue, should be abandoned as a part of the park, it does not follow that the lines laid down on the city map, before the project of a park in this vicinity had been suggested, should be re-adopted, and considerable advantages may be obtained, in our judgment, by adjusting them with reference to the park.

We have indicated on our study the manner in which this may be done. It will be seen that while the streets north of the reservoir follow the old lines, those south of it are set out at right angles to Flatbush avenue, instead of diagonally as formerly; and as Grand and Classon avenues cannot cross the park, they are stopped at Washington avenue.

This district, if re-arranged in the manner suggested, will most probably be occupied to a considerable extent by residences of a first-class character, and as the blocks will be sixty feet more than the usual width, it will be easy in execution, if thought desirable, to subdivide the property in such a way that, while on one street the lots will be of ordinary length, on the other they will be so much longer that ample room will be provided for stables that will have a convenient lane access between the two.

An open place or square is suggested at the junction of Grand and Washington avenues, and Washington avenue is proposed to be widened ten feet along the whole length of the property now owned by the Commissioners. A design is also shown for a possible future improvement opposite the park gate, in the vicinity of the present Willink property, so that Franklin avenue may be included in our general scheme for the arrangement of the approaches to this important entrance. As there is a fine distant view from the top of the reservoir, and as this structure belongs inalienably to the city, we also propose to reserve some of the ground about it so as to be able to flank it with agreeable groups of trees, and to connect it by means of a light foot-bridge over Flatbush avenue with the walks of the park, as indicated on our study. The formation of the ground is suitable for the purpose and the fine view to be obtained from the upper level of the reservoir can thus be associated with the attractions of the park.

In addition to the principal entrance, provision is made for gates to the park on Flatbush avenue, near the Willink property; on Franklin avenue, near the southeast corner of the proposed boundaries; at the junction of Franklin avenue, with the Coney Island road; at the junction of Sixteenth street and the Coney Island road, and from the junction of Ninth avenue and Fifteenth street. Another entrance is indicated on the Ninth avenue, opposite Third street, which can either lead into the park or connect simply with the zoological garden, as may be ultimately determined.

Improvements are suggested, in connection with three of these entrances, which seem to be necessary, for the purpose of securing easy and agreeable approaches; and the advantage proposed to be gained in each case will be so readily understood, by reference to the plan, that we deem further explanations in regard to this part of the design unnecessary.

Museums and Other Educational Edifices

Although the ground now held by your Commission, east of Flatbush avenue, does not appear to us desirable to be retained for the purpose for which it has been assigned, it will nevertheless be an advantage to the park, if a small section of it, abutting on Flatbush avenue and facing the park, remains in the possession of the city. We therefore desire to offer a suggestion as to the use to which it may be appropriated.

It is undesirable that any duties or responsibilities should be assumed by legislative bodies that can be equally well undertaken by citizens, either individually or associated in their private capacity. The exact limit of judicious legislation in this way cannot however be defined, and while there are many public responsibilities that clearly cannot be assumed by individual citizens, and many more that can, there are some few that are of an intermediate character, and that require special consideration. It is generally conceded that a system of popular education is an essential part of a republican government, for instance, but it is by no means determined what means of education should be secured to all, and to what extent the public can be taxed, with reasonable assurance of a saving to the tax payers through a reduction of taxes for courts, police, prisons and poorhouses, and the general cheapening of the necessaries of life by the increased capacity for productive labor of the whole community which may be obtained through the improvement of the educational system.

It is very desirable therefore that plans should, if possible, be adopted by our municipal bodies, which will admit of strict construction, and at the same time be no bar to the progressive improvement of our methods of education. At present, book learning and education are generally considered correlative terms, but the conviction is evidently fast gaining ground in the public mind, which has long been established with those who have given the most thorough consideration to the subject, that, although the ordinary chances of observation may be sufficient to make many branches of knowledge which are inculcated in books sufficiently intelligible, there are others, progress in which is of special value with reference to the enlargement of the mind and the development of healthy inclinations and habits, which cannot be pursued with much advantage in this second-hand way.

Hence, it may be anticipated that the common-school system of a large city will, sooner or later, be generally considered incomplete, unless ample opportunity is found within it for the direct exercise by every student of his perceptive faculties in regard to a large class of objects not likely to come under his ordinary observation. The idea of education, it must be confessed by all, unquestionably culminates in the development of the reflective faculties, but the reflective faculties—which are secondary—can never, it is obvious, be healthily exercised if the perceptive faculties—which are primary—are neglected and starved.

The question therefore is pertinent, even at present, whether the city, without absolutely assuming the whole expense and the whole control of undertakings for this end, may not wisely offer some encouragement to associations voluntarily formed by citizens for the purpose.

Having some such views in mind as these, when we were preparing the design of Central Park, we advocated the retention of the building near the boundary, north of the Artist's Gate, formerly used as an arsenal, simply because it would probably, if retained, be found to be of sufficient value to be converted into a suitable building for a museum, and although it was very inconveniently located for any such purpose, we felt that the opportunity was one that ought not to be lost. Our suggestion was adopted by the Commissioners, and the Historical Society has since asked for and obtained possession from them of this site and this building with the understanding that it is to be improved and converted into a public museum at the expense of the society.

We have before shown the impropriety, as a general rule, of placing edifices, which are not strictly auxilliary to the primary purpose of a park, within its boundaries, and this illustration is, of course, presented with no purpose of favoring their introduction but rather to show that they ought in some other way to be provided for in season. The suggestion we have to make in this case is that the stretch of ground abutting on Flatbush avenue, fronting towards the park (marked R. R. on the plan), and now in the possession of the Commissioners, should be distinctly set apart for such purposes as we have indicated. If this suggestion is accepted, the lots on this part of Flatbush avenue, will probably, in course of time, be occupied by handsome buildings, the objects of which will in some way be connected with the educational system of the city, but which will not be erected or owned by it, the terms on which the different sites would be given being such as to secure a share of control in the management of each institution, sufficient to ensure to the city an adequate return for the value of the land it parts with.

Suburban Connections

It will be observed that we have indicated the commencement of a road leading out of the west side of the circle, in connection with the southern entrance to the park. We have done so from a conviction, that a shaded pleasure drive in extension of that of the park, and free from the embarrassments which will inevitably be associated with a road partially occupied by a line of railway, and which is also used as a trotting course for fast horses, will soon be demanded by the frequenters of the park. Such a road, whatever may be the character of the country through which it passes, should be in itself of a picturesque character. It should, therefore, be neither very straight nor very level, and should be bordered by a small belt of trees and shrubbery.

We have made no special survey with reference to the course which should be followed by such a road, but the first objective point in view would unquestionably be the ocean beach, and this might very properly be its terminus. It has occured [sic] to us, however, that either from some point a little further east on the beach, thus made accessible by carriages from the park, or from a point more directly in connection with the park drives, a similar road may be demanded in the future which shall be carried through the rich country lying back of Brooklyn, until it can be turned, without striking through any densely occupied ground, so as to approach the East River, and finally reach the shore at or near Ravenswood. From this point, either by ferry or high bridges, it may be thrown over the two narrow straits into which the East River is divided in this neighborhood, and connection may thus be had with one of the broad streets leading directly into the Central Park, and thus with the system of somewhat similar sylvan roads leading northward, now being planned by the Commissioners of the Central Park. Such an arrangement would enable a carriage to be driven on the half of a summer's day, through the most interesting parts both of the cities of Brooklyn and New York, through their most attractive and characteristic suburbs, and through both their great parks; having a long stretch of the noble Hudson with the Palisades in the middle distance, and the Shawangunk range of mountains in the back-ground, in view at one end, and the broad Atlantic with its foaming breakers rolling on the beach, at the other.

The whole might be taken in a circuit without twice crossing the same ground, and would form a grand municipal promenade, hardly surpassed in the world either for extent or continuity of interest.

This suggestion forms no part of our plan and may seem premature, but there can be but little danger of too extended a prevision with reference to future improvements which may grow out of so important a work as that upon which your Commission is engaged, and we have, therefore, in the preparation of the design herewith submitted endeavored, as far as possible, to arrange for a proper connection with any undertakings of the character indicated which may hereafter be found to be required.

Respectfully,
OLMSTED, VAUX & Co.
Landscape Architects

January 24th, 1866

DOCUMENT IV

⇥⇥⇥⇤⇤⇤

FREDERICK LAW OLMSTED AND CALVERT VAUX

Report of the Landscape Architects and Superintendents to the President of the Board of Commissioners of Prospect Park, Brooklyn (1868)

⇥⇥⇥⇤⇤⇤

To the President of the Board of Commissioners of Prospect Park, Brooklyn:

SIR:—In our Annual Report of last year, we described the organization which had been made under instructions from your Board for carrying out the design of the Park upon the ground. This organization remains to the present time essentially unchanged.

In June last, Mr. J. P. Davis having resigned the position, Mr. C. C. Martin was appointed to the office of Engineer in Charge.

Development of the Design

During the year it has been found practicable to carry forward the design for the Park without intermission, although at many points the works, which it would have been most desirable to press to completion, have been suspended in consequence of the uncertainties in regard to boundary lines that still continue to embarrass operations.

So much of the land required for the Park as lies to the south of that upon which work was last year commenced, came into the actual possession of the Commissioners during the month of June last, and active operations were at once extended over a large part of the new territory.

A portion of the road system in this section of the ground has been developed, the carriage concourse proposed in our original design to be constructed on Briar Hill has been sub-graded and the ground in the vicinity of this concourse has been partially shaped. It was found practicable in execution to enlarge the area of this feature of the design, and the dimensions have been somewhat increased, it being evident that the position was one that would offer special attractions to visitors in carriages.

On the east side of the Park, north of the deer-paddock, the design as it stood last year has been so far modified in execution as to admit of the introduction of a series of arrangements adapted especially to meet the wants of children. The plan as approved, and now well advanced in execution, contemplates suitable accommodations for running sports and for playing various games, it also includes croquet grounds, a pond for the sailing of toy boats, and a maze.

In other respects but little variation has been made in the outline of the design from our first study.

Construction

You will find appended a full account of the progress of the methods used, and of the means and materials employed, which has been prepared by Mr. Martin and his principal aids, Mr. Bogart and Mr. Culyer.

Two arch-ways have been partially constructed during the year, and work has been commenced upon several other architectural features, our studies for which have been approved by the Board. The development in detail of this department of the work is under the more immediate charge of Mr. E. C. Miller, who has fulfilled the duties of Assistant Architect since the beginning of July last.

Public Use of the Park

It was found necessary in the spring to close the country roads by which the public had previously crossed the Park

territory, but on the 20th of October, a portion of the drive
at the east side was so far completed that, by making temporary connections with old roads, a thoroughfare for carriages
across the Park was again opened. At the same time regulations for the conduct of visitors and for the management of
the work with reference to the convenience of the public
were promulgated, and a beginning was made in the organization of a permanent body of Park-keepers, conjointly with
a body of gardeners, according to a plan which had some
time before been adopted by the Board. Although the short
piece of good road opened at this time was accessible with
difficulty, and the grounds through which it passed were in
a quite unfinished condition it was immediately resorted to
by visitors in large numbers. Besides those in carriages, many
came on horse-back, and although no walks had been opened,
many more on foot. A tabular statement of the number of
each class prepared from the returns of the gate-keepers is
given by Mr. Culyer. The fact is noted that a considerable
portion of the visitors evidently did not come merely from
motives of curiosity, but after their first visit, repeatedly returned. During all the remainder of the season, indeed, not
a few resorted to the Park as a daily habit, of whom some
came from the more distant parts of the town. Considering
the extreme inconvenience with which the Park is at present
reached and the very limited attractions which as yet it offers
this circumstance is a gratifying indication of the value which
it will hereafter possess.

The Park Way—Approaches and Connections

The unsatisfactory character of the approaches to the Park
has been recognized by your Board, from the outset of its
undertaking, as calculated to seriously detract from the value
of the service which it would otherwise be able to render
the city, and it has accordingly been an incidental part of
our duty to devise means of improvement. To do so it has
been necessary that we should extend our field of study beyond the territory under your jurisdiction. Our first suggestion

led, through the subsequent action of your Board, to the special appropriation of the ground necessary for the formation of the Plaza, and to the establishment of the several circular spaces by which amplitude, symmetry, and dignity of character was sought to be secured on the street side of each of the Park gates. Through the promptness of the necessary legislative action, and of the subsequent proceedings in regard to the Plaza, a very great advantage was gained at a comparatively small cost for the necessary land, much of the adjoining ground having since been sold in the open market at rates indicating an advance of several hundred per cent upon the prices paid by the city.

In our Preliminary Report, accompanying the first study of the plan of the Park, without making any definite recommendations, we suggested the leading features of a general scheme of routes of approach to and extension from the Park, through the suburbs, in which the sanitary recreative and domestic requirements of that portion of the people of the city living at the greatest distance from the Park should be especially provided for. In our Annual Report of last year portions of this project were somewhat more distinctly outlined, and the economical advantages were pointed out of preparing and adopting plans for the purpose well in advance of the public demand, which it was intended to anticipate, and while land properly situated might yet be selected in the suburbs of such moderate value that no private interests of much importance would be found to stand in antagonism in this respect to those of the public.

Relations of the Park to the Street Arrangements of the City

Your Board having brought these suggestions before the public they have during the last year attracted considerable attention. One of the minor recommendations has been already taken up by a body of citizens and an organized effort to carry it out is understood to be in progress. Under your instructions a topographical survey has also been made of a section of the ground to which the larger scheme applies, being that lying immediately east of the Park and extending from it to the city line, and a study has been prepared, also under your instructions and which is herewith presented, for a revision of a part of the present city map of this ground with a view to the introduction of the suggested improvement.

The period seems to have arrived, therefore, for a full and comprehensive inquiry as to the manner in which the scheme would, if carried out, affect the substantial and permanent interests of the citizens of Brooklyn and of the metropolis at large.

The project in its full conception is a large one, and it is at once conceded that it does not follow but anticipates the demand of the public; that it assumes an extension of the city of Brooklyn and a degree of wealth, taste, and refinement, to be likely to exist among its citizens which has not hitherto been definitely had in view, and that it is even based upon the presumption that the present street system, not only of Brooklyn but of other large towns, has serious defects for which, sooner or later, if these towns should continue to advance in wealth, remedies must be devised, the cost of which will be extravagantly increased by a long delay in the determination of their outlines.

Elements of Ordinary Street Arrangements

What is here referred to under the designation of our present street system, is essentially comprised in the two series of thoroughfares extending in straight lines to as great a distance within a town as is found practicable, one series crossing the other at right angles, or as nearly so as can be conveniently arranged. Each of the thoroughfares of this system consists of a way in the center, which is paved with reference solely to sustaining the transportation upon wheels of the heaviest merchandise, of a gutter on each side of this wheel-way, having occasional communication with underground channels for carrying off water, and a curb which restricts the passage of wheels from a raised way for the travel of persons on foot, the surface of which, to avoid their sinking in the mud, is commonly covered with flags or brick.

This is the system which is almost universally kept in view, not only in the enlargement of our older towns, but in the setting out of new; such, for instance, as are just being projected along the line of the Pacific Railroad. If modifications are admitted, it is because they are enforced by some special local conditions which are deemed, by those responsible for the arrangement, to be unfortunate. The reason for this is probably found chiefly in the fact, that it is a plan which is readily put on paper, easily comprehended, and easily staked out; it makes the office of an Engineer or Surveyor at the outset almost a sinecure, as far as the exercise of professional ability is concerned, and facilitates the operations of land speculators.

Its apparent simplicity on paper is often fallacious, and leads either to unnecessary taxation or to great permanent inconvenience. It is obviously incomplete, and wholly unsuited to the loading and unloading of goods which require storage, but, where it can be well carried out, offers very great advantages for the transportation of merchandise between distant points. It is also well adapted to equalize the advantages of different parts of a town, and thus avoid obstructions to improvement which mercenary jealousies might otherwise interpose.

In our judgment, advantages such as these have hitherto been pursued far too exclusively, but, as the presumption is always strong against any considerable innovation upon arrangements which have been long associated with the general conditions of prosperity and progress of all civilized communities, we desire, before giving reasons for this conviction, first, to remove any reasonable prejudice against the introduction of the entirely new elements into the street plan of Brooklyn, which we shall have to propose, by showing under what conditions of society and with reference to what very crude public requirements, compared with those which now exist, our present street arrangements have been devised.

Why Ordinary Arrangements Are Inadequate to Public Requirements

At present, large towns grow up because of the facilities they offer mankind for a voluntary exchange of service, in the form of merchandise; but nearly all the older European towns of importance, from which we have received the fashion of our present street arrangements, were formed either to strengthen or to resist a purpose involving the destruction of life and the plunder of merchandise. They were thus planned originally for objects wholly different from those now reckoned important by the towns which occupy the same sites, and an examination of the slow, struggling process by which they have been adapted to the present requirements of their people, may help us to account for some of the evils under which even here, in our large American towns, we are now suffering.

Historical Development of Existing Street Arrangements, First Stage

They were at the outset, in most cases, entrenched camps, in which a few huts were first built, with no thought of permanence, and still less with thought for the common convenience of their future citizens. The wealth of their founders consisted chiefly in cattle, and in the servants who were employed in herding and guarding these cattle, and the trails carelessly formed among the scattered huts within the entrenchments often became permanent foot-ways which, in some cases, were subsequently improved in essentially the same manner as the sidewalks of our streets now are, by the laying upon them of a series of flat stones, so that walkers need not sink in the mud. If the ground was hilly, and the grades of the paths steep, stairs were sometimes made by laying thicker slabs of stone across them. Convenience of communication on foot was, of course, the sole object of such improvements.

If, in these early times, any highways were more regularly laid out, it was simply with reference to defence. For example, although two nearly straight and comparatively broad-ways were early formed in Paris, so that reinforcements could be rapidly transferred from one gate to another when either should be suddenly attacked, no other passages were left among the houses which would admit of the introduction of wheeled traffic; nor in all the improvements which afterwards occurred, as the city advanced in population and wealth, were any of the original pathways widened and graded sufficiently for this purpose until long after America had been discovered, and the invention of printing and of fire-arms had introduced a new era of social progress.

The labor required for the construction of permanent town walls, and the advantage of being able to keep every part of them closely manned during an attack, made it desirable that they should not be unnecessarily extended. To admit of a separate domiciliation of families within them, therefore, the greatest practicable compactness in the arrangement of dwelling-houses soon became imperative. As families increased, the demand for additional house-room was first met by encroachments upon the passages which had been left between the original structures, and by adding upper stories, and extending these outward so as to overhang the street. Before this process had reached an extreme point, however, the town would begin to outgrow its walls, and habitations in the suburbs would occur, of two classes: first, those formed by poor herdsmen and others who, when no enemy was known to be near at hand, could safely sleep in a temporary shelter, calculating to take their chance in the town when danger came; and, second, those formed by princes, and other men of wealth and power, who could afford to build strongholds for the protection of their families and personal retainers, but who, in times of war, yet needed to be in close vicinity to the larger fighting forces of the town. Neither the castle nor the hovel being placed with any reference to the enlargement of the town, or to public convenience in any way, streets were formed through the suburbs, as they became denser,

in much the same way as they had been in the original settle-
ment; then, as the walls were extended, the military consideration again operated to enforce the idea of compactness in
every possible way.

The government of these towns also, however its forms
varied, was always essentially a military despotism of the most
direct and stringent character, under which the life, property,
health and comfort of the great body of their people were
matters, at best, of very subordinate consideration.

Thus the policy, the custom and the fashion was established
in the roots of our present form of society of regarding the
wants of a town, and planning to meet them, as if its population were a garrison, to be housed in a barrack, with only
such halls and passages in it, from door to door, as would
be necessary to turn it in, to sleep and feed, and turn it out,
to get its rations.

It naturally fell out that when at length the general advance
of society, in other respects, made it no longer necessary that
a man should build a castle, and control, as personal property,
the services of a numerous body of fighting men, in order
to live with some degree of safety in a house of his own,
apart from others, all the principal towns declined for a time
in wealth and population, because of the number of opulent
citizens who abandoned their old residences, and moved, with
servants and tenants, to make new settlements in the country.

The excessive suppression of personal independence and
individual inclinations which had before been required in
town-life caused a strong reactionary ambition to possess each
prosperous citizen to relieve himself as much as possible from
dependence upon and duties to society in general, and it became his aim to separate himself from all the human race
except such part as would treat him with deference. To secure
greater seclusion and at the same time opportunity for the
only forms of out-door recreation, which the rich, after the
days of jousts and tournaments, were accustomed to engage
in, all those who could command favor at Court, sought grants
of land abounding in the larger game, and planted their houses
in the midst of enclosures called parks, which not only kept

neighbors at a distance, but served as nurseries for objects of the chase.

The habits of the wealthy, under these circumstances, though often gross and arrogant, and sometimes recklessly extravagant, were far from luxurious, according to modern notions, and as, in order to realize as fully as possible the dream of independence, every country gentleman had his private chaplain, surgeon, farrier, tailor, weaver and spinner, raised his own wool, malt, barley and breadstuffs, killed his own beef, mutton and venison, and brewed his own ale, he was able to despise commerce and to avoid towns. The little finery his household coveted was accordingly brought to his door on pack-mules by traveling merchants. The vocation of a merchant, in its large, modern sense, was hardly known, and the trade of even the most considerable towns was, in all respects, very restricted. Thus the old foot-way streets still served all necessary requirements tolerably well.

As the advance of civilization continued, however, this disinclination to the exchange of service, of course, gave way; demands became more varied, and men of all classes were forced to take their place in the general organization of society in communities. In process of time the enlargement of popular freedom, the spread of knowledge by books, the abatement of religious persecutions, the voyages of circumnavigators, and finally the opening of America, India and the gold coast of Africa to European commerce, so fed the mercantile inclinations, that an entirely new class of towns, centres of manufacturing and of trade, grew upon the sites of the old ones. To these the wealthy and powerful were drawn, no longer for protection, but for the enjoyment of the luxuries which they found in them, while the more enterprising of the lower classes crowded into them to "seek their fortune."

Second Stage of Street Arrangements

Wagons gradually took the place of pack-trains in the distribution of goods through the country, and, as one man could manage a heavy load, when it was once stowed, as well as a light one, the wagons were made very large and strong, and required the employment of many horses.

In comparatively few town-streets could two of these wheeled merchantmen, with the enormous hamper they carried on each side, pass each other. The seats and hucksteries of slight wood-work with which the streets had been lined were swept away; but, as the population rapidly increased, while the house accommodation was so limited that its density, in the city of London, for instance, was probably three times as great as at present, any attempt to further widen the streets for the convenience of the wagoners had to encounter the strongest resistance from the house-holders.

Thus, without any material enlargement, the character of the streets was much changed. They frequently became quite unfit to walk in, the more so because they were used as the common place of deposit for all manner of rubbish and filth thrown out of the houses which was not systematically removed from them.

Although London then occupied not a fiftieth part of the ground which it does now, and green fields remained which had been carefully preserved for the practice of archery within a comparatively short distance of its central parts, to which the inhabitants much resorted for fresh air on summer evenings; although the river still ran clear, and there was much pleasure-boating upon it, the greater part of the inhabitants were so much confined in dark, ill-ventilated and noisome quarters, that they were literally decimated by disease as often as once in every two years, while at intervals fearful epidemics raged, at which times the mortality was much greater. During one of these, four thousand deaths occurred in a single night, and many streets were completely depopulated. All who could by any means do so, fled from the town, so that in a short time its population was reduced more than fifty per cent. It had not yet filled up after this calamity, when a fire occurred which raged unchecked during four days, and destroyed the houses and places of business of two hundred thousand of the citizens. Its progress was at length stayed by the widening of the streets across which it would have

advanced if the buildings which lined them had not been removed by the military.

Five-sixths of the area occupied by the old city was still
covered with smoking embers when the most distinguished
architect of the age seized the opportunity to urge a project
for laying out the street system of a new town upon the same
site. The most novel feature of this plan was the introduction
of certain main channel streets, ninety feet wide, in which
several wagons could be driven abreast upon straight courses
from one end of the city to the other. It was also proposed
that there should be a series of parallel and intersecting streets
sixty feet wide, with intermediate lanes of thirty feet. The
enormous advantages of such a system of streets over any
others then in use in the large towns of Europe were readily
demonstrated; it obtained the approval of the king himself,
and would have been adopted but for the incredible short-
sightedness of the merchants and real estate owners. These
obstinately refused to give themselves any concern about the
sacrifice of general inconvenience or the future advantages
to their city, which it was shown that a disregard of Wren's
suggestions would involve, but proceeded at once, as fast as
possible, without any concert of action, to build anew, each
man for himself, upon the ruins of his old warehouse. There
can be little question, that had the property-owners, at this
time, been wise enough to act as a body in reference to their
common interests, and to have allowed Wren to devise and
carry out a complete street system, intelligently adapted to
the requirements which he would have been certain to anticipate; as well as those which were already pressing, it would
have relieved the city of London of an incalculable expenditure
which has since been required to mend its street arrangements;
would have greatly lessened the weight of taxation, which
soon afterwards rose to be higher than in any other town
of the kingdom, and would have saved millions of people from
the misery of poverty and disease.

Although in a very few years after the rebuilding of the
city, its commerce advanced so much as to greatly aggravate
the inconveniencies under which street communication had

been previously carried on, the difficulties were allowed to grow greater and greater for fully a century more before anything was done calculated to essentially alleviate them. They seem to have been fully realized and to have been constantly deplored, nor were efforts of a certain kind wanting to remedy them: the direction of these efforts, however, shows how strongly a traditional standard of street convenience yet confused the judgment even of the most advanced. A town being still thought of as a collection of buildings all placed as closely as possible to one centre was also regarded as a place of necessarily inconvenient confinement, and therefore, of crowding, hustling and turbulence. An enlargement of the population of a town could only aggravate all the special troubles and dangers to which those living in it were subject, add to the number of its idle, thriftless, criminal and dangerous classes, and invite disease, disorder and treasonable tumults. As, therefore, to amplify the street arrangements or otherwise enlarge the public accommodations for trade or residence, would be to increase its attractions, the true policy was generally assumed to be in the other direction. In London, not only its own Corporation followed this policy, but Parliament and the Sovereign systematically did the same.

Once, for instance, a proclamation was issued, to forbid under heavy penalties the erection of any houses, except such as should be suitable for the residence of the gentry, within three miles of the town; another followed which interdicted householders from enlarging the accommodations for strangers within the town; another enjoined all persons who had houses in the country to quit the town within three weeks, while constant efforts were made to ship off those who had none to Ireland, Virginia, or Jamaica.

In spite of all, new houses were built on the sides of the old country roads, the suburban villages grew larger and larger till at length they were all one town with London and the population became twice as great and the commerce much more than twice as great as at the time of the great fire. Even when at last plans of real improvement began to be entertained it was no thought of resisting the increase of disease, pauperism and crime, by other means than fencing it out, that produced the change, but mainly the intolerable hindrance to commerce of the old fashioned arrangements. Though some refused to see it and still protested against the plans of improvement as wholly unnecessary, hazardous, reckless, and extravagant, and denounced those who urged them, as unprincipled speculators or visionary enthusiasts, the merchants generally could no longer avoid the conviction that their prosperity was seriously checked by the inadequacy of the thoroughfares of the town for the duty required of them. Parliament was therefore induced in the latter part of the last century, to authorize a series of measures which gradually brought about in the course of fifty years, larger and more important changes than had occurred before during many centuries.

As the definite aim of these changes was to get rid of certain inconveniences which had previously been classed among the necessary evils of large towns and as the measure with reference to which the purpose of their design was limited is thus clearly established it is evident that before we can realize the degree in which they were likely to approach the ultimatum of civilized requirement we need to know more exactly what the inconveniences in question amounted to.

It appears then that the imperfect pavements, never having been adequately revised since the days of hand-barrow and pack-horse transportation, were constantly being misplaced and the ground worn into deep ruts by the crushing weight of the wheels; the slops and offal matters thrown out of the houses were combined with the dung of the horses and the mud to make a tenacious puddle through which the people on foot had to drag their way in constant apprehension of being run down or crushed against the wall. In the principal streets strong posts were planted at intervals behind which active men were accustomed to dodge for safety as the wagons came upon them. Coaches had been introduced in the time of Elizabeth, but though simple, strong and rudely hung vehicles, they were considered to be very dangerous in the streets and their use within the town was for some time forbidden. Sedan chairs for all ordinary purposes superseded them and for a long time had been in common use by all except the poorer classes upon every occasion of going into the streets. When George the Third went in the state coach to open Parliament, the streets through which he passed were previously prepared by laying faggots in the ruts to make the motion easier. There was little or no sewerage or covered drainage, and heavy storms formed gullies of the ruts and often flooded the cellars destroying a great deal of merchandise.

This was the condition in which after several hundred years, the town had been left by the transformation of the passages, first occuring [sic] between the huts of the entrenched camp of a tribe of barbarians, from the serviceable foot ways of the early middle ages to the unserviceable wagon ways of the generation but one before the last.

Third Stage of Street Arrangements

To remedy its evils, in the construction of new streets, and the reconstruction of old, the original passage for people on foot was restored, but it was now split through the middle and set back with the house fronts on each side so as to admit of the introduction of a special roadway for horses and wheels, at a lower level. A curb was placed to guard the foot way from the wheels; gutters were used to collect the liquid and floating filth, and sewers were constructed which enabled the streams thus formed to be taken out of the streets before they became so large as to flood the sidewalks. At the same time an effort was made to so straighten and connect some of the streets that goods could be taken from one quarter of the town to another by direct courses, and without the necessity of doubling the horse-power at certain points in order to overcome the natural elevations of the ground.

Thus, just one hundred years after Wren's suggestions were rejected by the merchants, their grandsons began to make lame efforts to secure some small measure of the convenience which his plan had offered them.

A few of the latter improvements had been adopted in other towns at a somewhat earlier period than in London. In the plans of St. Petersburg and of Philadelphia, for instance, directness and unusual amplitude of road-way had been studied, and some of the free cities of Germany had, at an earlier date, possessed moderately broad and well-paved streets, but the exceptions do not affect the conclusion which we desire to enforce.

To fully understand the reason of this long neglect to make any wise preparation for the enlargement of population which it would seem must surely have been anticipated, we need to consider that while a rapid advance was all the time occurring from the state of things when a town was intended to be governed with little direct regard for the interests of any but a very few of its occupants, at the same time direct responsibility for the care of its interests was being diffused and held for shorter intervals, and was, consequently, less and less felt, as a motive to ingenuity and energy, by any one of the several individuals who partook in it. The theory and form of town government changed more slowly than the character and modes of life of those who were called upon to administer it, but an adherence to the antiquated forms was only calculated to make a personal duty, with reference to the actual new conditions of the people, less easily realized and less effectively operative. What is everybody's business is nobody's, and although of late years experts, with professional training in special branches, are not unfrequently engaged by municipal bodies to study particular requirements of the people, and invent means to satisfy them, still, as a general rule, improvements have come in most cities, when they have come at all, chiefly through the influence of individual energy, interested in behalf of special mercantile or speculative enterprises, by which the supineness of the elected and paid representatives of the common interests of the citizens has been overborne.

Erroneous View of the Necessary Disadvantages of Town Life

What is of more consequence, however, not merely that we may avoid injustice to our ancestors, but that we may realize the changes which have occurred in the standard of requirement, with reference to which the merits of a street system are now to be judged, is the fact that when these improvements were devised, it was still pardonable to take for granted that the larger the population of a town should be allowed to become, the greater would be the inconvenience and danger to which all who ventured to live in it would necessarily be subject, the more they would be exposed to epidemic diseases, the feebler, more sickly, and shorter their lives would be; the greater would be the danger of sweeping conflagrations; the larger the proportion of mendicants and criminals, and the more formidable, desperate and dangerous the mobs.

Evils of Town-Life Have Diminished as Towns Have Grown Larger

We now know that these assumptions were entirely fallacious, for, as a matter of fact, towns have gone on increasing, until there are many in Europe which are several times larger than the largest of the Middle Ages, and in the largest the amount of disease is not more than half as great as it formerly was; the chance of living to old age is much more than twice as great; epidemics are less frequent, less malignant and more controllable; sweeping fires are less common, less devastating and are much sooner got under; ruffians are much better held in check; mobs are less frequently formed, are less dangerous, and, when they arise, are suppressed more quickly and with less bloodshed; there is a smaller proportion of the population given over to vice and crime and a vastly larger proportion of well-educated, orderly, industrious and well-to-do citizens. These things are true, in the main, not of one town alone, but of every considerable town, from Turkey on the one side to China on the other, and the larger each town has grown, the greater, on an average, has been the gain. Even in Mahomedan Cairo, chiefly through the action of French engineers, the length of life of each inhabitant has, on an average, been doubled. The question, then, very naturally occurs: What are the causes and conditions of this amelioration? and Can it be expected to continue?

Reason for Anticipating an Accelerated Enlargement of Metropolitan Towns

If the enormous advance in the population of great towns which has been characteristic of our period of civilization, is due mainly to the increase of facilities for communication, transportation and exchange throughout the world, as there is every reason to believe that it is, we can but anticipate, in the immediate future, a still more rapid movement in the same direction.

We are now extending railroads over this continent at the rate of more than fifteen hundred miles a year, and before our next President takes his seat, we shall have applied an amount of labor which is represented by the enormous sum of two thousand millions of dollars, to this work, most of it preparatory, and more than half of it directed to the opening up of new lands to profitable cultivation. The productive capacity of the country thus laid open, and the demand upon commerce of its people, has scarcely yet begun to be manifested. We have but half made our first road to the Pacific, and we have only within a year begun to extend our steam navigation to Japan and China, where the demands upon civilized commerce of a frugal and industrious population, much larger than that of all Christendom, yet remain to be developed. We are ourselves but just awake to the value of the electric telegraph in lessening the risks of trade on a large scale, and giving it order and system. Thus, we seem to be just preparing to enter upon a new chapter of commercial and social progress, in which a comprehension of the advantages that arise from combination and co-operation will be the rule among merchants, and not, as heretofore, the exception.

Conditions under Which the Evils of Large Towns Have Diminished

The rapid enlargement of great towns which has hitherto occurred, must then be regarded as merely a premonition of the vastly greater enlargement that is to come. We see, therefore, how imperative, with reference to the interests of our race, is this question, whether as the enlargement of towns goes on the law of improvement is such that we may reasonably hope that life in them will continue to grow better, more orderly, more healthy? One thing seems to be certain, that the gain hitherto can be justly ascribed in very small part to direct action on the part of those responsible for the good management of the common interests of their several populations. Neither humanity nor the progress of invention and discovery, nor the advancement of science has had much to do with it. It can not even, in any great degree, be ascribed to the direct action of the law of supply and demand.

Shall we say, then, that it has depended on causes wholly beyond the exercise of human judgment, and that we may leave the future to take care of itself, as our fathers did? We are by no means justified in adopting such a conclusion, for, if we can not yet trace wholly to their causes, all the advantages we possess over our predecessors, we are able to reach the conviction, beyond all reasonable doubt, that at least, the larger share of the immunity from the visits of the plague and other forms of pestilence, and from sweeping fires, and the larger part of the improved general health and increased length of life which civilized towns have lately enjoyed is due to the abandonment of the old-fashioned compact way of building towns, and the gradual adoption of a custom of laying them out with much larger spaces open to the sun-light and fresh air; a custom the introduction of which was due to no intelligent anticipation of such results.

Evidence of this is found in the fact that the differing proportions between the dying and the living, the sick and the well, which are found to exist between towns where most of the people still live on narrow streets, and those in which the later fashions have been generally adopted; and between parts of the same town which are most crowded and those which are more open, are to this day nearly as great as between modern and ancient towns. For instance, in Liverpool, the constant influx of new-comers of a very poor and ignorant class from the other side of the Irish Channel, and the consequent demand for house-room, and the resulting value of the poor, old buildings which line the narrow streets, has, till recently, caused the progress of improvement to be much slower than in the much larger town of London, so that, while the average population of Liverpool is about 140,000 to the square mile, that of London is but 50,000; the average age at death in Liverpool is seventeen, and that in London, twenty-six. In the city of Brooklyn the number of deaths for each thousand of population that occurred this last year in the closer built parts, was twice as large as in those where the streets are wider and there are many gardens.

Comparisons of this kind have been made in such number, and the data for them have been drawn from such a large variety of localities in which the conditions of health in all other respects have been different, that no man charged, however temporarily and under whatever limitations, with municipal responsibilities, can be pardoned for ignoring the fact that the most serious drawback to the prosperity of town communities has always been dependent on conditions (quite unnecessary to exist in the present day) which have led to stagnation of air and excessive deprivation of sun-light.

Again, the fact that with every respiration of every living being a quantity is formed of a certain gas, which, if not dissipated, renders the air of any locality at first debilitating, after a time sickening, and at last deadly; and the fact that this gas is rapidly absorbed, and the atmosphere relieved of it by the action of leaves of trees, grass and herbs, was quite unknown to those who established the models which have been more or less distinctly followed in the present street arrangements of our great towns. It is most of all important, however, that we should remember that they were not as yet awake to the fact that large towns are a necessary result of an extensive intercourse between people possessing one class of the resources of wealth and prosperity and those possessing other classes, and that with each increase of the field of commerce certain large towns must grow larger, and consequently, that it is the duty of each generation living in these towns to give some consideration, in its plans, to the requirements of a larger body of people than it has itself to deal with directly.

Change in the Habits of Citizens Affecting the Structural Requirements of Towns

If, again, we consider the changes in the structure of towns which have occurred through the private action of individual citizens we shall find that they indicate the rise of a strong tide of requirements, the drift of which will either have to be fairly recognized in the public work of the present generation or it will, at no distant day, surely compel a revision of what is now done that will involve a large sacrifice of property.

Separation of Business and Domestic Life

In the last century comparatively few towns-people occupied dwellings distinctly separate from their place of business. A large majority of the citizens of Paris, London and of New York do so to-day, and the tendency to divisions of the town corresponding to this change of habits must rapidly increase with their further enlargement, because of the greater distance which will exist between their different parts. The reason is obvious: a business man, during his working-hours, has no occasion for domestic luxuries, but needs to have access to certain of his co-workers in the shortest practicable time, and with the smallest practicable expenditure of effort. He wants to be near a bank, for instance, or near the Corn Exchange, or near the Stock Exchange, or to shipping, or to a certain class of shops or manufactories. On the other hand, when not engaged in business, he has no occasion to be near his working place, but demands arrangements of a wholly different character. Families require to settle in certain localities in sufficient numbers to support those establishments which minister to their social and other wants, and yet are not willing to accept the conditions of town-life which were formerly deemed imperative, and which, in the business quarters, are yet, perhaps, in some degree, imperative, but demand as much of the luxuries of free air, space and abundant vegetation as, without loss of town-privileges, they can be enabled to secure.

Those parts of a town which are to any considerable extent occupied by the great agencies of commerce, or which, for any reason, are especially fitted for their occupation, are therefore sure to be more and more exclusively given up to them, and, although we can not anticipate all the subdivisions of a rapidly increasing town with confidence, we may safely assume that the general division of all the parts of every considerable town under the two great classifications of commercial and domestic, which began in the great European towns in the last century, will not only continue, but will become more and more distinct.

It can hardly be thought probable that street arrangements perfectly well adapted in all respects to the purposes to be served in one of these divisions are the very best in every particular that it would be possible to devise for those of the other.

Recreative Requirements and Distance of Suburbs

Another change in the habits of towns-people which also grows out of the greatly enlarged area already occupied by large towns, results from the fact that, owing to the great distances of the suburbs from the central parts, the great body of the inhabitants cannot so easily as formerly stroll out into the country in search of fresh air, quietness, and recreation. At the same time there is no doubt that the more intense intellectual activity, which prevails equally in the library, the work shop, and the counting-room, makes tranquilizing recreation more essential to continued health and strength than until lately it generally has been. Civilized men while they are gaining ground against certain acute forms of disease are growing more and more subject to other and more insidious enemies to their health and happiness and against these the remedy and preventive can not be found in medicine or in athletic recreations but only in sunlight and such forms of gentle exercise as are calculated to equalize the circulation and relieve the brain.

Change in the Character of Vehicles

Still another important change or class of changes in the habits of the people of towns may be referred to the much greater elaboration which has recently occurred in the division of labor and the consequent more perfect adaptation to the various purposes of life of many instruments in general use. A more striking illustration of this will not readily be found than is afforded by the light, elegant, easy carriages which have lately been seen in such numbers in your Park. When our present fashions of streets was introduced sedan chairs were yet, as we have shown, in general use for taking the air or making visits to neighbors. The few wheeled vehicles employed by the wealthy were exceedingly heavy and clumsy and adapted only to slow travel on rough roads, a speed of five miles an hour by what was called the "flying coach," being a matter for boasting. Now we have multifarious styles of vehicles in each of which a large number of different hands has been ingeniously directd to provide in all their several parts for the comfort, pleasure, and health with which they may be used. For the sake of elegance, as well as comfort and ease of draft, they are made extremely light and are supplied with pliant springs. They are consequently quite unfit to be used in streets adapted to the heavy wagons employed in commercial traffic, and can only be fully enjoyed in roads expressly prepared for them. In parks such roads are provided in connection with other arrangements for the health of the people.

Inadequate Domestic Access to Suburbs and Parks

The parks are no more accessible than the suburbs, however, from those quarters of the town occupied domestically, except by means of streets formed in precisely the same manner as those which pass through the quarters devoted to the heaviest commercial traffic. During the periods of transit, therefore, from house to house and between the houses and the Park there is little pleasure to be had in driving. Riding also, through the ordinary streets, is often not only far from pleasant, but, unless it is very slowly and carefully done, is hazardous to life and limb. Consequently much less enjoyment of the Park is possible to those who live at a distance than to those who live near it and its value to the population at large is correspondingly restricted. The difficulties of reaching the Park on foot or those who might enjoy and be benefited by the walk, are at the season of the year when it would otherwise be most attractive, even greater, for they must follow the heated flags and bear the reflected as well as the direct rays of the sun.

But we cannot expect, even if this objection were overcome, that all the inhabitants of a large town would go so far as the Park every day, or so often as it is desirable that they should take an agreeable stroll in the fresh air. On the other hand we cannot say that the transportation of merchandise should be altogether interdicted in the domestic quarters of a town, as it is in a park, and as it now is through certain streets of London and Paris during most hours of the day. On the contrary it is evidently desirable that every dwelling house should be accessible by means of suitable paved streets to heavy wheeled vehicles.

New Arrangements Demanded by Existing Requirements

It will be observed that each of the changes which we have examined points clearly towards the conclusion that the present street arrangements of every large town will at no very distant day require, not to be set aside, but to be supplemented, by a series of ways designed with express reference to the pleasure with which they may be used for walking, riding, and the driving of carriages; for rest, recreation, refreshment, and social intercourse, and that these ways must be so arranged that they will be conveniently accessible from every dwelling house and allow its occupants to pass from it to distant parts of the town, as, for instance, when they want to go to a park, without the necessity of travelling for any considerable distance through streets no more convenient for the purpose than our streets of the better class now are.

We may refuse to make timely provisions for such purposes in our suburbs, and we may by our refusal add prodigiously to the difficulty and the cost of their final introduction but it is no more probable, if great towns continue to grow greater, that such requirements as we have pointed out will not eventually be provided for than it was two hundred years ago that the obvious defects of the then existing street arrangements would continue to be permanently endured rather than that property should be destroyed which existed in the buildings by their sides.

The Position of Brooklyn

If we now take the case of Brooklyn we shall find that all the reasons for an advance upon the standards of the street arrangements of the last century which apply to great towns in general, are applicable to her special situation with particular emphasis.

With reference to general commerce, Brooklyn must be considered as a division merely of the port of New York. The city of New York is, in regard to building space, in the condition of a walled town. Brooklyn is New York outside the walls.

The length of suitable shore for shipping purposes which the city of New York possesses is limited. Many operations of commerce cannot be carried on in the northern parts of the island. It may be reckoned upon as certain that the centre of the commercial arrangements of the port will be in the lower part of New York island.

It may be also reckoned upon as certain that everywhere, within a limited distance back from its shores, all the ground will be required for commercial purposes. The amount of land enclosed by this commercial border remaining to be devoted to purposes of habitation will then be comparatively small and will be at a considerable distance north of the commercial centre, probably not nearer on an average than the upper part of the Central Park which is more than seven miles from the present Custom House. On each side of it, north, south, east, and west, will be warehouses and manufacturing and trading establishments, and, at a little greater distance, wharves and shipping.

The habitable part of New York island will then necessarily be built up with great compactness and will in every part be intersected with streets offering direct communication for the transportation of merchandise between one part of its commercial quarter and another.

If now, again, we look on the Long Island side of the port we find a line of shore ten miles in length which is also adapted to the requirements of shipping. It may be assumed that the land along this shore will be wanted, as well as that along the shore of New York island and for an equal distance back from the water, for mercantile and manufacturing purposes. Supposing that the district thus occupied shall, after a time, reach as far back as the corresponding district on New York island; in the rear of it, (and still at a distance from the commercial centre of the port, not half as great on an average as the Central Park), we find a stretch of ground generally elevated, the higher parts being at an average distance of more than a mile from any point to which merchandise can be brought by water. East of this elevation the ground slopes to the shore, not of a harbor or navigable river, but of the ocean itself. A shore in the highest degree attractive to those seeking recreation or health but offering no advantages for shipping, manufacturing or mercantile purposes. At present this slope is occupied chiefly by country seats, and the habitations of gardeners and farmers, and only through the most perverse neglect of the landowners of their own interests is it likely to be built upon for other purposes.

The Opportunity of Brooklyn

Here, then, there is ample room for an extension of the habitation part of the metropolis upon a plan fully adapted to the most intelligent requirements of modern town life. A large part of the elevated land which has been referred to lies not more than half as far from the commercial centre as the habitation district of New York island, the ground is better formed with reference to sanitary considerations; it is open to the sea breezes and lies in full view of the ocean; it can never be enclosed on all sides by commerce as the habitable part of New York island soon will be; and, its immediate back country being bounded by the sea, the commercial traffic through it is always likely to be light and will be easily provided for in a few special channels. Thus it seems set apart and guarded by nature as a place for the tranquil habitation of those whom the business of the world requires should reside within convenient access of the waters of New York harbor.

It does not follow, however, that it will be so occupied. In the drift of the population of towns it is generally found that natural advantages alone go for but little, and except in the part controlled by your Commission no other arrangements as yet exist with reference to the convenience, health, and pleasure of residents upon this land than such as would have been formed if it were desired to invite to it nothing but factories, ship yards, or the warehouses and offices of merchants. One or two streets were laid out through it some years ago with an avowed intention of being especially adapted to residences; they were so designed however, as to offer every advantage to commercial transportation and consequently for shops and factories but, except in mere width, without intelligent regard to the alleged purpose in view. They are nevertheless adapted to serve an important purpose in concentrating such commercial traffic as must pass through their neighborhoods and in furnishing sites for shops and public buildings which will in any case be needed to meet local requirements.

Upon the manner in which there are good grounds for confidence that the elevated district which has been indicated will be occupied in the future, depends the valuation which can justly and sagaciously be now placed upon it, and upon this valuation mainly depends the financial prosperity of the city of Brooklyn.

How the Opportunity May Be Misused and How Availed of

It would be a perfectly simple problem to cause this land to be given up in a few years almost exclusively to shanties, stables, breweries, distilleries, and swine-yards, and eventually to make the greater part of it a district corresponding, in the larger metropolis which is hereafter to exist on the shores of New York harbor, to that which the Five Points has been in the comparatively small town we have known.

The means by which it may be made a more suitable and attractive place of domestic residence than it is possible that any other point of the metropolis ever will be, are equally within command.

Influence of the Park on the Value of Property

The effect of what has already been done, under the direction of your Commission, has been to more than quadruple the value of a certain portion of this land, and we have thus an expression of the most simple character, in regard to the commercial estimate which, at this period in the history of towns, is placed upon the circumstance of convenient access from a residence to a public pleasure-ground, and upon the sanitary and social advantages of a habitation thus situated. The advance in value, in this case, is quite marked at a distance of a mile, and this local advantage has certainly not been attended by any falling back in the value of other land in Brooklyn.

If we analyze the conditions of this change in value, we shall find that it is not altogether, or even in any large degree, dependent upon mere vicinity to the sylvan and rural attractions of the Park, but in very large part, in the first place, upon the degree in which these attractions can be approached with security from the common annoyances of the streets, and, with pleasure in the approach itself. If, for instance, the greater part of the Park were long and narrow in form, other things being equal, the demand for building sites, fronting on this portion of it, would not, probably, be appreciably less than for those fronting on the broader parts. Secondly, the advance in value will be found to be largely dependent on the advantages of having near a residence, a place where, without reference to the sylvan attractions found in a large park, driving, riding, and walking can be conveniently pursued in association with pleasant people, and without the liability of encountering the unpleasant sights and sounds which must generally accompany those who seek rest, recreation or pleasure in the common streets.

There are other things to be valued in a Park besides these, but these are the main positive advantages which would make the value of a residence, if upon the Park, much greater than if at a distance from it.

How the Advantages of Vicinity to a Park
May Be Extended

So far, then, as it is practicable, without an enlargement of the Park in its full breadth and compass, to extend its attractions in these especial respects, so far is it also practicable to enlarge the district within which land will have a correspondingly increased attraction for domestic residences. The further the process can be carried, the more will Brooklyn, as a whole, become desirable as a place of residence, the higher will be the valuation of land, on an average, within the city, and the lighter will be the financial burden of the Corporation.

Example of a Fourth Stage of Street Arrangements

We come, then, to the question of the means by which such an extension can be accomplished. Although no perfect example can be referred to, there have been in Europe a few works by which a similar end, to a certain extent, has been reached. Of these, the most notable is the Avenue of the Empress, in Paris, which connects a palace and a pleasure-ground within the town, with a large park situated far out in the suburbs. This avenue, with its planted border, occupies so much ground (it is 429 feet in width) that it may be considered to constitute rather an intermediate pleasure-ground than a part of the general street system. It is lined with a series of detached villa residences, and building-lots facing upon it are much more valuable than those facing upon the Park.

The celebrated Linden Avenue, at Berlin, leads likewise from a palace and palace grounds, to a great rural park on the opposite side of the town, through the very midst of which it passes. The finest private residences and hotels of the town, as well as many public buildings, such as Art Galleries and Museums, front upon it, and it is equally convenient for all the ordinary purposes of a street with any other. It nevertheless differs essentially from an ordinary business street, in that the process which we have described, by which wagonways were introduced into the old streets, has been carried one step further, the wagon-way having itself been divided as the foot-way formerly was, and a space of ground having been introduced, within which there is a shaded walk or mall, and a bridle-road, with strips of turf and trees.

The Parkway—A Fifth Stage

The "Parkway" plan which we now propose advances still another step, the mall being again divided into two parts to make room for a central road-way, prepared with express reference to pleasure-riding and driving, the ordinary paved, traffic road-ways, with their flagged sidewalks remaining still on the outside of the public mall for pedestrians, as in the Berlin example. The plan in this way provides for each of the several requirements which we have thus far examined, giving access for the purposes of ordinary traffic to all the houses that front upon it, offering a special road for driving and riding without turning commercial vehicles from the right of way, and furnishing ample public walks, with room for seats, and with borders of turf in which trees may grow of the most stately character. It would contain six rows of trees, and the space from house to house being two hundred and sixty feet, would constitute a perfect barrier to the progress of fire.

Practicable Future Extensions of the Parkway

With modifications to adapt it to variations of the topography and the connecting street arrangements, the plan should eventually be extended from the Park, in one direction, to Fort Hamilton, where ground for a small Marine Promenade should be secured, overlooking the Narrows and the Bay; and in the other to Ravenswood, where it should be connected by a bridge with one of the broad streets leading on the New York side to the Central Park. A branch should extend from it to the ocean beach at Coney Island, and other branches might lead out from it to any points at which it should appear that large dwelling quarters were likely to be formed, at such a distance from the main stem that access to it from them would otherwise be inconvenient.

There are scarcely any houses at present standing on the general line indicated and it would pass nearly parallel to, and be everywhere within from fifteen to thirty minutes walk of the wharves of the East River. The distance between its extreme points would be about ten miles and the average distance of residences upon it from Wall Street would be about half the distance to the Central Park. Spacious and healthful accommodations for a population of 500,000 could be made within ten minutes walk of this Parkway.

Plan of the Parkway Neighborhood

Our plan, it will be observed, covers more ground than is necessarily required to be taken for the purposes which have been indicated. The object of this is that in addition to providing for an enlargement of the. Park advantages, throughout its whole extent, the Parkway may also constitute the centre of a continuous neighborhood of residences of a more than usually open, elegant, and healthy character. It is believed that such a neighborhood would not merely be more attractive, to the prosperous class generally, of the metropolis, than any which can be elsewhere formed within a much greater distance from the commercial centre, but that it will especially meet the requirements of an element in the community that is constantly growing larger and that is influenced by associations and natural tastes that unquestionably deserve to be fostered and encouraged. A typical case, for the sake of illustrating the class in view may be thus presented. A country boy receives a common school education, exhibits ability and at a comparatively early age finds himself engaged in business in a provincial town; as his experience and capacity increase he seeks enlarged opportunities for the exercise of his powers and being of superior calibre ultimately finds himself drawn by an irresistible magnetic force to the commercial cities; here he succeeds in becoming wealthy by close attention to his speciality and the sharp country boy becomes the keen city man. Trees and grass are, however, wrought into the very texture and fibre of his constitution and without being aware of it he feels day by day that his life needs a suggestion of the old country flavor to make it palatable as well as profitable. This is one aspect of the natural phenomena with which we are now attempting to deal; no broad question of country life in comparison with city life is involved; it is confessedly a question of delicate adjustment, but we feel confident that whenever and wherever, in the vicinity of New York, this delicate adjustment is best attended to, and the real needs of these city-bred country boys are most judiciously considered, there they will certainly throng. We do not of course mean to argue that the tastes to which we have referred are limited solely to citizens whose early life has been passed in the country, but only that the existence of the special social element thus typified gives one of the many assurances that such a scheme as the proposed Parkway neighborhood would be successful, if judiciously carried out within the lines suggested, before the demand is more or less perfectly met in some other locality.

It is clear that the house lots facing on the proposed Parkway would be desirable, and we assume that the most profitable arrangement would be to make them, say 100 feet wide, and of the full depth between two streets, convenient sites for stables being thus provided. The usual effect of such a plan of operations would be an occupation of the rear street by houses of inferior class, and it is with a view of avoiding any such unsatisfactory result that the design is extended over four blocks of ground. If the two outermost streets are widened to 100 feet and sidewalks shaded by double rows of trees introduced in connection with them, the house lots on these streets will be but little inferior to those immediately facing the Parkway, for they also will be of unusual depth and will be supplied with stable lots that can be entered from the street already mentioned, which should be made suitable for its special purpose, and with the idea that it is only to be occupied by such buildings as may be required in connection with the large lots which are intended to be arranged throughout back to back, with the stable street between them.

Thus, so far as this arrangement should be extended, there would be a series of lots adapted to be occupied by detached villas each in the midst of a small private garden. This arrangement would offer the largest advantages possible to be secured in a town residence, and there is no good reason why they should not be of a permanent character. With the modern advantages for locomotion which would be available, the departure from the old-fashioned compactness of towns might be carried to this extent, in that part of them devoted to residences, without any serious inconvenience. The unwholesome fashion of packing dwelling-houses closely in blocks grew, as we have shown, out of the defensive requirements of old towns; it may possibly be necessary to continue it under certain circumstances, as, for the reasons already indicated, on the island of New York, but where there is no necessary boundary, either natural or artificial, to the space which is

161

to be occupied by buildings, as is the case with Brooklyn, it is, to say the least, unwise to persist in arrangements which will permanently prevent any indulgence of this kind.

Those who availed themselves of the opportunity here proposed to be offered would not benefit themselves alone, but the whole community. The Romans seem to have been wiser than we have been in this particular. Rich people were offered every facility for surrounding their houses with open garden spaces, and the larger part of the Eternal City was composed of what we should now term detached villas, while in no part was it permitted that a new house, even though intended for the residence of slaves, should be built within five feet of walls previously erected.

How far it might be desirable for property-owners to extend the plan in the peculiar form suggested, is, of course, an open question, depending on the anticipated demand for lots of the size indicated, but it will be readily seen that as the proposed subdivisions are not of the ordinary contracted character, a comparatively small number of residents will suffice to fill up a considerable stretch of ground laid out in this way, and it is also evident that if, within a reasonable time, it should become certain that a specific number of blocks would be carried out on this plan, the lots included within the boundaries determined on would not require to be improved in regular succession, but would be selected with reference to slight, fancied advantages anywhere along the line, every purchaser feeling satisfied that the main question of good neighborhood had been settled on a satisfactory basis at the outset.

Advantages of the Parkway Likely to Be Secured to Brooklyn Exclusively

Having so fully described, in its principal aspects, the question of the desirability of developing, in Brooklyn, a plan of public improvement of the general character indicated, it may be proper for us to enquire whether the broad streets which are proposed to be opened on New York island under the name of Boulevards during the next few years, are calculated to interfere with the probable success of such a scheme.

While the Central Park was in its earlier stages of progress, a Commission was appointed to prepare a plan for laying out the upper end of New York island, and some years later this responsibility was transferred to the Central Park Commission, whose plan is published in their last annual report.

The same document contains an elaborate discussion of the subject by Mr. A. H. Green, on the part of the Board, and as our professional relations with the Commissioners have not been extended over this department of their work, and we are not aware of their intention in regard to this improvement, except so far as it is set forth in the plan and public statement above mentioned, we make, for the purposes of this Report, the subjoined quotation, which sets forth clearly the limitations that are to be recognized in New York as controlling the designs of the Commissioners:

"We occasionally, in some country city, see a wide street ornamented with umbrageous trees, having spaces of green interposed in its area, the portion used for travel being very limited. This arrangement is only possible where thronging population and crowding commerce are not at liberty to overlay and smother the laws that are made to secure the legitimate use of the public streets." [But] "it would seem inexpedient, at any rate, until some better permanent administration of our streets is secured, to attempt these fanciful arrangements to any great extent in a commercial city, under our form of government."

It is clear, therefore, that the Central Park Commissioners have no intention of carrying out, in New York, any such scheme as the "Parkway," and consequently, if, as we believe, the requirements that such a plan is designed to meet are already felt to exist in this community, Brooklyn can soon be made to offer some special advantages as a place of residence to that portion of our more wealthy and influential citizens, whose temperament, taste or education leads them to seek for a certain amount of rural satisfaction in connection with their city homes.

Although the plots of ground appropriated to the Brooklyn and Central Parks are entirely different in shape, while their landscape opportunities and general possibilities of design are equally dissimilar, a generic family resemblance will yet be found between the two pleasure-grounds, simply because they are both called into existence to meet the same class of wants, in the same class of people, at the same Metropolitan centre.

The Brooklyn Parkway, on the other hand, will, if executed, be a practical development of the ideas set forth in this Report, which seem to be particularly applicable to the city of Brooklyn, and which, as we have shown, are considered by those in authority to be unsuitable for development in the city of New York; it will consequently have no such family resemblance to the New York Boulevards as exists between the two parks, and its attractions will, for a time, at any rate, be of a special and somewhat individual character.

In pursuing the general question of approaches to the Park, in accordance with your instructions, we have thus been led to the examination of some other scarcely less important topics, and although the consideration of such problems as those we have adverted to can only come before your Commission in an indirect and incidental way, we have thought it best to lay the results of our study thus fully before you, because during the investigations and consultations of the past year it has become more and more evident that the early adoption of some such scheme as the "Parkway" would have the effect of adding very greatly to the advantages which your Commission is endeavoring to secure to the citizens of Brooklyn in the construction of the Park.

Respectfully,
OLMSTED, VAUX & CO.
Landscape Architects and Superintendents
Brooklyn
January 1st, 1868

PART THREE

STATEN ISLAND AND QUEENS

P UBLIC health needs were an important consideration in Olmsted's planning, for there was widespread medical and popular concern with such epidemic diseases as cholera and malaria throughout the Western world during the nineteenth century.[1] "The people of New York and its suburbs," Olmsted wrote, "are peculiarly cursed by conditions which tend to establish malarial troubles and are hard upon children, hundreds dying in consequence . . . as soon as extreme summer heat occurs."[2] In the absence of a well-developed "germ theory,"[3] and with the failure of "orthodox" medical treatments such as bloodletting, more "natural" cures were sought. Many of the health fads of the mid-nineteenth century which now seem ludicrous—various diets, water and electricity cures— were pragmatic efforts to remedy diseases for which science offered no satisfactory help at the time. This explains the emphasis on the natural environment in matters of health in Olmsted's reports on the outer areas of the city.

Document V, a plan for Staten Island, demonstrates how much Olmsted relied upon the expertise of public health physicians, sanitary engineers, and geologists. The very precise reports of the United States Coast and Geodetic Survey were models of environmental study for specialists in public health improvement. By analysis of water content, drainage patterns, and soil composition, the planners hoped to develop a water supply free from all impurities. It was believed that malarial diseases originated in stagnant deposits of subterranean water. The theory was that natural antidotes could be discovered through the study of wind directions, temperature, humidity, amount and quality of sunlight available, topography, and trees and shrubs. Thus, Olmsted's concern with the social and es-

[1] Charles E. Rosenberg, The Cholera Years (Chicago, 1963), passim.

[2] Olmsted to H. Y. Attrill and B. E. Smith, July 29, 1879, Olmsted Papers, p. 305. Hereafter cited as "Report on Rockaway Point." See Document VI below.

[3] It was not until 1883 that Robert Koch demonstrated that cholera vibrio was the true cause of the disease.

thetic aspects of nature was reinforced by a powerful—almost primitive—belief in the effectiveness of nature as a medical agent. Planning, it seemed to him, clearly depended upon the techniques of many disciplines.

Turning his attention in 1870 to a complete survey of the County of Richmond was like returning home. There, on a farm purchased for him by his father, he had lived and worked for six years. He had taken pride in his election in 1850 as Corresponding Secretary of the County Agricultural Society. It was therefore satisfying to be in a position to help the Island. Asked to advise concerning its potentialities for housing a national exhibition to rival the site of the Crystal Palace Exhibition at Sydenham, England, he declared it superior. "The view [see Illustration VIII] over the ocean, over the lower and upper bays, over the three cities is incomparably magnificent," he wrote. "There is nothing in the least like it at Sydenham or anywhere about London. In some states of the atmosphere it is one of the great sights of the world."[4]

The fact was, however, that since Olmsted had last lived there (in the 1850's), Staten Island had become infamous for ill health and understandably shunned by people who were terrified at even the rumor of an epidemic disease. This explains why the report places such great emphasis on matters of public health. Olmsted had the help of Dr. Elisha Harris, one of the foremost public health physicians in America. A graduate of the College of Physicians and Surgeons in New York, Harris had been Superintendent of the quarantine hospital on the Island. During the Civil War he had served under Olmsted on the staff of the Sanitary Commission and in 1864 helped to persuade the influential Citizens Association of New York City to sponsor a Council of Hygiene as a means of remedying the dangerously unsanitary condition of the city. In 1869 he organized New York City's first free public vaccination service.[5] Another distinguished member of the Com-

---

[4] Olmsted to C. K. Hamilton, July 22, 1870, Olmsted Papers.

[5] William Q. Maxwell, *Lincoln's Fifth Wheel: The Political History of the U.S. Sanitary Commission* (New York, 1956), pp. 333–334; Rosenberg, *Cholera Years*, pp. 187–188.

mission, and a close friend, was Henry Hobson Richardson, the noted American architect.

Just as important as the support of these men was the confidence of the Commission appointed by the state to oversee the report. In part, this confidence was based on the immediate financial successes of the Central and Prospect projects (real estate values rose enormously, as did tax revenues); the increased land value of Riverside, a suburb of Chicago which Olmsted and Vaux laid out; and his published address to the American Social Science Association (he was one of the founders) in the early part of 1870 on "Public Parks and the Enlargement of Towns." This paper, which enjoyed fairly wide distribution, was the most complete exposition Olmsted had ever made of the purposes and methods of planning cities. An influential member of the Commission wrote to him that "[more than] the general conversation in Committee yesterday and . . . a dozen conversations would have done, your paper 'On Parks' have enabled me, I think, to view your plans if I may say so, with *your* eyes and to see, in some sort, how it looks to *you*."[6]

The Commission surrendered direction of the survey to Olmsted, who took the opportunity to make it as thorough a report as possible. By carefully integrating the skills and knowledge of geologists, public health doctors, and sanitary engineers with the esthetic and social theory of cities which he had developed, Olmsted presented a model of what nineteenth-century cooperative planning could produce (see Illustration IX). The report was not adopted in its own time, and probably was not even considered when Staten Island, the City's last remaining undeveloped area, was laid open to ruthless land speculation by the construction of the Verrazano Bridge in 1964 (see Illustration X).

Document VI was a preliminary study done for private developers interested in the commercial possibility of Rockaway Point in Queens as a summer seaside resort. Ocean bathing, historically a health activity, assumed more importance

[6] Alvin C. Bradley to Frederick Law Olmsted, July 29, 1879, Olmsted Papers.

with the growth of cities (see Illustration XI) because of the increased incidence of disease each summer. In order to make Rockaway into a summer resort superior to its nearest competitor, Coney Island (see Illustration XIII), it would be necessary to rid it of mosquitoes and flies. "Flies," Olmsted noted, "are now bred in vast numbers in the privies and the slops, offal and waste thrown out at the back doors of the taverns, as well as in the dead fish, etc. on the strand."[7]

This Report indicates how seriously and conscientiously Olmsted undertook any project. His examination entailed a complete study of the district—of who lived there and who would be most likely to use it in the future. In addition, he spent nearly three full weeks on the site seeking "information from all local sources."[8] He was anxious to undertake the project because he believed "that Rockaway Point might be made not simply more attractive to the public than Coney Island, but quite the most complete and popular sea-side resort, *adapted to very large numbers*, in the world."[9]

In planning for comprehensive facilities, he urged the entrepreneurs to include a pavilion for those who could only afford to spend a day. He wanted Rockaway to become a meeting-place for all classes and tastes. Special provision was to be made for children, including "an elephant and a few camels to make tours," and "a pond in which . . . [to] sail small boats."[10] Streets would be designed to accommodate people in wheel chairs. He considered the carnival aspect of the resort, "such things as Punch and Judy and other puppet shows, circuses and minstrels, conjurers, performing birds, tents and enclosures for walking, leaping, and wrestling matches, quoits, Scotch games and travelling exhibitions of curiosities, scups, swings, flying horses and so on."[11]

Olmsted did not have an opportunity to execute his plans. He soon learned that the owners were more interested in quick

[7] Olmsted, "Report on Rockaway Point," p. 302.
[8] *Ibid.*, p. 301.
[9] *Ibid.*, p. 310.
[10] *Ibid.*, p. 321.
[11] *Ibid.*, pp. 323-324.

profits than in developing the area according to its natural potential.[12] America was experiencing rapid expansion in popular seaside resorts, brought on in part by the quick success of Coney Island. Olmsted noted the large crowds at the newly-opened beaches of Cape May, Newport, and Narragansett Pier, among others.[13] The Rockaway Point owners were not interested in careful planning when success—profit-making, that is—was guaranteed. The owners preferred to follow the example of Coney Island. Olmsted withdrew from the agreement.[14] Professional integrity would not bow to pleasing a client.

[12] Olmsted to H. Y. Attrill, Sept. 23, 1879, Olmsted Papers.
[13] Olmsted, "Report on Rockaway Point," p. 311.
[14] Olmsted to H. Y. Attrill and B. E. Smith, Sept. 23, 1879, Olmsted Papers.

DOCUMENT V

‹‹‹‹‹‹‹‹‹‹‹‹‹‹‹‹‹‹

FREDERICK LAW OLMSTED *et al.*

Report to the Staten Island Improvement Commission of a Preliminary Scheme of Improvements (1871)

‹‹‹‹‹‹‹‹‹‹‹‹‹‹‹‹‹‹

Report

Chapter I. *Questions of General Policy*

To the Staten Island Improvement Commission:

GENTLEMEN: We need, first of all, to so far forecast the future market of this metropolis for real estate, that we can be satisfied what of its demands Staten Island in particular may be prepared to supply with the greatest certainty of large, general, ultimate profit.

All possible demands of the future may, in the first place, be broadly divided under the heads of Commercial and Domestic; domestic being understood in this case to refer not only to dwellings but to whatever would administer directly to household economy, convenience and comfort, including stores, shops and markets, for local supply.

The eastern margin of the Island, from a little north of Tompkins landing nearly to the Yacht Club House, has advantages of a peculiar character for certain commercial purposes, deep water and good holding ground being found close off shore, and large shipping being less liable to be troubled by ice than at any other point in the harbor at which it can lie with equal safety and convenience in other respects. An extensive use of these advantages would lead to the building of a special class of warehouses, factories and shops along the shore. As, within narrow limits, this demand is liable to become an imperative one, the erection of many permanent and costly domestic buildings on this shore is not to be expected. The sooner, therefore, its commercial advantages are developed the better.

Beyond this district, we do not think that a commercial demand for real estate is ever likely to be of much importance, or that it should be courted, for the Island, and as we are advised that a different opinion is held by some of your Commission, we wish to explain why.

In any region where the value of land depends chiefly on its agricultural productiveness, as, a generation since was the case here, any undertakings that are calculated to improve its means of communication with a distant market, or to establish a market within it, can hardly fail to benefit the landowners, who, consequently, are often asked to aid in the introduction of them. Nearly all of the territory of the United States being in that condition, there is naturally a pretty strong public opinion about the interest and duty of landowners in this respect. But Staten Island is now very differently situated from the country in general. It has no difficulty in finding a market for its crops, or in finding shipping enough to move them. What advantages, then, can it expect to gain by courting commerce?

In answer we may be pointed to the value which real estate has acquired in the commercial quarter of New York Island. Staten Island has a much greater extent of shore on the same harbor than New York Island, and while it is considerably nearer the sea, it is also approachable to better advantage from the main land, especially by railways. Does it then seem unreasonable to expect that by adding certain artificial to its natural advantages, so much of the commerce of New York can be drawn to Staten Island, as will greatly advance the value of its real estate?

The question is how much—how many acres—of the whole

area of the island is likely ever to be actually occupied, do what you will, for commercial purposes? We think we can show that it is very little indeed.

If we look at the two parts of New York city as divided, say, at Fourteenth street, we shall see that one side is mainly occupied for commercial purposes, the other for domestic. Imagine, then, that this division had been made more perfect, and that it had not been confined to the politically limited New York city, but had included all of that larger New York, now numbering a population of nearly a million outside the city, which sends a deputation of men every day to its commercial quarter. Under this division it will be evident that the buildings of the domestic class not only already cover a great deal more ground, but that *their number and area of occupation is enlarging much more rapidly* than that of the commercial class, and this notwithstanding, perhaps, that the amount of business transacted, of goods exchanged, is larger than ever before.

It is not very difficult to see some reasons why this should be so, and why it is likely to continue.

In the progress of commerce, men of marked ability have more and more duties pressed upon them, and duties in undertakings of the most diverse character. The necessity of personal conference in regard to affairs requiring separate offices, gives increasing value to time during certain hours, and distance is for these purposes yet equivalent in the market to time. Hence vicinity to various offices becomes an increasing element of value.

The increasing specialization in business which often makes many sources of supply necessary to be called on for a purpose which could formerly be served by one, tends in the same general direction; the result being always an increasing motive to compactness.

At every center of commerce, consequently, more and more business tends to come under each roof, and, in the progress of building, walls are carried higher and higher, and deeper and deeper, so that now "vertical railways" are coming in vogue.

It may be thought that these observations apply only to commerce in a restricted sense, that is to say to exchanges and administration, and especially not to manufactures and shipping. The question is important because some think that it may be possible to establish a great manufacturing quarter of the metropolis on the island, and with this in view a different line of policy might be advised from that which we shall assume to be required. It is well known that conditions which make a difference of many years in the expectations of life with operatives are no obstacle of consequence to the success of manufactories. Let us then examine the facts.

There are between four and five thousand manufacturing establishments on New York Island, with an aggregate capital of about $70,000,000. Why are they on New York Island rather than anywhere else?

Not because of cheap land, cheap building materials, cheap food and lodging for operatives; not because of cheap coal, or wood, or waterpower, or taxes or insurances. For all manufacturing purposes in which these conditions are of primary importance, building sites must be sought far away, not only from New York but from Staten Island.

It is true that for certain of the latter class of purposes cheapness of transportation to and from the island of New York becomes also important. But the cost of transportation lies chiefly in the loading and unloading. Distance, within certain limits, extending far beyond Staten Island, counts but little. Moreover such disadvantages as distance establishes are lessened by every extension or improvement or addition to the roads, boats, telegraphs and mail facilities which connect the outer country with the town. They will be less in the future than they are at present. Thus the difficulty of establishing new centers or new sub-centers of manufacturing, like Newark, has, of late years, greatly increased and will continue to increase.

Dividing then, all manufacturing purposes for which land and buildings are liable to be required, into two classes, one of which economy will place at a comparatively remote distance, we see that, with respect to the other class, the same motives operate as with reference to buildings simply for the exchange and administrative offices of commerce—motives, namely, which favor a tendency to increasing compactness of association; to higher and deeper buildings, and to the occupation of less and less land relatively to the whole amount of the trade of the port.

The increasing use of large, deep, fast steamers, lying but a few days at the wharf, and each carrying in a year to and from any given hundred yards of shore ten times the burden of the old fashioned coasting craft, and the increasing employment of steam and machinery in handling and stowing cargoes, tends to make dock room of less and less value relatively to the whole amount of freighting business to be done at the port. General McClellan's plans will aid this tendency.

The length of shore front on navigable water within ten miles of the City Hall is about eighty miles, of which a tenth part only, and that all more than seven miles away, is on Staten Island; of the seventy miles perhaps twenty is now in constant demand for the accommodation of shipping; of the remaining fifty an important part, as yet unavailable for shipping, will soon be improved by undertakings in which the cities of New York and Brooklyn and leading railway corporations are now engaged. The land lying immediately back from the shore, to the extent of several thousand acres, is flat and easily adapted to manufacturing and other ordinary commercial purposes. It is on the other hand generally unattractive, and cannot easily be made, even tolerably, suitable for domestic purposes. We submit that at any rate of progress which past experience gives us reason to anticipate, and especially in view of the shrinking tendency in respect to ground-space which we have shown to exist, it will be a great many years before any considerable part of the land thus available and thus likely to be pressed on the market, will be required to be occupied by buildings, docks, or other structures for commercial purposes.

If not, then it is certainly impracticable, by any use of the taxable and other political resources of the county, to place Staten Island so successfully in competition for supplying the limited amount of land that is going to be wanted in the extension of the commerce of the port that any important favorable general effect upon the value of its real estate can be expected to be produced.

On the other hand, it is only necessary to go out on Long Island a little north and east from Brooklyn to see how harmful an effect is liable to result from a very moderate effort in that direction, many people of wealth who formerly lived there, having been driven away, and tracts of land formerly clothed with beauty laid waste almost as by an invading army, this being the result of a number of scattered manufactories. It is true that there are manufactures which would not be likely to have any such effect, but it is also true that manufacturing establishments started for one object are liable, after a time, to be adapted to another, and that those which have the greatest permanency in the outskirts of large towns are such as are most offensive, and destructive of value to the better class of domestic property near them. Illustrations of this are not wanting on Staten Island. It is also to be considered that it is very difficult to draw the line between a manufactory which is legally permissible, and one which is legally a nuisance, and that when capital has been once largely invested in any works, it is always a difficult and expensive undertaking for the public to remove or control them. The owners of property in the district we have referred to on Long Island, having first invited the introduction of manufactories, have of late years made great but vain exertions to cause the removal or suppression of many of them.

Turning now to the domestic division, is there, in the first place, any question that a tendency prevails precisely opposite to that which we have seen to be governing the commercial—a dispersing and colonizing tendency? If it is recollected that the people who inhabit the tenement-house districts of New York are very little to be taken into account, simply because they are just those who are least able to get what they want, and consequently manifest least what is generally wanted, for domestic purposes, we think there can be none.

A man who has probably made more money by suburban real estate improvements than any one else in the country, said to us lately, "I find that everywhere there has been the largest advance where the streets have been widest and the lots deepest, and if, where the determination of the width of streets and the depth and breadth of lots has been under my control during the last thirty years, I had, in every case, insisted on having them doubled, I should have been at least a million dollars the better for it. I will never again, if I can help it, have a street laid through or beside property of mine in the outer part of a town, less than a hundred feet wide, nor lay off lots less than fifty feet wide and a hundred and fifty feet deep, unless it is where I wish to draw commercial business or a poor class of people for a special purpose, as where hands are needed for a factory."

Is this experience and opinion exceptional? If so, why, over so large an extent of ground on New York Island, in Westchester and in Kings and Queens has the plan upon which land was laid out twenty thirty and forty years ago been discarded?

This plan was generally that of rectangular blocks of 25 × 100 feet lots, with streets of from fifty to seventy feet in width, a plan tolerably well adapted to purely commercial requirements. The new plans are less regular and will give larger blocks, wider streets, deeper lots and more open spaces. This, according to our reading of it, is simply an adjustment of the market to a rising demand of a special character for domestic purposes, which can be met on New York Island only by a compromise with the commercial demand, and consequently, at the best, but imperfectly, but which, with the small exception we have referred to, the whole of Staten Island may be adapted to supply in the most complete way and with great and speedy profit to its landowners.

From an examination of the recent census returns, which we have been permitted to make at the Marshal's office, it is ascertained that in one district, over twenty square miles in extent, about as far north from Wall street as the middle of Staten Island, there has been an increase of population during five years of over ninety-five per cent; in another sixteen miles distant, a little larger, forty-four per cent; in another twenty-five miles distant, or further than the most distant point of Staten Island, fifty-five per cent. These are all in Westchester County; and, from personal examination, we know that the larger part of the immigration has consisted of thrifty families, each carrying with it considerable capital, and almost invariably going into villas and cottages, with more or less extensive grounds.

There are a number of districts on Long Island and New Jersey where an increase of a similar character has occurred quite as large.[1]

The suburban travel (chiefly commutation), on five railways from which we have returns, has, during the last ten years, more than doubled the number of passengers, increasing from four to nine millions: on other routes the rate of increase is believed to have been still greater. On several of the suburban boat lines the travel has more than doubled in four years.

The out of town families, some member or members of each of which habitually visit the island of New York daily, now number fully three quarters of a million, and within two years will exceed the resident population of the city. What part of this number is strictly suburban, that is to say, resident in detached dwellings with sylvan surroundings yet supplied with a considerable share of urban convenience, it is not possible to ascertain, but it is certain that the proportion of this class is very rapidly enlarging.

[1] The increase in population on Staten Island in five years has been less than sixteen per cent. The average capital per head brought in and made available for taxation has been less than it has in some of the districts above referred to, which have increased much more rapidly. There are several districts in Westchester and Long Island, as near and as accessible as the most favored of these, which, as we perceive by the census returns, have either lost or failed to increase at all in population, and the real estate of which is believed to have fallen in value. We have either visited or had communication with physicians and intelligent citizens in each of these, and, in every case, the first reason given for the depression of their real estate is a reputation for unhealthfulness. [1871.]

Land held in farms fifteen to twenty years ago, since broken up into plots of from one to five acres, in the midst of attractive scenery, having a fair general reputation for healthfulness, approached by tolerable roads, and accessible in from half an hour to an hour from Wall Street, has almost invariably advanced in value at least five hundred per cent, and often a thousand.[2]

The tendency, thus indicated, is not peculiar to New York; it now prevails in every other large town, in London and Paris, as well as in Boston, Philadelphia, and in our Western cities. Everywhere townspeople have been lately tending to break town bounds. It may, to be sure, be regarded as a mere fashion, which, acting first on the richer and more luxurious classes, and sending them for the summer only to country seats, then taken up in a little different form by a large number of people of more moderate wealth, has at length fairly laid hold of the masses, in which case it must be expected to soon run out, and be followed by a reaction. But if it is a mere fashion, and has this liability, it is at least singular that it should for years, while sufficiently manifest, have been less powerful, and made its way more slowly at the Head Quarters of Fashion than generally elsewhere.

Regarding it not as a fashion but as a sensible and permanent common movement, the reason why it has been more subdued at Paris is not difficult to see. Obviously it is because at Paris the old theory of a town has been till now essentially maintained, which made it a fortress, enclosed it by walls, and necessarily surrounded the walls by a waste of land, in which domestic considerations were required to yield to military.

If we look closely at any large city, it is to be observed that this outward current is by no means setting all in one direction, nor does it benefit all points alike in any direction. Some districts are constantly avoided or fallen upon only by the thriftless, and for evident considerations of necessity rather than choice; others are passed clean over, so that sometimes

[2] This statement is made on the authority of Mr. Homer Morgan. [1871.]

land at a distance is more in demand than that lying between it and the point of departure. We shall hold not only that the general flow, but that all these leapings and turnings of the stream, wherever it has any strength and persistency, are the result of perfectly comprehensible laws, the working of which has been manifest in other forms for centuries. To agree on what class of improvements Staten Island requires in order to derive from it the greatest benefit, there must first be a common understanding of these laws. To carry out such agreement there must be a common faith in them, and in what they will, if heeded, ultimately accomplish. We shall briefly indicate, therefore, the general line of evidence which leads to the convictions in this respect which will govern our recommendations.

A century ago much of the filth which at present is taken off by sewers in most of our large towns was thrown out into the street, under the windows, in front even of the most noble mansions of the richest of cities, and often remained there for months polluting the air, and unquestionably greatly shortening the average period of life of their inmates. Less than a hundred years earlier, the dining rooms of the best houses in the healthiest city of England were at frequent intervals laid over with a wash of soot and small beer to hide the dirt which was allowed to remain upon them. Still another hundred years back we find the dining rooms of rich men's mansions strewed with rushes in order to absorb and partly cover the still greater amount of filth which was customarily permitted to accumulate on them, table-forks having then been but recently introduced, and such offal as bones, cartilage and apple-cores being often dropped from the fingers upon the floor.

We find from evidence, the character of which these facts illustrate that there is a fixed tendency among civilized men, to place more and more value upon the cleanliness and purity of the condition of their domestic life, and a little consideration will show that this law is not confined in its operation to the interior of dwellings, but extends to all that may surround or be associated with them.

Now it is impossible to have a high degree of cleanliness without great inconvenience and cost in connection with many conditions of commerce. Much that would be offensive in and about a dwelling house must be endured in and about a factory, a wharf, or even an office frequented by men engaged in many of the duties of commerce. Hence, in looking even but a little way back, we see how rapidly, since town walls have become generally less important, the tendency has been developed to separate domestic from commercial life. Late in the last century the largest bankers and merchants of London, Amsterdam and Paris, still maintained their domestic and commercial establishments under the same roof, and the Stewarts and Tiffanies of the day had a door opening between their show rooms and their family dining-rooms.

The constantly increasing distinctness of separation between the commercial division, and the compact domestic division, in all large modern towns, is one result of this law of progress; another is the gutters, gratings, sewers and water-works by which a large share of the filth which was formerly endured in and about the house is rapidly taken to a distance, and which have made it possible even to move about within the town without coming in direct contact with anything very obviously dirty. These improvements have been so great, and their results so beneficial, that the average length of life of the classes of the people who live the year through in the city of London has been doubled. But it has not yet been found practicable to keep the air of compactly-built parts of towns pure and sweet, and lives are yet shortened and made painful by the privation. It is doubtful if it will ever be possible to overcome the difficulty of doing so in localities of a certain density of population where the two great natural agents of disinfection, sunshine and foliage, cannot act largely and freely throughout the streets, and on each side of every house. In fact, beyond a certain point, density of residence is incompatible with a high degree of cleanliness or a high degree of health, comfort and civilization. The difficulty is vastly increased if to the thronging of mankind is added the liability of dust, dirt and unwholesome emanations of various

183

manufactories.³ Here then is one reason why our great cities will never be able to retain within narrow limits the families of those who are engaged in their exchanges and manufactures. They will be able to do so less and less. By modifying their plans, making larger blocks, wider streets and more numerous and broader public places and parks, they may bring the necessary evils of compact building within certain bounds, but the process must go much further than it has yet done, even in Paris, where, in fifteen years, $375,000,000 was spent in this way, or in London where $24,000,000 has just been spent on sewers alone, before the migration to a considerable distance from the commercial districts, of the classes most advanced in civilization, will cease to grow constantly larger.

There is one other motive element in this movement to which it is necessary to allude—the esthetic. There is no doubt that with the advance of civilization there is in the mental constitution of civilized men an increasing susceptibility to certain forms of beauty, especially to the beauty of nature, apart—so far as it is possible to regard it as ever apart—from associations of health and comfort. In what degree this element guides the suburban movement it is hard to say, but that it is of some consequence and increasing consequence, is proved by the extent to which it is abused in the course of catchpenny speculations. Nothing has been more common of late than to recommend building sites on account of the natural beauty of distant prospect which they possess, or the local attractiveness of the land itself which is offered for sale, when the process of building and of so called improvements in the neighborhood will assuredly destroy both. It may seem hardly necessary to say that views of woods which will soon be felled,

³ In nearly all large commercial towns in Europe great undertakings have been planned, and in some carried out, for securing more space in and about the dwellings of that part of their population which, by its avocations and its poverty, is practically precluded from moving into suburbs. Liverpool has recently expended over $5,000,000, and Glasgow has asked authority from Parliament to make a loan of $7,000,000, to be expended in the course of twenty years, for this purpose. [1871.]

streams which will be turned into sewers, meadows that will be built on, landscapes that may be shut off, are of no permanent value in a home, but it is certain that they are accepted as such in thousands of cases, and that they enter largely into the fictitious valuation of real estate which causes so much distrust and confusion in regard to permanent conditions of value.

There are few things which make greatly for the happiness of men concerning which they know so little of the process by which the happiness comes, and the conditions on which it depends, this as of the beauty of nature. It is the commonest experience that men destroy beauty under an idea that they are going to increase it.

But most men will, at first sight, prefer a coarse colored lithograph which is dear at a dollar to a Claude or a Murillo, which has, nevertheless, during hundreds of years been regarded as a treasure, and for which there are to-day not a few men who would gladly give many thousands of dollars. And it is probable that there are not a great many who, having the painting placed where they would see it, without any effort to force admiration, several times a day for some years, would not learn also to place something like the true market value upon it. Undoubtedly it is the same with the beauty of natural landscape, and the beauty of parks and gardens. Men do not know on what their enjoyment of one locality more than another depends, but they find that one permanently contents them more than another. And upon the degree of general contentment which can be assured to any community, will the value of the real estate of that community in the long run wholly depend.

In dealing with a question like this, of the most economical means of *permanent* improvement for a large area near a great center of business, nothing is more important than a realization of the utter folly of a policy which has heretofore been often followed with profit by individual speculators in a small way. To illustrate the danger of it we shall refer directly to local experiences.

Within the memory of several of your members, and since the childhood of most, the value of nearly all the land on Staten Island was established by reference solely to its advantages for fishing and agriculture. One-third of the appraisement of what were then the most valuable farms was due to the fishing rights which were sold with them. The demand for dwelling-sites by men engaged in business in New York began between 1830 and 1840. The probability of its increasing soon occurred to many persons, and upon this farms began to be bought and held idle "on speculation," along the East and North shore.

We propose to briefly and, of course, imperfectly, trace the history of a single district of from a thousand to fifteen hundred acres in extent, which, in the judgment of many, was at that time the most attractive of any on the island, or even perhaps of any on this side of the Atlantic. The land had been held for generations by the descendants of the original settlers. Their interests being divided between fishing and agriculture, but little of the ground was kept under the plough, most of it was in wood or broad greenswards. Old trees had an unusual value, ship builders from New York being wont to run down the bay, and select timber for special purposes in the woods, buying it standing. Hickories of a certain size and form were also in request for the fisheries. The woods were thus managed in a way not very common with farmers, a certain class of trees only being picked out and felled for ordinary purposes, and those promising special profit allowed to remain and spread broadly; the groves were therefore notable for their beauty, and something of this may be seen in portions of them yet remaining.

The owners of the land lived in quaint and cozy, low-roofed and broad-galleried cottages, approached by the most delightful class of summer roads, winding among the great trees, crossing clear brooks and skirting the smooth clean meadows. A man might search the world to find an alternative to the commercial town more complete or more pleasing. It was believed also by the best physicians of New York to be a place of distinguished healthfulness, and there is yet no reason to doubt that it was so. The apparent objections to it were merely the difficulties of access, the badness of the roads in the Winter and Spring, and the want of society.

The land traders, when their time came, promised to remedy these objections; a wharf was to be built, and direct stream communication established with New York, roads were to be constructed and each of the farms was to be divided into a number of places adapted to countryseats and villa sites, inviting to a good class of residents. This was chiefly undertaken by an association and so far as it was able to obtain possession of land it at once laid out a broad straight highway through it, crossing the shallow valleys upon low causeways. A wharf was also subsequently built, and direct steamboat communication for a short time maintained with the city. No substantial improvements in the way of drainage were made, however, nor was the slightest thought given, apparently, to securing to the public in the future any claim upon the preservation of the various elements of health and beauty which now gave the land really the better part of its value.

The expectations of profit of those who engaged in these enterprises were to a considerable extent realized. Numerous places were sold, houses built and grounds laid out. To the original reputation of the district for the beauty of its landscapes and its detailed and local rural charms was added a renown for the attractions of its villas, gardens and society. All choice sites rapidly advanced several fold in value.

Another class of changes began to be noticeable between 1845 and 1855. Such improvements as we have described had drawn not only a considerable number of families of great and moderate wealth, but also many with little or no accumulated means, who were employed as laborers and servants. The steam ferry made the island generally known to holiday excursionists. A lager beer garden was established to aid the ferry enterprise. The ground least saleable for villa residences began to be occupied by shops and small dwellings, stables and vegetable gardens, to make room for which fine trees were often felled. Several of the original suburban places became nearly enclosed by those of the later formation, and thus less valuable for their original purpose.

At length two or three factories were established in the neighborhood, increasing the demand for small lots for lodging houses, stores, and dram shops, thus still further lessening the attractiveness and the value of a certain part of the territory for suburban purposes. The means of livelihood of some of the later arrivals being precarious, when hard pressed they helped themselves to fuel, which they found first in the old farm rail fences, and then in the unenclosed woods which remained. Large tracts of these, consequently, were cleared soon afterwards by their owners. The construction of roads across the valleys had in several cases arrested the natural flow of water upon the surface, and some of the old water courses not only lost all their beauty, but, from the mingling of household wastes with the water made stagnant by obstructions, became disgusting and dangerous. Some places presently began to be known as unhealthy. All soon came under suspicion.

An intelligent stranger could now no longer possibly reach the parts which retained any of the original conditions of attraction, to look at a site offered him for a residence, without having the question raised:

"Suppose I come here, what grounds of confidence can I have that I shall not by-and-by find a dram-shop on my right, or a beer-garden on my left, or a factory chimney or warehouse cutting off this view of the water? Is this charming road sure not to be turned also into a common town street, strewn with garbage, and in place of these lovely woods, can I be certain that here also there will not soon be a field of stumps with shanties and goats and heaps of cinders? If so what is likely to be the future average value of land in this vicinity? Whatever advantages it still possesses over other districts about New York as a rural or suburban dwelling-place, it never can possess any for compact building at all superior to a hundred thousand acres elsewhere about the city. Looking either with reference to enjoyment of it as a place of residence, or as an investment for my children, I must be cautious not to be too much affected by superficial appearances. *What improvements have you here that tend to insure permanent healthfulness and permanent rural beauty?"*

We know that in certain cases, this course of reflection and inquiry has operated to prevent the sale of places, and we also know that since the conditions to which we have referred have been very distinctly manifest, the rent and market value of a large number has declined or at least ceased to advance, while at the same time, the number of people going out of town in search of places of residence has vastly increased.

There is another district on the island which, within twenty years, has been made accessible from the city in half the time that it was previously, taking contingencies into account and with reference to practical connection with the commercial center. It was believed, and confidently predicted by able business men that the completion of the railway, by which, mainly, this has been accomplished, would double its real-estate value. We find that, in fact, it is doubtful whether the gold value of land in this district has advanced at all. We know of several cases in which land has been recently bought at a price considerably less than that at which it was sold fifteen or twenty years ago.

Surely, it will be said, this is a very extraordinary case—a suburban district of great beauty, declining in value of real estate apparently because of being brought nearer to town, and this, at a period when in other directions suburban real-estate has been advancing five and ten fold in value! But it is not at all extraordinary that a suburban district loses attractiveness when the interests of its landowners are turned from agriculture to idle speculations. In this case obstructions to drainage have been permitted to occur and accumulate, common highways have been neglected, and hundreds of acres of beautiful woodland have been cut away, leaving bare, unsightly wastes in their place to mortify the eye, and making pestiferous swamps of low lands, the superabundant moisture of which was formerly sucked up and harmlessly evaporated by the foliage. The district is much less healthy, and the pleasure with which a family, having any feeling for natural beauty, can reside in it is not nearly as great as it was twenty years ago. Consequently it is less adapted to the market, and, of course, is all the time tending to fall, instead of rising in value.

We could easily enforce our argument by reference to several localities in various parts of the island, giving, if it were proper to do so, names and figures. We could point to one short piece of road laid out and "improved" in the usual way of land traders, in the midst of a district which had previously been flourishing, and by which a series of attractive, small villa sites was opened up and placed in the market. The local outlook was interesting. A pretty stream which ran near by skirted by a nice grove, was regarded as an advantage, as properly managed it certainly would have been. Access to broad distant land and water views was direct, short and convenient. More than twenty houses have been built on this road, the grove being cut away to make room for them. As population has come in malaria and other sanitary evils have been developed. The original builders have nearly all sold out and moved away. A real estate agent having charge of some of the houses tells us that for several years past there has been increasing difficulty in finding good tenants for them and rents have been largely reduced. The physicians inform us that this year, not one household upon this road has escaped a visit from diseases which are caused by poisoned air. In the densest wards of New York or London, there has been no larger percentage of preventable disease, and in none have diseases been found to fix themselves more firmly upon the system, and to offer stronger resistance to remedies.

Looking to see what had been the more indirect effect in the neighborhood we ascertained that a house which, during a long series of years, had been a favorite summer boarding-house—frequently rejecting for want of room more applicants than it was able to accommodate, had this year not been half filled. A large villa was pointed out to us, standing on an eminence overlooking the row of houses we have spoken of.

It had been sold by its original owner fifteen years ago at a certain price, since considerably improved, sold again last spring at one half the same price, had been unoccupied during the Summer except by a man hired to live in it, and is now offered at a reduction from the price paid for it last Spring.

We do not wish that our remarks should imply censure. However desirable and profitable it may be, where capital can be commanded, there is no obligation upon the owners of land to prepare it suitably for the residence of a community before putting it in the market, and very few, any where, are ever found disposed to do so. As long as the houses in any district stand well apart, with an abundance of trees about them, and only the more healthy situations are occupied, the dangers which threaten a closer neighborhood do not generally very distinctly appear. They may at least be guarded against by individual care. If, however, easy access from the city and low prices for land tempt immigration, with denser population the healthfulness of any locality is liable to become questionable; once established, from year to year the doubt increases; with its increase the prospect of any considerable future advance in the value of land diminishes. The owners at one time elated, become discouraged; they distrust the market value of radical improvements, and are more than ever unwilling to undertake them privately. At length, before they know it, a state of things is reached in which it becomes questionable whether any general combination, supposing it could be brought about, to secure them would effect a sufficient change in the reputation of the neighborhood to make it profitable.

It may be best to inquire here how far this doubt applies at this moment to Staten Island as a whole.

There are parts of the Island which now suffer from an undeserved reputation for unhealthfulness. There are various localities, further from the city, less attractive in landscape, and less healthy, which stand much higher in the real estate market. There are other places upon the Island, the reputation of which is locally worse, but concerning which we are obliged to say, after examining the physicians who practice in them, and after personal inquiries from house to house, that the worst has not been told. But whatever the shortcomings of public rumor toward them in particular, it is more than made up by the reputation which is fastening upon the Island in general. This growing bad reputation, damaging to the value of every acre upon it, we have found to be greater at a distance, and among people who had never seen it, than anywhere else. It is surprising how far it has already gone. It has been manifested in the most exaggerated form by new-comers from Europe and California. We have more than once seen it expressed in letters of travelers published in distant parts of the country.

Such a one in passing the healthiest part of the Island, including a locality of considerable breadth in which we find no evidence that a single case of malarial disease of local origin has ever been known, is led to exclaim, "What a Paradise!" whereupon his companions are represented as saying "Yes, if you don't find a Paradise on Staten Island it will not be because fever and ague will not do its best to help you," and the writer adds "It is quite true that this Island is as unhealthy as it is beautiful."

How is this to be arrested? How can it be prevented from going on from bad to worse? Never by voluntary individual exertions, never by local action, never by proceedings of one or two of the towns, for as long as a single locality remains in a state to justify it, it is impossible to prevent the undeserved reputation from being applied to the Island as a whole by the general public. And *if* it goes on, according to all experience, the consequences may, at no distant day, be absolutely disastrous. Nothing is more sorry than the fate of any district, which, lying near a great town, gets a bad character strongly fastened upon it. Capital avoids it in all forms except those in which its coming is resisted by all localities in which the hope of better things has not been abandoned. There is unquestionably a tendency to let things drift in this direction among some of the land-owners on Staten Island.

We may as well here as anywhere, perhaps, state our conviction that some of the local undertakings now in progress, which are expected to relieve real estate from the bad name which has been found to be growing upon it, are liable to result in still further disappointment, not only for the reason which has been given—namely the impossibility of inducing the general public, from which any considerable improvement of demand must come, to discriminate between good and bad localities upon the island—but also on account of the superficial character of these works, and the great expense and difficulty which will be found, if any attempt is made, to keep them in efficacious condition. This is so marked in some cases, that we are satisfied that the evil sought to be removed, will, in fact, be aggravated by them.

But let us ask what are the grounds of hope that Staten Island shall yet make head against this danger?

Harlem, ten years ago, had a place in public esteem much lower than Staten Island has yet reached. Its malarious condition was a constant subject of newspaper banter. Since then a very extensive and costly system of drainage has been carried out, and there is no more joking about Harlem flats. The old reputation seems already quite forgotten; and recent sales are reported at eight thousand dollars a lot for land which, ten years ago, before drainage and street improvements, was held and was unsaleable at five hundred.

The report, of your Committee on Organization, incidentally states that at New Brighton the value of real estate is higher, and has advanced more steadily during a series of years than at any other point on the Island. What is the reason of it? A large part of New Brighton is a remarkably well drained, and in all respects healthy district. It not only commands a magnificent view, but owing to the slope of the surface, it has been impossible to wholly cut off that view from any point. No part of it is compactly built upon. The houses are generally unobtrusive and inoffensive, wholly untownlike, and are surrounded by grounds with a variety of flourishing trees. Its roads are lighted, its wheelways macadamized, its gutters paved, its walks flagged and their slopes and borders neatly sodded.

If the reason is not to be found chiefly in these circum-

stances we think it will be difficult to account for the low
market value of some other land which we have seen—land
which, with good roads, could be reached as soon from New
York as that midway between Brighton and Tompkins landing; land which is equally elevated, which commands equally
fine distant views, which with drainage would be equally
healthy, but in the foreground of which there is a pond hole
and a raw bank and a gully, which fronts on a road of steep
grade, always toilsome to climb and in the Spring liable to
be almost impassable, and which is without gutters or sidewalks or gas. Land of this description can be bought at a
quarter of the price asked for that with which we compare
it at Brighton.

The hope of Staten Island lies in the certain large profits
of the substantial improvement of its low-priced lands.

But we have been met by men of large experience with
the remark: "Staten Island is on the wrong side of the town.
Fashion always goes one way and in New York it sets to
the North, just as in London it sets to the West."

It is perfectly true that the Eastern outskirts of London
are inhabited almost solely by very poor people, that the town
extends in that direction very slowly, and that the progress
of building in the finer class of residences has constantly been
to the Westward, but why? If fashion, what established the
fashion? Simply the fact that the town began to grow on
account of its commerce, that it stood at the head of ship
navigation on the river, that East of the uppermost anchorage,
the banks of the river were low and flat and the outlook
dreary, while to the West the ground was high and dry, and
there were most attractive landscapes.

So far as town houses are concerned the drift of fashion
to the Westward has thus been simply a matter of necessity;
beyond that there is no drift to the Westward. Ten miles
out of town to the Eastward there is as much of fashion and
wealth as there is at the same distance in the opposite direction.
The villas are as numerous and as fine. The noble seats of
Sir Culling Eardly Eardley, Lord Say and Seal, and the Duchess
of Sutherland are examples of them—and there are thousands

of fine places in the same general direction nearer than that to the town. Whoever has looked upon the country which was near to the South and East, from the terrace of the Crystal Palace at Sydenham, before the view of it was lost behind the host of suburban houses that have been lately built in that direction, will remember that here is a fine elevated, healthy, well-wooded district and that it is studded with villas, country seats and parks.

It is the same at Paris—the best quarter of the town is in the North, in the South are factories and factory people. But go *ten miles* to the Southward and you find the banks of the Marne entirely occupied by villas, and suburban villages, to which the Parisians who have no country seats resort for furnished apartments during the Summer. It is a beautifully wooded, healthy, and most attractive suburban district and fashion has nothing to say against it.

Is it fashion that prevents people from selecting Staten Island as a residence? We have known three cases this year in which families of wealth and high social standing, have, after looking at Staten Island, gone past it and found residences to the southward in Monmouth County, New Jersey. One of these had just abandoned a fine place at Newport, on account of the inconvenience of going there and returning. They went to a place south of and much more inconvenient than Staten Island, simply because of the advice of their physician, that it was more healthy.

We have, during this inquiry for your Commission, visited several of the more successful suburbs—suburbs in which real estate has advanced, and is advancing very much more rapidly than at any point on Staten Island. At none of these are there natural conditions as valuable, in some respects, as at various points on Staten Island; but on the whole we find reason to believe that the chances of securing health and happiness to a family in the long run are but little overrated in the market value of land.

We say but little, because there seems to be some reason to suspect that the long course of make-shifts to which the public has been subjected by men "making haste to be rich" on small capital, has at last had the natural effect of giving excessive market value to land, where the artificial requirements of a good suburban neighborhood are well provided for in a permanent way.

Evidence of this is not limited to the vicinity of New York Bay. Let us look to a point where sheer speculation has run wilder, and paper streets and paper towns have, for a time, been worth more than probably anywhere else for an equal period in the world. Recently two suburban speculations were started near Chicago, one at a distance of six, the other of nine miles from the town, each centering upon a station of the same railway, on land worth, at the time, from one to two hundred dollars an acre. The managers of one laid out their plan in the usual way, made streets of the prairie soil, with neat open ditches, and spaces for side-walks beside them; planted trees, hit upon a good name, got up their lithographs and advertised. The managers of the other borrowed a large sum of money at a high rate of interest, mortgaging not only the land they were to operate on, but other property for the purpose. With this they first underlaid their land with several miles of draining-pipe, then built macadamized roads with paved gutters, iron gratings, concrete side walks, and broad borders, frequently spreading into little greens and commons, planted picturesquely. All the natural wood and the banks of the stream which passed the place, were made public property, and shelters, seats, bathing and boat houses were provided upon it. An Artesian well was sunk, and with a steam-pump water sent to all parts of the property.

Before these improvements were nearly complete the owners began selling land upon the roads at twenty dollars, and soon afterwards advanced their price to thirty dollars, the front foot. The place has just been lighted with gas, the works being an independent undertaking, and no land can be bought at present on the improved roads at less than forty dollars. It is not two years since the work was begun. Over forty private houses have been already built upon the sites sold, a number of them at a contract price of over twenty thousand dollars. The engineer in charge of the works writes us, as to the effect on the neighborhood, that one tract, which is partially inclosed by the improved territory, and barely touches at a corner upon one of the macadamized roads, and which was valued two years ago at from $80 to $100, has been recently sold at $1,000, an acre. All surrounding property has advanced 200 per cent during the last year. With regard to the enterprise nearer town, it is a complete failure, it stands to-day as it did a year ago, not the first house having been built upon it.

We turn from this lesson in the West to another of equal significance which comes to us from the opposite quarter. East of the City of London, there are districts to which we have already referred, in which, among dust-heaps, brick and coal yards, and large waste places, there are clusters of habitations which from their wretchedness have been spoken of in Parliament as a national disgrace. Efforts have sometimes been made to relieve the dampness, which is the primary cause of the abandonment of these districts by every thing which is wholesome and decent; but, until recently, they had always been of a superficial penny-wise, pound-foolish character, resulting in disappointment. One such was alluded to by Mr. Dickens, in a description from which we draw, with slight contraction of the original, the following account:

"In such a neighborhood stands Jacob's Island, surrounded by a muddy ditch, known in these days as "Folly Ditch." A stranger looking from one of the wooden bridges thrown across it will see crazy wooden galleries common to the backs of half a dozen houses with holes from which to look upon the slime beneath; windows broken and patched; rooms so small, so filthy, so confined, that the air would seem too tainted even for the dirt and squalor which they shelter; wooden chambers thrusting themselves out above the mud, and threatening to fall into it—as some have done; dirt-besmeared walls and decaying foundations, every repulsive lineament of poverty, every loathsome indication of filth, rot and garbage; all these ornament the banks of 'Folly Ditch.' "

Six years ago it was determined by the authorities that one of the worst of these wretched eastern parishes should be, as far as the streets and public property were concerned, thoroughly improved. Matters were so bad that plans had previously been discussed for a wholesale deportation of the inhabitants. What actually was done included the construction of a sufficient number of deep under-ground drains, falling into a main, which extended to a distance, the road ways were macadamized, and tar concrete walks laid by the side of them, water was laid on, and gas lights provided for. To accomplish this, it was necessary to raise money by loans, payable in fifteen to twenty years. Mr. Fisher, the engineer, employed to superintend these improvements, is now in this country. He informs us that before they were well completed, the old shanties and pestilent rookeries began to be laid low through the voluntary action of the owners of the land, and that in place of them, now, less than six years from the outset of the work, may be seen hundreds of attractive cottages and villas, with neat grounds about them. A healthy and thriving population, able to bear a large taxation has come in, and although no exact statistics can at this moment be furnished us, there is no doubt of a great profit from the undertaking.

In the extended observation of the different members of our Board on both continents, not an instance is known in which similar results have failed to follow works of improvement judiciously adapted to provide good roads and walks, and well drained and healthful building sites, with attractive sylvan surroundings within convenient distance of any large town.

The effect of substantial suburban improvements, even where unnecessary for health, is not at all mysterious. The outgoing townspeople do not reduce their standard of comfort in any respect materially, and they soon become discontented if they go where the degree of study and forethought, and skill in management of household affairs which they are accustomed to use is very greatly augmented. People moving from the country to the town rapidly lay aside habits of careful provision in respect to many details of housekeeping. They keep but small supplies, and wait till they are nearly out before taking thought for their replenishment. It is nothing to call or send to the grocer's or the butcher's or the baker's, when anything which they supply is found to be wanted. But the distance of a quarter of a mile over a bad country road is a much greater difficulty to a housekeeper than three or four miles upon a clean firm flagged street. A well fifty feet deep comes as a severe blow often repeated. Kerosene lamps all over the house and utter darkness outside the door give constant anxiety. Considerations of health being equal, it is the degree in which objections of this class to a residence prevail, here and there, that chiefly determine the direction of the suburban currents.

There is no doubt of an increasing domestic demand for land divided on a larger scale than has hitherto been generally adopted, or than is desirable, where commercial convenience is the primary consideration. A question remains as to the extent of the enlargement demanded?

Of this, the course of reasoning we have followed enables us, perhaps, to form some idea. Houses, for instance, must be so far apart, that the air of each shall be absolutely free from contamination arising from any other or from the highways; the highways must be so far apart, so spacious, so furnished or flanked with trees that organic waste can not be carried from them, to an injurious extent, into the houses between them; that the air passing across them shall be quickly disinfected or screened of whatever it takes up that is filthy. If a highway is short—taking little or no through traffic, requiring a wheel way of not more than 22 feet, the minimum thus reached would but little exceed the space of the ordinary town arrangements, except in the size of lots.

What then, is required to be possessed by each family, for its private use, out of doors, beyond what can commonly be had within towns?

We answer that a high state of health, or a sound moral condition can never be acquired by children or preserved by adults under the requirements of success which modern town life tends to impose, where it can not be made easy and convenient to spend considerable time out of walls—more time than can honestly be spent in idleness or in occupations which, with us, are deemed consistent with publicity. For this purpose there needs to be attached to every house a series of out-of-door apartments, not open to public view, in which direct exposure to sun and wind may, when desired, be avoided, and in which various ordinary household occupations may be carried on. One of these should connect with the kitchen, another with the social rooms of the family; there should be turf on which young children can walk, and fall without injury, on which girls can romp without soiling their dresses; there should be a dry walk for damp weather, a sheltered walk for windy weather, and a sheltered sitting place for conversation, needle work, reading, teaching, and meditation.

We repeat, that with the exciting and engrossing interests of the stage of society which we are now reaching, arrangements such as these are essential to a high state of health in a family. Every physician will endorse this statement. We can dispense with them as our ancestors could dispense with chimneys and table forks, with cotton and silks, with potatoes, sugar, coffee and tea; but it will cost us more to dispense with them than to obtain them, and learn to use them. Sooner or later all civilized people will learn to use them.

These requirements involve no large amount of land; but the minimum can not be much less than twice that of our present ordinary town lot.

How much must be added to this in order to admit of any degree of artistic luxury and completeness will depend very much on situation. With good, shaded highways, walks not liable to be overthronged, it is not at all necessary that the house should command fine distant or general views, it is rather better that stand-points for these should be possessed by each family in common with others, at some little distance from the house, so as to afford inducement and occasion for going more out from it, and for realizing and keeping up acquaintances by the eye at least, with the community. To give children a fair chance to develop their individual tastes and talents, however, without disturbance to neighbors, even with the most wholesome family discipline, the space of private ground must be enlarged, under most circumstances, to at least what would be inclosed in a parallelogram of fifty by one hundred and fifty feet. Where less than this is taken it will soon be from necessities of poverty, not choice.

It is not desirable that the lot should be a parallelogram or of any regular and uniform shape, on the contrary, it will be more satisfactory if it is not. It is much easier to fit a house and grounds agreeably upon a space of land, the sides of which are not parallel and the angles equal than upon one of the ordinary town-lot form.

Can we get any idea of the maximum? Suppose that two, three, or four hundred thousand families are to be in competition for land, each needing to have one member, at least, spend the larger part of each day in close proximity to the center of business; obviously the maximum for each will eventually be fixed chiefly by considerations of the cost of the land, established by competition, within certain limits of distance; and the limits of distance as far as time of passage is concerned will be, up to a certain point, constantly enlarging in every direction.

Yet we do not think that the progress of invention is to tell so much in the improvement of the speed with which distances can be overcome as in the cheapness, frequency, regularity and *comfort* of transportation. The question will be between cost of passage and cost of land; the nearer, other things being equal, the more valuable the land and the less of it must be accepted for what each man can afford to pay. But the measure of cost for passage will not be wholly in the value of time required for it and the fare; the incidental occupation of the time will be an important item. At present there is scarcely a suburb of New York the time to reach which from Wall Street, is not, on an average, worse than lost, that is to say, so far from being passed profitably, it is passed most expensively—at great cost of nervous energy, health and comfort. An addition of ten per cent to the cost of running the Staten Island ferry boats, with good roads and walks from the landings, would make it possible for most men to be in the way of gaining health, of receiving enjoyment, of spending their time profitably, doing two-thirds of all that would be given to the necessity of passing from Wall Street to their home.[4] Nothing like this can, as yet, be asserted of any railway line of exit from the town, and there is no reason to suppose that any form of land communication will ever be invented by which, without vastly larger cost, it will be possible to make the time occupied as valuable as it may be now made in water conveyance.

The greatest improvement will probably occur, however upon common highways, which there is no difficulty in carrying to the point at which one horse can do the work which must be given to three on our present roads. It is not improbable, also, that steam omnibuses will soon come into use, and that these, running from landings and stations, at a speed of ten or twelve miles an hour, will call at all houses on the highroads, whenever required, as the old coaches did. There are, at this moment, no practical difficulties in the way of this method, except those with which any new arrangement of general public utility has to contend. There are already in different parts of the world over four hundred steam carriages working successfully on common roads. But better and generally wider roads are the first requirement.

When there shall be, as there soon will, two or three hundred thousand families to be provided with houses out of town, the least space wanted by each of which shall be what we have named—and when the possibility shall be realized of occupying the best part of an hour's time of transit not uncomfortably, competition will then fix such a price upon all land within an hour's distance of the city, that only men of exceptional wealth, and tastes for rural domestic life, will think it best to pay for the use of more than eight or ten times as much of it as the amount we have named as the minimum

[4] The boats have most uncomfortable seats, are badly ventilated, and at night badly lighted. Being, also, short-handed, or with inadequate organization of service for their duty, passengers suffer from disorder and nuisances which might easily be prevented. These little matters make all the difference between misery and comfort to many, especially many women. The landings and houses are in every way the reverse of attractive and convenient. [1871.]

for health. The ordinary size of the house lot which will soon be most in demand in the suburbs may thus be approximately estimated. Along the shores, where sites can be reached by a short walk from the steamboat landings, it will probably be from quarter to half an acre. Wherever there is a tendency to reduce it much below this, men will prefer to spend more time on the passage, go farther and enjoy the use of more space. At a distance from boat landings, a larger area will be generally wanted to compensate for the greater trouble of land conveyance, and men who can afford to keep horses will also be able to afford to buy more land. Sites then will be in demand large enough to admit of some luxury of personal property in local landscape. The maximum, under ordinary circumstances, within an hour of Wall Street, on elevated land, and in a healthy and well furnished neighborhood, is not, in our judgment, likely to permanently exceed five acres. The average for all the more attractive parts of Staten Island, clear to its furthest extremity, beyond distances within an easy walk from the shore, would be less than that, but certainly not less than one acre. If the interior land should be cut up in smaller plots than an acre, most people will prefer to pass a little more time on the public conveyances, and go further. This is to be inferred from the readiness with which thousands are now induced to travel by the most fatiguing and expensive means of conveyance to much greater distances than Tottenville, to gain no advantage except that of controlling a little more land for their money.

If our reasoning has been good, we have thus determined with some approach to definiteness for what form of real estate there is likely to be in the early future the largest demand in the vicinity of New York. To what extent that demand shall go, and how rapidly it shall be developed is a question in all probability of the completeness and rapidity with which a supply shall be provided for it to be fed upon. In any locality where such building sites have been provided as we have described, from a quarter of an acre to five acres in extent, well drained and in all respects healthy; approached quickly, cheaply, and with any tolerable degree of comfort from New

York; where good service of tradesmen and public servants may be had, where water and gas may be laid on, where pleasant natural scenery is accessible, and where these characteristics extend over a sufficient breadth of country to give assurance of a suburban domestic neighborhood of a permanent character—in any locality which comes near offering these advantages—the indications of experience all are that if twenty thousand building sites could be put in the market, there would be twenty thousand families glad to buy them at once, at prices a good deal more than double the present average value of all the land on Staten Island—and it is hardly to be doubted that if they did so, there would be one hundred thousand people healthier, happier, richer and better for the bargains. We do not know where one such site can be had near New York to-day at ten times the average value of land on Staten Island.

The result of our study thus far has been to suggest a doubt whether there is any safe intermediate ground between an abandonment of the Island to the condition of an outskirt quarter of the metropolis, which, while it may increase in number of population, will lose in quality—an outskirt which will tend constantly to compare less and less favorably with the more fortunate suburbs—and an undertaking of improvement which will be likely to give it the first rank among them for healthfulness and general convenience, and which will have the result we have described, of causing twenty thousand detached villas and cottages, to be soon built upon it by capital to be brought from without and thus made available for local taxation.

We will go further and say that we have been led far toward the conviction that the position of the Island with reference to the center of business, and its natural attractions, are such, that if it could be relieved of its bad reputation in one single particular, the public would accept temporary inconvenience in other respects, taking the risk of delay in improvement of access, of roads, of water supply, and of other common suburban requirements, and that the Island, relieved from the single disadvantage to which we refer, would rapidly advance to the position of the best suburb, and its real estate command the highest rates of the market.

The one particular to which we refer is of course its unhealthfulness, and its special unhealthfulness depends simply and solely upon malaria. Aside from malarial troubles it has always been the healthiest suburb of New York.

The problem of malaria will be considered in a second letter. Without present argument upon the latter point, therefore, the views of general policy which we now desire to commend to you may be briefly re-stated as follows:

The value placed by the more far-sighted, prudent and prosperous part of the public, first on healthfulness, second on convenience, third on beauty, especially on rural beauty, in choosing their residence is constantly and rapidly increasing. This increase does not depend on fashion but on fixed laws of civilized progress, it is then likely to continue and may be depended upon as permanent.

The territory conveniently accessible from New York which has any prospect of retaining an agreeable rural character, and which is now free from malaria is limited. The rural territory which is likely soon to be retrieved from malaria is still more limited.

If Staten Island can be freed from malaria, it will be a comparatively easy matter to make it the healthiest, and at the same time the most convenient and most beautiful suburb of New York.

As soon as this character can be established for it a practically unlimited demand for its real estate will occur—a demand which will rapidly multiply the value of every acre of land upon it.

Chapter II. Malaria and Conditions of Health

The danger that great discouragement and depression may result from the adoption of plans for the relief of the Island from malaria, which should eventually prove to have been inadequate, has impressed us with a strong conviction of the importance of investigating the questions involved in this part of our duty as thoroughly as time would admit.

We believe it to be impracticable to secure complete relief from malaria solely by any system of public works. There can be little hope of success therefore, unless a substantial agreement of opinion, among the leading property holders, can be reached in regard to many questions which are involved in the study of the problem.

For this reason we are desirous to present you the results of our enquiries in a form adapted, as far as possible, to set at rest such doubts as we know are commonly entertained by others in regard, more especially, to the extent of ground on the Island in which there is a liability to encounter malaria; as to the degree of harm which is liable to result from encountering it, as to its sources, as to the practicability of obtaining relief from it, and as to the means of doing so.

Fortunately for this purpose, one of our number, Dr. Harris, had several years since undertaken a special inquiry as to certain of the phenomena associated with malarial disease, had enlisted the aid of a number of physicians and others resident in different parts of the Island, and had entered into correspondence with several scientific investigators in different parts of the country and abroad, for the purpose of interchanging the results of observations on the subject. He was therefore, fairly well prepared at the outset to answer the class of inquiries which most interest the public.

Since the appointment of our Board, and more or less accompanied by others of our number, he has visited all parts of the Island anew, observing, it is believed, every acre of its surface, for the purpose of verifying and enlarging the information previously obtained, and for conference with the medical faculty and intelligent citizens generally on the subject. He has also been assisted in his examination by Doctor J. S. Newberry, State Geologist of Ohio, and Professor of Geology in the Columbia College School of Mines, who is not only eminent in his special branch of science, but having practiced medicine in the malarial regions of the West, and thus been led to give particular attention to the influence of geological conditions upon health, is unquestionably the first authority in the country on certain of the points involved.

After two months of constant searching inquiry, made with these advantages, and with, we are confident, an entirely unbiased, candid, and cautious disposition of mind we feel prepared to report certain conclusions with a reasonable degree of confidence.

We should be glad, were it possible to lay before you full minutes of the evidence which has influenced the judgment that we shall express upon the practical questions to which the problem gives rise, both that obtained from persons direct and from medical and scientific records; but as, on account of its volumnious [sic] and frequently minutely technical character, this is out of the question, we have adopted the course of propounding a final series of questions to our medical associate with a view of presenting you, in a comprehensive and wholly intelligible form, answers which shall embody the more significant results of the general study which has been given the subject. Should it be desired, we are prepared to give much more detailed and specific evidence on most of the important points discussed.

The report of questions and answers which follows has been deliberately reviewed and approved, not only by Doctor Harris but by several other medical gentlemen of the island, and the opinions expressed may, we believe, be regarded with confidence as those to which the closest observation and the most cautious and responsible study of the questions presented has led. These remarks apply more especially to matters of medical opinion. For others, all the members of our Board may be considered as equally responsible.

Q. What is Malaria?

A. A poison in the atmosphere of certain localities which is recognized only by its effects, of which ague and fever is an example.

Q. Besides ague and fever what other effects of this poison are observed on Staten Island?

A. Disturbance of sleep and general uneasiness, rheumatic and neuralgic pains, lassitude, and a marked disturbance of the digestive organs and the vital energies, are commonly complained of in the localities where fever and ague prevails. They are mitigated or removed by the same antidotes, and are in most cases unquestionably due also to malaria. The most virulent form of disease produced by malarial poison upon the island is pernicious congestive fever which, where proper antidotes have not been quickly administered, has sometimes proved fatal. This has occurred in but few neighborhoods and rarely.

Q. In what proportion of the households upon the island, do forms of suffering or discomfort occur which physicians attribute to this poison?

A. Disregarding certain localities which are in general comparatively safe, amounting altogether to not more than one tenth of its area, it must be said that the population is almost universally affected in some degree by malaria. The effect of it has been sufficiently decided within the last six months in about three-fourths of the households to induce the inmates to consult a physician; of the fraction referred to as comparatively safe very little can be said to be perfectly secure against malaria wafted, under certain atmospheric conditions, from the other parts.

Q. Are those who have suffered from the more severe forms and persistent influence of malarial disease permanently enfeebled or constitutionally injured thereby, as a general rule?

A. As an invariable rule.

Q. Are other animals than man affected by malarial poisoning?

A. Frequently and decidedly, on Staten Island. (See appendix.)

Q. Are young children affected by it?

A. There have been numerous cases of late on Staten Island, in malarious places, in which infants only a few days old have suffered severely. They have been born with the poison in their system.

Q. Is it probable that malarial poisoning in many cases where it does not very distinctly appear, that is to say, by the ordinary symptoms, acts harmfully by stimulating, complicating and increasing other diseased tendencies?

A. It certainly does so.

Q. The tendency to drunkenness or to a morbid desire for stimulants for instance?

A. Yes.

Q. It exerts a general demoralizing and debilitating influence?

A. Yes.

Q. Does it appear that malaria is increasing on the island—affecting more people and acting over a larger part of the surface?

A. It does, so far as mere extent of its effects and the frequency of its prevalence are concerned.

Q. And is that the case looking back through a number of years and independently of seasons of an unusual character?

A. It is. In the early part of the present century, and as late as thirty-four or thirty-five years ago, malarial disease was almost unknown, except in occasional years, in localities where it now prevails every year. Dr. Spencer of Westfield, for instance, says that from 1835 to 1839, he did not meet with a single case, and considered the island free from malaria. In 1839 he first began to meet with evidence of its presence. It has now, for a series of years, been very prevalent in the same localities. Dr. Spencer's field of observations extended from Gifford's and Fresh Kills to Ward's Point. Dr. Edgar, the President of the County Medical Society, and the physician of longest experience on the island, states that the "malarial years" occur more frequently since 1845, but that there were occasional intense malarial epidemics in earlier times, as far back as 1827. He believes the malaria now more constant, but usually less intense. Dr. William C. Anderson, whose observations have been very extensive, thinks that the malarial nurseries are more numerous and extensive than formerly.

Q. Setting aside special conditions, such as unusual heat or drought, do the evils of malaria appear to be increasing year by year?

A. Yes.

Q. Are there any instances in which regions at one time free, or nearly so, of malarial poison, have gradually become highly malarious?

A. There are lands which at one time maintained large communities in fair healthfulness, and that have since been almost completely depopulated by the gradual inroads of malaria. This is well known to be the case in parts of the Campagna, near Rome, for instance.

Q. What is known of the causes of malaria?

A. Sir Thomas Watson has, perhaps, given the best statement of the conditions positively known to be most constantly necessary for the production of malaria. He says: "For producing malaria it appears to be requisite that there should be a surface capable of absorbing moisture, and that this surface should be flooded or soaked with water and then dried; the higher the temperature and the quicker this drying process, the more plentiful, the more virulent, the poison that is evolved."

Q. Our attention has been called to a statement cut from a newspaper, as follows:

"M. P. Bolestra has communicated to the French Academy some observations on ague poison. He says, that in examining marsh water he always finds, in proportion to its degree of putrifaction, a granular microphyte, somewhat resembling in form the Cactus Peruvianus. It is always accompanied by a considerable quantity of small spores $\frac{1}{1000}$ of a millimeter in diameter, greenish-yellow and transparent, and also by sporangia or vesicles, containing spores from $\frac{2}{100}$ to $\frac{2}{300}$ of a millimeter in diameter, and of very characteristic form. This plant grows on the surface of the water; when young, it is rainbow-like in tints, and looks like spots of oil. At the low temperature of cellars, and in water containing no vegetation, it develops slowly, but in contact with air and exposed to solar rays it grows fast, disengaging small gas bubbles. A few drops of arsenious acid, sulphite of soda, or still better, neutral sulphate of quinine stops its vegetation at the surface of the water: the spores become thin and transparent, and the sporangia alter so they would not be recognized. These changes may be seen under the microscope. M. Bolestra states that these spores can be found in marsh air. He caught ague twice during his researches—once after having been exposed to air from water in fermentation, covered with fresh algæ in full vegetation, mixed with an extraordinary quantity of spores. He thinks these spores constitute the ague poison."

It is a fact that such oil-like spots are to be frequently seen upon the edge of pools of water near which malarial disease is understood to prevail in the island. What is to be thought of the theory?

A. There are two hypotheses used in accounting for the production of malaria, one is that sustained by the observations which have been read, the other, that malaria is produced directly or indirectly by certain gases or volatile emanations, the nature and combinations of which are yet undetermined, but which are evolved by decaying vegetable matter under the required conditions of temperature and moisture.

Q. In either case the point where danger begins, and the manner in which it spreads would be the same, would they not?

A. Yes, and in this respect we have to deal with malarial diseases precisely as with other fevers. We understand only the physical conditions under which the fever occurs, the factor-like relations of these conditions, the results they produce, and the means by which the local causes can be prevented.

Q. Is it at all improbable that malaria is produced by something thrown off by a microscopic plant which is liable to be reproduced whenever its seeds are carried by the wind to situations where they may be washed into the midst of dead vegetation, and afterwards find a somewhat warm moisture, such as might on a hot summer's day be produced by the direct rays of the sun on the edge of a marsh or pond, or even under turf, or a bed of rotting leaves, where the soil had lately been water-soaked?

A. While it has, as yet, by no means been proved, such an hypothesis is not improbable. On the contrary, it fits the conditions, under which malaria oftenest arises, better perhaps than any other that has been suggested. Prof. Niemeyer, the most recent of writers on the subject, says it must be so. Dr. Daniel Drake, who spent an active life studying malarial diseases, says, that this hypothesis is better sustained than any other, but is not yet proved. In the latter is the true state of the evidence.

Q. Adopting this hypothesis, what would be the effect of the shade of trees falling upon damp ground with reference to the propagation of the supposed plant?

A. By preventing as great a degree of heat as would otherwise occur, it might hinder its growth and propagation.

Q. What would be the effect of foliage upon the dissemination of the poison?

A. It is probable that the spores or germs would be arrested by and fasten to the foliage. But inasmuch as foliage evolves oxygen and volatile aromatic material, it is believed that the poison is more or less neutralized in passing through foliage. That electrified or active condition which is termed ozone, and which is abundant in the vicinity of flourishing trees, tends to destroy malaria.

Q. What is the effect of foliage on dampness of the soil?

A. No tree can live without drawing moisture from the soil. Experiments have been recently made with great care by Pettenkofer, at Munich, to determine the amount evaporated by a single tree. It is proved that a common spreading tree, such as may grow by the roadside, discharges from its leaves eight and a half times as much water during the Summer, as commonly falls in rain upon the surface of the ground covered by its branches. The tree experimented upon was an oak. More succulent trees, as the elms, maples, and hickories, probably discharge more than that, especially in this climate.

Q. The roots of trees then, wherever they go, act as underdrains to draw water from the soil and discharge it into the atmosphere?

A. Yes, so long as covered with living foliage. Professor Pettenkofer's experiments have proved that during the first three months of summer the activity of this process of evaporation from the foliage is greatest. And those experiments scientifically explain the fact which has long been known, and which can be witnessed upon thousands of acres on Staten Island, that wherever forests are cut away, and brushwood allowed to remain there will be an increase of stagnant ground-water. Large and flourishing trees when standing fairly separated from each other so as to have ample foliage, as formerly at Clifton, act with amazing certainty and power in preventing the stagnation and increase of ground-water. We see how this occurs, by sucking up at the roots, and throwing off by the leaves—in vapor—eight times as much as the total rainfall on the same area.

Q. And in this way one of the conditions which all investigators are agreed is necessary to the production of malaria, may be prevented from occurring?

A. Yes, adopting the cryptogamous hypothesis, we should say that drainage might cause the death of all the sprouts from seeds deposited on the soil the previous year, as it would those of flags or cat-tails.

Q. Are instances known in which drainage, having been by any means made less effective, districts have thereby been made more subject to malarial disease?

A. Many such instances are known, not only in history like that of the Campagna, but in the records of our civil courts, in the cases which have come up for legal adjudication because of negligence to prevent the occasional overflowing or saturation of lands.

Q. Are instances known in which regions once populous and prosperous have been reduced to absolute desolation and waste by the progress of malarial poisoning?

A. There are many such. Even the Campagna, now a waste and uninhabitable, had at one period, when drained, twenty-three flourishing towns.

Q. Are there instances in which malarial poisoning, once having been common in any region, has been made less common or entirely ceased?

A. Numerous instances.

Q. Has this been the result of the use of artificial means, or of conditions which may be artificially produced?

A. Yes, always.

Q. Can these conditions be generally reduced to these two; thorough drainage and an increased growth of foliage?

A. Yes, and as the cases stand, it would be entirely correct to say that such a result has been reached only by deep and thorough drainage. Trees and tillage are adjuvants.

Q. What are the main facts of the evidence to which you referred, supplied by the region about Rome?

A. The districts soaked by the waters flowing from the Palatine, Aventine and Tarpeian Hills were for centuries excessively malarious. The elder Tarquin carried deep subterranean channels through them by which the stagnant water of the ground was collected and turned into the Tiber. They immediately became healthy and were for a long time occupied by a large population. After the invasion of the Goths the care of the drains was neglected, they gradually became obstructed and so remain to the present day. For hundreds of years these districts have in consequence been made almost unhabitable by malaria. There is a similar history of other districts about Rome, and within the city itself the records are numerous and complete which show: *first*, the prevalence for centuries of malaria; *second* the construction of drains, followed by freedom for centuries from malaria; *third* the destruction or obstruction of the drains followed again for centuries by malaria.

Q. There have been some similar experiences in France, have there not?

A. Yes, at Bordeaux and Rochefort, and in large districts of the Lorraine.

Q. And in England?

A. Many in England. In large districts where ague and fever was common twenty or thirty years ago, since the general adoption by the farmers of the system of thorough-drainage for crops, it has quite disappeared. This is true of parts of Essex, Lincolnshire, Cambridgeshire, Kent and Sussex; also of Stirlingshire and Perthshire in Scotland. There are remarkable instances also in Ireland. Hundreds of cases might be cited, in our own country, in which the disappearance of malarial disease has followed close upon land drainage, several in the western part of the State of New York. Batavia was at one time so malarious that its prosperity was seriously threatened. A public meeting was held at which a physician, Dr. J. B. Cotes, advised the drainage of some water soaked land near the town. The work was commenced by subscription, but had not proceeded far, when the profit of it became so evident that the owners of the land carried it out on their own account. Malarial disease began at once to be less prevalent and during the last sixteen years the town has been essentially free from it. Shawneetown, on the Wabash, suffered fearfully from malaria until after 1838. In the construction of a railway through it one seventh of all the men engaged died. A ditch, which at one point had to be cut to a depth of forty feet, having been opened through the town it at once became healthy and has since so remained. The terribly malarial effects that attend upon the wet-system of rice culture; and, on the other hand the speedy relief that has followed the substitution of dry-culture, are facts well known.

An illustration of another character is furnished us by Doctor Hertzog, a pupil of Professor Von Pettenkofer, the highest authority in Europe on this subject. The King of Bavaria had two stud-farms, on one of which it was found that the horses were constantly liable to fall into low condition, while on the other, with the same rules of management, they were in excellent health. The best veterinary surgeons were consulted, and many experiments in diet and regimen tried without success. Rough coats, bad digestion, sudden mysterious deaths, and a general low tone continued to prevail. Professor Von Pettenkofer, hearing of the circumstances, obtained leave to examine the subsoil of the locality. He ascertained that though superficially dry, it was a little below the surface completely saturated. He urged that the farm should be thorough-drained with tile laid not less than four feet below the surface. This was done at once, the following year the horses recovered, and there were no further complaints.

In a recent letter to me from Prof. James Law, of the Cornell University, he states that "the various forms of 'anthrax' and the 'brand' or splenic disease, are indigenous among domestic animals pastured on wet and malarial lands. These diseases, and the blackleg and other distressing maladies have disappeared whenever the lands have been thoroughly drained. In Potsdam, Prussia, the domestic animals were formerly deciminated by such diseases, but they have disappeared since the lands have been drained. Also at Elahaff, near Douanwerth, where these maladies were formerly rife, they have totally disappeared since the wet lands were drained as Prof. Von Pettenkofer advised."

Q. What is the character of the evidence that connects the occurrence of malarial disease with decaying vegetation?

A. Perhaps the most conclusive is that afforded first at the town of Urbs Vetus in Italy, which from its elevated situation might have been expected to be free from malaria, nevertheless suffered terribly. An eminent physician, Dr. Lancisi, detected the cause of it and secured an ordinance forbidding the rotting of flax near the town; malaria immediately and permanently disappeared. This experience led to the prevention of flax rotting in ditches in France, Ireland, and other countries, always with the same desired result.

Q. Is there an unusual amount of stagnant water, and water-soaked soil during every period of dry warm weather, in the immediate vicinity of each of the localities distinguished in the medical records of Staten Island for extraordinary malaria?

A. Yes, without exception.

Q. One of the largest of these districts, as you have informed us heretofore, lies near the railway on the South side. We know by personal inspection and otherwise that several hundred acres of woodland (estimated by a resident as over a thousand) have been cleared in that vicinity during the last ten years, much of it low and sedgy land. We are also informed that the construction of the railway caused obstructions to the natural water-courses from some parts of this low land. Must the increase of malaria in this vicinity be attributed wholly to these two circumstances?

A. It is to be attributed mainly to these, but also to the dropping out of cultivation of much land formerly valued and well tilled for farming purposes, but lately held only for speculation, to some extent by non-residents, water consequently finds its way more slowly through the soil; soils that once bore good crops when under the plow now bear sedge-grasses, and retentive subsoils have been formed near the surface, where formerly the plow and spade prevented this mischief. I have witnessed the same evil in certain undrained paper-city lands in Kings, Queens and Westchester counties, where malaria is quite as troublesome as on Staten Island.

Q. Do you consider that the prevalence of malarial disease on the Island is chiefly to be attributed to the difficulty with which rain water finds its way below the surface, to a depth where it will remain too cool to admit of the generation of the malarial poison?

A. That difficulty is a primary condition.

Q. What is there in the soil of Staten Island which makes it difficult for water to soak through it?

A. The drift which covers the greater part of Staten Island as well as the opposite shores of Long Island and parts of New Jersey contains, even where it is apparently most sandy, particles of feldspathic clay, ordinarily in a condition of impalpable fineness, but which were originally deposited in the form of silt. When wet, these particles expand, and, coming in contact one with another, form a slime or puddle, filling what would otherwise be the waterducts between the larger grains of sand and other particles composing the soil. The dust of the serpentine ridges which form the elevated points of the Island has a similar property. A certain form of iron (hydrous oxide), in a finely pulverized condition is also abundantly diffused in the soils of the Island; where this is washed in with the argillaceous, feldspathic or serpentine debris, it forms with it a kind of cement, impenetrable by water.

Q. The elements of this cement are in the first place washed together by rain water, but when thus properly commingled have the property of resisting its passage?

A. Yes.

Q. Does this occur upon the surface?

A. Sometimes; there are remarkable instances near the iron mines at Centreville, for instance, where rushes may be seen growing on the crowns of hills, but it is not general except where a considerable body of water is often collected by depressions of the surface, and where it evaporates slowly.

Q. Why not generally upon the surface?

A. The form of iron which has been referred to, is changed by the action of oxygen, and another form is taken which is pulverulent, and through which water passes freely. The air penetrates soil near the surface when it is not covered by water, especially when it is under tillage, and oxygen is thus transfused through it to a certain depth. Going down six or eight inches the indurated form of iron may often be found in scales, more often as a dark stain in a plate or hardpan of sand, gravel and clay, which it firmly holds together. The soil below this pan may often be found dry when that above it is mirey. I have, during the past dry Autumn, seen in various cuttings of earth-banks, an upper or second stratum yielding a constant stream of water of super-saturation, running off from a thin impervious "hard pan," while the gravel or the sand immediately beneath, and for several feet in depth, not only was not saturated, but was loose and dry. In digging drains or wells the pan is often broken through by the pick, and thrown out in pieces which appear as hard as if they had been broken out of an old water-cemented cistern wall. They will bear a sharp rap with a walking stick without fracture. Place one of these upon a plate in a dry airy room and after a day or two it will have quite disappeared. In its place will be a little heap of loose grey and reddish loam.

Q. In the western part of the Island there are extensive tracts of sandy surface, apparently very open, yet we hear complaints of malaria upon them. What is the difficulty in those cases?

A. They are frequently underlaid with the same hard-pan. The most deadly malaria is often found under such circumstances. That is the condition of the celebrated malarial plains of Walcheren in Holland.

Q. With the liability to the formation, a few inches below the surface, of a water-cement by the process which has been described, how can under drains act to relieve the surface of water? Why would there not soon be a water-holding pan above them?

A. It is a well proved fact that the earth immediately in contact with the drains, if not naturally porous, soon becomes so; if they are laid in clay the withdrawal of the water which would escape by the open joints of the drain will cause the clay to shrink and open in many fine fissures, as may often be seen in a clay bank by the road side. These fissures as soon as the water has ceased to run through them will be filled with air. Gradually, after several rains perhaps, they will extend until they have reached the water-holding pan and penetrate it; giving the air opportunity to reach and decompose the cement from below. They would behave precisely like the masses of hard-pan laid up to dry, falling into masses of powder.

Q. And tillage facilitates a similar action in dry weather from above?

A. Yes.

Q. Pools of water from twenty to fifty or a hundred yards in width are common upon the Island. Are they generally liable during droughts in the hot season to become "stagnant" in the common acceptation of the term, that is, productive of cryptograms, and of malarial poison?

A. There are upwards of a thousand such pond-holes upon the Island, and excepting in excessively wet and cloudy summers they inevitably produce vast quantities of algæ and other chryptogamous plants which are continually reproducing and decaying, and the more rapidly as the quantity of water decreases by evaporation. Such places are malarial nurseries for the Island.

Q. And, contrary to the usual belief, they are more common on the higher parts, and in rolling ground with an apparently open sandy surface than on the long and gentle, nearly level slopes?

A. Yes. They are frequent on the ridges, and on several square miles of the western parts of the Island, a space of twenty acres can hardly be found without what is called a pond-hole upon it, that is a basin, the bottom of which is cemented and covered with a vegetable deposit, often several feet in depth, sometimes covered with water and sometimes simply saturated. These are even more frequent, midway between the waters enclosing the Island than near its circumfeıence.

Q. Are the rims of these basins often rocky?

A. Not one has a complete rim of rock in place, and only a very few of them have any rock near them. They could in most cases be drained of water by a pipe laid five or six feet from the surface of the rim of the ground about them. In this respect the Island is more fortunate than any other district of equal extent, no further removed from the city. To relieve some portions of our suburban districts upon Long Island, Westchester and Queens Counties, and New Jersey, from malaria, deep excavation and works of far more formidable character and cost will be required. Unfortunate as the reputation of Staten Island is for malaria, the sources of it can be more speedily and completely removed than those in other suburban districts.

Q. We were told by citizens of Northfield that in the low flat district between New Springville, Graniteville and Morning-Star Road, over which the waters of the Willow Brook are spread, that deep drainage would be impracticable on account of a natural dam of rock. What are the facts in that case?

A. There is an impervious ridge of trap rock thickly overlaid by diluvial gravel, extending from the shore near Port Richmond to Long Neck, between which and the upland, east of Springville, there is an extensive basin which receives, from Willow Brook and other sources, some two million gallons of water a day, which, in some cases covers large surfaces, making marshes; in others, saturates the soil just below the surface. In dry weather much of this water stagnates and breeds malaria, and the whole district, together with its borders is at night, or whenever the sun is obscured, very chilly. There is in this quarter, consequently, a special liability to pulmonary complaints (as well as to malarial), which are comparatively rare in the greater part of the Island. For this, as well as other reasons, it is very desirable that the region in question should be relieved of its excessive dampness. There are two methods of operating for this purpose. The inflowing streams should be controlled and deflected from it, and it should be drained. Professor Newberry assisted me in a careful examination of the supposed obstacles, and is of the opinion that there is nothing in the way of the perfect drainage of the whole area to any depth desirable for sanitary or agricultural purposes. It only requires a little care in engineering the course and grade of the outlets. Most of the land but. for its dampness is very fertile, and by drainage would be rendered available for highly salubrious residences, and profitable culture. Much of it is now worse than useless, as the emanations from it unfavorably affect the health of an important part of the town of Northfield and the reputation of the whole Island.

Q. Are there any basins on the higher parts of the Island formed by ridges of the serpentine rocks?

A. None such are found which are due to the rock. The serpentine ledges will not, like trap or granite, hold water. On the contrary, the serpentine and talcose rocks as they are found on this Island, are very remarkably absorptive rocks. (See Statements of Experiments in Appendix.)

Q. All the class of rocks which are commonly referred to on Staten Island as serpentine have also the property of changing temperature much more slowly than most rocks have they not?

A. Yes. They are peculiarly non-radiating. That is, the serpentine rocks when of the varieties we see on this island, namely, the soft steatite, dolomite, talc and magnesia, transmit heat very slowly, but retain it tenaciously.

Q. Is it for this reason they are valued for the beds of ovens and in the form of soap-stone are formed into stoves and foot-warmers? That is to say because, although they heat up more slowly, they retain heat and yield it as a gentle warmth for a very much longer time than iron or any ordinary hard building stone?

A. That is the reason.

Q. These qualities pertain to the whole of the elevated masses of serpentine which we find on Staten Island?

A. Yes, and this ridge of soap-stone and porous magnesian rock extends from New Brighton Point to St. Andrew's Church and the Fresh Kills at Richmond village.

Q. These masses are, in effect, two ridges of rocks, which are projected boldly to a height of from two to nearly four hundred feet above tide level, and together are nearly seven miles in length, surrounded by a low sloping base of drift and alluvium, and at a distance of a mile or two by tidal water; must they not on account of their singularly absorptive and singularly non-radiating qualities have considerable influence upon the local climate.

A. There are facts which indicate a certain degree of influence highly favorable to health from them, but, they are complicated by the phenomena produced by the superficial conditions which have been described, and which would be removed by thorough-drainage. We are warranted in stating that if these rocky ridges were of granite or trap, and exposed as they would be, they would vastly increase some of the conditions which now render some of the uplands unhealthful. *The* rocks we actually have on this Island are highly favorable to this natural requirements for healthfulness. They are even more favorable than chalk cliffs or sandstone would be in the situation.

Q. How do they affect the local climate?

A. Their effect, if not contracted by the superficial conditions referred to, must be at all times a moderating one. By absorbing moisture, they would tend in cold damp periods to limit the reduction of temperature at the surface of the ground, by exhaling moisture, they would equally tend to restrain the elevation of temperature in hot dry periods. Radiating heat more slowly than other rocks, or than ordinary soils and substrata of soils they would tend to give unusual length to the process of a general change of temperature. They would for instance, part with less heat late in the day or early at night than is usually given off from the Earth's surface, and *more* late at night, when the temperature of the air is coolest—thus moderating the common chilliness of the latter part of the night. When this chilliness is extreme delicate persons are often most unfavorably affected by it. They would tend to prolong the Autumn and to make the changes of Spring less sudden, extreme and trying.

Q. You say they would do so. Are such effects observable at all as a matter of fact?

A. They are, distinctly—have been often remarked by observing men, and the advantages thus sometimes gained by delicate persons in certain parts of the Island are recognized by the older physicians upon it. They would be much more marked were it not for the hard-pan crust which so generally is found in the soil, and which has precisely the opposite qualities.

Q. Which opposite qualities may be completely changed by thorough drainage?

A. Yes, not may be only—they have been already to a certain extent in several places.

Q. South of this are there anywhere on the coast masses of rock found having strikingly absorptive or non-radiating qualities?

A. In Florida, the coral reefs.

Q. Any to the North?

A. Nowhere on the coast.

Q. Is there not a somewhat similar quality in the rock which forms the mass of the Isle of Wight, and does it not aid to give it its special reputation for healthfulness?

A. Yes, but the elevated parts of the Isle of Wight, as well as other health resorts in chalk cliff regions, are barren wastes in comparison with the Staten Island hills, and less healthful than Staten Island could be made.

Q. Do you know what the effect of that reputation for salubrity in the Isle of Wight has been?

A. It has brought families of the most intelligent and refined classes and many wealthy persons to build and permanently reside upon that island; large numbers of such residents have gone thither from all portions of Great Britain, and various other countries, and thus a great value has been given to the land which would otherwise have remained almost worthless.

Q. Below one of the principal ranges of hills (sometimes called Grimes Hill, formerly and more properly "Signal Hill") in which serpentine rock and iron ore both appear in large masses, there is a broad stretch of flattish land upon which the passage of water flowing from the hills is evidently slow and often obstructed. The character of the herbage and the moss on the trees also indicate a saturated soil. According to our hypothesis this district (the Clove Valley, Concord flats and Rocky Hollow) should be a seed bed of malaria. How do medical records bear out the suggestion?

A. The facts are that at some points, where the evidence of an arrested flow of water and of water-soaked soil over considerable areas is most obvious, malarial disease not only prevails but fever of a pernicious type, has occurred more than once during the past five years. There are records of its occurrence, in the same localities, going back to 1827. The amount of malarial disease, of the common types, has been increasing, however, as woods have been felled, and the surface of cleared land has been less cultivated. There are but few households in or near these flatlands which have not suffered from malarial disease of late years. The same is true of most of the flatter surfaces below the hills throughout the Island.

Q. Is the malarial poison generated in these beds liable to be wafted up to and over the high ridges which overlook them?

A. It is. They are nurseries of evil to all more elevated grounds which chance to be so situated as to receive currents of air from them.

Q. Are there any facts going to show that persons resident in houses at a considerable elevation above these seed beds are poisoned by malaria while at their residences?

A. Facts such as this for instance—a physician reports that he has recently visited a lady who for weeks suffered from malarial poisoning; she has scarcely been out from her own elevated grounds, not at all at night, and has lived wholly in the second story of her house, at an elevation of three hundred feet above tide water and two hundred and fifty above the lowest point of the malarious valley upon which her windows open, and from which they are half a mile distant.

Q. There is reported to be about six thousand acres of salt marsh on the shore of the Island, chiefly on the continental side. Is this malarious, and if so, can it be rendered harmless by drainage?

A. The actual salt marsh, that is to say, marsh reached by the tide from the sea, is not more than thirty-five hundred acres in extent, and there is no evidence that this is in the least malarious. The immediate margins of such marshes in fact, are, in some cases, where well drained and cultivated, exceptionally free from malarial diseases. In others such marginal land, once malarial, has been rendered healthy by drainage, the salt marsh remaining undrained. Little streams flow from the upland into most of the salt marshes, the channels of which are generally tortuous and obstructed. The fresh water pools and marshes thus formed above the salt marshes are often highly malarious. Little estuaries at the head of salt inlets such as are found at Factoryville, at Richmond Valley, at the outlet of Taylor's Brook and near Seguine's Point are also apt to be malarious. In all these cases however it is the fresh, and not the salt water, that establishes the condition of malaria. From personal inspection and inquiry, I judge that the quantity of such back water marsh, which is not actually salt, may be estimated at about two thousand acres.

Q. Are ponds of water, which have no visible outflow, sources of malaria, even though the water in them is never exhausted by evaporation?

A. There are a few such ponds on the island, in which there is seldom any appearance of algae or other vegetable growths. Such ponds, in some parts, are usually quite deep, and they are, to some extent, supplied by springs. In these there is a constant circulation between the deep cold parts and the surface, so that the water in them seems nowhere to become sufficiently stagnant and warm for the evolution of malaria. But such condition is seldom met with, and ponds can be kept from becoming malarial only by care. If, in an extremely hot period, the water should reach a temperature of sixty or sixty-five degrees Fahrenheit, and much vegetable waste were in and around it, malaria would probably be produced.

Q. Are such ponds unfavorable to health?

A. Provided there were no shallow bays opening upon them the soil of which they soaked, and that their shores did not greatly contract in Summer, leaving long slopes covered with decaying organic matter to putrify in the sun, they would be generally favorable to health. The necessary conditions of healthfulness in ponds, which have a value for their effect in landscapes, could easily be established and maintained artificially, but they seldom are so. What commonly occurs is indicated in the record here exhibited, which gives a series of measurement made upon the margin of a pond at frequent intervals during the Summer. The pond is nearly circular, and on May 15th measured 64 feet in diameter. On June 3d the diameter was 5 feet less, the water having receded 2 feet 6 inches, leaving a border of offensive matter. June 10th the water had receded from original outline 5 feet.

June 17	5 6	Aug.		2 14	Sept. 2	12	
" 24	5	" 8		12	" 7	12 4	
July 3	8	. " 11		15	" 14	12 6	
" 9	5	" 19		15	" 28	14	
" 16	7	" 25		15	" 30	13	
" 21	8 6	" 28		12	Oct. 3	12	
" 24	12 5				" 7	12 6	
					" 15	12 8	
					" 18	10	

It will be seen that with every shower, and according to the varying degree of sun-heat, the width of the exposed margin varied, but that not till the 18th of October did the water return to the original margin. Conditions more exactly in accordance with those laid down by Sir Thomas Watson, as necessary to the production of malaria could hardly be contrived, and, as before said, there are probably at least a thousand shallow-edged ponds on the Island in which a similar process occurs every Summer. The pond-hole to which the foregoing records relate is situated in Westfield, and the observations were undertaken simply to ascertain the facts for the information of a sanitary officer in the year 1869.

Q. We have seen many open drains leading from the ponds—many miles of them altogether. In frequent cases they simply reduce the depth of water, not wholly removing it from the surface; in others they barely take the water off the foul bottom, and in most cases where drains of this class have been made more than one season we have found them obstructed. A landowner who had himself made a great many, and who was extremely dissatisfied with the result stated that nine times out of ten some obstruction began to form within a week after they were made, the causes at the beginning being various, sometimes the work of birds or beasts, sometimes of children, sometimes of sportsmen or ramblers who throw in stepping stones, sometimes the lodging of reeds, brush or leaves, sometimes the caving down of the bank. What is the effect of such drains?

A. In all the instances named, and in by far the larger number of cases, in which open drains have been made on the Island, their effect has been to increase malaria by opening to the sun a larger extent of soil, thinly covered by water, or not all covered but saturated, either at or a little below the surface exposed. Open drains are usually succeeded by increase of malaria for a time immediately succeeding their construction, but such is not the case with good tile drains.

Q. And many of the smaller water-courses, farm ditches and road gutters, gullies and culverts being of the same character, do they have the same effect?

A. Yes. Being easily obstructed they form pools, keeping the soil saturated, under conditions favorable to the collection of decaying vegetation.[5]

[5] The following observation taken from the Minutes of Information, laid before Parliament in 1852, with regard to the open water courses in the districts of the country surrounding London, apply to all the old brook channels on Staten Island, near which a considerable number

Q. Road side ditches, then, as at present formed, are often a nuisance?

A. Yes.

Q. It is generally believed that the *immediate* effect of drainage is to increase malaria. Is that a necessary result of it?

A. It is not. Unless some special precautions are taken, there is danger that malaria will be increased for a short period if drainage is executed during hot dry weather, none if it is carried on in the Autumn. In any case, the danger can be overcome by applying some cheap disinfectant to the newly exposed soil. This has been proved in the extensive operations of Mr. Orange Judd and Mr. Poppenhusen during the last two years near Flushing.

Q. How extended are the records of observation and experience upon which the views are based which have been expressed regarding the origin of malaria in damp and warm decaying vegetation, and the practicability of its eradication where established, by the means indicated?

A. Observations have been making in several localities of Europe almost constantly for centuries, and as malaria has frequently been very destructive to the strength of armies, and monastic organizations, and has frustrated plans of colonization, the investigation of its causes and the records of observations thereupon are by no means limited to those of medical men. The records of observations fill thousands of pages of our most trustworthy medical and historical literature.

---

of suburban residences have been established.

"When there are no floods the water . . . moves sluggishly over uneven bottoms, or lodges in stagnant pools in these ditches, giving off insalubrious effluvia. . . . Many of the ditches are used for the outfalls for the drainage of suburban houses, and with the addition of such house drainage the effluvium becomes at times highly noxious and even fatal. The courses of these open water-courses were marked by excessive ravages of the cholera amongst the population living near them.

With regard to wayside drains of the common form, it was remarked that they were open to similar objections, "namely their unsuitableness to small runs of water; wide bottoms intended to be flat, but so irregularly shaped as to impede effectually the current of all but very large floods of water with considerable flows." [1871.]

Q. Can the fact be explained that the same conditions which on Staten Island apparently give rise to malaria, fail to do so a short distance to the northward?

A. There are a number of trees and plants which are common on Staten Island, but which are very rare, or not found at all north of it. There are others that ripen reproducing seed here which, while they will grow from seed ripened here, will not themselves produce ripe seed much further North, unless perhaps in an unusually warm dry Summer, such as this has been. Such facts are, perhaps, not more unaccountable than that of the special liability of this immediate vicinity to malaria; difference of climate, which seems slight as defined by the thermometer, is adequate to account for great differences of vegetation, and in respect to malaria. As a matter of fact, malarial disease is not at all rare much to the northward of this, and in those parts commonly exempt from it, it often breaks out when from any unusual circumstance, such as the drawing down of a pond at midsummer, a large surface of rich and saturated soil is exposed to be more than usually heated. Such has been the case near Plymouth on the coast, and near Northampton in the interior, of Massachusetts. Such is at present the case in localities near some of the tributary ponds of the Croton Aqueduct, where it has been unknown before, but has been induced by an unusual lowering of the pond-water.

Q. Understanding that all marshy places and stagnant pools of water, not salt, are sources of malaria which may be remedied by drainage, would their drainage relieve the Island from malarial disease, or would the poison continue to arise from sources not superficially evident, especially from damp ground, the subsoil of which is a hard pan or of a tenacious character?

A. Malaria is liable to arise from such grounds. The thorough-drainage of all retentive soils can alone insure absolute safety.

Q. By thorough-drainage is meant under drainage, adequate to prevent the soil from remaining saturated with water after rain has ceased to fall?

A. Yes; a soil that remains saturated for a day after rain ceases (except in frost), is not thoroughly and sanitarily drained. Sanitary drainage, like agricultural drainage, requires open-jointed pipes, so laid down as to preclude such saturation.

Q. It is generally understood, in districts where thorough-drainage is general, that a common open-jointed tile, after the cracking process (in the stiff soil), which has been described, will completely free soil from water, except such as is held in the pores of its particles, in a space about ten feet wide for every foot of distance from the surface at which it is laid, estimating approximately for ordinary circumstances. If, then, tile are laid thirty feet apart and three feet deep, or forty feet apart and four feet deep, is it to be expected that the locality so treated will be rendered perfectly safe against malaria of local origin?

A. Yes; that may reasonably be expected under all ordinary circumstances.

Q. Would a less thorough drainage be adequate?

A. It should not be possible for the soil to long remain saturated within two feet of the surface near a dwelling. If it is, exhalations, causing disease, will be liable to rise from it. To make sure against this danger, drains must be laid little, if any, less than three feet, below the surface. Where there are or have been ponds with accumulations of vegetable matter in the bottom, the drains should be carried, if practicable, below the vegetable matter, and, at any rate, four to five feet below the top of it, otherwise there will be a liability, from the unusual porosity of the soil, to moist exhalations rising through it.

Q. Where the foundations of a dwelling and the land about it for a certain space have been thoroughly underdrained, and where considerable foliage interposes between such a space and any exterior source of malaria, are the liabilities to malarial disease greatly reduced, and, in general, is there little danger that malarial disease would be contracted by its inmates, except by exposure outside their own ground?

A. Instances of exemption so obtained are not unfrequent, even in the midst of very malarious districts, but they somewhat rarely occur, unless where several adjoining properties are so improved; that is to say, where the land is thorough-drained over a somewhat larger space than an ordinary house lot. Examples are furnished in the four adjoining drained farms of Messrs. Garretson, Underhill, Cortelyou, and Mrs. Banker, near Fresh Kills, and on the estate of Mr. Crooke, near Gifford's. Adjoining each of these there has been much malarial disease, but the people living upon them, to the number of seventy, have scarcely had a symptom of it. In another quarter the adjoining places of Messrs. Meyers, Simonson and Luling may be referred to. They were formerly very malarious, and the families living on them before their drainage, since living elsewhere, on the island, continue to suffer from malarial poison, there first contracted. The families which remained upon them after their thorough-drainage, recovered, and have since suffered not at all, and those who have moved to them since their drainage have lived for years upon them without suffering at all from any form of malarial trouble. Beyond the influence of the underdrains, the neighborhood is still highly malarious.

Q. The difficulty of obtaining outlets by which the water collected would be at once removed harmlessly to a distance, is one of the obstacles to efficient private drainage, is it not?

A. No doubt it is. For example, none of the property on the Fingerboard Road, or upon Pennsylvania Avenue, can find outlet for necessary drainage except by artificial channels through other property.

Q. Malarial poison being established in a locality where there is excessive moisture upon the surface, and where decaying vegetable matter, and the liability to a considerable degree of heat from the direct rays of the sun occur together, and these conditions being maintained through a series of years, is there reason to believe that something from the organic waste of a large and increasing population being added to them, malarial poison is increased?

A. Yes; not only so, but to malarial poison others are added which come from domestic wastes, and the compound effects are of a very dangerous character, often causing incurable diseases and fatal epidemics.

Q. Are all persons, of whatever habits, when living, or passing near the places where these poisonous compounds form in the air, liable to suffer from them?

A. They are. Good habits, good houses, and good food can not insure protection against such sources of danger.

Q. And the distance to which they may be wafted, without losing fatal power, can it be strictly limited? May it, under special conditions of the atmosphere, be much extended?

A. Yes. Malaria may be wafted overland and up hill sides some distance. There is ample proof that when favored with a warm and moist atmosphere the malarial poison may be wafted for a mile or more, especially when borne along the course of valleys and hill sides.

Q. We have seen several localities on the east and north shores, where the conditions exist under which these fatal compounds are liable to be generated, have we not?

A. Yes.

Q. Generally they are to be found near the outlets of the island streams, are they not?

A. Yes.

Q. As communities enlarge near these streams, it will be essential to safety that these household wastes should not be discharged into them, will it not?

A. Yes.

Q. And will the planting or preservation of trees on their banks be a reasonable precaution against malaria?

A. It will.

Q. Other things being equal, no trees being planted, no drainage of consequence effected, is malaria likely to increase on this island with an increase of population, and is it thus likely to grow more and more unhealthy?

A. More than liable. If no efficient preventive measures are taken, it is practically sure to do so—practically sure, with any considerable increase of population, to become extremely unhealthy. The exceptions will be found only where there is exceptionally good drainage, natural or artificial.

Q. On the other hand, can we feel wholly confident that the removal or prevention of stagnant water, or of prolonged

232

saturation, in conjunction with a high Summer temperature, in all places where dead vegetation occurs above or immediately below the surface, would be followed by the relief of the island from malarial disease in all its forms?

A. There can be no reasonable doubt of it.

Q. Would such relief be complete and immediate?

A. Yes; but in very retentive soils drains do not always instantly remove saturation of the surface for reasons already indicated.

Q. If all the small shallow ponds, and all the marshy places in which water stands above the surface, or in which its presence just below the surface is obvious, during the Summer, were drained, so that water could not stand in them, within three feet of the surface, would the island be freed from malaria within a year?

A. The liability to contract malarial disease would at least be reduced in a very important degree within that time. It might take longer to eradicate the poison from the system of those who had previously taken it, and as the soil of the island in most districts may now be supposed to contain the seeds of malaria, which only require favorable circumstances to become sources for the evolution of the poison, it is probable that in all localities where the subsoil is at all impervious, and the surface is apt to remain long saturated, malaria would still be produced to a limited extent. The total amount of the malarial element in the air of the island would perhaps be reduced by the drainage of all places where water is obviously stagnant close beneath or upon the surface, of all rush-bearing land, for example, as well as pond-holes, to one-tenth what it is at present. Almost any person, in ordinary health, would resist what remained, and the number of those who would be affected by it would gradually become less.

Q. Your statement would seem to imply that the resisting power of the system was gradually sapped where a man lives exposed to a high degree of malaria—and supposing the degree of malaria to be reduced, his resisting power gradually increases. Is that the accepted view?

A. It is. Experience indicates that a general, even though

not absolutely complete extinction of the common sources of malaria, would have the effect which has been stated. The amount of the malarial disease might be quickly reduced to possibly one-tenth what it now is. A slow and gradual reduction below this would subsequently follow, the rate of reduction being a fluctuating one, varying with the seasons.

Q. That statement, that the resisting powers of a man become less, the more malaria he is exposed to, and that his resisting powers become greater, the more attenuated the malaria he is exposed to, seems to be at variance with the common notion that a man may become acclimated to malaria. Is that notion not accepted by physicians?

A. What is termed acclimatization, and hardening in malarial regions is attended by such impairment of constitutional health as to be as undesirable as fever and ague itself.

Q. So long as the people of Long Island and New Jersey opposite, neglect drainage, what danger would there be of malaria produced there, drifting to Staten Island and destroying the benefits of drainage upon it?

A. None what ever. Staten Island is wholly responsible for the malaria under which it suffers, and it commands within itself the complete remedy for it; malaria seldom travels far over salt-water, never at all except under the influence of a current of highly-heated air. Numerous cases in proof of this might be cited from the records of our military posts and naval stations. The fact is well established.

Q. Can you refer to instances in which belts of trees have been found to protect localities near them from malarial poison?

A. To many. Augusta, Georgia, may be mentioned as one in which a large community was kept nearly free from malarial diseases for many years, by a surrounding border of forest trees left for that purpose. A portion of these trees having been felled, malarial troubles immediately afflicted many households.[6]

[6] The surrounding of houses by trees at a little distance is desirable, but the shading of houses by trees in the midst of malarial districts seems to increase the liability of their inmates to be poisoned. [1871.]

Q. To what diseases, apart from those attributable to imperfect drainage, if any, is Staten Island subject, more than the adjacent continent, the comparison being especially with parts equally distant from New York?

A. None; pulmonary catarrhs which prevail in certain localities to an unusual degree, are attributable to excessive ground-moisture, and would be relieved by drainage. The same is true of rheumatic and neuralgic affections which prevail in some damp localities.

Q. To what diseases if any less in parts where ground moisture, either from natural or artificial causes, is not excessive?

A. Pulmonary diseases, especially consumption;[7] all continued fevers, especially typhoid fevers; degenerative diseases, as scrofula and cancer; uterine diseases both of tissue and function.

Q. Is the Island generally believed by those physicians who have been long resident upon it to possess certain special and peculiar advantages in this respect?

A. It is. Where there is no complication from malaria, the greater part of the Island is unquestionably a sanitarium for persons afflicted by, or having a tendency to any of the several classes of disease which have been named, and still more especially for overtaxed nervous systems, and mentally overworked persons. In all its non-malarial positions, this island is, unquestionably, one 'of the most healthful places in the world, and the most invigorating of any of the suburbs of New York. There have been an extraordinary number of instances of prolonged vigor and great age among the native Staten Islanders, especially in families who have lived in those parts, while up to this time there has been little or no malaria.

Q. Is the advantage which the Island is reputed to possess in respect to consumption, due at all to the malarial elements of its climate?

A. Not at all. *Malaria has no advantages.* This Island is freest from pulmonary consumption in the dwellings and dis-

---

[7] This remark is limited to the early stages and the cause of consumption, namely, the deposit and progress of the tubercles. [1871.]

235

tricts where there is no malaria. There is most suffering from it where there is most malaria. Consumption is known to be particularly associated with wetness of grounds about dwellings.

Q. Would this advantage, in respect to pulmonary complaints, be increased, or lessened, and in what degree by the same means that would relieve the Island of malaria?

A. Greatly increased.

Q. The same means being used, what in general terms might be anticipated of the quality of the air upon the Island, with respect to the counteraction of the effects of the irritating, wasting, and debilitating conditions to which men spending their days in the crowded parts of a large town are specially subject?

A. The air of the Island where not at all malarious, has an effect more decidedly remedial to that class of ailments than any other within easy distance from the city.

Q. Thoroughly drained, would the condition of Staten Island be such that physicians might generally be expected to recommend it as a place to be resorted to on account of its special sanitary advantages?

A. They would undoubtedly do so, and people would come to it from far and wide, as they now do in England to the Channel Islands on account of their climate.

Q. It appears then that simply by thorough-drainage it might be transformed from a region threatened with devastation, to a region offering really unparalleled advantages of residence to large numbers of persons?

A. Unquestionably it might.

Q. Thorough-drainage being accomplished, and trees being generally planted on the road-sides, what might we say are the number of chances in a thousand that malarial diseases would not only entirely disappear from the Island, but that it would become as healthy as the elevated regions of the Continent at some distance from the sea, to which people resort on account of their supposed healthfulness; the granite hills of New England for instance?

A. There is not one chance in a thousand that it would

fail to become more healthful than any of them. The drainage being really thorough, reasonable caution being used to prevent common nuisances, and the occupation of the land being such as to favor a considerable growth of foliage and clean cultivation, it is perfectly reasonable to anticipate that no place on the continent would equal Staten Island in healthfulness. There are perhaps a few localities, and but a few, which could be rendered equally healthy by similar means.

Chapter III. Practical Recommendations

Our undertaking is to suggest to you a series of propositions, which, if you should see fit to adopt them, will serve to determine, approximately, the place, scope, and general proportions and relations of the more controlling features of a practicable plan for the improvement of Staten Island.

WE start with the conviction which it was the principal object of our first chapter to justify, that the improvements required to secure the greatest possible prosperity to your Island, are such as will present the largest number of sites for dwellings, furnished with urban public conveniences and associated with permanent and generally available advantages of landscape and sylvan beauty, all accessible with regularity and comfort from the business quarter of New York, and all preeminently healthful.

In regard to this last condition we have in our second chapter distinguished two groups of facts, a disposition to look at which apart, accounts for the conflicting opinions often expressed in regard to the chances of health upon the island.

These two groups of easily observed sanitary facts—those which exhibit the effects of a subtle and generally weak poison, pervading the air of the larger part of the island, and the field of which is surely extending, and those which indicate special exemption from certain classes of ailments, and which account for numerous instances of remarkably prolonged vigor and longevity, especially in the older stock of islanders, we have connected with two corresponding series of topographical and geological facts.

The central element of one of these groups is that of a great mass of absorptive non-radiating rock[8] and of a strong argillaceous and ferruginous soil situated in the midst of a natural air tunnel opening from the humid and equably tempered reservoir of the ocean; the central element of the other is that of the thin metallic, nonabsorptive and strongly radiating crust which under a condition of prolonged saturation is formed within your superficial soil.

There are three circumstances attending and resulting from this condition of saturation of the surface which need your distinct recognition.

First, while it has, chiefly because of the topographical changes which have attended the increase of population, the holding of land on speculation and the decline of agriculture, been much more general of late years, it has always been sufficiently so to prevent a realization of the special advantages inherent in the geological structure of the island the proper effects of which, though not wholly lost, have yet remained indistinct, undemonstrable, and, from a commercial point of view valueless. Disclosed and developed their commercial value would be very great.

Second, under certain circumstances, and in combination with other causes, it produces the air poison, concerning which we find that from year to year it is increasing, at the same time that the appreciation of its evils by the more intelligent, thrifty and able portion of the public, and the general prejudice against localities where they are liable to be incurred, is also increasing. Put the two conditions together and they

[8] A statement of trials made at our suggestion, at the School of Mines, to test the absorbent qualities of the rock, is expected to be received in time to be inserted in the Appendix. A measurement of radiative or heat-holding qualities is making, the result of which will not probably be reached in time for this report, but Prof. Newberry authorizes us to say that it is so far advanced as to justify a general conclusion, and that this sustains our conviction that these qualities are sufficiently distinct and extraordinary to account for special local climatic conditions upon this island. [1871.]

involve ruin to Staten Island, unless its tendency to grow more
and more malarious can be reversed. For it may be assumed
with perfect confidence that, whatever has been the case heretofore, no man of average intelligence, unless under compulsion
of poverty, will, in the early future, move from New York
Island to any suburban district which is commonly reputed to
be malarious. It may also be assumed that so long as any part
of the island deserves the reputation of being malarious, that
reputation will practically attach to all parts.

Third, the condition of a prolonged and high saturation
of the soil, is so distributed over the island, the seed-beds in
which malaria is chiefly propagated are so scattered, and the
poison so pervasive that there is little or no inducement to
improvement by individual or local enterprise. Again and again
we hear of properties selling at less than the cost of improvements which have been made on them, solely because those
who would dwell in them cannot be assured of exemption
from the danger of malaria propagated elsewhere.

To recapitulate; this condition of saturation of the soil locks
up a treasure such as no other suburb, and probably, no other
community in North America, can possess; it poisons the air
and threatens the ruin of the island by prejudicing the public
against all parts of it as a residence, and it forbids private
enterprise and capital from being employed to overcome these
two evils.

Here lies, then, the arch enemy of your island. There are
two ways of dealing with him. One is to deny his existence,
or to insist that his power for evil is local and restricted, and
a matter of limited individual and local concern; to say that
there are some truths which it is not best to utter, to curse
those who make any public admission of your actual suffering
and danger, and generally to play the penny-wise, pound-
foolish poltroon.

The other is to look all the facts fairly in the face, study
them deliberately and fully, and then devise and steadily pursue whatever course shall be necessary to a success which
shall be really worth something. A conviction that the last
is the wiser way has given existence to your Commission.

The means by which saturation of the soil may be prevented, to the extent required to lay open the locked-up wealth
of the island, are well established. During the last thirty years
they have been applied with invariable success upon not less,
probably, than a million acres of land. They consist in the
laying of a sufficient number of open-jointed pipes, generally
from three to four feet below the surface, so connected and
graded as to form unbroken descending channels for water;
this is *thorough-drainage*. The cost may be estimated at one
hundred dollars an acre. Elsewhere the primary object of the
operation has not been sanitary benefit but increased agricultural productiveness. The effect is not to make the soil, previously liable to saturation, on an average necessarily dryer, but
more porous and permeable, so that it will hold and transmit
water, in moderate and desirable quantity, not only downward
but upward as well, as a lamp wick does oil. A district of
country that has been thorough-drained is less dry during
periods of drought than it was before. Its spring is hastened,
its autumn prolonged, its winter delayed and shortened; the
temperature of the soil at these seasons being elevated from
ten to fifteen degrees of Fahrenheit, while in extremely hot,
dry weather, the surface must be cooler than before.[9] Its productiveness in nearly all ordinary farm crops is increased,
never less than sixteen per cent, and not unfrequently more
than doubled. In view of these and other agricultural advantages great sums of money have elsewhere been spent by land
owners in thorough-drainage. But where agricultural productiveness is so small an element in the value of land as it is
generally on Staten Island this inducement will not operate.
The motive of personal and family safety and comfort, and
of gaining an advanced demand for healthful land would do
so, to a certain extent, immediately, but for two reasons, one
of which, the danger of wafted malaria, we have named; the

[9] We know of no experiments on this last point, but theoretically
it must be so, and we have no doubt that it could be proved by
trial with the thermometer. All our other statements as to the effect
of drainage rest on abundant, accurately measured experience. [1871.]

other is the frequent difficulty and cost of obtaining good outlets for private drains.

Let these two difficulties be overcome—and we know that many land owners are prepared to begin thorough-draining. Once begun at many points, and its advantages in giving increased value to land made evident, it would soon become frequent, and then rapidly general. Overcome these two difficulties, then, and you may look forward with confidence to a not very distant period when your hidden treasure shall have been unlocked, and Staten Island be known of all men as the healthiest dwelling place of the metropolis, and probably the healthiest in the whole country. Every other desirable improvement will follow, provided only the way to it is not obstructed by ill-considered, time-serving, catch-penny plans of "improvement."

The overcoming by public means of these two obstacles, which it is certain that private means will not overcome, we hold to present so much the most important problems for your study, that all others beside are insignificant.

Let us face the first.

The principal source of malaria upon the island is to be found in the dishes of the surface where water accumulates in the form of puddles, ponds and swamps. Though by no means the only source, it may be reasonably assumed that if this were overcome, the poison in the air would be so much diluted that it would rarely produce fever and ague, and it would be possible by local thorough-drainage, especially if free-spreading trees should be common, to perfectly guard any private place of an acre or more in extent, and certainly any considerable neighborhood in which the land-owners would combine for the purpose, against wafted malaria. It may also be reasonably assumed that if the more distinct effects of malaria should thus become no longer common on any part of the island, a fair general reputation for healthfulness would return to it; that it would at least compare favorably with any other suburb accessible in the same time from Wall Street. Private enterprise might then be depended on to carry forward the work of improvement to the higher ultimate stage which is desired.

All propagating grounds of malaria then, of the character we have indicated, must be abolished and prevented, and this can be accomplished only by their legally enforced under-draining.

To compel private citizens to open a conduit from every dish in the surface of their land all the way to the sea or to a natural safe outlet would be obviously unfair. To undertake directly the under draining by public administration of every such dish would involve an interference with ordinary privileges of property very undesirable. A mixed system, therefore, seems to be essential—a system, that is to say, in which the public shall supply certain advantages now wanting to private undertakings and with the offer of which it shall make compulsory the abatement of every distinct malarial nuisance on private ground.

The public should provide safe and convenient outfalls at the general charge of the whole Island, from the sea up to the point where *direct* benefit to the land-owners would result from the laying of under-drains. Beyond that point it should cause pipes to be carried on to the malarial dishes, either by undertakings of the land-owners personally, or by its own agents, the cost in either case, except for engineering and superintendence, to be a charge upon the land directly benefited.

This having been done, outfalls for thorough-drainage would have been generally provided; where they were wanting they should be supplied; it might then be best, in order to hasten an advance toward the end finally to be attained, to offer a release during a series of years, from a part of the taxation which would otherwise fall upon land which should be thorough-drained.

Although we have spoken of the public outfall drains as of two classes, and as if they might be constructed in two periods, there is no doubt that the localities to be reached in the first stage are so scattered and so frequent throughout the Island, and the incidental advantages of every rod of such drains which may be laid are so great, that economy would require that the process should be [a] continuous one. The only important question that remains then in our present duty regarding them, is as to their form, size, extent and frequency. This we shall take up later in the present report.

We can not pass from the general consideration of this subject, however, without again expressing our deliberate opinion, and offering you our most earnest advice, that, if it is thought necessary to neglect everything else that we shall recommend in order to relieve the island of malaria, everything else should be neglected. Nothing threatens your interests, nothing even now compares in importance as a drawback to your prosperity, with this evil of saturated surfaces. Do not think that we undervalue other means of improvement when we say that ten times the money it would cost to carry out our suggestions in this respect, put into roads and railways and steamboats, would ultimately bring you not nearly as much profit. We doubt, indeed, if this Hydra be not soon manfully dealt with, whether cheap, rapid, frequent communication with New York would be at all a benefit to the island. It would not bring a class of people here in large numbers who would be able and willing to pay an advanced price for land and for improvements. It might bring, and it might tend to make the island a miserable, squalid lodging place for, ignorant, uncircumspect, unthrifty men. In short, blocking the way to all suitable improvements, it might fix a character upon the island such as would destroy all hope of any great advance in the value of its real estate.

Once put the island in the way of some relief from this danger, and the value of other means of improvement can not be too highly estimated; but you cannot build without a foundation, and this must be the foundation of all improvement for Staten Island. We feel that if we cannot convince you of this, all our advice must go for nothing.

At the outset of our inquiry, facts came to our knowledge which impressed us with the conviction that, second only to the problem of malaria—a long way following it, but a long way preceding everything else—would be the problem of providing water for household use in considerable parts of the island.

The difficulties of obtaining wholesome water in sufficient quantity, are here and there already so great, especially on the eastern part of the island, even in favorable seasons, that they are fully overcome only by the more enterprising, intelligent, and well-to-do householders. The water from some wells in constant use near the shore is perceptibly brackish, that from some others is impregnated with salts of magnesia, and has a decided action on the bowels. At some points wells have been sunk to a great depth without reaching springs; there are others, the labor of drawing water from which is so great, on account of their depth, that it puts a strong check on the consumption of the water they yield, which after all is liable to be turbid. But the worst misfortune is that of the liability to organic impurity of the water used where population is growing somewhat dense; this has, without doubt, already been in some cases a cause of fatal disorders, and it is quite certain that with no great enlargement of population, it would render the whole community of the island especially liable to suffer from dangerous epidemic diseases. (See analysis of water from a well in Edgewater in appendix.)

None of these conditions are general, nor do their consequences, as yet, perhaps, seriously affect your prosperity; but if the island advances as we expect it to do, the localities and the number of people in each affected by them will increase, and some means of radical relief will, before many years, be demanded. The direction from which this is to come should be anticipated by your Commission, and in all your plans a way for it at least carefully left open.

The high and comparatively narrow ridge which forms the larger part of the island, presenting no large interior basins, suggests the impracticability of collecting any considerable supply of fresh water within it, except from wells, which would involve a very costly system of pumping. Nor is there any near point on the main land from which it could be conveniently obtained. It has given us, therefore, great pleasure to find that there are opportunities within the island of collecting a considerable supply of water on the surface of the best possible quality. Before the amount of it can be estimated with any approach to exactness, a careful series of gaugings will need to be made. As favorable an opportunity as the present for this purpose is not likely to occur again for many years, on account of the protracted drought of the last season, and we strongly advise you to provide for it immediately. We are only now able to express the opinion that the sources of supply which we are about to indicate would, under a proper system of conservancy, meet all the requirements for pure, fresh water, of a much larger population than at present occupies all of the island north and east of Richmond.

On the ridge line of the range of hills, the south slope of which merges upon the plain of New Dorp, three prominent knolls are observable. To the middle one, which is that due north of the Moravian Church, and near the old Egbert and Sharrot homesteads, we shall have frequent occasion to refer, and as it stands upon and overlooks the site of the old manor of Governor Dongan, we shall distinguish it as the Dongan knoll. Standing upon it, a valley may be seen, or rather a gentle dell, mainly of pastured fields, but with some beautiful woodlands, descending to the north-west. The water collected on its slopes forms a series of springs, and half-way down a living stream known as Willow Brook, which, near the bottom, being dammed, drives the works of a little machine shop, beyond which it spreads out, forming the chilly district of Northfield, which has already been described. We shall refer to this as the Manor Dale.

A little to the left is the head of another dale trending to the west, the upper waters of which supply the pretty beech-shaded mill-pond north of Egbertville, and the lower that of Ketchum's Grist Mill. We shall distinguish this as the Mills Dale. The water of both streams can be taken by gravity into the Manor Dale at a point well above the swamp east of Springville, where a dam would form an impounding reservoir for all the water gathered by the two dales. An incidental advantage of such an arrangement would be the arrest of the waters which go to form the chilly district of Northfield, thus making its drainage and reclamation a much easier undertaking.

From a point a few hundred yards to the eastward of the head of the Manor Dale, another gentle depression of the surface may be observed, having a more winding course than the two before described, widening at the distance of half a mile into the west fork of the Little Clove Valley, and finally discharging its waters into the beautiful pool known as Martling's Pond, being the lower of Britton's two Clove Valley iceponds. We shall refer to this as the Martling Dale. A large and deep impounding reservoir can be formed to hold the waters which it collects, and those also which flow from the Silver Lake valley, and all the northern and central hillsides of the Clove, by a dam constructed at or near that now existing by Britton's ice house in the Glen, but which could, if desired, be easily made to raise the water twenty feet above the surface of the present pond.

Martling's Pond now supplies a considerable share of the ice consumed upon the island, and the quality of the water is well-known and held in high popular esteem. The present dam having raised it so as to flood a considerable area of bogs and bushes, and as it is surrounded and overhung by trees, the leaves of which have drifted into it, the analysis of its waters by no means indicates the degree of purity which it is easily practicable to secure in them. A similar observation applies to the water taken from above Ketchum's dam. It is evident that all these waters are of high rank, but that the latter is of really remarkable excellence, superior to most of the streams which contribute to the Croton, and fully equal to the best. To the eye it is perfectly clear, limpid and sparkling, and the analysis shows that it is soft and possesses every desirable quality in an extraordinary degree. We regard the fact as one of great value to the island.

We have no doubt that whenever a system of water works for the eastern part of the island is fully studied, the several dales which we have described and named will be relied upon to collect the principal part, if not all, of the water.

Neither have we any doubt that, if no measures are soon taken to secure certain public rights and properties in those dales, the practicability and economy of securing a large supply of water of good quality from them will be seriously impaired. What measures they should be we shall hereafter discuss.

We now turn to the question of public communications.

Our object, at present is, chiefly, to discern why Staten Island in all its parts does not gain, at least as much, from the general suburban movement, as any of the more favored districts, and to contrive means for overcoming what we find to be the more important obstacles. Difficulties of access to its shores from New York do not appear to be properly classed among these. We have had special opportunities for ascertaining the motives which have influenced many suburban residents in their choice of locality, and have used them diligently, but have known of no single instances in which the scale has been turned against the island by advantages of access offered elsewhere. We have heard a great many encomiums on the healthfulness, on the water privileges, on the scenery, and on the local roads of the places preferred, but never observed any enthusiasm in regard to the conveyance from town; on the contrary, we have often heard it referred to with disgust and indignation. It costs a great deal more in watchfulness, in time, in money, in fatigue, in irregularity, vexation and disappointment, in the course of the year, for a man who has business daily in New York, to go to any point on the range of hills between Riverdale and Scarborough, for instance, where during the last ten years or more land has been advancing in market value at the rate of 5 per cent a month, than to large districts of Staten Island where it is doubtful if it has advanced enough to cover interest, insurances and decay of improvements.

It is not to be denied that the ferry arrangements of Staten Island are singularly bare, rude, unattractive in appearance, and inconvenient compared with what they easily might be; but, looking well ahead, this rather tells to the advantage of the island than otherwise. It is quite impossible by the most lavish use of capital to overcome the limitations of room and of many conditions of comfort to great numbers of people when they are thronging out of town upon narrow iron lines extending through the town itself (and in this sense Brooklyn and the New Jersey towns are parts of the town). And this is especially the case when the first objects of management in the organizations which control them are the movement of freight and of through passengers. The opportunities of enlargement and of adding increased appliances of comfort are as unlimited on the ferries as they are in a country house. There can never be the most distant approach to what a very little capital and skilled architectural study would accomplish for them in the means of access, for instance, to Mr. Stewart's Garden City speculation on Long Island, or to any of the inland suburbs.

We have, therefore, at present, nothing to do with the matter of external communications, except as it is necessary to anticipate improvements in them which would affect the question of the best way to improve the internal communications of the island.[10]

[10] The reason given us by the managers of the ferries for their being fitted only to meet the barest necessities of passage to and from New York, by those who are compelled to use them or live somewhere else than in Staten Island, is that, at present, their receipts do not so far exceed their running expenses as to justify an investment of capital in appliances of convenience, comfort and attractiveness. It is encouraging, therefore, to learn, as we do by returns made by the companies to the Police Department, that the business of the ferries is increasing a great deal faster than the population of the island, the fares collected on the "Staten Island Ferry" being but 912,500 in 1861, while in 1870 they were 2,500,000. On the North Shore Line the business has exactly doubled in five years. In a few years more, therefore, some essential improvements may be reasonably looked for. It is added, and certainly not without reason, that complaints of the means of travel across the bay do not come with a very good grace when made in behalf of a community the civil service of which provides no better facilities for travel than are generally found on shore on Staten Island. Undoubtedly the boats are centuries ahead of the common roads, many of which illustrate in every particular of location, construc-

We may assume that, as soon as any considerable impulse to general improvement on the island has been established, by means which it is the object of this report to suggest, the more radical defects of the present system of communication with New York will, through force of public opinion, competition or otherwise, be put in the way of remedy.

What are the radical defects—that is to say, the defects seriously prejudicial to the Island, and which cannot be remedied simply by a little more study and capital applied to the appointments, furniture and organization of the boats and ferry-landings? They are, preëminently, the liability to occasional, however rare, irregularity and the risk of accident. The weight of defect in these respects depends almost wholly on the force of conditions likely to throw the boats out of their usual course and time. It may be argued that as it is, irregularity occurs so seldom and is commonly so slight, that it is hardly worth considering as an objection to the Island as a dwelling place, and that all risk of personal injury from accidents might be insured against at a premium infinitesimally small. But those upon whom this irregularity and this risk is liable to weigh most are not controlled in their estimates of it by the calculations of actuaries, they are nervous women, with strong affections and ingeniously tormenting imaginations, and before twenty thousand more of them can be established in Staten Island homes, there will be a very strong demand that all possible obstacles to absolute regularity and punctuality in running the boats, and especially all possible apologies for abruptly taking off or suspending the usual trips of the boats, shall be overcome and guarded against.

There has been for twenty years or more a settled conviction among intelligent men in all parts of the island that this would be accomplished by the establishment of a landing and a direct "bee line" ferry at the point of the island nearest

tion and maintenance the result of exactly reversing all established rules for good roads. Costly expedients are now being introduced in road-mending on the island, which have been elsewhere tried hundreds of times always resulting in disappointment and disgust. [1871.]

to New York. The harbor on this line is less liable to be packed with ice than on any other, and the course being straight, the channel broad all the way, and no strong lateral tide-drifts, as in the East and North rivers, except close at the landings, the elements of difficulty in pilotage are less than in going to the Brooklyn or Jersey shore.

Mr. John C. Thompson, whose practical experience and special attention to questions of ferry management gives a value to his judgment which we cannot claim for our own in this matter, says in answer to our inquiry, that upon this line "the route being short and straight, neither storms, ice nor fogs need cause interruption. The passage can be made [by the present boats] in fifteen to twenty minutes." To run half hourly from the present landings would involve an expenditure, Mr. Thompson supposes, of $300,000 for new boats, as it would require two extra boats to keep up a line of four with certainty, besides doubling daily running expenses. A single powerful, large boat could be built for less than half that amount and put upon the short line, which would be able under all ordinary circumstances to make the passage from pier to pier in fifteen minutes, and there have been no conditions of weather in twenty years when such a boat could not have comfortably made the passage in less than half an hour. The suggestion does not involve the suspension of the existing ferries, but it offers to the people of all parts of the island the alternative of a line *shorter and surer* than any of the existing lines can be, on which to fall back whenever desirable. Mr. Thompson would advise that the direct boat run from 4, 5, or 6 A.M. according to season, from the island, until 7½ P.M. from the city, and that the boats on the old routes run as at present, or oftener, till 8 P.M., after which they might cease running, the trips of the direct boat being continued till after midnight at least, leaving the island on the hour and the city on the half hour.

Supplemented, as, of course, it would be by railways on both sides of the island, it appears that the existing facilities of communication with New York can in this way be made essentially better, regarding especially the one point of liability to unexpected detentions, than they could by doubling the number of boats, and the working expenses upon the old lines.

We say that this opportunity has been long seen and can-vassed by intelligent property owners in all parts of the island, but, although universally looked upon with favor and hope, it is no more practically agitated now than it was twenty years ago. The reason it makes no progress seems to be, that the existing highway system, if the word 'system' is not a misnomer, has been formed without reference to it. New Brighton Point cannot be made accessible, with any tolerable approach to directness and ease of grade, from distant parts of the Island without a widening and straightening and re-grading of some existing highways, the construction of some new ones, and more or less injury to many established property interests. The difficulty of overcoming these obstacles, seems hitherto to have continually increased faster than the disposition to engage with them.

We now proceed to the discussion of what should be called for, in an improved highway plan for the Island.

We have in our first chapter given our reasons for assuming that it is quite practicable and desirable to make the whole island essentially a city of detached dwellings, with only such shops, stores, factories, and buildings for other purposes, as may, advantageously or inoffensively to the great body of the residents, be associated with them. We shall further assume that each of these dwelling sites needs to be provided with ways of communication as direct and at the same time as agreeable as possible, (1st.) with New York City; (2nd.) with those situations, nearest each, which are most suitable and most likely to be chosen as the sites of churches, schools, and shops; (3rd.) with those parts of the Island which are likely to be most attractive for visits of recreation, whether in pleasure-driving, riding, or walking.

We shall likewise assume as probable the eventual construction of a railway from some point near New York, either Jersey City or Ellis Island, to a point on the North shore of Staten Island.

Also, the construction of a railway from the short ferry

landing westward, which shall cross the Fresh Kills marshes near their narrowest point, and thence be carried in a moderately direct course until it makes a junction, not far from Tottenville, with the present railway on the south side; also, that this latter will be extended to New Brighton.[11]

There are two classes of sites at present upon the island which have special value for villa dwellings—1st. Those upon the border lowlands, from which, or from the immediate vicinity of which, views over the water are commanded that are not likely to be obstructed in the future by buildings or plantations; 2nd. Those upon eminences in the interior which overlook the low lands, and in or near which there is permanent command of expanded landscapes, including portions of the surrounding waters. Keeping in view the general interest of advancing the reputation for beauty and convenience of the Island as a whole, and of increasing its average real estate taxable valuation, it must be conceded that, other things being equal, those improvements will be of the most value, which, while directly serving the general convenience, shall incidentally give new and special advantages to property of a more secluded character.

It is also to be considered that any thing that is *beautiful* upon the Island, and which is laid open to public view, is of value to the public, and that no dwelling, however remote from it, can wholly fail to be advanced in value, by reason, first, of the right of its occupants to avail themselves of it, and, second, of its general influence in an advertising way for the Island. Public roads, then, which while serving as well as possible their primary purpose, incidentally give pleasing prospects to those passing along them are, on that account especially, of more public value and tend to advance the general reputation of the island and to increase the taxable value of all its real estate. We shall assume this also to be conceded.

[11] A suitable place for the railway bridge over the Kills, occurs near York Avenue. Should it be located much to the west of this, we assume that the west side railway would be extended by a branch line to the short ferry landing, and that this, in any case, must be the chief point of concentration of common road traffic with New York. [1871.]

Finally, we shall take for granted that a definite plan of improved highways is wanted forthwith, which, while it can be realized at an early day if desirable, may also for the most part be carried out gradually, as the advance in population and wealth of the island shall be found to justify; that it is to be general and comprehensive rather than local or detailed; that it is to block out the entire island with a frame-work of highways, between which private taste and enterprise may be fully exercised without disturbing the economy of the general plan; that the purpose is to guide and facilitate improvement, and, as far as possible, not to hamper or restrict it; and in brief, to furnish a chart of future progress to which individuals may refer and conform their improvements, with assurance that in pursuing their private designs they are also contributing to a complete and harmonious whole, every step toward which, wherever made, tends to the general advantage and benefit.

Great detail in the plan is to be avoided, because once adopted it is intended to become, to that extent, binding upon the land owners, restricting in a certain degree their liberty of action in respect to their property. If such restraint be carried to an extent beyond the absolute requirements of the general public interest, it will be felt as an invasion of private rights, and possibly engender serious opposition.

In devising, under this series of assumptions, a system of highways for Staten Island, it is almost necessary at the outset to take up the problem *de novo*—that is to say, to regard the island as so much territory, conformed, populated, situated and affiliated as now, with prospects in the near future such as are conceded to it, but as entirely without ways for inter-communication; and then, having devised a plan, comprehensive and complete, as best suited to its present wants and its reasonable future expectations, to proceed to adapt such plan to existing conditions by engrafting it upon them. By such method the present highways will be put to their utmost availability; while the transition from the old system to the new will be effected with less of disturbance and, by consequence, less of expense to individuals in readjusting their communications to the new order, than by radical and sweeping changes.

As some slight classification of roads will need to be used, we must explain why we avoid the terms "avenue" and "boulevard." Avenue, formerly used to designate a straight, level approach between formal plantations, was in an evil day used to designate a town street of unusual breadth and directness, also adapted to be planted with trees. For purposes of misrepresentation in regard to paper towns it was afterwards applied with even less propriety; it has reached the lowest point of degradation and abuse when applied, as it now is, by official sign board on Staten Island to a narrow lane leading to a stable. All association of dignity and wealth which once belonged to the word are lost and it henceforth suggests nothing but clap-trap. The only useful significance of the designation, Boulevard, which is the French for the English word bulwark, and properly applied to streets of extraordinary breadth, formed on the site of the old town bulwarks of Europe, is already similarly destroyed past recovery, it being now applied all around New York to wretched dirt roads fifty feet wide. Instead of these we shall use the old term "high roads" for such public ways as are likely to be in daily use by large bodies of the general public, and which are designed to form main channels between the different principal quarters of the island.

New York being the focus of the principal travel of the island it becomes a primal necessity that the high-roads take that direction, and reach to points of nearest or at least quickest approach thereto, and that they be sufficient in number and size to provide all parts of the island with the most direct and ample lines of approach to those points. Such a road fixed with regard to present location of population and existing facilities of communication with New York, would be drawn from Tottenville, by the most direct line practicable, to or near Silver Lake, and thence to the two ferry landings at present nearest New York, Tompkins and Brighton.

We find that with little bending from a straight line, the topography of the island admits of the construction of such a road upon easy grades without heavy work to obtain them. The most difficult division would be that between Silver Lake and Tompkins Landing. By a slight deviation from the route of the present road, the grade here can be brought to 1 in 25 without much excavation. On this grade with good construction a horse can trot down or up with a moderate load, with speed and safety. At no other point would the grade need to be as steep as this, and it could, with some quite short expections, be kept below 1 in 40.

This road would divide the present town of Westfield into two nearly equal parts, and with a few additional lateral roads, would take the greater part of the common wheel travel of that town to the ferries. Hence we shall speak of it as the Westfield High Road. If well constructed it would lead to a great increase of this travel and by shortening the way to the early markets in town would considerably increase the agricultural value of its land, as we are assured by leading market gardeners of the town. It would pass through and open up a district of Castletown and Middletown now the most secluded on the island, and which is accessible by direct roads from no point on the shore; a district nevertheless possessing great landscape attractions, and much of which would without doubt be at once greatly advanced in value by its construction. It would occupy an axial position with reference to the island as a whole, being at all points nearly equidistant between shores.

It could be made to terminate at the proposed short ferry landing without increasing grades, and we propose that it should be so laid out. As compared with present roads, it would shorten the distance to the landing from its junction with the old Manor Road half a mile; with the road near Ketchum's Mill, three quarters of a mile; with the Rossville Road near Marshland, a mile and a half, and from Tottenville, a mile and a quarter. Its width should nowhere be less than one hundred feet, and as the throng upon it would be constantly enlarging as the ferry was approached, from the middle of the island, east, it should be from 120 to 150 feet wide. Of course we refer to the requirements of the distant future, with regard to which its limits should be established. Within these limits a wheelway of ordinary breadth only would need to be soon constructed. The borders should be graded, and made neat, and utilized at once in the manner we shall hereafter indicate.

The Westfield High-road, as thus proposed, falls, it will be observed, to the northward of the main central ridge, or back bone, of the island. This ridge extends only from the Fresh Kills near Richmond to Stapleton, but while its altitude is melted away in gentle slopes to the northward toward the Sound, permitting in that quarter the greatest freedom in the location of roads, it descends toward the sea on the south, in steep and broken declivities, impracticable for roads for rapid travel. As a route toward New York it will therefore be of no direct value to the residents of the greater part of the extensive and populous district of Southfield lying between the crest and the bay.

It becomes necessary therefore to provide for them another high-road, for which purpose the course of the present Richmond Road would be generally satisfactory. This road was originally laid out 99 feet wide, but as the result of a long series of encroachments is now at many points less than 30. We are advised that the county can compel the restoration of the land appropriated from it to private purposes, and if it should be thought necessary to adopt it as one of the high-roads of a new system, this would be a necessary proceeding. It would involve the removal of a number of buildings, and the destruction of a good deal of property, and, the encroachments having been made for the most part generations ago, would bear hardly on many good citizens. We should rather suggest that the lines of this road be but slightly modified, where especially desirable, and, if practicable, that so much of the land originally appropriated to it as is not required for public convenience, should be formally released to the present owners of the adjoining properties. If your Commission should be disposed to adopt this policy, we would recommend a course nearly parallel with the Richmond Road to be adopted for the Southfield high-road, and at such a distance east and south from it as would make the best division of lands. With efficient drainage arrangements this would admit of greater directness and better grades, and would better accomplish all general public purposes.

Before reaching the broken ground near the Black Horse, this road would fork, one branch leading off to Egbertville and Richmond, the other running nearly parallel with the Amboy Road, as will hereafter be proposed.

The present Philadelphia Turnpike or Long Neck Road would serve as a north branch of the Westfield or central high-road. But, still further to the north, there is a large and already very populous district at too great a distance to make use of it as a route to the short ferry. Another high road is, therefore, required to be laid out on a line between this and the north shore, (to which it would be mainly parallel,) dividing the distance into three parts. The dwellers upon the southern third may be expected to use the Long Neck Road, and a course for the additional or Northfield high-road, which would serve the largest number of house sites to the best advantage, will be not far from the line which would divide the other two-thirds. In approaching New Brighton, however, considerations of grade will demand a curve to the north, and not, far west of Jersey Street, probably, the line should merge in that of the present Terrace Road, at the point which would be chosen for a bridge.

Such a class of improvements as are contemplated in this report, will make Staten Island a resort of pleasure travel from all quarters, and, as the great suburban population west of Newark Bay would find the most convenient route of access to it by way of Elizabethport, and as this also will be a point of connection for visitors from all the West, it will be desirable to lay out the western part of the Northfield high-road with a view to its serving as a general approach road from that direction. Its terminus should, therefore, be fixed with reference to a suitable position for a bridge, if that should be found feasible.

Immediately about the short ferry landing at New Brighton Point, where the travel by the three high-roads would be concentrated, there should be an open space of sufficient extent to admit a large concourse of people, on foot and in carriages, to assemble and wait without the necessity of dangerous or uncomfortable crowding. For this purpose it should have an area of not less than two by four hundred feet.

It is beyond our province to suggest what rights or privileges the county can hold or offer to this proposed ferry line. The improvidence of possessing no rights in respect to means of communication, upon which its future prosperity may be very greatly dependent, in view of the arrogance and unscrupulousness with which the business of public carriers is now often conducted, it is unnecessary to argue.

A road along the shore where none exists has been so long called for and the occasion for it is so generally admitted, that we need not state its advantages. It is most required along the south shore, where some fifteen years ago it was agreed that it should be made, the project having been defeated, as we believe it had been once or twice before, by the determined resistance of one or two land owners who approved the purpose in general, but demanded more consideration for their private convenience at the points where it crossed their property.

As such a road would not, in general, be on a line leading directly toward New York, or to any point of much business on the island, and as it would be the only road from which a near view of the lower bay could be obtained, it would necessarily become a route of pleasure travel as well as a neighborhood road, and the object of presenting the sea to view fully and to the best advantage, should be prominent in determining its route. For this reason, beginning at the end of New York Avenue, Clifton, it should be carried with all convenient directness to the shore, and thence follow as near the beach as economy of construction would admit, so that private buildings and plantations could not be interposed to obstruct the seaward prospect.

After reaching a point on New Dorp Plains, where, owing to the flooding of the ground in Spring tides, it would be necessary to divert it to a considerable distance from the shore, it should be laid out chiefly with regard to neighborhood convenience until the hill district north of the Great Kills is reached; at this point a junction would be formed with the Southfield high-road, after which, as it is impracticable, in going west, to follow the shore on the beach, and would be unadvisable on the bank near the beach, on account of its liability to be encroached upon by the sea, it will be an object to keep sufficiently high to overlook the buildings on the lower slope near the shore. This will establish a road intermediate between the present Amboy road and the beach, and will generally divide property advantageously. From New Dorp westward to Prince's Bay, it would serve as an extension of the Southfield high-road, and be a direct route to the short ferry as well as to all the east side ferry landings, for residents along the shore. From Prince's Bay it would pass near the shore to Ward's Point, thence to Tottenville, thence along the west side to the shore road on the north side.

With respect to the internal plan of this road, we would express our general satisfaction with the suggestions of Mr. Root, with whom it has been a matter of special consideration, and whose views are before the public.

Routes will next be required to and between the high-roads, as well as to the railway stations and ferry landings, their general direction being transverse to that of the high-roads, though it will be better that they shall, as far as practicable, approach the high-roads in the direction toward New York; speed with carriages in that direction being everywhere more of an object than in any other, and as the time thus gained in driving, supposing that it involved in some cases the reverse rule in respect to the approach to railway stations, would be offset by nothing appreciable in locomotive travel.

The course of these cross-roads would be generally nearly parallel, with such deflection from directness only as would be required to secure ease of grade and convenience of drainage, at little cost for excavation and embankment. Their course will generally be coincident also with that of the trend of the valleys and of the currents of the water courses on the hill-sides. This fact will, to a certain extent, influence their location between stations and landings. The present village streets, especially those along the north shore, would establish the initial point for a considerable number, particularly such of them as lead to the ferry landings. In the interior, each railway station would establish an objective point for a road approaching from each side. At present, stations occur at intervals of one mile on the south side track, that being the distance apart at which the old transverse highways of the island are generally found. It is to be expected that in the early future, if the interior of the island increases in population at all rapidly, double the present number of stations, each to be called at by alternate trains, will be demanded. These will be established as nearly as practicable midway of those existing, and it being assumed that the same rule will serve on the projected North Side Railway, the position of roads at half-mile intervals is thus approximately indicated.

Taking the ferry landings, the positions and probable positions of railway stations, the lines of water courses and intermediate ridges which it would be necessary to accommodate, and the advantage of maintaining, where practicable, an approximate equidistance between the roads, a series of lines would be formed, which, with the intersecting high-roads, would subsect the whole island into blocks having a general width of half a mile, and an average length of about a mile.

This having been accomplished, the question is in order whether a judicious limit has not been reached, and whether the further extension of our plan had not better be left to local and private enterprise? We shall leave this question open to your Commission, taking care in further elaboration to avoid as far as possible any elements which will involve additional highways as a necessity. We shall, however, offer reasons why in our judgment it may be best to proceed one step further with the general plan, doubling again the number of cross-roads.

Looking forward a brief space, and making but moderate allowance for the effect of increased facilities of access and conveniences of housekeeping, and of the advertising influence of the mere adoption of a broad and comprehensive scheme of improvement, and especially for the consequences which will result from the adoption of means adapted to relieve the island of malaria, and give it for the first time the full benefit of its unequalled latent advantages of climate—making the least hopeful allowance for the effect of these proposed improvements, an early large demand for land in the interior and back parts of the island must be anticipated, and of a different character from any that has yet been experienced.

We have endeavored to show more particularly in our first chapter, the space which each of the largest class of purchasers will be likely to want. Along the shore, especially near the steamboat landings, and in the interior near the railway stations and existing villages, the competition for land for domestic business purposes and for the residence of those to whom distance from the boat or station would be objectionable, may be sufficient to make it desirable that it should be readily divisible into lots of from one to two hundred feet in depth. Elsewhere, universally, it should be practicable, without a special process of laying out roads, to divide all land into villa plots as small at least as five acres. With roads averaging half a mile apart, plots of five acres, each occupying half the space between two roads would necessarily have a depth of disproportionate length to their frontage, being 1300 feet to 170, which would be generally objected to. With roads laid out at a quarter of a mile apart, a five acre lot would have a depth of 660 feet, with a front of 330 feet, which is a very good proportion. Again, if lots of about one acre are required, they would be obtained with 150 feet front on streets opened at intervals of 600 feet between the laterals of the general system. Another reason remains, before stating which, however, it will be necessary to advance our drainage plan.

We have argued that thorough-drainage must be the first object of any valuable scheme of general improvement for the island, and have admitted that such drainage must be effected largely by individual undertakings. It is quite evident, however, that not much can be expected of individuals, unless suitable channels are open to them at no great distance for taking away the water which their private drains are designed to collect. Nor can much be expected of volunteer associated efforts for this purpose so long as they shall remain hampered by the almost insurmountable difficulty of first obtaining unity of opinion, concert of action, and equality of convenience, among a considerable number of neighbors. All may be convinced and resolved, but the moment when all are agreed as to all the particulars necessary to be settled, and when all are prepared to incur the expense, is never reached. The establishment of public drains at frequent intervals would obviate these difficulties by allowing each individual to consult his own convenience as to time, and the same means would provide outlets for the proper drainage of the highways, without which good roads are an impossibility.

Precisely at what intervals such public drains should be constructed, is a question depending on the peculiar conformation of the surface and character of the underlying strata, to be determined only by a careful examination of each particular area. Convenience and efficiency, however, require, in our judgment, that in no case should any land-owner be compelled to carry the main of his private drainage more than a quarter of a mile before reaching an outlet in a public drain. This would require public drains to be formed at a distance apart, never exceeding half a mile, throughout the island, and this we shall assume as a maximum.

We have already shown the objections to open drains, saying nothing of the inconvenience and danger which they occasion otherwise; the prime object of drainage is liable to be defeated, and the evils designed to be remedied by their construction to be aggravated, whenever the flow of water in them is obstructed. Obstruction is constantly liable to occur from vegetation growing in their channels and along their margins, from leaves and other debris delivered by the winds, from the treading down of the banks by cattle seeking water, cool standing places and lush herbage in hot weather; from stepping-stones thrown in by wanderers; from the fall of neglected bridging, and from carelessness in conducting agricultural operations on their banks. Open drains, therefore, are to be avoided as far as practicable, the limit of practicability being one of expense.

The common form of roadside gutter is inefficient, expensive to keep in order, especially on steep hill-sides, and it is often liable, as we have shown, to all the objections which apply generally to open drains.

That roadside gutters may be kept moderately narrow, shallow, smooth and tidy, no large volume of water must be allowed to accumulate in them. They must therefore be provided, at frequent intervals, with outlets to the general system of public drains.

It is obviously undesirable that public drains should cross private fields or pleasure-grounds, where this can be conveniently avoided.

In the larger part of the island the drainage system has to be adapted to two quite distinct districts; the first a highland district, having frequent slopes, which end, often abruptly, in the low-land plain which forms the second. In the descent of these slopes a drain-pipe of given calibre would carry much more water than it would upon the grade at which it would be necessary to lay it on the plain below, and a volume of water which would move with lazy flow in a ditch of given dimensions on the plain, if turned into a similar channel upon the hill sides, unless it were made very expensively or were laid out in a very long and circuitous course, would soon establish a gully; it is, therefore, especially desirable to avoid the necessity of a resort to open drains above the base of the higher and steeper hills. We estimate that all the drainage water which can be collected upon the hills (certain extraordinary circumstances, to be hereafter provided for, being excepted) might, if required, be carried across the lower ground by a series of open drains half a mile apart, and above these in pipes which, even at the point of discharge, need never exceed 15 inches in calibre. (If the drains were to be placed much further than half a mile apart, a far more expensive pipeage would be required near the base of the hills, the rate of cost increasing much more rapidly than the size.)

But although 15 inch pipes, half a mile apart, would take all the water of the hills under ordinary circumstances, economy, safety and convenience would be greatly better consulted, in many cases, by the use of smaller pipe at more frequent intervals. This gives the additional reason which was promised for providing in your plan for highways at a less distance than half a mile. It would not be desirable to construct the intermediate roads, or lay drains upon all the lines proposed to be established for them, at once, but in the study of the drainage system it would be a great convenience and matter of economy to be free to do so occasionally.

Where there are existing highways, or where they are immediately required, crossing the lowland regions in a direction transverse to the shore line, at intervals of quarter of a mile or less, as generally along the north and east sides of the island, it is to be presumed that pipes would be laid in them; as a general rule they would not need in these cases to exceed eight inches of calibre, as by means of lateral channels each volume of water descending from the hills could be distributed, on reaching the flatter grades, to a number of outlets.

We are now prepared to define a considerable part of the framework of a highway and drainage plan, which we present in a series of propositions, as follows:

Scheme of Improvements to Be Had in View in the Study of a New Plan for Staten Island

I

Westfield High-road.—A highway not less than one hundred feet wide from Tottenville to New Brighton Point, by the most direct course which shall be found consistent with ease of grade and reasonable economy of construction.

II

Northfield High-road.—A similar highway from the western part of Northfield to New Brighton Point.

I. Calvert Vaux (1824–1895), June, 1868. Vaux was Olmsted's partner in planning many of the landscape designs for New York City. He—like Olmsted—considered spaces to be more significant than solids in the urban scene. Even though Vaux, an architect, designed a number of important New York City buildings, he believed that his real contribution was in the field of landscape architecture. (Courtesy of The New-York Historical Society, New York City.)

II. New York and its environs, 1867. (Engraving by R. Kupfer; courtesy of The New-York Historical Society, New York City.)

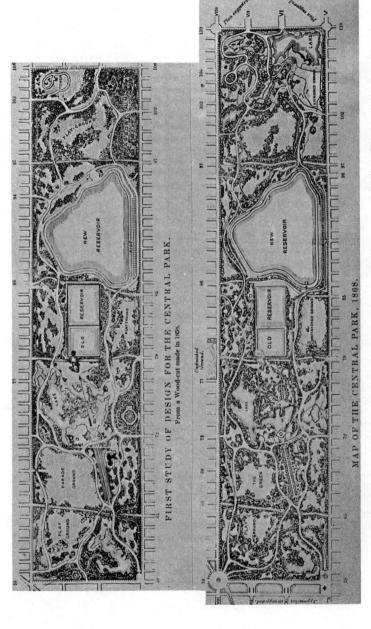

FIRST STUDY OF DESIGN FOR THE CENTRAL PARK.
From a Wood-cut made in 1858.

MAP OF THE CENTRAL PARK, 1868.

III. Comparative designs of Central Park, 1858 and 1868. (Courtesy of The Garden Library, Dumbarton Oaks, Washington, D.C.)

IV. Central Park, 1863. (Lithograph by John Bachman[n]; courtesy of The New-York Historical Society, New York City.)

V. Bird's-eye view of New York City, with parts of Williamsburgh and Brooklyn, 1859. (Lithograph by John Bachman[n]; courtesy of The New-York Historical Society, New York City.)

VI. Design for Prospect Park, 1866–1867. (Courtesy of The
Garden Library, Dumbarton Oaks, Washington, D.C.)

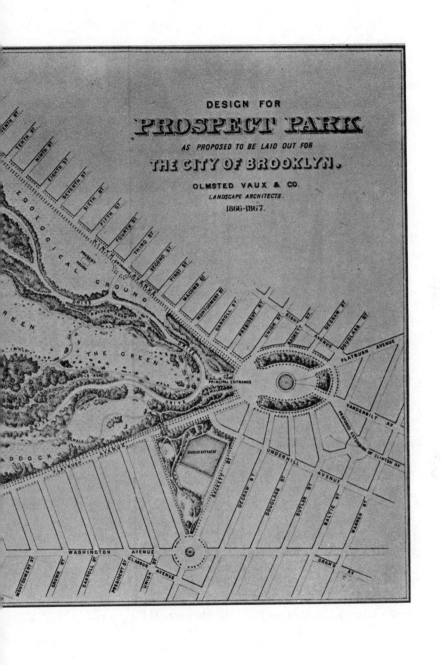

DESIGN FOR

PROSPECT PARK

AS PROPOSED TO BE LAID OUT FOR

THE CITY OF BROOKLYN.

OLMSTED VAUX & CO.

LANDSCAPE ARCHITECTS.

1866-1867.

VII. Constructing Prospect Park in 1867. (Courtesy of The
Garden Library, Dumbarton Oaks, Washington, D.C.)

VIII. Panorama of the harbor of New York, Staten Island, and the Narrows, 1854. (Lithograph by Goupil & Co.; courtesy of The New-York Historical Society, New York City.)

IX. "Central Park Fifty Years From Now." Cartoon by Rollin Kirby in the *New York World*, May 22, 1925. (Courtesy of The New-York Historical Society, New York City, and the *World Journal Tribune*.)

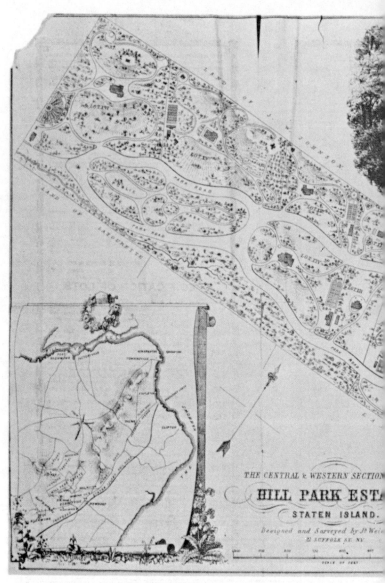

X. Central and western sections of the Hill Park Estate, Staten Island, designed and surveyed by Jacob Weidenmann about 1870. The design of the Hill Park Estate, done by Olmsted's friend and one-time partner, exemplifies the pattern of residential land development which Olmsted desired for Staten Island in 1870.

VIEW OF HILL PARK HOUSE.

LITH. OF G. W. LEWIS 125 FULTON ST. N.Y.

Unfortunately, the maps and diagrams which must have accompanied Olmsted's own plan for Staten Island have not been found. None were printed with the Report. (Courtesy of The Staten Island Institute of Arts and Sciences.)

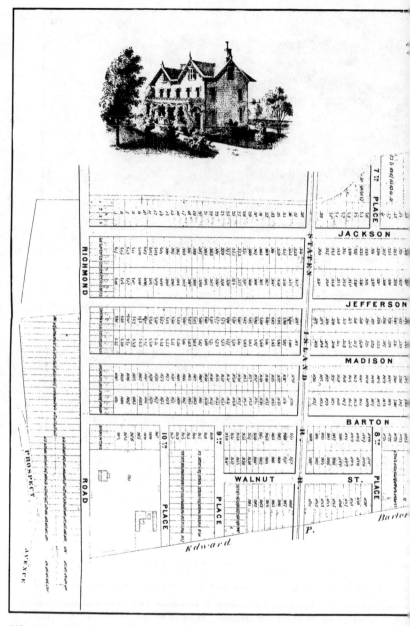

XI. Map of the Ocean View Land Improvement Company of Staten Island, about 1860. This map illustrates the grid method (still in use) of residential land division — much deplored by Olmsted — which was being used on Staten Island. (Courtesy of The Staten Island Institute of Arts and Sciences.)

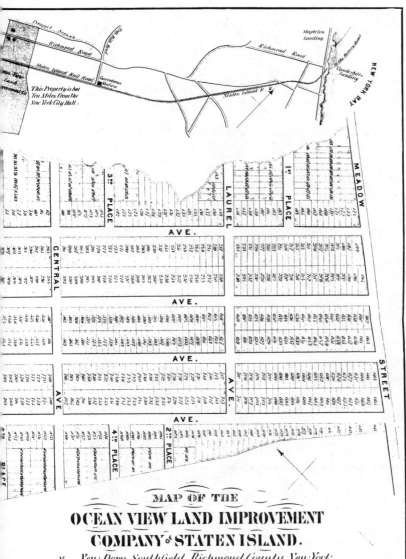

MAP OF THE

OCEAN VIEW LAND IMPROVEMENT

COMPANY of STATEN ISLAND.

Near New Dorp, Southfield, Richmond County, New York.

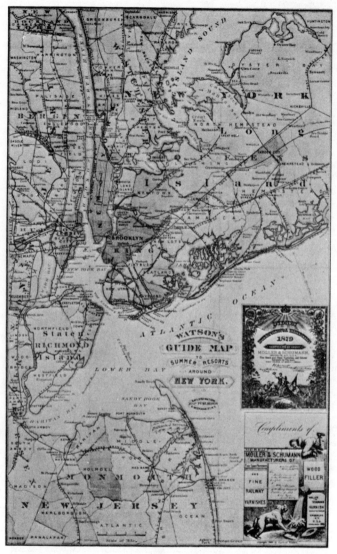

XII. Guide map to New York City summer resorts, about 1879. Summertime recreation became so popular an activity for New York City residents—as for other urban dwellers —by the 1870's that maps were provided illustrating the different routes to urban resort areas. It is interesting to note that many of the street-railways terminated in such places. (Published by Gaylord Watson; courtesy of The New-York Historical Society, New York City.)

XIII. Central Park, 1864. An attempt to break the grid. (Lithograph by Martel; courtesy of The New-York Historical Society, New York City.)

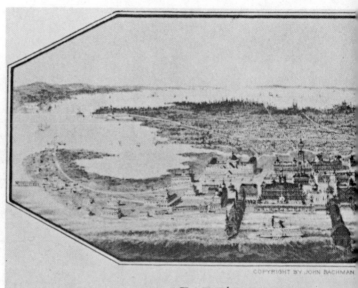

BIRD'SEYE VIEW

BIRD'SEYE VIEW

XIV. Bird's-eye views of Coney Island and Rockaway, n.d. Coney Island and Rockaway Beach, both developed in the 1870's, were and are two of the principal oceanside resorts for New York City residents. (By John Bachman[n]; courtesy of The New-York Historical Society, New York City.)

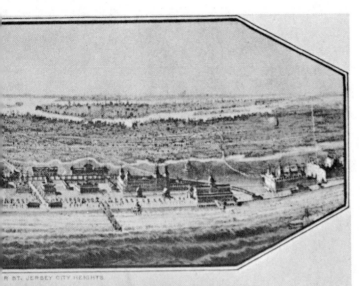

CONEY ISLAND.

OF ROCKAWAY.

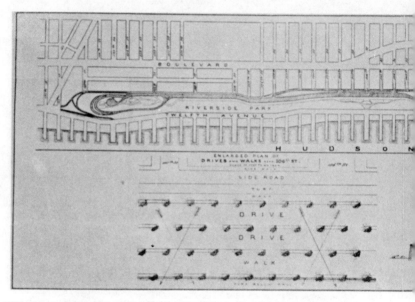

XV. Map of the Riverside District, 1875. A plan for Riverside Park
and Avenue. (Courtesy of The Garden Library, Dumbarton Oaks,
Washington, D.C.)

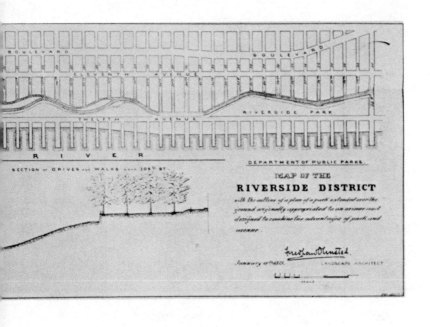

BOULEVARD   BOULEVARD

E L E V E N T H   A V E N U E

T W E L F T H   A V E N U E   R I V E R S I D E   P A R K

R I V E R

SECTION of DRIVES and WALKS near 108th ST.

DEPARTMENT OF PUBLIC PARKS.

MAP OF THE

RIVERSIDE DISTRICT

with the outline of a plan of a park extended over the
ground originally appropriated to an avenue and
designed to combine the advantages of park and
avenue.

Fred Law Olmsted.

January 11th 1871.   LANDSCAPE ARCHITECT

SCALE

XVI. A topographical map "of that part of Westchester County adjacent to the City and County of New York," 1873. This map, undertaken in the late 1860's, was done under Olmsted's supervision in anticipation of the annexation of part of that county to the City of New York. (Courtesy of The Garden Library, Dumbarton Oaks, Washington, D.C.)

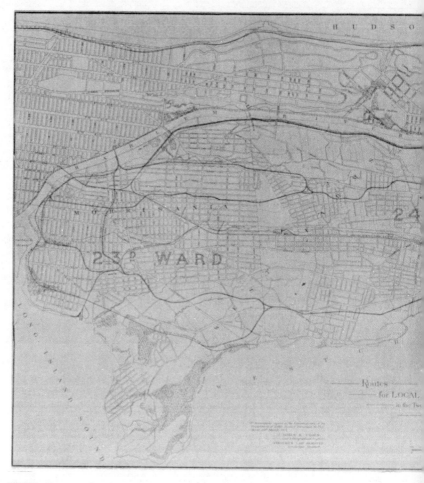

XVII. Routes for local steam transit in the Twenty-third and Twenty-fourth Wards of New York City, 1877. (Courtesy of The Garden Library, Dumbarton Oaks, Washington, D.C.)

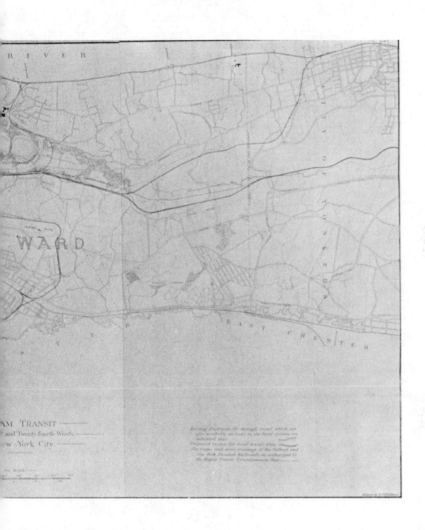

R I V E R

WARD

EAST CHESTER

IF "IMPROVEMENT" PLANS
HAD GOBBLED CENTRAL PARK

IF the various persons who have sought to invade Central Park in the last sixty years, for projects in themselves often worthy, oftener grotesque, and frequently purely commercial, had had their way, there would now be nothing left of the park except a few walks and drives, and a lake on which steamboats and full-rigged ships would be plying.

The park was a new institution in 1860, but already it had become apparent that there were plenty of people in New York who saw in this large expanse of ground only room for profitable private enterprise. The Board of Commissioners for Central Park reported in that year that "the demands of people who wish to advance their business interests by means of the park are most astounding."

The accompanying chart gives a birds-eye view of Central Park as it would look if all these enterprises had been carried into effect, although it fails to represent the case fully, since the park would not have had room for all of them.

Digging of a trench system as a publicity scheme for the Third Liberty Loan, just authorized, is the first actual use of the park for other than park purposes, except the construction of the Metropolitan Museum of Art, but suggestions for its utilization have ranged all the way from the installation of

a speedway for the sportive rich and an academy of design for the art artists to the granting of concessions for private amusement enterprises.

Of the plans shown on the accompanying chart, many are unnumbered—the churches for which park space has been sought again and again. They, alone, would almost obliterate the park if they had been permitted. Following are some of the more audacious projects:

No. 1 is an outdoor theatre, proposed in 1911, which would have seated anywhere from 25,000 to 100,000 persons at heavy strain to the vocal cords of the actors. No. 2 is the stadium for athletic games in the old Croton Reservoir, which was first proposed in 1912, and has lately been revived to be countered by the proposal of the construction of an Italian sunken garden in that space. No. 3 is a marionette theatre for the southern portion of the park. No. 4 is a street railway, suggested as long ago as the civil war.

No. 5, the use of the lake for the voyagings of a full-rigged ship by way of me-

morial of ancient times, or a steamboat as illustrative of modern progress, was proposed more than half a century ago. About the same time it was suggested that the park should be used as a burial ground for the city's distinguished dead, and years later there was strong support for the location there of Grant's Tomb, eventually built on Riverside Drive.

No. 13 is, perhaps, the most visionary scheme of all. It was proposed in 1904 by Robert B. Roosevelt, who wanted to cut up the whole park into building lots.

In 1910 recreation experts demanded (No. 17) free swimming baths, a big lawn with a free wading pool, and heaps for children, and a baseball ground. Other interests at the same time proposed a free opera house. In the previous year the Academy of Design asked for 30,000 square feet, including the Arsenal site, for its buildings. (No. 18.)

XVIII. "If 'Improvement' Plans Had Gobbled Central Park," 1918. This cartoon from the *New York Times*, March 31, 1918, demonstrates the almost constant effort to make Central Park into something other than its original designers intended and suggests the resistance of an

Many Other Proposed Grabs Are Not
Shown in the Picture, for Lack of Room

enlightened public to such distortions. During the 1880's and early 90's, while Olmsted was still active, his opposition was effectively felt against all such destructive innovations. (Courtesy of the *New York Times*.)

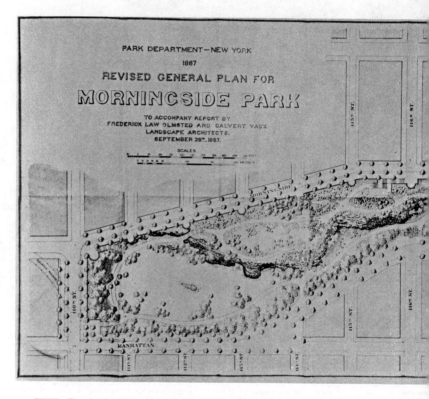

XIX. Revised general plan for Morningside Park, 1887. (Courtesy of The Garden Library, Dumbarton Oaks, Washington, D.C.)

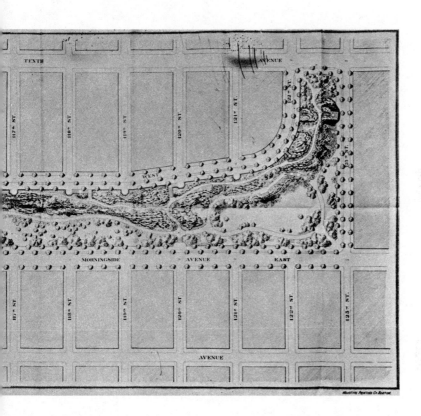

III

Southfield High-road.—A similar highway from the western part of Southfield to New Brighton Point.

IV

Brighton Place.—At the point of junction of the three high-roads, above specified, an open place on the water side, not less than four hundred feet in length upon the shore and two hundred feet deep.

V

Shore Road.—A road not less than one hundred feet wide leading from the south end of New York Avenue, Clifton, southward to the shore; thence, westward, along the shore, or as near it as a reasonable economy will admit, to New Dorp Plains, then curving to the northward so as to make a convenient junction with the Southfield high-road north or north-east of the Great Kills; thence, westward, keeping the Bay in view, to Tottenville; thence, along the shore, or as near the shore, either upon salt marsh or upland, as shall be found consistent with moderate directness and economy, until a connection is made with the existing shore road on the north side of the island.

VI

Transverse Roads.—Roads not less than fifty feet wide crossing the highroads wherever the topography admits, at intervals not exceeding, on an average, half a mile, nor nearer together, on an average, than a quarter of a mile.

VII

Public Drains.—Public Drains, at intervals not exceeding half a mile, nor nearer together, on an average, than quarter of a mile, throughout the Island; the salt marshes alone excepted, to be adapted to serve as outfalls for the thorough-drainage of all the lands between them, and also to receive the surface drainage of the highways.

VIII

Under Drains and Road Drains.—Wherever the public drains will be required to receive no more water than can be safely carried in a pipe of fifteen inches calibre, they may be covered drains, laid as far as practicable within the bounds of public highways.

It may be presumed that under the last rule, drainage would begin near the "divide" of the water shed, with three inch tile of common brick clay, laid with collars; and that in most cases a close six inch pipe, laid on each side of the road, would be the largest required, until an open water course, natural or artificial, should be reached. A cheap form of silt-basin, made probably of cement, would be placed at intervals of from two to three hundred feet, into which land-owners would be permitted to carry their mains. The surface drainage of the roads would reach the pipe also through the silt-basin, entering it by a grating on the surface; this grating in the rural districts might be of wood. To avoid the expense of a gutter of stone, which would nearly double the ordinary cost per foot of the system, we should propose that highways out of villages be generally laid out of sufficient width to admit of their being constructed with turf gutters. These have elsewhere been found adequate to the duty that would be required, and with the arrangement suggested, would be liable to gully probably on no grade necessary to be adopted on the island. Assuming a wheel-way of twenty-two feet as the minimum for the most secluded neighborhood roads, the gutters would require as much as four feet on each side, beyond which, the turf should be extended with a very flat slope four feet further, to admit trees to be grown healthfully and without inconvenience. The advantage of fairly grown road side trees, as an adjunct to the drainage system and as air purifiers, has been sufficiently shown, their advantage as embellishments needs no argument. The arguments against them are all based on the assumption of a bad ground plan and an ignorant and inconsiderate administration. We assume that in all roads to be hereafter laid out proper provision will be made for them. In a highway fifty feet wide, there would remain six feet on each side of the tree border for walks. The gutters should be kept free at public expense, and should be adapted in form to be rapidly mowed, rolled and swept by a small horse machine of special construction, which would make the cost of keeping them from five to ten dollars a year per mile of road. Whenever business upon any such road so much increases, that twenty-two feet should be found inconveniently narrow for a wheelway, stone or brick, gutters could be substituted for turf, and iron for wooden gratings, and the wheelway enlarged to thirty feet. The sidewalks could also be extended and flagged to the curb if necessary, making them ten feet wide. These remarks are intended to show simply the practicability of applying the general plan to the highways not more than fifty feet wide, that is to say, the narrowest neighborhood roads, without excessively expensive details. Its adaptation to wider roads, and especially to the high-roads, needs no explanation.

It remains to define the form of the open drains which shall be used where the amount of water to be provided for is liable to exceed the capacity of a fifteen inch under drain, the object being to reduce the necessary evils to the lowest point which shall consist with economy of original construction. The inside slopes of the canals of this state, approved by half a century of experience, have two of base to one of vertical measurement; channels for drainage not being subject to the abrasion of boats, may not require as much, but it is a common sense rule that no side slope should be formed artificially with a greater slope than is established by nature where banks of similar material are undermined by streams. An examination will show that a slope of at most one to one is that fixed as a *maximum* in the ordinary material of the island. We therefore add the following to our series of propositions.

IX

Open Public Drains.—Open drains either to be boxed, or to be cut with side slopes of never less than one foot horizontal to one of vertical measurement, and whenever such side slopes are impracticable, to have smooth floors of firm material, and such wall as may be necessary to prevent caving or crumbling of sides.

The danger of air-poisons rising from all water courses which are liable to run dry, or nearly so, in the heat of summer, especially if there are many dwellings near them, has been fully explained; without further argument, therefore, we add:

X

Natural Water Courses.—The beds of all open water courses to be made sufficiently firm, smooth and dishing towards the deepest part of the channel, to prevent any lodgment of the water, as the streams shrink in summer, in pools where it will be liable to stagnate.

XI

Occasional Flood Courses.—Wherever any open drain or water course is liable to great fluctuations of service, as to flood by storm, and stagnation by drought, provision if practicable, to be made for laying a pipe below such open drain, the use of the open drain being to dispose safely of floods which the pipe cannot carry.

Certain extreme cases above alluded to remain to be specially provided for. The water, for example, falling during a heavy storm upon the eastern side of Signal Hill, is mainly collected before it reaches the bottom, in a series of depressions, and then combined in one stream, the outlet of which is near Stapelton Landing. Generally in summer, the channel of this stream, south of the head of Rocky Hollow, is dry on the surface, and even below that point it often carries, in time of drought, nothing but a driblet, which breeds deadly poison; yet in a single night it has risen so rapidly as to burst its banks and destroy property to the amount of many thousand dollars, and even cause loss of life. Here, then, are two extreme conditions to be provided for in the same locality, and in each case the question whether our scheme is adequate, may be a matter of life and death. That the present arrangements are really murderous, there can be no doubt.

The cost of providing a covered conduit sufficient for all occasions, would be very large.

It has occurred to us that a channel for a part of this water might be opened to the southward, and we find that this can be done by a light excavation. For ordinary conditions a moderate sized pipe-drain might be laid below the present bed of the stream, as already proposed, and instead of a deep open trench sufficient for storm waters, which, would be very costly to maintain, and always liable to become a nuisance, we should propose a broad and gently sloped turfed depression. At certain points, as at the mouth of the Clove for instance, this depression would be made sufficiently large and deep to serve as a storage pond, taking up a large body of water during heavy storms, and giving out north and south no more than conduits of moderate size below would be adapted to carry with safety. The object of the arrangement, it will be readily seen, is to avoid what would otherwise be the dilemma of a very expensive system of large covered drains, or a very inconvenient and dangerous system of large and deep open drains, canals in fact. The ground required in this case is now mainly swampy, a "seed bed of malaria," and of little value. The arrangement proposed would make it wholesome, useful, and ornamental.

It will be obvious that the plan proposed by Mr. Root, before referred to, for the shore road, may be readily modified, whenever circumstances shall render it desirable, so as to admit of the introduction of such an arrangement as has been described, the exterior highway lines being expanded and the central row of trees carried around the depression. The plan has also the advantage that if between any two crossing roads it should, for any future village purpose, become desirable to establish a market place or open ground, or merely to gain additional wheelway room, it can be readily done by removing the central row of trees. Should such a necessity arise where the proposed depression has been introduced, it could also be met by the construction of a sufficiently large culvert or pipe drain, and covering and levelling up above and about it, to the grade desired.

An arrangement of this nature, nearly continuous, but varying in breadth and depth, would have considerable advantages if introduced parallel to and a little below the steep slopes terminating the highland district, as all the water flowing from them might thus be arrested and distributed as before suggested to find its way thence to the sea through any required number of channels of moderate capacity.

In many situations where its use would be thus desirable, the land is at present unoccupied by houses, uncultivated, often boggy, and generally highly malarious, and would probably be the last in which proper remedies would be applied by private enterprise, because being low, it would, even if improved, be the last to be selected for private residences. For these reasons we are disposed to think that it might profitably. be made a somewhat prominent and important feature of the general plan of roads, especially about the base of the hills. It may be well, therefore to try to realize its landscape character a little more distinctly.

This may be done by imagining that a shallow stream has formerly flowed upon the course to be followed by a highway, close upon the banks of which trees have grown picturesquely and that back of the trees on each side a roadway and walks have been formed. The water of the stream having been cut off, and turf having established itself in the old bed, the result would have the character of the safety-valley we suggest. For a short time after storms it would be covered with water which would rise through occasional outlets from the pipe drain below; soon subsiding, it would leave the turf perfect, and available as a continuous pleasure ground. At certain points this plan has other advantages which will be hereafter indicated.

We give you the suggestion as our 12th proposition.

XII

Flood Regulators.—On any line of drainage which it may be desirable to follow in laying out a public highway, and the stream of which is liable to great fluctuations, a sufficiently deep and broad valley, or depression of the surface, to serve as a catch-water drain, safety pond and flood regulator; the surface of the ground being sodded and otherwise prepared, so as to have an agreeable appearance, and whenever practicable, fitted to serve as a public green, the road way being carried on each side of the depressed ground.

It may be noticed that each of the high roads as proposed to be laid out, with no object in view except that of offering the shortest practicable route to New York from the greatest number of house sites on the Island, will, if properly drained and constructed and especially if wisely embellished in planting, incidentally make available and attractive a series of sites fronting upon itself, upon ground which is now mainly useless, unoccupied by houses, uncultivated, and of which there is less prospect that it will be soon turned to much account in the ordinary course of improvement than almost any other on the island. Beyond, at furthest, the first mile, the value of land required to be taken would be low and the benefit to adjoining property would be more than enough to compensate the cost of the roads, provided always that adequate measures are at the same time taken to lift the character of the Island as a whole in public esteem.

It will also appear, if the whole system which has been thus far suggested, is carefully studied, that it is calculated to bring especially into public notice and favor the very districts which have been pointed out as those having the most advantages for collecting, storing and distributing water. Two, if not three or more of the safety-valley roads, which would take especially the character of pleasure roads, would lead toward them, the Westfield high-road would run for four miles through or beside two of the dales, and would cross the third, and both the Northfield and Southfield high-roads would, by short, necessary and important branches, connect with them.

There is no room for doubt then that if the general suggestions of our report thus far should be carried out, there will be a rapid and large rise in value in the land of these dales. A paint mill, a tobacco manufactory and a large brewery, have already been established hard by one of them. There are five places of burial, three of them recently established, upon the hills overlooking them, though fortunately only one drains toward them, and there are already within a mile of them settlements much too dense to consist with the preservation of water collected on the surface in a state of wholesome purity. Not only will all the dale land rise much in value, then, but its occupation in such a way or in such degree of domestic density as would destroy its suitability as a field of water collection will almost certainly occur before many years.

We have before referred to the peculiar situation of the island, in that, while likely to be the residence of a large and closely settled population, its authorities can not fall back for water, as is usually done, upon collecting basins in elevated highland pastures, where serious sources of contamination are easily guarded against.

We show by analysis that already in the denser settlements along the shore the well water contains nearly five times the amount of organic and dangerous impurity that is found in the water collected by the surface of these dales. (See Appendix, pp. 102–104 [285–288].)

It will be evident, upon a review of all the circumstances, that the value of these dales, if held as public property, will by and by be almost beyond price, while the cost to the public of obtaining them is liable soon to be vastly greater than at present. The immediate duty thus suggested is in our judgment of the most imperative character and gives grounds of justification, which could not well be made stronger, for throwing upon posterity some share of the cost.

We are by no means prepared to completely plan a water system for the island. Our figures of elevation are taken from the coast survey chart, which gives nothing within contours of twenty feet. We have not been able to properly guage the streams, and all our data must be taken as roughly approximate. Under any conceivable plan, however, large places will be wanted at several points in these three dales for impounding ponds and other essential parts of an aqueduct system, as will all the land occupied by and adjoining the streams flowing through them. If not absolutely essential to hold a large area on either side of the water courses from end to end, it will be quite necessary to restrict the amount and the character of its occupation, and it will certainly be desirable to keep it entirely free from dwellings and stables. Observing that your Commission contemplates a public park, (having appointed a committee on that subject,) the question occurs whether there would be any objection to its use as a public ground for recreation. We are fortunately able to answer it with confidence, a similar question having been raised some years since in Pennsylvania, and having been referred by the legislature to a Commission of leading citizens of Philadelphia. They obtained the assistance of the best engineers, chemists and sanitarians of the country and their decision was that with proper care such use-of a water preserving ground was unobjectionable. The result gives the City of Philadelphia a noble suburban park of nearly three thousand acres, this being the extent of the area sloping towards the impounding pond of the Fairmount Water Works, which it had been thought desirable to especially guard from sources of contamination.

In the case of Staten Island, it would be a simple plan for the public to form a park similarly designed, to include nearly all of the valleys and hill sides which would constitute the areas of precipitation for the water to be collected. Such a park for the Eastern water works would be four miles in length and at least one in average breadth, the Western part of the island still remaining to be provided for. It would occupy a moderately central position, would turn to good use a large extent of land which is at present benefiting nobody, but is much of it a nuisance, and relatively to the City of New York would possess somewhat of the character of the great suburban parks about London, Paris, and Berlin. This plan has great attractions, but it involves the purchase of a large extent of valuable real estate on the upper hill sides, and although we are confident that, as has happened in all similar cases, the advance in taxable value of the surrounding properties would eventually more than compensate for the required outlay, provided a thorough-drainage system should at the same time have been carried out over the whole island, we are constrained to doubt the practicability of so large an undertaking.

We propose, instead, that highways should be laid out on the slopes of the three dales we have indicated, one on each side of each, in such a manner as to leave the water-course generally midway between the two, the intermediate dale-bottom being in the upper parts not more than three or four hundred feet wide, but becoming gradually broader as the points are approached which would be suitable for impounding reservoirs, about and above which there would in each case be a large meadow. This space we should propose to clear of buildings, (there are none upon it now of much value), thin out the trees to open groups, and with little or no grading lay it down to grass. The ground thus prepared would have much the character of the safety-valleys before described, ex-cept that it must be broader and more diversified. We shall speak of it as the Water Glade.

The outlines of the water-glade would be curving in cor-respondence with the present forms of the inclosing hills, its bounding roads being carried down the slopes, always upon easy grades, giving occasion for a series of small bays and headlands on its border.

Outside the bounding road we should recommend that an-other space, having a depth of fully three hundred feet, should be acquired, which should be cleared of everything likely to occasion contamination, and the surface prepared as might be found most desirable for the collection and discharge of water upon the water-glade, by culverts under the highway. This having been done, and the ground on each side of all branches of the water-course being reserved, the remainder of the exterior ground, which we shall designate the Overdale, might be disposed of on long building leases, or possibly sold with certain rights reserved, also with restrictions against burial of the dead, against various manufactures, limiting the number of dwellings, providing against cellars, manure pits or cess-pools, unless cemented, and with cemented outlets to a common pipe which would be provided in the highway, to discharge below the impounding ponds, and under whatever other conditions should, upon careful consideration, be thought desirable. There would perhaps be three hundred acres of the Overdale, which when properly prepared and regulated, might safely be occupied by detached dwellings.

On the south side of Dongan-knoll there is a favorable place for a distributing reservoir for the upper hill country, and we should propose to acquire this ground and connect it, together with the knoll itself, with the heads of each of the water-glades.

We should also recommend the acquisition of a tract of land of from five to ten acres suitable for a distributing reservoir for Clifton, which would be found at an elevation of two hundred feet on Fox Hill, and another with reference to Stapleton and New Brighton at some point on Signal Hill.

The Martling Dale lies exactly on the line of the proposed Westfield High road, which would here constitute part of the bounding highway of its water-glade. The west end of the Millsdale would extend to the Fresh Kills near Richmond. The Manor Dale would be reached by a short branch from the Northfield High-road, and thus opened to pleasure travel from Jersey as well as New York. By carrying a branch of the drainage valley proposed to be formed below the hills at Concord up the Clove, this feature in the Southfield High-road would become to all appearances a branch of the water-glade; we should propose to extend it in one fork to the reservoir ground at Fox Hill, about which a drive and walk constituting a local promenade for Clifton should be formed, and in another, east of the Oldtown road, to the Shore-road at the South beach, where, as already suggested, it would merge in the central feature of Mr. Root's plan. We should propose a similar connection with the proposed reservoir ground on Signal Hill, the distance to which would not exceed half a mile probably, and a third branch following down the glen below the Martling Pond to the North shore, by which means some of the most charming sylvan scenery on the island would be appropriated at little cost and with great incidental advantages to the neighborhood.

To the amount of land which should be acquired and held by the public simply from considerations of economy and prudence with regard to water supply and drainage, an addition of a tenth would enable a pleasure-ground to be laid out, which, if less desirable than the large park before suggested, would certainly have a highly interesting and attractive, as well as wholly original character.

One element in the value of a park is the advantage which house sites fronting upon it have in not looking directly upon the face of other houses but rather upon a permanent verdure. This advantage our plan would secure to a frontage from fifteen to twenty miles in length, (not counting the Shore-road, much of which would have an outlook finer than that upon any park). Regarded as a park scheme, much of the Glade is already very charmingly planted, the western landscape as seen from all parts of the Manor Dale has great breadth and beauty, while from the Dongan-knoll, which is the central feature of the system, the views, with some little improvement of the foregrounds, would be really magnificent, comprehending a grand sweep of the horizon in blue water on one side, in blue hills on the other.

The advantages of such a public ground in giving increased value to all property on the island we hardly need argue. It is sometimes said, however, that the island is a park in itself and has no need of any special public ground. It may be pertinent, therefore, to recall the fact that no part of the island is today more of a park than Rocky Hollow, or the Bloomingdale road north of Union Square, or the greater part of the Twenty-first Ward of New York, was fifty years ago. Nowhere on Staten Island is there a landscape or even a glimpse of agreeable scenery which belongs permanently to the public—which no man has the right to obstruct and destroy in pursuance of private and selfish ends.

Without advocating the immediate construction of waterworks, we may observe that the measure we propose would give Staten Island control of an opportunity for supplying its eastern and northern parts with pure water at a smaller cost for original construction of works and annual maintenance and extension, than a similar advantage could probably be obtained by any other considerable rural suburban district.

The conditions upon which this opportunity depends, beyond those which we have already emphasized, are to be found mainly in the nearness of the sources of water to the points at which its distribution will be required; the commanding height attainable for distributing reservoirs, by which the requirements of size and consequent cost of pipeage may be kept low; the location of the communities to be served within a circular sweep of short radius from the center of the system—the situation of the Dongan-knoll being almost exactly equidistant from tide water at Factoryville on the north, and New Dorp on the south, Stapleton on the east, and the Fresh Kills near Richmond on the west;—and finally in the limit to outward and scattered extension which is imposed by the sounds and bays, and the certainty that the principal increase of population will tend to bring the point of greatest average annual consumption constantly nearer the principal point of supply.

We submit that the Island cannot afford to run the least risk of losing this opportunity.

The preparation of the Glade and its connections with the safety valleys and the distributing reservoirs, so far as necessary to give unity of character to the whole territory proposed to be acquired for the public, as a pleasure ground system, would involve very little expense for construction. The ground simply requires the treatment that a farmer would ordinarily use for making a permanent meadow. We propose no constructed interior roads or walks, and the general character aimed at being that of a rural common rather than a park, the turf would be cropped by sheep, and its maintenance involve no expense. The bounding road would be a common highway, and the expense of its maintenance would be a charge upon the householders of the Overdale fronting upon it.

The propositions in respect to this subject which we present for your formal consideration, are almost necessarily somewhat indefinite in terms, the object being to leave much freedom for further study.

277

XIII

Eastern Water Preserve and Public Common.—A system of water works for the eastern part of the Island to be had in view, the suggestion being favored of appropriating to this purpose so much as is desirable of the ground designated in the report before the Commission as the Martling-dale, the Manor-dale and the Mill-dale, with reference to Impounding Reservoirs, and the preservation of the purity of the water to be collected in them. An appropriation to be made of from five to ten acres of ground upon Fox Hill and upon Signal Hill, selected with reference to the double purpose of distributing reservoirs and public recreation grounds, and these sites to be connected by arms from fifty to one hundred and fifty feet wide, with the ground proposed to be appropriated as a water preserve, and the whole designed to serve as a public common.

The system of water works which has been indicated has been studied especially with reference to supplying the population dwelling east of the Kills, (Fresh and Great). It might for a time contribute also to the supply of the community living west of the Kills. But the necessity of an aqueduct supply will not nearly as soon, probably, be pressing in that part of the island, and when it is so it will doubtless be thought prudent to provide for it from local sources. These will be found in the water-shed of Benham's Brook and Lemon Creek, the collections of each of which may be united in one scheme to supply the whole, or perhaps better, may be used distinctively for separate districts. The amount of water estimated to be due from both, supposing the usual yield, would be adequate under proper conservance to meet the necessary requirements of a population many times as large as the present. There are elevations centrally situated within the districts of altitude sufficient to give the water satisfactory distribution by gravitation. The early acquisition of ground for this purpose would, it is believed, be a measure of prudence and economy. Nor would its early appropriation as a public common, maintained as heretofore suggested, be without considerable

278

advantages. We submit therefore our last proposition as follows:

XIV

Western Water Preserve and Public Common.—Suitable grounds for the collection, storage and distribution of the waters of Lemon Creek and Benham Brook, to be selected and laid off, and these to be of the extent required to admit of a system of conservation and management, in all respects similar to that proposed to be had in view for the Eastern Water Works.

It may be acceptable to you to learn that while very great interest in our duty and a disposition to assist us has been generally manifested by citizens of the island, for which we are grateful, we have seen no evidence of an intention to unworthily influence our judgment. We have received no hint from any person, in the Commission or out of it, of private or local interests, nor was there a soul beside ourselves who, before this reading, had any knowledge of our intended recommendations.

We beg to return thanks, on your behalf, to Doctor H. I. Bowditch, of Boston; to Professor J. S. Newberry, of the School of Mines; Prof. C. F. Chandler, of Columbia College; to Professor A. F. Liautard, of New York; and Professor James Law, of the Cornell University; to Messrs. G. K. Radford, of Buffalo, L. Y. Schermerhorn, of Chicago, H. D. Fisher, of New York, Civil Engineers, and to S. C. Hawley, Chief Clerk of the Police Department, R. S. Guernsey, Esq., and Homer Morgan, Esq., of New York, and to Messrs. Crooke, Elliott, Meyer, Minthorne Tompkins, John C. Thompson, D. R. Hitchcock, Jacob Garretson, and Peter L. Cortelyou, of the Island, for valuable contributions.

We are also under obligations, in your behalf, to the physicians of the Island generally, and more especially to the following gentlemen, who have answered our inquiries with painstaking care, or otherwise particularly aided us: Doctors Edgar, Golder, Spencer, E. and G. Hubbard, and Andrews, of Westfield; Doctors Anderson, Lea and Richardson, of Edgewater; Doctors Walser, Bogart and Van Rensselaer, of New Brighton; Doctor Clark, of West Brighton; Doctor Martindale, of Port Richmond; Doctor Satterthwaite, of Mariner's Harbor, and Doctors Ephraim Clark, and Isaac L. Millspaugh, of Southfield.

We shall conclude by gathering in one scheme the several propositions to which our study has led. It is by no means intended to cover all obvious requirements of improvement, but to establish a framework, and give a key to the character of what should be had in view. Accepting the estimate which we have taken, and have attempted to justify, of the opportunities and dangers of the island, we believe that we have given you good reasons for adopting each proposition.

With the problem of ways and means for carrying out the proposition we have nothing to do, nor, as we understand, has your Commission, further than as it affects the question of its practicability; and even on that point the question is not merely what is practicable now, but what is to be practicable? What can be expected of Staten Island? It is for you to determine whether our recommendations assume too much or too little in this respect.

We respectfully recommend you to adopt the following:

Scheme of Improvements to Be Had in View in the Study of a New Plan for Staten Island

I

Westfield High-road.—A highway not less than one hundred feet wide from Tottenville to New Brighton Point, by the most direct course which shall be found consistent with ease of grade and reasonable economy of construction.

II

Northfield High-road.—A similar highway from the western part of Northfield to New Brighton Point.

III

Southfield High-road.—A similar highway from the western part of Southfield to New Brighton Point.

IV

Brighton Place.—At the point of junction of the three high-roads, above specified, on an open place on the water side, not less than four hundred feet in length upon the shore and two hundred feet deep.

V

Shore Road.—A road not less than one hundred feet wide leading from the south end of New York Avenue, Clifton, southward to the shore; thence, westward, along the shore, or as near it as a reasonable economy will admit, to New Dorp Plains, then curving to the northward so as to make a convenient junction with the Southfield highroad north or north-east of the Great Kills; thence, westward, keeping the Bay in view, to Tottenville; thence, along the shore, or as near the shore, either upon salt marsh or upland, as shall be found consistent with moderate directness and economy, until a connection is made with the existing shore road on the north side of the island.

VI

Transverse Roads.—Roads not less than fifty feet wide crossing the high-roads wherever the topography admits, at intervals not exceeding, on an average, half a mile, nor nearer together, on an average, than a quarter of a mile.

VII

Public Drains.—Public Drains, at intervals not exceeding half a mile, nor nearer together, on an average, than quarter of a mile, throughout the Island, the salt marshes alone excepted, to be adapted to serve as outfalls for the thorough-drainage of all the lands between them, and also to receive the surface drainage of the highways.

VIII

Under Drain and Road Drains.—Wherever the public drains will be required to receive no more water than can be safely carried in a pipe of fifteen inches calibre, they may be covered drains, laid as far as practicable within the bounds of public highways.

IX

Open Public Drains.—Open drains either to be boxed, or to be cut with side slopes of never less than one foot horizontal to one of vertical measurement, and whenever such side slopes are impracticable, to have smooth floors of firm material, and such wall as may be necessary to prevent caving or crumbling of sides.

X

Natural Water Courses.—The beds of all open water courses to be made sufficiently firm, smooth and dishing towards the deepest part of the channel, to prevent any lodgment of the water, as the streams shrink in summer, in ponds where it will be liable to stagnate.

XI

Occasional Flood Courses.—Wherever any open drain or water course is liable to great fluctuations of service, as to flood by storm, and stagnation by drought, provision, if practicable, to be made for laying a pipe below such open drain, the use of the open drain being to dispose safely of floods which the pipe cannot carry.

XII

Flood Regulators.—On any line of drainage which it may be desirable to follow in laying out a public highway, and the stream of which is liable to great fluctuations, a sufficiently deep and broad valley, or depression of the surface, to serve

282

as a catch water drain, safety pond and flood regulator; the surface of the ground being sodded and otherwise prepared, so as to have an agreeable appearance, and whenever practicable, fitted to serve as a public green, the road way being carried on each side of the depressed ground.

XIII

Eastern Water Preserve and Public Common.—A system of water works for the eastern part of the Island to be had in view, the suggestion being favored of appropriating to this purpose so much as is desirable of the ground designated in the report before the Commission as the Martling-dale, the Manor-dale and the Mill-dale, with reference to the Impounding Reservoirs, and the preservation of the purity of the water to be collected in them. An appropriation to be made of from five to ten acres of ground upon Fox Hill and upon Signal Hill, selected with reference to the double purpose of distributing reservoirs and public recreation grounds, and these sites may be connected by arms from fifty to one hundred and fifty feet wide, with the ground proposed to be appropriated as a water preserve, and the whole designed to serve as a public common.

XIV

Western Water Preserve and Public Common.—Suitable grounds for the collection, storage and distribution of the waters of Lemon Creek and Benham Brook, to be selected and laid off, and these to be of the extent required to admit of a system of conservation and management, in all respects similar to that proposed to be had in view for the Eastern Water Works.

Respectfully,
FRED. LAW OLMSTED,
ELISHA HARRIS,
J. M. TROWBRIDGE,
H. H. RICHARDSON

Appendix

I. COMPARATIVE PROGRESS OF POPULATION OF STATEN ISLAND AND OF OTHER SUBURBS

SUMMARY OF THE CENSUS

RICHMOND COUNTY	1865	1870	DIFFERENCE
Castleton	7,883	9,519	1,636
Middletown	6,866	7,589	723
Northfield	5,201	5,949	748
Southfield	4,407	5,072	675
Westfield	4,052	4,905	853
Totals	28,409	33,044	4,635

TOWNS IN WESTCHESTER COUNTY	1865	1870	DIFFERENCE
Yonkers	12,756	18,320	5,564
Westchester	3,026	6,166	3,140
West Farms	7,333	9,334	2,001
Morrisania	11,691	19,637	7,946
Rye	4,675	7,152	2,477
Cortlandt, including Peekskill	9,393	11,695	2,302
Greenburgh, including Tarrytown	8,463	10,876	2,413
Ossining, including Sing-Sing	6,223	7,798	1,515
Eastchester	5,615	7,494	1,879
W. Plains	2,122	3,000	878
Bedford	3,465	3,700	235
New Rochelle	3,968	3,901	67 less

TOWNS ON LONG ISLAND	1865	1870	DIFFERENCE
Flushing	10,813	14,673	3,860
New Lots	5,009	9,805	4,796
Gravesend and Flatlands	3,531	4,417	886
New Utrecht	3,394	3,298	96 less.

II. ANALYSIS OF WATERS, BY PROFESSOR
C. F. CHANDLER, OF THE SCHOOL OF MINES

Note—Samples 1, 2, 3, 4 and 5 were selected as follows, under the supervision of this board, and were forwarded to PROF. CHANDLER, under seal, and with no other description than the above numbers. They were obtained during a time of unusual drought, and consequently may be considered as fairly representing the particular characteristics of the water-supply in each of the localities, or from each of the sources we here describe:

DESCRIPTIVE LISTS OF THE WATERS SUBMITTED TO
PROFESSOR CHANDLER FOR CHEMICAL ANALYSIS

Sample No. 1.—From a well in Amos street, Clifton, about twenty feet above tide level; depth nine feet in the ordinary gravel and earth of that district. Well, clean, with clean surroundings, the surface near it being paved and cemented but the subsoil exposed to the ordinary results of defective drainage. Quantity 5 gallons, taken December 10th, 1870.

Sample No. 2.—From a shallow well-spring at the dam of the Millpond of Standrig's machine shop, on Willow Brook, about fifty-five feet above tide level; Northfield. Quantity, 6 gallons, taken December 9th, 1870.

Sample No. 3.—From principal inlet of Ketchum's millpond, near the road from New Springville to Richmond. The inlet receives some fresh drainage from swamp ditches recently opened, and the surface wash of some soft magnesian rocks, which give the chief impurities. Taken at a point about sixty feet above tide level. Quantity 5 gallons. December 10th, 1870.

Sample No. 4.—From the upper pond of Abraham Britton, Esq., on east side of Clove road, two days after heavy rain. Height about one hundred and thirty-five feet above tide-level. Quantity, 6 gallons. December 15th, 1870.

Sample No. 5.—From a well near Franklin avenue, at a

285

point about one hundred feet above tide-level, and from a clean excavation forty feet deep in the magnesian or soapstone rock of the locality. Quantity, 2 quarts, taken December 15th, 1870.

Remark.—The wells (Nos. 1 & 5), are regarded as fair examples of the village and villa wells. The samples 2, 3 and 4, are specimens of the present natural outflowings from the several dales described in the report.

Laboratory of the School of Mines,
New York, January 12, 1871

Certificate of the Analysis of the Samples of Water from Staten Island, marked Nos. 1, 2, 3, 4 and 5, submitted to me for examination, contain in one U. S. Wine Gallon of 231 Cubic inches

Grains	No. 1	No. 2	No. 3	No. 4	No. 5
Potassa	0.529	0.140	0.091	0.106	
Soda	2.822	0.369	0.345	0.362	
Lime	1.819	0.816	0.846	0.851	
Magnesia	4.397	0.332	1.960	1.149	
Chlorine	3.156	0.486	0.546	0.546	0.728
Sulphuric Acid	2.018	0.140	0.198	0.158	
Silica	1.429	0.804	0.937	0.385	
Oxide of Iron and Alumina	0.233	0.041	0.088	0.204	
Carbonic Acid	5.451	1.447	2.660	1.813	
	21.854	4.575	7.671	5.574	
Oxygen equivalent to Chlorine	0.711	0.109	0.123	0.123	
Total Inorganic matter as left by evaporation	21.143	4.466	7.548	5.451	8.519
Organic and Volatile matter	4.283	0.816	0.734	1.397	0.812
Total Impurities left by evaporation	25.426	5.282	8.282	6.848	9.331
Carbonic Acid holding Carbonates in solution as Bicarbonates	5.451	1.447	2.660	1.813	
Water in Bicarbonates	2.230	0.391	1.088	0.742	
Total impurities in solution	33.107	7.120	12.030	9.403	

These bases and acids exist in the water in the following combinations:—

Grains	No. 1	No. 2	No. 3	No. 4	No. 5
Chloride of Sodium	5.200	0.697	0.651	0.683	
Chloride of Magnesium	none	0.084	0.203	0.177	
Sulphate of Potassa	0.979	0.260	0.169	0.195	
Sulphate of Soda	0.152	none	none	none	
Sulphate of Lime	2.520	0.035	0.205	0.116	
Bicarbonate of Lime	2.354	3.299	2.203	2.326	
Bicarbonate of Magnesia	15.957	1.084	6.841	3.920	
Oxide of Iron and Alumina	0.233	0.041	0.087	0.204	
Silica	1.429	0.804	0.937	0.385	
Organic and Volatile Matter	4.283	0.816	0.734	1.397	
Total Impurities as they exist in solution	33.107	7.120	12.030	9.403	
Hardness—Carbonate of Lime or its equivalent	4.130	1.430	1.350	1.380	4.210
Oxygen required to oxidise the *putrescent* organic matter	0.050	0.020	0.020	0.070	0.040

GENTLEMEN.—As I am not informed of the particular sources from which these samples were obtained, I must necessarily limit my remarks upon them to the chemical composition of the waters as developed by my analyses.

Sample No. 1 is a very impure water, it contains an unusually large proportion of organic matter, which, while it is, perhaps, not specially dangerous at present, is liable at times to be a prolific source of disease.

Besides the organic matter this water contains a large amount of alkaline and earthy salts. The former are not specially objectionable, while the latter are anything but desirable. These lime and magnesia salts are injurious in waters intended for domestic purposes; (1) as they render the water "hard," and destroy a certain portion of the soap, when they are used in washing; (2) because when food is prepared with such waters, the full effect of the application of heat is not obtained, meat and vegetables do not become as tender and perfectly digestible as when boiled in soft water; (3), that salts are believed by physicians to cause, when present, in unusual quantity, certain very troublesome diseases, such as indigestion, diarrhœa and dysentery, and even goitre.

This water is probably drawn from the neighborhood of dwellings, and perhaps of stables, and I regard it as unsuitable for domestic use.

Samples numbered 2, 3 and 4 are of very good quality. They contain about the same quantity of organic matter as is usually found in the sources from which the Croton and Ridgewood waters are drawn. The alkaline and earthy salts are not excessive, though there is a marked choice between these three samples of water. No. 2 is decidedly the best of the three; it is remarkably pure, and is of equal quality with the Croton.

Next in the order of purity stands No. 4. No. 3 contains an amount of earthy salts which places it near the dividing line between the good and the impure waters. If the supply of Nos. 2 and 4 is sufficient for the public wants, it would perhaps be advisable to rely entirely upon them, though I think No. 3 may be used with safety.

No. 5 is of about the same quality as No. 3, though somewhat inferior to it, as it contains a larger quantity of alkaline and earthy salts than any of the others, except No. 1, and more magnesia than is desirable; yet it is not contaminated by organic matter.

The *softness* of numbers 2, 3 and 4 is remarkable, and is an important element in a supply for domestic purposes, for the reasons already mentioned.

Respectfully yours,
C. F. CHANDLER,
Professor of Analytical and Applied Chemistry
To the Advisory Board,
Staten Island Improvement Commission

III. STEAM ON COMMON ROADS

The following extract from an official report of a very cautiously conducted trial of road locomotives is here given, on account of its bearing upon the question of the probable future value of roads of unusual breadth and easy grades, especially when they are continuations of important routes of water transportation, as would be the case with the proposed high-roads, and some of the cross roads, leading inland from landings on the island. There seems little room for doubt that upon firm, broad roads of easy grades, steam can now be used for the carriage of freight more economically than horses. If roads should now be laid out of ordinary width and grades, upon such routes, leading to localities which are likely to increase very much in pōpulation, a demand is very likely to arise, in the early future, for widening and reducing them, which can only be met at the cost of much destruction of property fronting upon them.

The report gives the result of a trial of one of AVELING & PORTER's Road Locomotives, undertaken by M. Tresca, for the French Conservatoire Imperial des Arts-et-Métiers, at the instigation of the Director, General Morin, and in concert with Professor Fleeming Jenkin, Fellow of the Royal Society of London. The engine, "La Ville de Senlis," with which these experiments were made, is of 14 horse-power nominal, and as will be seen, *drew a load of nearly* 80 *tons, of* 2,240 *lbs. each ton,* (exclusive of the engine,) whereas her power is stated to be "40 to 50 tons." The trial of the engine took place at the Sugar Manufactory of Messrs. Lallouette & Co., of Beaurain, near Senlis:

"Messrs. AVELING & PORTER, who have applied themselves to the construction of Traction Engines, have already made a great number for business purposes; so, as it was impossible for us to make sufficiently prolonged trials of these machines at the Exposition, we gladly availed ourselves of an occasion offered at the Sugar Manufactory of Messrs. Lallouette & Co., of Beaurain, near Senlis, to witness a traction experiment with a very heavy load; and we took the necessary steps to register all the mechanical elements of the question.

"These experiments were, moreover, made in concert with Professor Fleeming Jenkin, Fellow of the Royal Society of London, who went into all details, and whose presence gives to the results arrived at, a character of security that increases their importance.

"The motive power of the engine consists of a single cylinder, 11 inches diameter, with a piston stroke of 14 inches.

"The diameter of the driving wheels being 6.50 feet, the ground gone over by every turn of the wheels should be 20.07 feet; and we shall see, in fact, by the numbers shown on the wheel indicator, that the actual ground passed over differs very little from this number. The width of face of the driving wheels is 18 inches; they each form a veritable roller, bearing upon a great surface and preventing the destruction that might be found from the passage over them of so great a weight, of macadamized roads.

"These wheels work free upon the axle, and are only keyed to it by means of a strong pin of 2.36 inches diameter at the projecting end, which it is necessary to draw out a short distance to unlock the wheels when going around curves. This mode of connection, as simple as it is strong, is exceedingly convenient, and appeared entirely to answer the purpose intended. The two front wheels are only 3 feet 8 inches in diameter, and 12 inches wide on the face, but when the engine is on a level road they only carry 7-29ths of the total weight; those on the driving axle accounting thus for 22-29ths of this weight.

"The locomotive is, besides, provided with a fifth, steering wheel in front, or rather a thin disc of 2 1-2 feet diameter, which acts on the road by its own weight and by that of a triangular frame, fixed, by means of a horizontal joint, on the front part of the engine. The weight of all this apparatus is 6 cwt. 1 qr. 16 lb. only. This fifth wheel cannot exercise any injurious action upon the ground; but slight as the friction is, it is sufficient for moving the fore carriage which carries it, guided by the hand of the steerer, and by a very slight effort, in any required direction, The entirely effectual arrangement of the steering wheel is not one of the least interesting features of the engine in question."

After giving a long and technical description of the Locomotive Boiler, and the large amount of heating surface provided,—which in a 14 H. P. engine reaches 273 1-4 square feet,—the report proceeds to detail the particulars of the load drawn:—

"In order to form a load, six wagons were filled with coal, the total weight of which added to the weight of the wagons, was 59 tons 14 cwt. 3 qr. The trial consisted of drawing this load from Beaurain to Senlis, and then from Senlis to Beaurain, a distance of 7.45 miles, presenting inclines and descents which in some instances were as great as 1 in 30. On the departure of the train the following conditions of the engine were noted:—

Fuel on the locomotive, 5 cwt. (560 lbs.)

Water in tenders, 375.47 gallons.

Level of the water in boiler below brass case of glass tube, 0.39 inches.

Steam pressure on starting, 97 lbs. per square inch."

Time occupied in the run from Beaurain to Senlis (7.45 miles,) 3h. 3m.

CONDITIONS ASCERTAINED ON ARRIVAL:

Fuel remaining on the engine = 1c. 1q. 16lb.(156 lbs.)

Ashes and Cinders . . . . = 1c. 0q. 14lb.(126 lbs.)

Water in the Tender after having refilled the boiler to the level of starting, 125 galls. which gives a consumption of 278.78 galls.

Pressure on arriving 90 lbs. per square inch," corresponding to 7-12 atmospheres, (French measure.)

"The facility with which this journey from Beaurain to Senlis, (7.45 miles) was accomplished, led us to suppose that the limit of traction power had not been sustained. It was believed that *two additional wagons* might still be attached, which Mr. Aveling had gone to fetch with the locomotive from the sugar factory at Beaurain. He set out at 3.25 P. M. and returned at 4.15 P. M. with another load, which was yoked on to the principal train.

"In consequence of this addition the total weight of the load drawn was raised to 79 tons 19 cwt. 1 qr. The adherent weight consisting of only 22-29ths that of the locomotive, we may call the total load equal to 7.65 times the adherent weight.

"In spite of these unfavorable conditions *the engine started very well and hauled the load on level ground and up slight inclines 1 in 250.*

"The care with which we registered the time of passing each kilometric post may appear excessive, but our motive was to ascertain convincingly if the engine, loaded as it was, had not slipped over any portion of the road. The total distance was 7.44 miles, and the counter marked 2.037 revolutions, which brings it to 19.29 feet of displacement per revolution. The figure is so near the exact figure, 6.12 miles, that *it may be considered no abnormal slip took place*, the slight observed difference not being greater than 4 per cent of the external circumference of the wheel.

"To sum up: The engine La Ville de Senlis drew in a regular manner, upon a good road slightly undulating, a total load of 59 tons. The co-efficient of traction may be approximately estimated at 1-40, which would bring the mean strain to nearly 39 1-2 cwt., taking into account the weight of the locomotive.

"This mean effort, developed at a speed of 3.54 feet per second, brings the valuation of effective work to 15,623 foot-pounds per second, or to 27.61 horse-power. This figure will appear high if it be compared with the consumption of fuel, which was 3c. 2q. 13 lbs. (405 lbs.) in three hours and three minutes, say, 132.15 lbs., per hour of actual traveling. This consumption represents only 4.40 lbs. of coal per horse-power and per hour.

"The corresponding consumption of water is not less than 132.22 gallons per hour of actual travelling. With the present tenders, which can hold 396 gallons of water, it is necessary to replenish them every 6 1-2 to 7 1-2 miles. The co-efficient of adherence may be estimated on the road gone over at 0.3

of the adherent weight. The adherence resulting therefrom was only necessary for the working of the engine up inclines of 0.030 (1 in 33 to 1 in 30) and at starting.

"*The load of 79 19-20ths tons which the engine drew on level ground is not the limit of what it can draw under these conditions.*

"A speed of 2.48 miles per hour appears suitable for traffic of this nature, and renders the manœuvres so easy that the train is well managed by a superintendent, an engine driver, and an assistant solely employed to guide the steering wheel in front.

"Done by the Engineer Sub-Director of the Conservatoire Imperial des Arts-et-Métiers.

H. Tresca,

General Morin

"*Approved—The Director,*

"*Paris, 15th January, 1868.*"

Note.—M. Tresca adds to his report some facts as to this engine, furnished by Messrs. Lallouette & Co.

From these it appears that it had only been worked half of the previous season, but during that time "it had conveyed 2,460 1-2 tons of beet-root from the weighbridge to the factory; a distance of 2.48 miles. It drew each journey 3 wagons loaded with 24t. 12cwt. 0q. 11lbs. of beet root, and the engine made 4 journeys and back; thus effecting the transport of 98 1-2 tons per diem.

The expenditure of fuel was not more than 9c. 3q. 10 lbs. (1,102 lbs) of coal for the 8 journeys,[12] and the trains were well managed by a driver and two assistants.

IV. VENTILATION OF THE FERRY BOATS

EXTRACT FROM A LETTER FROM L. W. LEEDS, ENGINEER
OF VENTILATION AND HEATING

Mr. Leeds was consulted as to whether by any simple expedient, the sickening air often found in the saloons of the

[12] Equal to 2 1-2 lbs. per ton. The ton referred to is 2,240 lbs. [1871.]

Staten Island ferry boats, when crowded and artificially heated, could be avoided without introducing draughts of cold air.

In reply he remarks:

"I think the uncomfortable feelings experienced in the upper saloon are much owing to the way in which it is warmed. The thin floor is exposed to the current of cold air sweeping through the carriage way below, and to keep up a tolerable average of heat, the upper part of the cabin must be highly heated, making the head hot and feet cold. To remedy this, I should think, it would be necessary to ceil below the floor, and that being done, it would be very desirable to pass a current of heated air beneath it, [in the interspace]; there appears to be an abundance for that purpose that now escapes around the smokepipe, and which might be utilized in that way.

There is also abundant power to create any amount of draught of heated air through the saloon, even when densely crowded, that may be desirable. But I do not believe that this alone would satisfy most persons, they need fresh, moderately cool air for breathing, and warmth to be supplied in a great measure by radiation or by contact with a warmed floor."

V. AGRICULTURAL EFFECTS OF THOROUGH-DRAINAGE

The large Gold Medal of the Highland and Agricultural Society of Scotland was last fall awarded to William W. Hozier, a farmer of Tannochside, for a paper entitled "Practical Remarks on Agricultural Drainage." At the conclusion of the paper, the author, after proving the greatly enlarged yield which has followed thorough-drainage, says:

"Nor is increased productiveness the only benefit therefrom accruing. By thorough-draining all the operations of agriculture are rendered less dependent on the variations of the weather; and farming, instead of being a hazardous game of chance, approaches to a certainty as nearly as any out-door occupation can be held to do in an unsettled climate. Drained land can be earlier ploughed in spring and, becoming sooner workable after rainy weather, the seed is sown betimes, and the crops arriving earlier at maturity, harvest is expedited and the crop saved before the advent of bad weather. Stock can be sooner placed in pastures in the spring, and left out later in the autumn, thereby securing the advantages of a prolonged season. . . . Owing to [the] increase of temperature [in the soil], germination is speedier, growth more rapid, and the quality of the crops enhanced. Drained land even acquires the power of producing crops which cannot possibly thrive on undrained land. The growth of wheat has thus been rendered certain, where formerly it was precarious. . . . It counteracts the evil influence of drought in summer, . . . while in winter the openness of the pores, which it induces, permits the frost to penetrate deeper and to pulverize the soil more thoroughly. Everywhere its introduction tends to the farmer's benefit by lessening the expense of seed and labor, and by adding to the fertility and consequent value of the land. The very climate is improved; dense and chilly fogs are dispelled. . . . Even diseases, such as rheumatism, ague and intermittent fevers, often disappear on its introduction. Cattle and sheep are more comfortable and, consequently, become healthier. In some Highland farms the diminution of casualties from 'braxy' has been found more than sufficient to cover the entire cost of draining."

The *Boston Journal,* of Chemistry, reports a trial made in this country in April, in which a difference in the temperature of the soil of the drained and the undrained part of a field, at four inches from the surface was found to be 13°, the condition in all other respects being as nearly as possible alike. Corn would germinate and grow on the drained and not on the undrained side of the field.

VI. EFFECTS OF SATURATED SOIL ON BRUTES

Prof. Liautard, of the New York College of Veterinary Surgeons, confirms, from personal observation, our statement that domestic animals, both of common and high bred stock, suffer much from malaria on Staten Island and other districts having highly saturated soils, about New York, and has kindly furnished the following letter:

To the Advisory Board of the Staten Island Improvement Commission:

GENTLEMEN: In reply to your inquiries, I beg leave to state that marshy and other malarious localities have always been regarded by observing veterinary physicians as being injurious to domestic animals as well as men. I need not delay here to quote authorities upon this subject; they are abundant in the records of our profession.

Carbuncular fever, various putrid affections that tend to gangrenous termination, anæmia, hydræmia, catarrhal affections, periodic opthalmias, grease, canker of the feet, etc., etc. Such are the diseases which, according to the seasons, affect animals inhabiting malarious localities. These very serious forms of disease show themselves during the summer months and in the autumn, when the marshy or other wet grounds are partially dried, and especially when the animals are turned out in the fields at evening, or during the night and morning—the periods when the air is loaded with vapor, and when the malarial elements are present in their highest proportion, and are saturated in the dews.

The growth of vegetation in marshy and malarial grounds is generally very active; the plants in such localities are usually large and watery, but containing little of nutritive elements. Animals fed with such herbage generally have very large and tumid bellies, their skin is thick, hard, and covered with long, rough hair (rough coated), the feet are flat and spreading, and the hoof material thin and brittle. Their blood contains an unhealthy proportion of watery elements; the lymphatic glands are excessively developed and swollen. Such animals may be larger framed, but they will be anaemic and feeble. Such animals—chronically poisoned by malaria—are thus already constitutionally and structurally predisposed to blood diseases, as also to diseases of the lymphatic and circulatory systems. Horses are thus predisposed to, and readily suffer from "distemper," influenza, periodic ophthalmia, canker, glanders and farcy. Horned cattle, particularly in the spring, are often, from such poisoning, found suffering from anæmia, hydræmia, and parasitic diseases; and when thus associated with malarial empoisonments, such maladies generally appear under the entozoötic or epizoötic forms.

In regard to the question, "How is the malarial poison received into the system by domestic animals?" we find that the skin, being protected as it is by the rough, long coat of hair and by the thick epidermis, is less liable than in human beings to absorb malaria. But the digestive apparatus offers a more ready way for receiving the poison. Animals, in drinking the water of marshy or other malarial grounds, eating the herbage during the night—especially in morning hours—of plants covered with saturated dew, introduce into their digestive cavities the pathogenic malarial element, which is soon absorbed and made operative for evil in the blood. The pulmonary mucous membrane is likewise an open door for the introduction of paludal malaria, and, as we know, that delicate membrane has a great power of absorption, both for liquid and gaseous elements. M. Roche, in a treatise published in 1852, states that "an adult horse, breathing at an average of 10 or 12 times per minute, would, in 24 hours, introduce into his organism, by respiration alone, from 6 to 7 *litres* of malarial elements."

I have the honor to be,
Gentlemen,
Respectfully yours,
ALEXANDRE F. LIAUTARD, M.D., V.S.

VII. SANITARY GEOLOGY

NOTE FROM PROFESSOR NEWBERRY UPON THE GEOLOGY OF STATEN ISLAND IN RELATION TO WATER-SUPPLY AND SANITARY DRAINAGE

The following note from Professor Newberry sustains the view presented in the Report, of the drainage, even in the most difficult situations upon the island, and of the absorptive and reservoir character of the great central ridge of loose sepentine rock:

School of Mines of Columbia College,
New York, January 10th, 1871

F. L. Olmsted, Esq., Chairman Advisory Board, Staten Island Improvement Commission:

DEAR SIR:—In reply to your inquiry I would say that one result of my hasty reconnoissance of Staten Island was to convince me that geological causes exert an important influence on its salubrity. The geological conditions are important, mainly as they affect the drainage and water supply; and they are—very briefly stated—1st. a' peculiar topography, apparently the result of glacial drift action, in which an unusual number of small, detached water-basins or pond-holes are a conspicuous feature; 2d. A hard-pan subsoil, more than usually retentive of moisture; 3d. The nature and relations of the different belts of rock which traverse the Island. These rocks are serpentine, sandstone, and trap rocks, which differ greatly in their power of absorption and retention of water, and their conductibility of heat. How much they differ in these respects can only be determined by experiments now in progress, for your Board; but we know that they differ in a marked degree. The serpentine is granular and porous in texture, and generally loose and open in structure, so that it promptly absorbs surfacewater, and promotes natural drainage; while at the same time it is the great reservoir from which a water-supply must come. The sandstone has much the same physical characters, and whatever influence it exerts is similar to that of the serpentine, but it nowhere shows itself at the surface, and I only infer that it is present from what I know of the geology of the neighboring country. The trap is a very close and impervious rock, and is a ready conductor of heat. It is therefore an undesirable element in the geology of the Island. The belt it occupies is however, very narrow, and cuts only one side of the Island; the ridge it forms is also very low, and while it is the rim of certain water-basins which must be drained to be salubrious, such basins are relatively small, and I was

298

led to believe, by what I saw of them, by no means beyond the reach of reclamation. The cretaceous clays which underline so much of the western part of the Island, are nearly impervious to water, and hence when underlying regular slopes must form a salubrious substratum. When scooped out into basins they, like the trap rock, will retain water with great tenacity.

On the whole the effect of my visit was to give me a more hopeful view than I had before entertained of the sanitary problem before you. As it seems to me, thorough-drainage would remove nearly all the causes of insalubrity of the Island. To be effectual this drainage must be intelligently planned, and thoroughly carried out. It will cost money, but by bringing into market so much beautiful country, so near New York, I should say that it would many times repay its cost.

Yours, very truly,
J. S. Newberry

VIII. RESULTS OF EXPERIMENTS ON THE ABSORPTIVE CAPACITY OF STATEN ISLAND SERPENTINE, BY PROFESSOR J. S. NEWBERRY

School of Mines, Columbia College, New York, Jan. 27th, 1871

Specimen No. 1.   Compact Variety:
"   No. 2.   Granular, porous variety from near surface

	Loss in weight, per cent.	
	No. 1.	No. 2.
Air-dried by remaining two weeks in Columbia College cabinet, then Dried in air bath at 212° Fahr. 5 hours	1.13	2.90

	Gain in weight, per cent.	
	No. 1.	No. 2.
Saturated with water, then allowed to drain till surface was dry	12.84	28.41

For comparison I give below results of similar experiments on two well known varieties of sandstone.

No. 1, Amherst, Ohio; No. 2, Bass Island, Lake Superior, artificially dried and then saturated with water.

	Weight—per cent.
No. 1 absorbed	6.268
No. 2 "	6.718

From these experiments it will be seen

1st. That when exposed in dry air this Serpentine spontaneously parts with nearly all its moisture.

2d. That its capacity for absorbing moisture is remarkable, almost equal indeed to that of Carbonate of Magnesia; the most compact variety absorbing *twice,* and the most porous *four times* as much water as average sandstones, generally regarded as the most porous of all our rocks.

The absorptive power of an average Limestone,—that of Athens, Ill.,—is 1.901 per cent. of its weight. Of Milwaukee Brick 17.118 per cent. of its weight.

The gain on saturation, of these specimens of serpentine rock, would be nearly double their volume.

DOCUMENT VI

FREDERICK LAW OLMSTED

Report of a Preliminary Survey of Rockaway Point (1879)

➤➤➤➤➤➤➤➤➤➤➤➤

209 West Forty Sixth Street
New York
30th July, 1879

H. Y. Attrill, Esq.
B. E. Smith, Esq.

GENTLEMEN:

On the 8th instant I received your instructions to examine Rockaway Point; consider the opportunities it offers for making a place of summer resort, more particularly as compared with those of Coney Island, and to suggest how they might be most profitably turned to account.

I have since spent nearly three weeks on the Point and have sought information from all local sources. The topographical survey in progress is not so far advanced that I can make much use of its results and my estimates of distances and quantities must be subject to correction, but they will be found, I believe, sufficiently accurate for your present purpose.

Objectionable Circumstances

This being a report for your private information, I shall speak first of circumstances unfavorable to your object which you are liable to have underestimated.

BARREN ISLAND

First the stench of decayed fish is perceptible on the Point whenever the wind sets toward it from Barren Island which it frequently does at night. It might be prejudicial to a hotel even at the East end. Coney Island lying to the westward of Barren Island suffers less from this source because Easterly winds are less frequent in summer and, being more violent, when they occur the odor is apt to be dissipated before reaching the hotels.

FLIES AND MOSQUITOS

Next as to flies and muskitoes [sic]. These are always to be found in countless numbers among the bushes. I am assured that in passing through the thickets even in January, clouds of muskitoes [sic] are stirred up. They swarm to the seaside in summer whenever there is not a fresh breeze. They have been annoying at the Surf House nearly every night. The residents are cautious in speaking of them, but it is admitted that they have, at times, been an intolerable pest.

Flies also swarm on the Point and at times during my visit it has been difficult to take a meal because of them, they so covered the food and filled the air.

I think it practicable to so far abate both these nuisances that they will be of no serious prejudice to your object.

Flies are now bred in vast numbers in the privies and the slops, offal and waste thrown out at the back doors of the taverns, as well as in the dead fish, etc. on the strand.

Mosquitos are generated in stagnant water and find their proper sustenance while in the larvae state only in decaying matters at the bottom of pools or puddles. They mature and harbor, after taking the insect form, in bushes and herbage where they can escape from wind. Much of the eastern part of the Point presents exactly the conditions most favorable to their propagation, in moist hollows in which shallow pools form with every shower, surrounded on all sides by dense thickets, with sand hills to make a lee for every wind.

How to Be Obviated

I am not likely to undervalue the beauty of the natural low growth of the Point and it goes against my professional grain, as I know it will disappoint your expectations, that I should advise you that it had better be sacrificed. But in doing so I only express my reluctant judgment of the risk which it involves of bringing a dangerous reputation upon your property. You had better burn every living thing, level every sand-hill and give the breeze a clear sweep rather than build a great establishment and have your guests even once driven away by these pests, and the newspapers tell the story, as newspapers would.

LOW GROUND

By clearing off the bushes, draining the low ground and providing for the prompt removal of decaying matters, there is every reason to suppose that you may avoid the danger. Thorough measures, and perhaps rather costly measures, for drainage, sewerage and the washing away of all manner of filth, which are needed for this, are, as I shall presently show, for other reasons of the first importance.

Relative Elevation of Different Parts

Lastly, I must point out that though you have a certain extent of better building ground than was originally found at Coney Island, the advantages of the Point in this respect may not be quite as extensive as you have supposed, for the reason that the sand-hills are so disposed and so conspicuous that in any view at the east end a deceptive idea is obtained of the general elevation of the land.

North of the line of dunes which protects it in storms from the wash of the surf and, from a line half a mile from the East end to the extreme west, very little of the property is a foot above ordinary high-water and probably nine tenths of it is occasionally flooded. The relative standing of different parts as affected by this consideration may be seen in Diagram

No. 1.[1] In this, the part lettered A, shows an area (lying just back of the sea-beach) which consists of an undulating ridge of sand often 20 feet in height. There a plateau might be formed of local material at a distance of from one to two hundred feet from ordinary high-water-mark on the beach, having a length of three quarters of a mile, a depth of a hundred and fifty feet and an elevation of ten feet above high-water of spring tides.

This narrow district along the beach is the best building-ground upon the property. I will compare it later with the ground correspondingly situated on Coney Island.

Further to the southwest, the same ridge continues with much less average elevation. Still, at several points upon it, there are sites suitable for large hotels. The block on the diagram, lettered B indicates the district now referred to.

The space lettered C represents an average elevation of at least three feet above that of any considerable part of the property lying west of it, and is, in all respects, the best site for shops and residences, and nearly all buildings not desirable to be more closely connected with the beach. To prevent an inconsiderate occupation of any part of it which would stand in the way of good final arrangements, lines of streets and lots of various depths, suitable to different objects, should be laid down at once, to which all constructions and all sales and leases of land may conform.

GAINING LAND

In the remainder of the property there are numerous hillocks but no considerable space which is more than a few inches above ordinary high water. Most of it is marshy, but I have not found any miry. By dyking on the Bay side and closing a few gaps in the sand-hills through which water above the general level of the sea is urged in great storms, and by some drainage through tide-gates, aided, if necessary, by wind-

[1] This diagram, as well as others referred to in this document, have not been located.

mill pumps, a large part of this area, (say 450 acres) may be reclaimed. It will then be available for many purposes, but hardly desirable for large hotels or residences. The westernmost part is liable to be swept by the sea and no building would for the present be safe upon it in a severe storm with spring tides and ice afloat in the bay, unless set upon strong piles well above the present surface. The extreme point is gaining, however, and there is good reason to expect that it will continue to gain both in extent and elevation. Not improbably within two years the capabilities and value of this last district will be decidedly greater than at present.

Dyking the bay side of the Point might be expected to accelerate the extension and elevation of the extreme point by strengthening the westerly current after a storm and increasing and carrying further out the eddy in the edge of which sand is deposited.

Need of Large Sewer Arrangements

Before passing from the subject of the elevation of the property, I will observe that communities occupying such low ground, and especially temporary and shifting communities, are particularly open to contageous [sic] and endemic diseases. (As an outbreak of one of these would be liable to be magnified by rumor, raise a panic, empty the hotels and create a permanent prejudice against the place, no unnecessary risk of it should be taken.[)] This danger, as well as that from flies and mosquitos, is to be mainly provided against by abundant water supply and efficient sewerage and plumbing. The need of these to the highest success of your proposed enterprise will appear from this consideration.

A REFUGE FROM MALARIA

The people of New York and its suburbs are peculiarly cursed by conditions which tend to establish malarial troubles and are hard upon children, hundreds dying in consequence of them every year as soon as extreme summer heat occurs.

There is no place as near and easily and cheaply accessible from New York as Rockaway Point, which is also as far removed from conditions of the same class, or in which, barring the liabilities which I have pointed out, conditions exist as favorable for recovery and the working off of malarial and diarrhetic trouble. It is at least five times as far removed from local malarial conditions as any part of Coney Island; ten times as far as parts of it, and is separated from them, as Coney Island is not, by a body of water so large that it will be recognized by Sanitarians as a perfect barrier to their influence. There is no other locality equally secure in this respect within twice the distance. Whenever this fact is well understood by physicians it will much recommend the Point as a place of summer resort and no risk should be taken, in order to save outlay in sewerage arrangements or otherwise, of sacrificing this advantage.

PLACE FOR SEWER DISCHARGE

To avoid fouling the Bay water for bathing, the nearest point at which sewage should be discharged is a mile west from your eastern boundary. As the sewers must be carried below the level of high-water, an efficient and economical arrangement will require expert planning and the matter should have early and careful study.

The sewage of the Brighton and Manhattan Beach Hotels is discharged into Sheepshead Bay at a distance of about 3000 feet by twelve inch pipes. Complaint is made of the arrangement and a larger sewer to convey it further, with steampump to secure a better discharge is projected. Both houses are supplied through pipes with water pumped upon the main land. The first large hotel upon the Island was supplied at first from local wells, but whenever much drawn upon the water became brackish. A special Company to bring a much more abundant supply of water to the Island is reputed to be forming.

I have now stated all the difficulties and drawbacks, for your purpose, of the property which I can suppose are not already patent to you. I will proceed to show some of its advantages more especially as compared with Coney Island.

Qualities of the Sea Beach

The beach in both cases varies so much with different conditions of wind that in some particulars it is difficult to generalize accurately about it, but the same winds produce like results in each case, and I shall speak of what appears common with ordinary tides and the usual summer breezes.

SLOPE—REGULARITY—TEXTURE

At Rockaway Point for a mile and a half the beach has a more regular slope. The breakers ordinarily reach it more unbroken and with equal force of wind are a little larger. There is usually a larger proportion of powdered shell in the composition of the surface stratum; it is consequently firmer, finer in grain, and it is less apt to be pebbly.

PURITY OF WATER

The water being further from the outflows of the Hudson, Raritan and other streams and the sewers of New York, Brooklyn, and the New Jersey towns must be supposed to be purer sea-water.

MERITS OF THE WHOLE

This part of the beach is not only a better bathing beach than any part of Coney Island but better than the beach to the eastward which gave Rockaway its old reputation and which I find is generally preferred, by those who have had experience of both, to the Coney Island beach. I have watched it and tested it in all states of tide and I do not think that it has a fault from which it is possible that a sea beach shall be always free. I do not know that there is anywhere a better bathing beach.

UNDERTOW

Beyond a point a mile and a half to the westward of your east line the beach has a longer slope, but for another mile and a half is still an excellent bathing beach, quite as good as that of the favorite bathing resorts further east, or those of Coney Island. I find no more evidence of "undertow" than at Coney Island.

THE OFF-SHORE BAR

The statement above that the breakers are larger than at Coney Island may suggest that they are likely to do more damage along shore as well as make bathing more dangerous. This is not the case in any appreciable degree for this reason. At a distance of about a hundred and fifty yards from the shore and parallel with it is a bar upon which, with the ordinary afternoon sea-breeze, the waves pass undisturbed, but if the wind freshens and the waves run higher and deeper, they are checked or broken upon it and consequently come to the shore with abated force. I have three times seen this illustrated during my visit and Captain Donn of the Coast Survey tells me that the bar has been long established and is to be considered a permanent circumstance. Winter storms sometimes work gaps through it, but these are quickly repaired, and it is never broken during the bathing season.

The Lagoon Side

YACHTING—FISHING—SHOOTING

On the opposite side of the Point and at a distance of 450 yards from the Ocean, your property fronts again upon the lagoons of Jamaica Bay. Vessels drawing twelve feet of water can run in at the lowest ebb of the tide from the open sea, find a land-locked harbor, and come to a wharf at a hundred yards from the shore. Small craft can come to the natural banks. The lagoons offer twenty square miles of quiet water surface which can be used without danger of sea-sickness and which is otherwise well adapted to and much frequented by sailing and rowing parties. They are also celebrated for their fishing and shooting advantages. I have seen their value in all these respects fully demonstrated during my visit.

STILL-WATER BATHING

At the nearest point of the lagoons to the best bathing place upon the ocean there is a smooth soft, clean, gently-sloping, sandy beach admirably adapted for still-water bathing for delicate persons and all who find the surf unpleasant. Further to the westward there are other such beaches on your property.

Relative Defects of Coney Island

At Coney Island not only are all these advantages growing out of the lagoons wanting, but the ground immediately back of the principal hotels and upon which some of their dependencies stand is a marsh intersected by narrow creeks and washed by the tide, disagreeable if not even repellant [*sic*]. There is nothing which invites to yachting or boating, nor off the beach to walking, driving or riding. Embankments are now being formed adjoining to and back of the hotels upon the marsh with sand drawn from the beach and loam from the main land, and it is reported that in one case a large operation of this character is intended, with a design for pleasure grounds, in which ponds for amusement with boats will be a feature; showing that the need is felt of the class of advantages which you so abundantly possess.

Coolness of the Point at Night

This large body of water in your rear in place of the narrow marsh gives you also the advantage of cooler nights when the wind is northerly. A gentleman who has spent much time at Coney Island tells me that during periods of northerly wind he has often found it as warm there as at New York.

I have heard the same said of Long Branch. With northerly winds I have found an agreeable coolness in the air at Rockaway.

The Driving Beach

One other advantage of your property I find in the beach to the eastward of it. At low-water the drive along this beach, after passing the group of inns, for a distance of five miles is surely one of the finest of the kind in the world. It is better than that from the Cliff House at the Golden Gate and equal to that of the celebrated Lynn Beach. A finer riding course cannot be imagined.

It is to be noted, however, that nowhere along this beach are the same advantages to be found for a summer hotel as those you possess; the land in the rear being less elevated and the space between extreme low and extreme high water two or three times as broad—an advantage for driving, a disadvantage for bathing.

The Opportunity on the Whole

For the reasons I have thus sufficiently indicated and having due regard to the accessibility which is promised, it is my opinion that Rockaway Point might be made not simply more attractive to the public than Coney Island, but quite the most complete and popular sea-side resort, *adapted to very large numbers,* in the world.

It should not be forgotten that forty years ago "The Beach at Rockaway" was the most fashionable sea-shore resort in America, drawing visitors from all parts of the country, and that only three years ago, with poorer accommodations, it had more visitors than Coney Island; 50,000 coming to it in one day. Considering the present furor for Coney Island and its numerous superior approaches the fact that Rockaway even now draws 20,000 a day is significant as to its undeveloped capabilities.

In discussing how a property of these capabilities should be dealt with in order to secure the largest profit, the chief difficulty I find lies in an apprehension that such measures as a prudent estimate of immediate results may call for, may restrict and embarrass such a development of its value as will be justified when its merits shall have been established in the estimation of the public.

New York But Partially Drawn upon

There is, in my judgment, sound reason for believing that a much larger number of visitors may yet be drawn to a suitable resort upon the sea shore than has yet been known at Coney Island.

The fame which in two years three or four independent undertakings more boldly and liberally designed than any of the class before them brought to Coney Island has drawn many thousands to the seashore who never before left home for recreation; thousands besides who had hitherto gone for their summer recreation elsewhere than to the seashore; and thousands more who had before been accustomed to go to other resorts on the sea-shore. Yet there is no reason to suppose that this success has been obtained at any serious and permanant cost to other like enterprises. It seems rather to have stimulated the business at various points. A substantial hotel of brick 800 feet in length has just been opened at Cape May. Newport, Narraganset[t] Pier and other resorts to the eastward are reported to have more visitors than ever before. The Telegram of today reports that the number of visitors at Long Branch, both of lodgers at the hotels and of "excursionists" coming for a day, has never been as large as it is now.

THE MARKET YET TO BE OPENED

The growth of the business does not come exclusively, though it does largely, from the great cities. It is evident that the field is opening very widely. Of the visitors to Rockaway during my stay there parties of a few hundred each have come from Connecticut; from Central New York; from distant points of New Jersey and from Eastern and Western Pennsylvania. I have talked with those engaged in getting up such parties and am assured on intelligent grounds that these hundreds are not unlikely soon to be thousands.

Again, I have observed a statement, and it seems to me true, that more than three quarters of all the visitors to Brighton Beach have thus far come from Brooklyn and that much more than double as many people come to the Island as a whole from Brooklyn in proportion to population as from New York. It must be inferred that with better provisions, better knowledge of them, better facilities of transport and better times there may be vastly greater number[s] of people drawn out from New York to the seashore than there yet has been.

That the enlargement of the business shall be attracted chiefly to Rockaway Point the main requirement is that those coming there shall carry a more decided and pleasurable impression of its adaptation to public wants than they can obtain elsewhere.

Distribution of Visitors at Coney Island

By observing how and in what degree different points at Coney Island are occupied, something is to be learned of the manner in which visitors are acted upon in this way.

Within certain definable limits it is evident that substantially all take their pleasure alike. All, for instance, enjoy the outlook upon the sea; the great expanse. All enjoy the dash and sparkle of the breakers close at hand. All enjoy to feel the full force of the sea-breeze and nearly all enjoy to take their pleasure in these things while walking slowly up and down the beach, or if the sun is hot, the verandas of the hotels. Beyond these the inclinations of visitors are diversified and they rapidly divide off, according to their tastes and dispositions, as affected by age, sex, education and means.

Out of 50,000 visitors on a fine day at least 49,000 will have stood or strolled before the end of it on the beach or the verandas; nearly that number on both. But I do not suppose from what I have seen that more than 10,000 of these will have taken a "square meal" at the hotels or more than 1,000 have paid for a room. I doubt if 20,000 will generally have paid for anything at all at the hotels. Rarely 10,000 pay for baths. Then come a variety of special provisions for the public entertainment of which each draws a few. The aquarium, the Prospect Tower, the Race Course, the Ballroom, the shooting Galleries, Billiard Rooms and so on down to the Mud Pie establishment Aunt Sally and the Scups. Not one in a hundred of all who attend the concerts or walk on the verandas may be seen at any of these, yet few fail to see and be pleased with some of them, and each contributes to a general gay, grand, popular holiday effect and thus to make people of all tastes and of all classes go away satisfied, inspired to come again, and to stimulate their neighbors to come.

Indirect Influence of the Hotels

Hence in forming the general scheme of a resort of this class it would be a wild mistake to measure the value of an object by the money it is likely to directly bring in, or even by the degree in which it is to be voluntarily used by visitors. It may be, as I have said, that at Coney Island much less than half the visitors on a particular day contribute anything to the revenue of the hotels. But to a man who does not enter the hotels, who even does not use their free verandas, they are by no means an unimportant element in his experience and will influence very much the story he will tell of the place. That is to say, these great, gay, complex structures, if they do not feed his belly do feed his eyes. They please his fancy. He feels them, with all the rest, to be admirable and they help perhaps as much as everything else to the common exclamation, "It's a Great Place!"

And, in the long run, the revenue of the hotels is dependent on the common fame of the place and will, in some degree, rise or fall according to the satisfaction taken in it even by men who directly contribute nothing to it.

The Loss through Divided Interests

Looked at in this light it will be evident that the capital invested in the hotels might have been much more profitably

313

used had it been under one control and had the prospective value of the common fame of the place been appreciated.

For example, with reference to general popular admiration of the place, nothing perhaps is more talked of or accounts for more, than the single circumstance of the length of the verandas. "Such a glorious piazza!" you hear people exclaim again and again. Yet the longest hardly exceeds four hundred yards. If all the verandas on the island had been set end to end it would have made one more than a mile in length.

Let it be supposed that the four principal buildings for public entertainment on the island instead of being set a quarter of a mile apart and one obscured from the other by petty structures, had been skillfully grouped together with a view to producing a single strong impression of the same kind which has been more or less judiciously aimed at in the composition of each. Suppose that the several bathing establishments connected with them had been in like manner consolidated and brought into range and harmony of effect with the mass and that the small buildings for various purposes which huddle about them had been added and then suppose that a single spacious arcade had been carried along the entire front of the whole. Let this have been done by an architect alive to the opportunity and it is certain that at no greater cost and at no sacrifice of convenience a result might have been obtained which in its effect in pleasing the fancy and producing a strong impression of spaciousness, liberality and adequacy to the public needs, would have been a much more marked success than has in fact been realized on Coney Island.

Coney Island No Model for Rockaway Point

Hence, as you are situated, with a frontage of four miles on the ocean beach and another frontage of four miles upon the Lagoons; with every important advantage which Coney Island possesses and many of great value which she lacks and with the opportunity of a far broader and more comprehensive organization of all the elements of your improvements with reference to general effect, it would be a mistake to look closely upon Coney Island as a model or to take the numbers which it has drawn as the measure of those for which you should make provision.

THE HOTEL ELEMENT TOO PROMINENT

Successful as the arrangements of Coney Island have been it is apparent that they were not contrived either as a whole, or (except in a few later constructions) in particular parts, with direct regard to the character and extent of the business which has actually been drawn to them. From fifty to a hundred thousand people, largely in families, in which the little children have to be taken care of without the aid of hired nurses, often come to the island in a day. At the same time there may not be upon it more than one thousand such visitors as usually fill a first-class hotel. Yet it is apparent that the plans of the central, most conspicuous, most famous and most costly constructions upon the island have been conceived in the first instance wholly from the point of view of the ordinary hotel-keeper.

THE PAVILION TOO INSIGNIFICANT

Both at Manhattan Beach and at Brighton Beach there is a building known as the Pavillion specially prepared for visitors who do not want a room and do not want regular meals. But they are comparatively plain and inconspicuous structures; are set on one side, are evident after-thoughts; and the hotels have as distinctly the aspect of hotels simply, as if they had been designed for Saratoga or Niagara. The great outlay for music, for turf, and for flowers is all for the hotels. The ground about the Pavillions is shabby and neglected.

The Pavilion Should Be Primary, Hotel Secondary

Now the class of people for whose use the Pavillions are more especially intended do not as individuals spend much money; they are not at all the sort of people whom first-class hotel keepers like to fill up with because of their frugality

315

and the small number of "extras" they call for. But of the class of men who are well able, and who are growing rapidly to be more disposed than they have hitherto been to come with their "wives, their cousins, their sisters, and their aunts" and more especially their little children for an occasional holiday to the seashore, there are in New York and its various suburbs and in all the country penetrated by the railways and steam boat routes centering at New York not hundreds merely to one of those for whom first class hotels are more particularly designed, but absolutely thousands.

I have not any doubt that your best policy is to provide directly, frankly, ostensibly and with manifest pride, as the foremost matter of your enterprise, for the accommodation and gratification of immense numbers of this class—the great industrious, moderately-thriving, decent, self-respecting class, the children of which mainly fill the common schools. Even with the very unsuitable provisions which now exist, the business of the inns at Rockaway Point has at once a large increase when the Public Schools of New York close and their profitable season ends abruptly when the schools open again.

RELATIVE POSITION FOR HOTEL

I do not mean that ample and wholly suitable provision, even surpassing that made at Coney Island, should not also be made for the more free-spending and luxurious class, but that the larger profit on the whole would be found in placing the hotel for these where it would not seem intended to be the focus of attraction; even by giving it a slightly retired and reserved, if not exclusive character.

Hardly anyone at a pleasure resort does not prefer to command occasional quiet and an opportunity to draw himself well away from a multitude. Hardly anyone, on the other hand, does not like, in his own good time, to join a great festive throng. It is better then, not to complicate the problem of the festive arrangements with the problem of the hotel. It is only necessary that there should be convenient communication between the two.

It is to be remembered that large numbers and apparent expectation and preparation for large numbers go far to secure large numbers, as is so well established in respect to theatres and all public shows and exhibitions. The gregarious instinct of human beings is as evident as that of crows or buffaloes, and that immense numbers are drawn to a play or a concert or a preacher does not stand in the way of rich, exclusive, refined people's being drawn with the rest. Unless there is some special element of rowdyism or coarseness in the crowd, of which there is always less danger in the case of a very large than of a moderate sized assembly, the gregarious disposition manifests itself in the rich quite as much as in the poor and this equally whether it is the Black Crook or a sermon that is the centre of attraction.

ORIGINALITY DESIRABLE

This idea, thoroughly-well carried out, of remanding the hotel element of a watering place to its proper subordinate position and magnifying and glorifying the Pavillion element would have this incidental advantage, that the new place would not seem to be quite so much Coney Island over again as there is danger that it otherwise must be. It should be remembered how much Coney Island owes to the immense gratuitous advertising which it has received from the newspapers. There is nothing newspapers are more averse to than repeating an old story. Every element of originality that you can secure, whether it be novel in its purpose or simply novel through the advance made in carrying out in a large and grand way purposes previously realized more cautiously and contractedly, will compel the Press to help you, will compel people to talk about you. Nothing can be more fatal than failure in this respect.

SITE FOR PRINCIPAL BUILDINGS

A realization of the topographical conditions which the diagram (No. 1) before you is intended to broadly exhibit will lean no doubt as to where you should aim to fix the centre of attraction and provide most amply for the public accommodation. The division marked by the letter A is your most elevated and finest ground and that which will be first closely approached by rail from New York. There is no area on the sea-coast from New York to beyond Far Rockaway and none on the New Jersey coast for a much greater distance from New York than Long Branch which is quite as well adapted for a building or a range of buildings close upon the strand and from which an equally simple sweeping ocean overlook may be secured.

CONSOLIDATION

Make the most that is practicable of these three elements— the great breadth of the ocean view, the surf tumbling at your feet and the expression of amplitude and liberality in your provision for general public entertainment, and you will not only stand in advance of any other place of summer resort but all competition must be permanently at disadvantage. And I advise you to bring all your main structures into one line, partly for the reason which I have already suggested and partly to avoid the flanking out of the view of the sea as the view from the hotels is flanked out by the bath houses, railway-stations and other structures at Manhattan Beach.

PROXIMITY TO STRAND

Finally, I advise you to place the front of this range as near to the Strand as shall be found consistent with perfect security and convenience. That is to say, as your guests come to enjoy the sea-shore, I advise you to place your principal accommodations for them as closely as practicable to the sea-shore.

This would give you another distinction. It is not a customary arrangement and it is not partly because it is not generally practicable. From the veranda and the lower windows of the Manhattan Beach House the beach can not be seen and all the glory of the surf breaking upon it is lost. It is the same at Cables' and at the principal hotels at Long Branch. To visitors who come to stay but a few hours at most upon the seashore of a hot day the deprivation seems almost a cruelty.

COMPARATIVE ADVANTAGES OF NEAR AND DISTANT SITES

Is it compensated by the customary front flower-garden? I question the art which under such circumstances places such an object as a flower-garden where to be enjoyed it must be in competition with and through distraction from such another object as the ocean. I question if it does not involve an unnecessary incongruity with sea-coast scenery which it would be better under any circumstances to avoid.

If a garden is desirable in connection with a sea-coast house to occupy all the ground between the house and the beach with it is to place it where as an object of interest from the windows it is least needed, where it must be formed and maintained at the greatest cost and where perfection of plant-growth is, at whatever cost, least likely to be secured.

In sketch No. 2 you will see more distinctly the position which I have thus recommended to be held for your principal architectural demonstration. (The dark space on the right marked A) Within the limits indicated a range of buildings can be stretched out nearly three-quarters of a mile in length. According to the depth and height adopted for them their entire capacity might be less than that of the two principal hotels with their dependencies on Coney Island, or it might be greater.

For convenience of reference in what is to follow I will call this proposed range of buildings facing the Strand, the Terrace, and will now proceed to point out the best positions for other provisions of a large Summer Resort which cannot, or for various reasons should not, be incorporated with it.

Railway Station

Referring again to sketch No. II, the terminal railway station of the roads from New York will be observed (F) fixed upon a direct prolongation of the present tracks and to avoid bringing unnecessary noise near the Terrace at a distance from the latter of 200 yards. A narrow-guage road leads each way from it, the southern branch showing two way-stations in the rear of the Terrace.

Steamboat Wharf

The Steamboat Wharf (L) is at the point where boats of 10 feet draft can come nearest to the shore, and a straight, broad street leads directly from it, passing the main railway station, to the Terrace.

Village Plot

The ground immediately to the West (I) is proposed to be reserved for a village plot for all shops and residences for which close association with the beach is not important.

Dyke and Reclaimed Land

The northern line of narrow-guage railway is to follow down the northern shore of the Point upon an embankment which will form a dyke. Of the land thus to be reclaimed, the highest and firmest is on the ocean side of the Point half a mile to a mile west of the Terrace. Here (J) provision is made for an enclosed Exhibition Ground with a mile race track; buildings for spectators and a level sward for cricket, base and foot ball; arrangements for acrobatic performances, school and club festivals, fireworks, etc., the whole as much as practicable open to the sea breeze and accessible by special trains direct from New York and Brooklyn.

Military Parade

Still further West an area of nearly 200 acres (O) is proposed to be adapted to military maneuvres on a larger scale than is practicable on any Parade Ground in the country.

I assume that, with the advantages that could be offered, brigades would be likely to be drawn from New York and Brooklyn, and Regiments from a greater distance, to camp upon the Point, forming an attraction for other visitors. They could be landed from boats or the railway upon the ground. This being for maneuvres in line and column, the region further West, (P) consisting largely of low, broken sand-hills with slight growth of vegetation, will be suitable for skirmish practice. A range for rifle and light artillery target practice being desirable, not only for military but for general use, the best position for it is shown just west of the Steamboat Landing at K. The extreme length of this range would be 1200 yards, which is equal to the longest in the country.

Ground for Various Entertainments

An intermediate area, marked Q, is proposed to be enclosed for a variety of objects by which the attractions of the Point would be increased. I have in mind for this some of the more popular features of European Zoological Gardens.

DAIRY

In several of these there is, for example, a model dairy in which cows are exhibited in a luxurious stable and milk from them, as well as other dairy products, as cream-cheese, ice creams and custard made on the spot, are sold to visitors.

WATERFOWL

Another establishment would be for the breeding of large numbers of swans, geese and ducks, the greater number to be sent out during the day to give greater interest to the lagoon water. A large poultry yard and dove-cote would be another. An elephant and a few camels to make tours, carrying children, would be desirable. A pond in which children could sail small boats.

FISH POND

A fish pond and a house for fish dinners would be placed near the railway station and the boat-landing on the shore. At this house there should be large glass tanks from which guests could select the fish to be served to them.

AQUARIUM

A grotto of artificial stone leading into a subterranean aquarium, in which day light would come to the visitor only through tanks in which the fish would be seen, after the style of that last year in the Paris Exposition. Each of these features, as I intend it, would be a novelty and would be particularly pleasing to the large class of people who would come to the Point with their children. They would probably be directly profitable in admission fees, sales and charges, but their chief profit would be indirect in swelling the general tide of popular interest in the locality.

WHEEL-CHAIRS

I may here barely touch upon several matters of detail in most of which every place of summer resort in America is deficient as compared with many like places of repute in Europe. For example, at one where I spent a week or two, years ago, there were hundreds of wheel-chairs held to let, and they were more used by visitors than public carriages. The streets of the town were adapted to them, there being slopes instead of curbs at the crossings. I think from experience at the Philadelphia Exhibition, that they would be much liked here and that there would be no difficulty in managing so that one could travel in them without a jar from the steamboat landing to and along the whole length of the Terrace if not further. Other desirable equipment would be pony phaetons for the beach with broad-tired wheels, and riding ponies and donkeys to let. The beach and surf should be thoroughly illuminated for a distance of a mile. This could be accomplished by the use of low-grade electric lights set at frequent intervals along the veranda of the Terrace, with clear glass toward the sea and opaque glass toward the buildings.

VARIOUS MOVEABLE ENTERTAINMENTS

Fireworks, except what are called fixed or exhibition pieces, appear to the best advantage when seen at a greater distance than is usual in exhibition grounds and best of all when fired over water. A nightly display of colored fires, bombs and rockets from a hulk moored so far off-shore that they would be well seen from the ends as well as the centre of the Terrace would be very attractive.

A mere squirt of water such as commonly passes for a fountain at our hotels is a poor thing and especially so if it comes from coarse and pretentious iron-work. But as an abundant supply of water and a powerful pumping engine will be needed for reasons I have given and also to guard against fires, it would add but little to the cost for hydraulic works to provide some simple fountains, both wall and jet, which would be an element of great splendor. Of course, they should be on the landside, not the sea side of the buildings.

On the strand, however, gay awnings thrown out from the veranda of the Terrace at frequent intervals with comfortable seats under them will not be out of place and elsewhere numerous public seats with awnings fixed to them will be desirable. A provision of row-boats much more gaily painted and furnished than is usual would give an element of life to the lagoon side. There are several additions which could be made to the ordinary bathing arrangements which would be gratefully regarded by the public, but these are details for the future.

The district along the shore West of the Terrace I advise to be given with suitable preparation to shows, hucksteries and means of amusement such as can be accommodated with slight temporary buildings, or none at all, so that the ground will remain available whenever required for adding to the length of the Terrace or for another detached hotel and bath-house. I mean such things as Punch and Judy and other puppet shows, circuses and minstrels, conjurers, performing birds, tents and enclosures for walking, leaping, and wrestling matches, quoits, Scotch games and travelling exhibitions of curiosities, scups, swings, flying horses and so on. I would take care that they were so arranged and displayed with bright colored awnings and bunting and in such positions with reference to the beach, that without being obtrusive or offensive they would add to the general festive character of the scene.

COTTAGES AND CAMPING GROUND

Still further West beyond Mr. Degraw's villa site, I suggest a range of small cottages or cabins and beyond these again, where the ground near the beach is too low for slight houses to stand safely during the winter, a provision of tents to be let with all requirements for camping. I believe that well organized, under a superintendent and a police officer who would have their headquarters at a store at which supplies would be sold the Campers, such an arrangement would find many patrons, single, by clubs and in families, and that the whole affair would not only pay fairly in rent of tents, etc., but add another object of interest to the Point.

I have thus sufficiently for the present set forth the germ of a general plan and what seems to me to be the best disposition for various purposes of the different parts of the property.

Drawing No. III shows to a larger scale and with more suggestion of detail the proposed position of the Terrace group, the Stations, Landings, Still-water Baths, the Village Plot, the Hotel Garden and Play Grounds. The walk from the Terrace to the Station and Steamboat Wharf is designed to be shaded by a trellis and vine foliage.

CONCERT GARDEN

A Concert Garden is suggested, in connection with the Terrace, in which a large audience would occupy the ground where in the afternoon it would be shaded. Great amphitheatrical galleries are suggested to be carried around this space in which, suitably divided, open to the breeze from the North and South and with a view over the ocean, the principal business corresponding to that of the Pavillions and restaurants of Coney Island would be done.

PROVISION AGAINST FIRE

A continuous arcade along the entire front of the Terrace is indicated. At points where the different sections of the Terrace could be desirably separated, the supports of the arcade might be of iron and the roof and floor moveable, with a view of guarding against sweeping fires in winter.

Sketch No. IV, shows the general design with some modifications and more elaborately than No. II.

All the drawings are to be regarded simply as elementary suggestions of matters of general design to serve as a basis for a more mature discussion of your scheme.

It would be inexpedient to proceed further except in consultation with an architect to whom you would entrust the design of the buildings.

I am, Gentlemen,
Your obedient Servant
FREDERICK LAW OLMSTED
Landscape Architect

209 West Forty Sixth Street,
New York, 30th July, 1879

PART FOUR

>>

UPPER MANHATTAN AND THE BRONX

T HE 1870's in New York City were difficult years for Olmsted. It was clear that his principal objectives for the metropolis would not be accepted. His main intent, that physical planning be guided by social—rather than economic—needs, had been defeated. If Olmsted had succeeded, it would have signified a revolutionary change in attitude and law regarding the purpose of cities and the use of urban land and other resources. The principle involved was that land was God's gift—meant for public use—and not a commodity to be exploited for private gain. Only with this point of view, he felt, would it be possible to plan for maximum social benefits in keeping with the natural endowments of the environment.

Olmsted considered the "grid system"—introduced into New York City by the Plan of 1807—the epitome of the evil of commercialism, and responsible for the obliteration of the natural beauty of Manhattan Island. Under this system, which was standard in most American cities, parallel lines divided the city into neat parcels intended for quick sale. There was no concern for either the use of the land or for its geographic features. The entire environment was reduced to commercial status, whereas Olmsted wanted to plan primarily for communities and for the social institutions required by a great democratic metropolis (see Illustration XII).

But this was not to be. The Board of Commissioners of Central Park, influenced by Andrew Haswell Green and others, rejected the concept as too visionary and impractical. "It would seem inexpedient, at any rate," Green wrote, ". . . to attempt these fanciful arrangements to any great extent in a commercial city, under our form of government."[1] Furthermore, it would impede the amalgamation of the Greater City of New York because of the time needed to execute such a plan and the political and legal battles which would have

[1] Andrew H. Green, "Communication to the Commissioners of the Central Park," *Tenth Annual Report of the Board of Commissioners of the Central Park,* (New York, 1867), p. 142.

329

to be fought. The city was moving northward. For Green the question was not what kind of city there was to be, but rather how to physically integrate into the City of New York "the growing populations of Westchester (see Illustration XV) on the north and east, and those of the Jersey shore on the west."[2] And for this purpose he considered the grid system fundamentally sound. It had generally served the City adequately, encouraging rapid land development and spread of population.[3] Finally, Green and his supporters on the Park Commission argued that the designation of park land for public use was in itself sufficient evidence of social planning.

It was Olmsted's official responsibility as Architect and Superintendent to the Park Commission to provide plans whether or not he accepted the underlying social policy. As a professional, he did his best to solve the technical problems of each project assigned to him and Vaux. He tried to make optimum use of designated lands although he often considered a project unrelated to a broader purpose. Documents VII and VIII display the techniques used in his plans for Morningside and Riverside Parks (see Illustration XIV) in the rapidly growing upper wards of the city. Document VII indicates as well what he thought of merely providing another park without considering the overall needs of the metropolis. "The city is still deficient in many provisions," he wrote, "which unquestionably will soon be urged upon it by advancing civilization. . . . Unfortunately Morningside Park but adds another public ground chosen without the slightest reference to any of these special requirements of the city, and happens to be singularly incapable of being adapted to them."[4]

In 1874 New York City, by state legislation, annexed the western portion of Westchester County, which later (in 1898) became part of the Bronx. The annexation had been

[2] *Ibid.,* p. 132.
[3] *Ibid.,* p. 125.
[4] Frederick Law Olmsted and Calvert Vaux, *Preliminary Study of a Design for the Laying Out of Morningside Park* (Board of the Department of Public Parks, Document 50, Oct. 11, 1873 [New York, 1873]), pp. 334–335. See Document VII below.

planned for some time. It was the first official step toward the political and administrative consolidation of the Greater City of New York. Documents IX and X discuss the plan for this area, designated as the twenty-third and twenty-fourth wards of New York City, and clearly state the function which Olmsted believed this part of the City ought to serve. He probably understood that this would be his last opportunity to influence the development of the metropolitan region.

He urged the Commission to reject the grid system. Instead, he asked them to consider the kind of social institutions which the City needed and the natural features of the area, which he felt would never be suitable for commerce or industry. He warned the Commission that continued disregard for the social basis of planning was crippling to the City. "So far as the plan of New York remains to be formed," he wrote, "it would be inexcusable that it should not be the plan of a Metropolis; adapted to serve, and serve well, every legitimate interest of the wide world; not of ordinary commerce only, but of humanity, religion, art, science and scholarship."[5] To placate the Commission, however, he avoided specific recommendations. Olmsted's plan was one of general outline, guided by the need for a rapid system of transportation and an interlocking road system to preserve the natural form of the land. His ingenuity in adapting the steam railway (see Illustration XVI) indicates that technical changes in methods of communication need not be an insurmountable obstacle to esthetic design.

A year after the proposal was submitted, Olmsted was dismissed by the Board.

[5] Frederick Law Olmsted and J. James R. Croes, *Preliminary Report of the Landscape Architect and the Civil and Topographical Engineer, upon the Laying Out of the Twenty-third and Twenty-fourth Wards* (Board of the Department of Public Parks, Document 72, Dec. 20, 1876 [New York, 1876]), p. 352. See Document IX below.

DOCUMENT VII

FREDERICK LAW OLMSTED AND CALVERT VAUX

Document No. 50 of the Board of the Department
of Public Parks: A Preliminary Study by the
Landscape Architect[s] of a Design for the
Laying Out of Morningside Park (1873)

October 11, 1873

The Landscape Architect submitted a preliminary study
of a design for the laying out of Morningside Park, together
with a report and an estimate of the cost of carrying same
into effect.

The report and estimate were ordered to be printed as
a document of the Board, accompanied with photo-lithographs
of the plan presented therewith.

WM. IRWIN,
Secretary D. P. P.

Department of Public Parks,
Office of Design and Superintendence,
New York, 11th October, 1873

To the Hon Salem H. Wales, President of the Board:

SIR:—I have the honor to present a preliminary report
on the improvement of Morningside Park.

The city property which has received this designation is
a strip of steep hill-side, equal in length to the distance from

the Battery to the City Hall, or about three-quarters of a mile; its width for the most part is less than that of the planted part of Union Square (100 yards). The only surfaces within it, not steeply inclined, are in two small patches lying widely apart, against the northeast and southeast corners respectively; most of the remainder being precipitous hill side, formed by the rounded face of a ledge of gneiss, difficult, unsafe, and in parts, impracticable to travel over. At one point only a break of this ledge occurs about three hundred feet in length, and here the slope is sufficiently gentle to allow the hill to be mounted with moderate directness. The difference of elevation between the west and the east sides is a little less than one hundred feet, and the western boundary is to be a public highway carried at a still higher level and generally supported by a nearly vertical stone wall, which, at some points, is thirty feet in height. There will, consequently, be no view from the Park to the westward, and from the accessible parts the view to the eastward will be cut off whenever the adjoining valuable private lands shall be built upon.

In studying the practical public uses for which ground of this kind is available, they will be found unusually limited.

The city is still deficient in many provisons which unquestionably will soon be urged upon it by advancing civilization: such as already exist in the principal towns of Europe, and for which considerable spaces of open ground are necessary. New York, for example, has no ground for the athletic exercises of young men, the open spaces of the Central Park not being suitable for this purpose, and being already devoted to the athletic education of the children of the city, for whose use they will eventually prove much too small—no grand promenade, the Central Park roads and walks being designed for rural and not for urban recreation. It has no proper market places, no fair grounds nor places adapted to the display of fireworks or other exhibitions. Within four miles of Morningside Park there is no ground suitable to exercises in arms, civic receptions, or any great public ceremonies. There is no ground in the city or its suburbs adapted to special education in general botanical science, arboriculture, horticulture, pharmacy or zoology, nor have any of the thirty-five reservations, large and small, termed parks, in New York and Brooklyn, been selected for or devoted to any of these purposes. Unfortunately Morningside Park but adds another public ground chosen without the slightest reference to any of these special requirements of the city, and happens to be singularly incapable of being adapted to them.

Having the Central Park on one side, Mt. Morris on another, Riverside on the third, the most distant being but a thousand yards away and the nearest less than two hundred, there is no part of the city in which there is less occasion for another ground adapted simply to the airing of young children, and to general strolling and lounging of the residents of the neighborhood, and should its plan have no other very evident motive, it would be hard to justify the maintenance of any public park in this situation at the general expense of the city.

Studying the ground in search of opportunities for serving larger interests, a series of circumstances are to be observed, as follows:

First.—Although no distant or expanded view can be controlled within the limits of the Park itself, from the public highway which overhangs it on the west, as before described, a prospect will be had (above the house-tops of that quarter of the town now growing on the Harlem plain) far out across a wide range of beautiful country, and over the waters and islands of the river and sound, the eastern sea-gate of the metropolis.

It is not from one point alone, but from all parts of the road, that this fine view may be enjoyed. It is only to be regretted that the advantage which it thus possesses had not been recognized in laying out the new highway, and more importance given to it by an increased breadth. Even as it stands, however, there is ample space for several thousand persons to make use of it at a time while moving in carriages or on foot, and with proper management, it may be made a public resort of no small importance in the general system of grounds for the healthful recreation of the city.

Taking this terrace road in connection with the ground below it, the latter will be found to serve a very important purpose, for had it remained private property, it would in time unquestionably have been used in such a manner as to utterly destroy the special advantage to the public of the highway.

This consideration will be found to have an essential bearing on the question of the laying out of the ground, for if those portions of it lying immediately below the terrace road should be planted as in conventional landscape gardening, the view would be as entirely cut off in a few years by lofty trees as if the ground were covered with tall buildings.

Second.—The break in the general face of the ledge, before referred to, presents a position considerably elevated above, yet easily approached from the lower side of the Park. A retaining wall of moderate extent, connecting the two opposite piers of rock, would here make practicable an esplanade or level space 500 feet long and over 1000 feet deep, which might be turned to account in various ways. It would, for example, form a fine site for any structure of such moderate elevation, that it would present no obstruction to the view from the terrace road above. The introduction of an artificial feature of this character, with the suitable decoration of the retaining wall and staircases ascending it, would enhance, by contrast, the effect of the natural bold and rugged elements of the Park.

Third.—The natural conditions of the Morningside site are of a similar character, but rather inferior in interest to those of the northern portion of the Central Park. The two being not three minutes walk apart, for many years to come the greater number of visitors will probably reach it by way of the Central Park. It is desirable, then, as a matter of art, that Morningside Park should be, if possible, so treated as to contrast with the nearer parts of Central Park, and not produce the effect of a small and weak pendant of the older and more important ground. It is particularly desirable that the southeast angle should offer a direct and inviting entrance upon a scene strikingly interesting in character. The topographical conditions just here are, as it happens, unusual. With the construction of the necessary embankments of the street and avenue, a considerable basin will be formed of a generally triangular outline, two sides being steeply sloping; the third, a natural and quite picturesque cliff of rock, which is a prominent object in approaching from the direction of the Central Park. The earth at its base is light and easy of excavation, and in the process of grading in the vicnity, will be needed as material of embankment. The ground rises behind the rock on the north and west, and it will thus be seen that an area can here be formed about two acres in extent, which would be remarkably well protected from winds. The local conditions indicated offer advantages such as are possessed nowhere else by the city for either of two purposes:

It is, namely, admirably suited to a small enclosure in which some of the tamer tropical animals could be allowed to graze, and in which suitable accommodations for lodging them throughout the year could be placed, or to a special garden for the display of what are known as sub-tropical plants. The latter is probably the simpler and more immediately attractive suggestion.

With respect to an entrance at this point, there are some special difficulties to be met. The sidewalk of the street, will be 20 feet above the adjoining surface of the park, and from the angle the street grade descends rapidly to the north, and ascends to the west. Under these circumstances, an architectural construction of an original character is desirable to supply such an entrance as is required.

Fourth.—Although there are rocky points on the Central Park more interesting perhaps than any that can here be found, by a moderate excavation of the alluvial deposit along the base of the steep rocks between the line of 116th and 120th streets, a walk may be obtained, which, with skillful management of the materials at hand, may present a greater continuity of picturesque rocky border than an equal distance of walk on any other park possessed by the city.

Fifth.—Near the northwest end, the whole breadth of the park is occupied by masses of rock, like a craggy mountain side. There is no soil for the support of large trees, but the conditions are well fitted for the advantageous display of the very interesting forms of vegetation technically termed Alpine plants.

Sixth.—Argument is hardly necessary to prove that by no appropriate treatment could a ground having the natural features of Morningside Park, be made a safe and reputable place of resort at night. At least access to all the precipitous and rocky parts should be rigidly prevented by suitable barriers.

The six general considerations which have been thus developed, may be regarded as supplying the specifications to which a plan should conform, and in which provisions for meeting them should be agreeably related and combined.

In examining the study of a design here presented it will be necessary to bear in mind the extreme steepness of the ground, as it is impossible to represent on a plan (in which every object is assumed to be looked at directly from above) the nearly perpendicular faces of the rocks that, seen from below, will be such important features of the park.

The principal parts of the plan will be easily recognized as follows:

Beginning the examination at the point nearest the Central Park, an enlargement of the sidewalk at the angle formed by the junction of the street and avenue will be seen forming a balcony looking into the basin which has been described, and also serving as the upper landing of a double staircase, descending 22 feet, to a paved court below. From wall fountains under the balcony, water flows into a large semi-circular basin. On the other side, the court opens upon a body of water, which by an arrangement of points and islands, is designed to be seen in vistas radiating from its centre, and terminating at interesting points of the high rocks opposite.

Aquatic plants break the surface of these little lagoons, and they are overhung by luxuriant and intricate foliage of tropical character, of apparently natural growth from their

338

banks. These will be backed and protected by thickets of large but inconspicuous hardy shrubs. Walks lead out laterally from the entrance court, which are carried on the opposite face of these thickets, but, at certain points, openings occur, from which other vistas are seen of a like character to those which extend from the court. The rare plants, while seen to advantage, will be out of reach, and secure from injury by visitors.

Further to the right occurs the break in the outcrop of the ledge which has been described.

The suggested esplanade, the larger part of it occupied by a building, will here be seen, forming the most prominent object in the plan. A series of staircases, steps and walks will be noticed leading to the level of its site from two points on the terrace-road above, and from three in the avenue below. Passages are thus formed from the upper to the lower borders of the Park, the elevation being overcome by a convenient combination of stairs and sloping walks. Between the two entrances on the upper and the three on the lower side of the Park a distinct district is here designed, which is treated in an urban and gardenesque style. A fountain and flower beds will be observed, and, in connection with the architectural elements of the stairs, terrace and arcade, admirable positions will be found for the display of statues and other works of art, such as private munificence may hereafter offer for the purpose. The whole is so arranged that the walks leading north and south into other parts of the Park can be closed by gates, and this division, being well lighted, may then be left open for free passage at all times during the night, all due precaution being taken for safety both against accidents and violence.

The principal walk leading northward from this district will be observed near the middle of the plan, and is designed, as required by the fourth specification, to be formed in an excavation along the foot of the ledge. Although broad and not indirect in course, it is to be deeply shaded and to have a wild, picturesque and secluded character until it reaches the second walk, crossing from east to west, at 120th street. Immediately beyond this point it opens upon the only quiet,

339

sunny lawn on the Park. This is bordered by shrubbery and flowering plants, and a chalet for refreshments is built on the rocks overhanging it on the west.

Leading westward from the lawn, the walk ascends, by steps, a rocky defile, the Alpine ground of the fifth specification, beyond which, the entrances to the Park from Tenth avenue are reached.

A mall, nowhere less than twenty feet wide, surrounds the Park, and is separated from it by a parapet wall, over which, at intervals, views into the Park can be enjoyed. The mall is planted with a double row of trees, is furnished with seats, and is to be well lighted, that it may be safely used at night when the rugged and more obscure parts of the Park are closed.

On the upper side of the Park, at the best points for enjoying the distant prospect to the eastward, balconies are built out, from four of which staircases give access to walks in the Park below. At 120th street, a third crossing is arranged, to be lighted and kept open at night.

Fourteen entrances to the Park will be observed, in the arrangement of which there is much variety of character.

Between two of these, on the eastern avenue opposite the esplanade, the outer roadway is widened so as to form a bay in which carriages may stand for the accommodation of visitors without interruption of general movement in the highway.

It will be recognized that the variety of scenery in the several divisions of the Park which have been indicated, is very marked, but that the transition from one to another is nowhere abrupt and sensational. The visitor passes through the exotic luxuriance of the tropical garden; thence through dense masses of foliage he comes upon the terrace district, with its striking architectural and floral decorations; then through the wild, picturesque and sombre walk along the foot of the ledge; then along the bright open lawn, simple in character but highly cultivated; then, mounting the craggy hillside, with its low growth of brilliant Alpine plants springing from the crevices of the rocks, and by a stairway up the vine-covered wall, he reaches the terrace road mall. By this he may return to the point of starting, enjoying in a further walk of half a mile the broad distant view which is the crowning attraction of the Park.

Respectfully,
FRED. LAW OLMSTED,
L. Architect;
For himself and CALVERT VAUX,
Late Consulting L. A.

DOCUMENT VIII

→»→»→»«←«←«←

FREDERICK LAW OLMSTED

Document No. 60 of the Board of the Department of Public Parks: Report of the Landscape Architect upon the Construction of Riverside Park and Avenue (1875)

→»→»→»«←«←«←

January 20, 1875

Report of the Landscape Architect upon the construction of Riverside Park and Avenue.

Ordered to be printed as a document of the Board.

W. IRWIN,
Secretary, D. P. P.

Department of Public Parks,
Office of Design and Superintendence,
New York, 15th January, 1875

To the Hon. Henry G. Stebbins, President of the Board:

SIR:—I have the honor to present a map of the Riverside territory belonging to the city, with the main outlines of a plan for its improvement.

What I have designated as the Riverside *territory* consists of two divisions: first, a strip uniformly 100 feet wide along its eastern side, named Riverside Avenue, and originally intended to be treated as other avenues of the city; second, a body of land of variable breadth named Riverside Park.

343

Nearly all of the ground on both of these parts of the territory slopes with a rapid inclination to the west, so much so that the originally proposed avenue would require to be supported on the lower side by a strong retaining wall, generally not less than twenty feet in height.

The avenue (as laid out in 1868) has a very crooked course, as is shown by the following line, representing a part of it equal in length to that part of Broadway south of Canal street.

Its variations of grade are also frequent, a change between ascent and descent occurring thirteen times, as represented by the following line (200 feet vertical; 4,000, horizontal, to one inch).

Many of the grades are severe, there being nine sharper than one in twenty, and on which trotting would be impracticable.

On each side of this avenue there is to be, at an average distance of less than two hundred yards, another avenue, straight in course, of better grades and equally wide. These others would amply provide for through and heavy travel, and the breadth of 100 feet on Riverside Avenue, as originally designed, is therefore only required on the presumption that it will be used for the same purpose as the Park—that is to say, as a pleasure resort.

344

The advantage of the Riverside territory for this purpose lies in its command of views over the Hudson, which at several points are of great interest, and in its airiness.

This advantage is least, and will eventually be wholly lost, on its lower or westerly side, and is greatest, and will alone be of permanent value to the city, on its higher parts—that is to say: 1st, that part originally assigned to the avenue, and 2d, that part originally assigned to the park which, if the avenue should be built, would be close under its supporting wall (a, in the diagram).

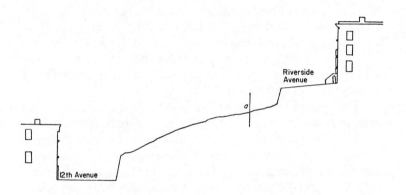

This part of the park, inclined as it would be to the west, with a wall of masonry on the east, would, when it might otherwise be most agreeable, be found insupportably hot, unless planted with large trees.

Trees upon it would, however, completely intercept the view over it from the avenue as originally planned.

This view being cut off, the avenue, with its steep grades and frequent undulations, would be the least attractive of all the avenues of the city for pleasure driving.

For this reason the Department was advised, in 1873, that the imaginary line by which the site for the avenue was divided from the site for the park should be disregarded, and a plan prepared, with a view to utilize, in the greatest degree practicable, the advantages offered by the territory, *as a whole,* for the several purposes—first, of a means of access to the property on its east side; second, of a pleasure drive, commanding a fine view over the river, airy and shaded; third, of a foot promenade, commanding the same view, and also airy and shaded.

This proposition, after full consideration, received the unanimous approval of the Park Commissioners; it has since, also after cautious consideration, received that of all their successors; of the Commissioner of Public Works; of all citizens interested, who have accepted the invitation of the Commissioners to examine the matter; of the Legislature of 1873, which passed a bill based upon it; and of the Senate Committee on Cities, of 1874, which recommended a bill intended to provide for it, which failed to pass solely because of a question which arose under it as to the division of duties between the Departments of Parks and of Public Works.

The plan of which an outline is given in the accompanying map is prepared in accordance with the proposition which has been stated; that is to say, it is a plan for a combination of the avenue with the park. Comparing such a plan with one for a separate improvement of the two parts of the territory as originally intended, the general aim being as nearly as possible the same in both cases, the advantages which would be had under the combination plan, may be partly and moderately stated as follows:

1st. It would be less costly.

2d. The carriage way would, at all the more important points, command the view over the river, and would generally command better views; would be better shaded; would be breezier and cooler; would conveniently accommodate a much larger number of carriages, and would have much better grades. (See appended note, p. 9.)

3d. The accommodation for people on foot would be ampler; would have better views; would be better shaded; would have better grades, and would be more cheaply and efficiently policed.

In short the cost of the property under the new plan will

346

be less than under the old, while its value to the city will be immeasurably greater.

There is a part of the Riverside territory to which the above observations do not apply, the park as originally arranged under the act of 1867, not being continuous from the north to the south end, but the whole breadth from Eighty-fifth to Eighty-eighth streets being assigned to the avenue, the west line of which was made to coincide with the east line of Twelfth avenue, but with a difference of elevation of 65 feet.

A plan for dealing with this district has been prepared, under instructions from the Department of Public Works, by Mr. Leopold Eidlitz, drawings of which, by favor of the designer, I am permitted herewith to present. It is proposed by this plan that instead of filling up with earth the great space over which the avenue would need to be constructed, it should be utilized as a building suitable for a market or other public purpose, the walls of which would thus have at this point the character of a terrace, commanding fine views of the river.

It is not necessary that this plan should be carried out at present, but it has been thought best in designing the adjoining ground to keep it in view, and the dotted lines on the map imperfectly show how by means of it, the two parts of the general walk and drive system which has been described would be connected.

Respectfully,
FRED. LAW OLMSTED,
Landscape Architect

Note as to Grades

On the Central Park it is found that the majority of horses are walked wherever the grade of the drives is steeper than 1 in 26. On the new Riverside plan, from Seventy-second to One hundred and twenty-seventh Streets (3 miles), there

347

is no grade steeper than 1 in 28. More than an eighth part
of that distance, on the old plan of the avenue, is on grades
steeper than 1 in 20. On the descent from One hundred and
twenty-seventh Street to Twelfth Avenue, the new plan offers
a road with a grade of 1 in 20; the only road in the old
is steeper than 1 in 10. By the following diagrams the differences of grade between the points indicated will be evident,
the full line showing the old, the dotted line, the new grades.

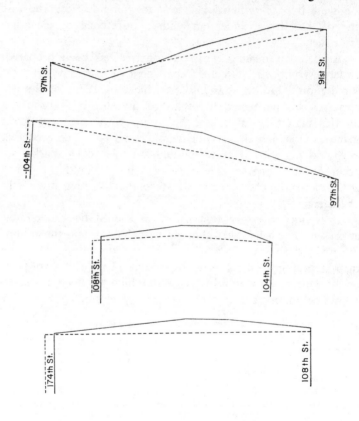

DOCUMENT IX

>>>->>>->>><<<-<<<-<<<

Frederick Law Olmsted and J. James R. Croes

Document No. 72 of the Board of the Department of Public Parks: I. Preliminary Report of the Landscape Architect and the Civil and Topographical Engineer, upon the Laying Out of the Twenty-third and Twenty-fourth Wards; II. Report Accompanying a Plan for Laying Out That Part of the Twenty-fourth Ward, Lying West of the Riverdale Road (1876)

>>>->>>->>><<<-<<<-<<<

December 20, 1876

1. Preliminary Report of the Landscape Architect and the Civil and Topographical Engineer, upon the laying out of the Twenty-third and Twenty-fourth Wards.

2. Report of the Landscape Architect and the Civil and Topographical Engineer, accompanying a plan for laying out that part of the Twenty-fourth Ward, lying west of the Riverdale Road.

Ordered printed as a document of the Board.

Wm. Irwin,
Secretary D. P. P.

349

I. Preliminary Report of the Landscape Architect and the Civil and Topographical Engineer, upon the Laying Out of the Twenty-third and Twenty-fourth Wards

City of New York,
Department of Public Parks,
15th November, 1876

The Hon. William R. Martin, President of the Board:

Sir:—The undersigned have the honor to present a report introductory to a series of plans for laying out the new wards of the city. The first of these plans can, if desired, be laid before the Board at its next meeting; a second and third are in preparation, and the whole series is in progress of study.

The great advance northward in the building of New York, since 1807, has been strictly according to the street plan which a commission of its citizens then laid down for it. The objections at first hotly urged against this plan (chiefly by property holders whose lands it would divide inconveniently, whose lawns and gardens it would destroy and whose houses it would leave in awkward positions), have long since been generally forgotten, and so far as streets have been opened and houses built upon them, the system has apparently met all popular requirements. Habits and customs accommodated to it have become fixed upon the people of the city. Property divisions have been generally adjusted to it, and innumerable transfers and pledges of real estate have been made under it with a degree of ease and simplicity probably without parallel. All the enormous changes in the modes of commerce, of means of communication, and of the styles of domestic life which the century has seen, have made but one slight local variation from it necessary.

These facts, taken by themselves, may seem to leave little room for doubt that the system was admirably contrived for its purpose, and that, as far as can be reasonably expected of any product of human skill, it remains perfect.

There are probably but few men in the community who, in the course of a busy life, have given any slight attention, and but slight attention, to the subject, who are not in the habit of taking this view of it, and in whom, consequently, a pre-judgment is not in some degree deeply rooted in favor of the system. That it should be extended, whenever practicable, over that part of the city not yet laid out, and where this is forbidden by extraordinary difficulties of topography, that no greater variation should be made from it than is necessary to bring the cost of preparing streets within reasonable limits of expense, seems, to all such persons, a matter of course.

All the work of the undersigned will, nevertheless, have been done under the influence of a quite different conviction and its results can only be fairly judged, after a candid and patient balancing of the advantages to be gained, and the advantages to be lost by the adoption of a variety of proposed arrangements always differing, and often differing widely from those with which commissioners and the community are familiar under the regular system.

They, therefore, wish to submit, in advance of any plans, a few general considerations adapted, as they think, to give a different impression of the merits of the system from that which appears to be ordinarily accepted, and by which the Commission has hitherto, to some extent, almost necessarily been influenced.

New York, when the system in question was adopted, though vaguely anticipating something of the greatness that has since been thrust upon her, viewed all questions of her own civic equipment, very nearly from the position which a small, poor, remote provincial village would now be expected to take.

The city had no gas, water or sewer system. The privies of the best houses were placed, for good reasons, as far away from them as possible, in a back yard, over a loose-bottomed cesspool. If the house stood in a closely built block, the contents of the cesspool, when necessary to be removed, were taken to the street in buckets carried through the house; the garbage of the house was often thrown, with its sweepings and soiled water into the street before the front door, to be there devoured by swine, droves of which were allowed to run at large for the purpose.

Under these circumstances, it was not to be expected that, if the utmost human wisdom had been used in the preparation of the plan, means would be aptly devised for all such ends as a commission charged with a similar duty at the present day must necessarily have before it.

So far as the plan of New York remains to be formed, it would be inexcusable that it should not be the plan of a Metropolis; adapted to serve, and serve well, every legitimate interest of the wide world; not of ordinary commerce only, but of humanity, religion, art, science and scholarship.

If a house to be used for many different purposes must have many rooms and passages of various dimensions and variously lighted and furnished, not less must such a metropolis be specially adapted at different points to different ends.

This it may chance to be if laid out by the old cow-path method, or more surely if laid out in greater or less part with carefully directed intention to the purpose, such as is now being used for instance in London, Paris, Vienna, Florence, and Rome.

There seems to be good authority for the story that the system of 1807 was hit upon by the chance occurrence of a mason's sieve near the map of the ground to be laid out. It was taken up and placed upon the map, and the question being asked "what do you want better than that?" no one was able to answer. This may not be the whole story of the plan, but the result is the same as if it were. That is to say, some two thousand blocks were provided, each theoretically 200 feet wide, no more, no less; and ever since, if a building site is wanted, whether with a view to a church or a blast furnace, an opera house or a toy shop, there is, of intention, no better a place in one of these blocks than in another.

If a proposed cathedral, military depot, great manufacturing enterprise, house of religious seclusion or seat of learning needs a space of ground more than sixty-six yards in extent from north to south, the system forbids that it shall be built in New York.

On the other hand it equally forbids a museum, library, theatre, exchange, post office or hotel, unless of great breadth, to be lighted or to open upon streets from opposite sides.

There are numerous structures, both public and private, in London and Paris, and most other large towns of Europe, which could not be built in New York, for want of a site of suitable extent and proportions.

The Trustees of Columbia College sought for years to obtain the privilege of consolidating two of the uniform blocks of the system, into which their own property had been divided, in order to erect sufficient buildings for their purpose, in one unbroken group, but it was denied them.

There is no place under the system in New York where a stately building can be looked up to from base to turret, none where it can even be seen full in the face and all at once taken in by the eye; none where it can be viewed in advantageous perspective. The few tolerable sites for noble buildings north of Grace Church and within the built part of the city remain, because Broadway, laid out curvilinearly, in free adaptation to natural circumstances, had already become too important a thoroughfare to be obliterated for the system.

Such distinctive advantage of position as Rome gives St. Peter's, Paris the Madeleine, London St. Paul's, New York, under her system, gives to nothing.

But, if New York is poor in opportunities of this class, there is another of even greater importance in which she is notoriously still poorer. Decent, wholesome, tidy dwellings for people who are struggling to maintain an honorable independence are more to be desired in a city than great churches, convents or colleges. They are sadly wanting in New York, and why? It is commonly said because the situation of the city, cramped between two rivers, makes land too valuable to be occupied by small houses. This is properly a reason why land, at least in the lower part of the island, should be economized, and buildings arranged compactly. The rigid uniformity of the system of 1807 requires that no building lot shall be more than 100 feet in depth, none less. The clerk or mechanic and his young family, wishing to live modestly in a house by themselves, without servants, is provided for in this respect no otherwise than the wealthy merchant, who, with a large family and numerous servants, wishes to display works of art, to form a large library, and to enjoy the company of many guests.

In New York, lots of 100 feet in depth cannot be afforded for small, cheap houses. The ground-rent would be in too large proportion to that of the betterments. In no prosperous old city are families of moderate means found living, except temporarily in the outskirts, in separate houses on undivided blocks measuring 200 feet from thoroughfare to thoroughfare. It is hardly to be hoped that they ever will be in New York under the plan of 1807.[1]

The inflexibility of the New York plan, and the nature of the disadvantages which grow out of it, may be better recognized upon an examination of certain peculiarities with which Commissioners must be familiar as distinguishing the city.

These are to be found, for instance, in the position usually occupied by the kitchen and menial offices of even the better class of houses; in the manner in which supplies are conveyed to them, and dust, ashes, rubbish and garbage removed. This class of peculiarities grows out of the absence from the New York system of the alley, or court, by which in all other great towns large private dwelling houses are usually made accessible in the rear.[2]

[1] Various attempts have been made on a small scale to get the better of this difficulty, the most successful being the introduction of an alley by which a tier of 100 feet lots is divided into two of 42 feet each, one tier facing upon the back of the other. A philanthropic scheme is now under discussion for cutting up a whole block into short lots for poor men's houses by 16-feet alleys. [1876.]

[2] THE SANITARIAN, for January, 1877, received as this is printing,

It is true, that in other cities, as they become dense and land valuable, the alleys and courts come to be much used as streets, that is to say, small houses and shops, as well as stables are built facing upon them, and the dwellings only of people of considerable wealth are carried through to them from the streets proper. But this practice does not do away with the general custom of a yard accessible from the alley by an independent passage, and of placing the kitchen and offices of all large houses in a semi-detached building. Out of this custom come the greater ease and economy with which streets are elsewhere kept in decent order, and the bad reputation which New York has always had in this respect; and again, the fact that New York houses of the better class, much more than those of other cities, are apt to be pervaded with kitchen odors.

Another peculiarity of New York, is to be found in the much less breadth and greater depth of most of the modern dwellings of the better sort. There are many houses not much wider than the hovels of other cities, which yet have sixty or seventy feet of depth, and fifty to sixty feet of height, with sculptured stone fronts and elaborately wrought doors. This incongruity results from the circumstance that a yard at the back .of the house, when no longer needed for a privy and where there is no alley to communicate with it, has little value; consequently, to economize ground-rent, two house lots

---

contains the following professional notes on Boston, by Doctor E. H. Janes: "The streets of Boston present· quite a contrast with those of New York in point of cleanliness." "Their system of alleys, by which access is obtained to the rear yards, renders it unnecessary to disfigure the sidewalks, or defile the gutters and pavements with every variety of house refuse and filth. At the appointed time the cartman rings the bell at the rear gate, receives from the housemaid the garbage, deposits it in a water-tight cart. . . . The garbage is taken to the country and used for feeding swine. The ashes are collected in a similar way, and, being entirely separate from garbage, or any putrescent matter, can be used for filling low ground. . . . I wish some such system could be adopted with us, as I am confident it would reduce the rate of mortality among our tenement house population." [1877.]

of the size originally contemplated are divided into three or four, and houses stretched out upon them so as to occupy as much of the space as the Board of Health, guarding against manifest peril of public pestilence, will allow.

The same cubic space is now obtained in a lot of 1,700 square feet, or even 1,300, as formerly on one of 2,500, and the depth between the front and rear windows of houses of corresponding area has been nearly doubled.

That this change has been forced also by the street system, and is not a matter of fashion, nor the result of a caprice in popular tastes, is evident from the fact that no corresponding method has obtained in other cities, new or old, nor however situated; none, for example, in London, Liverpool, Philadelphia, Baltimore, Buffalo, Chicago, or San Francisco.

The practice is one that defies the architect to produce habitable rooms of pleasing or dignified proportions, but this is the least of its evils, for in the middle parts of all these deep, narrow cubes, there must be a large amount of ill-ventilated space, which can only be imperfectly lighted through distant skylights, or by an unwholesome combustion of gas. This space being consequently the least valuable for other purposes, is generally assigned to water-closets, for which the position is in other respects the worst that could be adopted.

Still other, and perhaps even graver, misfortunes to the city might be named which could have been avoided by a different arrangement of its streets. The main object of this report will, however, have been secured, if the conviction has been shown to be justified that an attempt to make all parts of a great city equally convenient for all uses, is far from being prescribed by any soundly economical policy.

"Equally convenient," in this case, implies equally inconvenient. "As far as practicable," means within reasonable limits of expense. But there are no reasonable limits of expense for such an undertaking. Even on a flat alluvial site, like that of Chicago, it is essentially wasteful and extravagant. In proportion as a site is rugged and rocky it is only more decidedly so; not simply because in this case it involves greater unneces-

sary cost, but because variety of surface offers variety of opportunity, and such an undertaking often deliberately throws
away forever what might otherwise be distinctive properties
of great value.

The important question in dealing with a site of greatly
varied topography is, whether, and in what manner, advantage
can be so taken of the different topographical conditions it
offers, that all classes of legitimate enterprises can be favored,
each in due proportion to the interest which all citizens have
in its economical and successful prosecution.

It would be easy, of course, to attempt too much in this
respect, but the range of practicability is more limited than
at first thought may be supposed. The value of a particular
situation for a certain purpose may be determined as far as
the depth which is left available for building is concerned,
by the distance apart of two adjoining streets, and as far as
aspect, accessibility to the public, and the cost of transportation
to and fro, are concerned, by their courses and grades; but
as to the breadth of ground that shall be available for any
particular purpose, as to the manner in which it shall be graded
and otherwise dealt with; whether it shall be cut down or
filled up, terraced, or used in a more natural form—these are
questions which the street system must necessarily leave to
be settled by private judgment under the stimulus of
competition.

Hence, while it is held that the capability of the ground
should be studied for purposes more or less distinctly to be
classed apart, and that, as topographical conditions vary, it
should be laid out with reference to one class or another,
an extended, exact, and dogmatic classification for this purpose
is not to be apprehended.

A judicious laying out of the annexed territory requires
a certain effort of forecast as to what the city is to be in
the future. In this respect, there is a great danger in attempting too much as in attempting too little. Before New York
can have doubled its present population, new motive powers

and means of transit, new methods of building, new professions and trades, and new departures in sanitary science, if not in political science, are likely to have appeared. If half its present territory should then be built up and occupied as closely as its seven more populous wards now are, the other half would need to lodge but one-seventh of its total population. Assuming that in this other half there should be but a moderate degree of urban density along the river side and near the railway stations, there would still remain several square miles of land which could only be occupied by scattered buildings. It is, then, premature, to say the least, to attempt to overcome any topographical difficulty that may be presented to a perfectly compact and urban occupation of every acre of the ground to be laid out.

Respectfully,
Fred. Law Olmsted,
Landscape Architect
J. James R. Croes,
Civil and Topographical Engineer

II. Report of the Landscape Architect and the Civil and Topographical Engineer, Accompanying a Plan for Laying Out That Part of the Twenty-fourth Ward Lying West of the Riverdale Road

City of New York,
Department of Public Parks,
21st November, 1876

The Hon. William R. Martin, President of the Board:

Sir:—The undersigned have now the honor to submit, as the first of a series, a plan for a primary road system for that part of the new wards lying west of the Riverdale Road.

358

The Commission has had the problem of laying out this district under debate since 1872. It has heretofore at various times called four engineers into its counsels upon it, and has considered five separate plans covering the ground wholly or in part. Much difference of opinion and something of partizanship with regard to these plans has appeared, and conflicting private interests concerned in the issues developed have been urged with warmth.

These, with other circumstances, the force of which the Commission will recognize, made it desirable that the purely professional and official character of the duty given the undersigned should be strictly guarded, and that for the time being, they should keep out of view any private ends to be affected.

For this reason, and also because it would be impracticable to give a fair hearing to every one concerned, they have, since they took the matter in hand, declined conversation upon it, have denied all requests for an examination of their study plans, and have neither expressed opinions nor accepted advice upon the subject.

They are now, consequently, under obligations to explain more fully than might otherwise be thought necessary, the grounds upon which the judgments have been formed which are embodied in the plan herewith presented.

In a previous report the objections have been indicated which prevail with them against one of the ruling motives upon which New York, so far as built during the present century, has been laid out and upon which most American cities are now building; the motive, that is to say, of securing in all quarters as nearly as practicable without excessive expense, an equality of advantages for all purposes.

They proceed, on the contrary, with the conviction that the principle of a division of labor may, with advantage, be measurably applied to the plan of a city; one part of it being laid out with a view to the development of one class of utilities, another to a different class, according as natural circumstances favor.

Under the first method, the great variety of topographical conditions found in the site of New York is regarded as a misfortune to be overcome, under the latter, as an advantage to be made available.

Having in view all the territory to be occupied before laying out any part of it, according to the preferred method, the topography of that part is to be questioned as for what class of private undertakings it is comparatively unsuitable, and as for what it is comparatively suitable.

I. The District to Be Laid Out

The district lies within and forms the larger part of the great promontory, the shank of which is crossed by the line dividing Yonkers from New York, and which terminates three miles to the southward in the abrupt headland of Spuyten Duyvil. Its ridge line seldom drops much below an elevation of 200 feet, and its highest point, which is also the highest in the city, is 282 feet above tide.

Its surface is much broken by ledges, and there are numerous steep declivities on its hillsides which can rarely be directly ascended without encountering a grade of from 15 to 25 in a hundred. Its ruggedness has prevented its being occupied for agricultural purposes, except very sparsely, and it is largely wooded and wild.

The only noticeable improvements have been made in connection with a number of private villas, and with a large convent and seminary, the grounds of which were also first prepared for a private pleasure ground.

That the district is not more generally occupied in this manner, is due first, to the uncertainty which exists as to how it is to be laid out and generally built over; second, to the fact that it is affected by malaria, of a mild type, however, and resulting entirely from superficial conditions easily to be removed; third, to its lack of suitable roads. The local scenery is everywhere pleasing, except as it is marred artificially. Generally, it is highly picturesque, with aspects of grandeur, and from nearly all parts, broad, distant prospects are commanded of an extended, interesting, and even very impressive character.

II. The Unsuitability of the District for the More Common Purposes of the City

To what needs of the city is such ground as has been described, well adapted?

The authors of the five plans for laying it out, of which transcripts upon a uniform scale are herewith exhibited, all knew well, from much experience, the convenience of the ordinary city division of real estate, and each plan represents an amount of patient and ingenious study in fitting streets of rectilinear or nearly rectilinear courses, to the highly curvilinear contours of the topography, that can be fully appreciated only by those who have had some experience in similar tasks.

Under neither of these plans could any considerable part of the ground to which it applies be subdivided into building sites of the usual form and dimensions of city real estate, or be built upon advantageously in compact ranges. This may be considered as conclusive testimony that the attempt to lay it out with such a purpose in view, would be impracticable.

The ascent of the slopes will be nowhere easy, and two horses, on an average, will be required within it to accomplish the work, which, in most other parts of the city, could be done by one.

There will be no thoroughfares adapted either to heavy teaming or to rapid driving, and in none of the plans heretofore prepared, is a single short-cut proposed across the district.

On these grounds, it may be concluded that factories, (at least of heavy goods), shops, warehouses, or stores for general trade, except possibly to a limited extent at the foot of the slopes, can be brought here only by some forced and costly process. The city holds much better ground for them in large quantity elsewhere.

The nearest part of the district is ten miles away from the present centre of population, and within that distance, there is but little other ground in which the call for houses of low rent for families of small means, could not be more economically met. The cost of preparing each site for such a house, and rendering it accessible, would be excessive, and the average space which would be appropriated for each, would be much larger than would be elsewhere required.

III. The Question of a Permanent Suburban Quarter

There remains to be considered the question of its further general and permanent occupation by that class of citizens to whom the confinement, noise, and purely artificial conditions of the compact city are oppressive, and who are able to indulge in the luxury of a villa or suburban cottage residence.

What are the chances of its being occupied in this manner advantageously?

IV. The Possibility of a Permanent Suburban Quarter

Of course, although manufactories and commercial buildings on a large scale are not to be apprehended, a perfectly uninterrupted succession of private villas and cottages is not to be hoped for. Here and there a shop or a range of shops will be necessary, but being adapted only for local custom, they are not likely to be lofty or excessively obtrusive. Now and again buildings for other purposes would probably occur; a school with its play grounds, a church set in a proper churchyard; a higher institution of learning with its green quadrangle, academic grove or campus; a public hall, library or museum; a convent with its courts and gardens; a surburban inn or boarding-house with its terrace, commanding grand prospects over the Hudson. All who have lived abroad know how buildings of these classes and many others may come into a villa suburb (their sites being chosen so as to gain an advantage from appropriate natural circumstances), in such a manner as not to disturb but to give point and emphasis to its proper aspect.

The nearest approach to urban building likely to be frequent, if once the general character proposed is obtained for the district, would be what the English call a terrace, a range of dwellings set back from the public street and reached by a loop-road, the crescent-shaped intermediate space being either a quiet slope of turf, a parterre of flowers, a play ground for children, or, if the topography favors, a picturesque rocky declivity treated perhaps as a fernery or Alpine garden. There will be, whatever the plan of roads, a great number of situations well adapted to such an arrangement, and which could be made suitable for no other except at much greater cost.

Old neighborhoods, more or less of the character indicated, are to be found near almost every great city of Europe, and there are towns like Bath, Leamington, and Brighton, and scores on the continent, noteable parts of which have had something of it for generations past, and hold it still.

But in none of these cases, except perhaps that of one of the suburban quarters of Edinburgh, were the natural conditions nearly as unfavorable for the more common manner of town building, and at the same time as favorable for a permanent, highly picturesque neighborhood, combining the conveniences of the town with the charms and healthfulness of the country.

It is not to be doubted that the promontory may, throughout its whole extent, be so laid out and occupied as to have an interest and attractiveness far excelling in its kind that of any other locality in America; nor that, if this result can be secured, it will hold great numbers of wealthy people within the city who would otherwise go away from it to find homes to suit them, and will draw many to it from without the city. Its effect will, in this respect, be similar to that which has been experienced from the Central Park, but with this difference, that the gain to the city will be in conditions the cost of which will have been mainly defrayed by the voluntary and self-directed contributions of the private owners of the land, not from the public treasury.

It may be questioned whether, even in a locality as yet so remote from dense building and so rugged in its topography, the demand for land for various other purposes will not, in time, crowd out all rural and picturesque elements, and whether, for this reason, it would be prudent to lay it out with exclusive reference to suburban uses? All that can be said in reply, is that thus far in the history of other great cities there is nothing to sustain such a doubt.

After a certain degree of density has been attained, the proportion of people who are disposed and able to live under suburban conditions, relatively to those who may be content or obliged to live under rigidly urban conditions, becomes larger the larger the town, but there is yet no city in the world so large that it has not luxurious suburban quarters much nearer to its centre than is the promontory, even to the outer part of New York as now densely built. London has fairly grown around and stretched beyond some clusters of fine old suburban residences without seriously disturbing them. There are private gardens in which the town is almost lost sight of at not many minutes walk from Hyde Park. Within a range from the heart of Old London of less than one-third the distance of Riverdale from the City Hall, there are hundreds of acres of gardens and villa and cottage grounds; and, with a city adding much more annually to her population than New York, costly villas are every year built, and villa neighborhoods are steadily enlarged without becoming less distinctly suburban in character.

Districts of villas exist and others are forming also but a little way from dense parts of Paris. Under Haussmann, roads were laid out expressly for villas closely adjoining the grand route between the Champs Elysées and the Bois de Boulogne, every site upon which is now occupied by a semi-rural residence. Other and extensive districts of the same class have been laid out since with confident reference to permanence as an integral element of the attractions of the city.

V. The Advantages Offered by the Proposition to the City

It is reasonable to infer that New York will have such quarters. It remains a question whether they shall be formed by a co-operation of public and private work, or by private enterprise in making the best of unsuitable public arrangements.

The importance of the question will be recognized if it is considered what a difference there would now be in the attractiveness, and consequently in the wealth of the city, if twenty-five years ago, when it was quite practicable, Fifth avenue from Madison Square to the Central Park, had been laid out fifty feet wider than it is, with slightly better grades, a pad for riding horses, broad sidewalks and an avenue of trees.

It will cost much less to lay out and prepare the promontory admirably as a permanent suburb than to prepare it tolerably for any other use.

A given sum expended upon it for the purpose will have important results much sooner than if expended for any other.

All other purposes which the city needs to have in view can be provided for at much less cost and much more conveniently in other parts of its present territory.

Treated as a suburb, the district is likely to make larger contributions to the city treasury, and to begin to contribute to it in important amount sooner than if treated in any other way.

What is meant by treating the district as a suburb is, that the development of a distinctly suburban and picturesque character should everywhere be kept frankly in view as a source of wealth, and that the roads should be adapted to a population living less densely, and with which pleasure driving and walking are to be, relatively to heavy teaming, more important than in the streets of the compact city.

If the policy which has been indicated does not, upon reflection, fully commend itself to the Commission, the plan now submitted is not entitled to further examination. It is professedly adapted to no other.

If, however, the soundness of the policy is accepted, the manner in which the district should be laid out, in order to its success, remains to be considered.

VI. The Question of Laying Out a Specially Picturesque and Convenient Suburb

The custom of laying out roads in the outskirts of cities only upon right lines, under any circumstances which leave it possible to do so, is so strongly fixed in our country that the Commission cannot entertain the idea of abandoning it before carefully weighing what is to be gained and lost by doing so. It should remember, however, that the custom is largely due to the disposition of land owners, to act on the imagination, by showing lots which, as represented on paper, differ in no respect from the most valuable in the city, and thus to feed the pernicious propensity which prevails among the ignorant for gambling on small means under the name of speculation in real estate.

Again, it is to be remembered that it is not customary to think of the laying out of any part of a city as a matter in the smallest degree of esthetic design; but, if the policy of carrying on a series of constructions in a manner sympathetic with picturesque landscape effects has any claims to adoption by the Commission, it necessarily involves a serious application, in however humble a way, of the laws and the spirit of art.

The more tangible and weighty advantage to be urged in favor of keeping as nearly as practicable to straight lines of road, is one commonly expressed under one of the following specifications.

1st. That of the comparative ease and simplicity of the business of laying out the roads.

2d. That of the comparative rapidity and convenience with which surveyors' measurements and calculations are made when dealing with straight lines.

366

3d. That of the greater convenience of a straight front when land is to be divided or described with a view to sale or mortgage.

It is not questioned that these advantages should be waived in the case of very difficult topography, such as must often occur on the promontory. (It will be observed that each of the six plans before the Commission proposes a considerable extent of curved line.) It apparently follows that whether the straight street should yield to the winding road at any point, when it is otherwise desirable, is, at the worst, a question of employing surveyors competent to deal with curved lines. No plan has been proposed to the Commission for laying out the promontory, under which a local surveyor to whom curved lines were a serious matter, could honestly earn his living. The whole amount of the class of expenses in question, under the most difficult circumstances, would be relatively inconsiderable, and if any essential, permanent advantage to the community is at stake, regard for them should not be allowed to obstruct the very best arrangement that can be devised.

The third specification above refers to the facility which straightness in a street gives for laying off properties in lots the dimensions of which may be expressed in two numbers, and to the convenience of the custom, to which this advantage is essential, of dividing property for sale in a series of parallelograms of uniform length of frontage, as in the case of city lots. As to this custom, it is to be remembered that if it should be generally adhered to on the promontory it would not affect the desired result favorably, but otherwise, for this reason.

In broken and rolling ground, and especially in rocky ground, sites for houses can be well chosen only with an intelligent consideration of local circumstances. If a hundred lots are to be laid off, each one hundred feet wide, and with the dividing lines all at right angles with the street line, in many parts of the promontory the dividing lines will so occur, that on not half the lots will an entirely satisfactory site for a building be found, and, on several, building will be impracticable until after much labor has been given to transform the natural surface. Let the same property, on the other hand, be laid out with a judicious adjustment of lines to the local conditions, and an equal number of lots may be made of it, each offering an admirable and conveniently approached site. Of course, however, they will vary in size.

As to the general attractiveness of the region, and as to the total or average value of all its real estate, there are certain well established principles by which men of taste throughout the civilized world, when living among rural or even rus-urban conditions are almost invariably guided when laying out the private carriage approaches to their houses.[3] The motives growing out of well established experience which enforce this practice, apply equally in the case of a common approach to two houses as to one, and if to two, equally to twenty or to two hundred. Though the propriety may be questioned of advancing toward a house indirectly when it is situated on a plain, there is no question that in a hilly country the principles referred to always lead to the use in roads of winding courses in greater or less degree of correspondence with the natural surface.

VII. The Economical Advantages of the Proposition

The comparative economy of straight and winding roads is partly a question of what is desirable under given circumstances as to grades. The shortest line between two points is not always that which can be passed over at the least cost of time or in wear and tear.

A carriage load that requires two horses and a given strength of harness to be drawn over a road with grades by which one foot in elevation is overcome in ten feet of distance, as in the case of some of the present roads of the promontory, can be as easily and safely drawn by one horse and with a harness one-half lighter on a road in which twenty-four

[3] Exceptions occur when the approach is short, crosses flat ground, and can be seen from end to end in one symmetrical composition with the house; conditions to which there will be none corresponding in the roads of the promontory. [1876.]

feet is allowed for overcoming the same elevation. If a man in haste at a given point wishes to drive a horse of ordinary quality with a light wagon to another point 180 feet higher on a hillside, he can do so in shorter time upon a curved road 800 yards in length than upon a straight road of 600 yards.

If the hillsides of the promontory are to be occupied chiefly by families in comfortable circumstances it is evident that for the great majority of occasions a road carried between two points, one at a greater elevation than another, upon a curve regulated by the curve of the hillside along which it will be passing, though longer horizontally will be passed over in shorter time, and with less wear and tear, than a straight road between the same points. The straight road might, because it was the shortest, cost less for construction. The probabilities are, that ploughing straight through whatever was in the way, it would cost more. But, whether so or not, in running along an alternately swelling and retreating surface, the more unswerving the course the more it would be necessary in grading the road to cut through the protuberances and to fill across the depressions.

From this consideration it follows, that unless a level can be kept, which in this district it rarely can for any distance, access will be had from a road laid on natural lines to adjoining building sites with much less violence and at less cost, on an average, than it can from a straight road, and, again, that the amount of walling, sloping, turfing or other operations necessary to a tidy road-side, or the attractive presentation of the adjoining properties will be less with the winding than the straight road.

VIII. The Immediate Convenience of the Proposition

One advantage to be gained by adopting winding and picturesque roads, as far as conveniently practicable, rather than straight and formal streets remains to be suggested.

Formal streets, especially when far extended on a straight line at an even grade, their every line of curb, sidewalk and lamp-posts, being truly set, and when bounded by continuous walls of stately houses, have an imposing effect, and satisfy good taste. But in streets which, by alternate cuttings and embankments, are carried, here through woods, there across open fields, here are flanked by the ragged face of blasted ledges or raw banks of earth, there by a varied prospect, even when fine houses are occasionally built fronting upon them, straightness gives no dignity and expresses little but incongruity and imperfection.

To make such a street tolerable to the eye it needs from the beginning as perfect lines and as perfect surfaces in its curbs, gutters and lamp-posts, pavement and flagging, as the densely occupied street of the city. If a cheap temporary wheel-way is made in it, or temporary sidewalks, any deviation from a straight line, or even any short flexions of grade in them are unsatisfactory. If trees are set between the walks and the wheel-way they seem out of place, and add to a general expression of untidiness, incompleteness, disorder and shiftlessness, unless they are evenly spaced in continuous lines parallel with all the other features. The slightest disarrangement of such a road, scattered patches of grass and weeds, a sucker growth of trees and bushes on the bordering banks, even the general heaving outward and inward of the fences that form its outlines, all claim attention as defects and shortcomings from what is attempted.

Nothing of this is true of roads laid out with a natural motive. The wheel-way may have a somewhat variable width, as economy shall require; its grade may dip and rise within a hundred yards; the courses of the walks may vary a little from that of the wheel-way, may rise a little in a cutting or fall a little on an embankment, may rise on one side and fall on the other; wild plants may spring up, here and there, in random tufts, or, again, the roadsides be all filled out (as some in the district now are), with a thick growth of low brambles, ferns, asters, gentians, golden-rods; roadside trees may be irregularly spaced and of various sizes and species, great opposite small, ash over against maple, elm bending to oak; fine old trees may be left standing, and, to save them, the wheel-way carried a little to the right or left, or slightly raised or lowered. It may be desirable, simply for convenience sake, to go to the expense of avoiding such conditions, but, as a matter of taste, they are far from blemishes; they add to other charms of picturesqueness, and they are a concession to nature, tending to an effect not of incongruity and incompleteness, but of consistent and happy landscape composition.

Hence, roads on natural lines, which may be so far worked, at moderate cost as to meet the ordinary requirements of convenience of a considerable community, will much sooner and more uninterruptedly give results of a presentable, comely and attractive character. In this manner, indeed, the most agreeable roads in the world have been made.

IX. General Requirements

Adopting the general conclusion which has thus been sustained, there is still much room for difference of judgment as to the location of roads, their breadth and grades.

The existing divisions of land, the positions of houses, of fences, of roads, have been determined without regard to such an occupation of the district as is now to be prepared for. Individual interests, based on existing arrangements, must necessarily be, in greater or less degree, at issue with those general and lasting interests of the public of which the Commission is the guardian. There must be limits within which the latter are so far paramount that not the least compromise between the two is admissible. To keep on the safe side of those limits, it has appeared to the undersigned best to perfect a conclusion, in the first place, as to what roads are necessary as routes, or links in routes, of extended, general and unquestionably desirable, in distinction from local and limited, communication. This they have done in the plan now presented, except that they have adopted the judgment of the Board, as heretofore indicated, on three points not materially affecting the general design.

X. By-Roads

If the Commission should substantially adopt the system, and afterwards think proper to consult the judgment and wishes of each land-owner as to cross roads or by-roads, it can do so with confidence, that no conclusions to which it may then be led can be seriously detrimental to the general interests. Any one of the divisions left by the plan might even be subdivided, for example, by rectilinear roads without destroying the consistency and harmony or lessening the convenience, of the main system. If, on the other hand, such minor roads within any division should, in order not to mar a series of natural building sites, be made very indirect and circuitous, the worst result would be a slight inconvenience to a few residents within the division and those calling upon them, which, to these, would be compensated by the greater beauty and local convenience of the buildings. The public in general, keeping to the primary roads, would suffer no inconvenience.

It is believed, too, that the proprietors will be much better able to form a sound judgment as to the requirements of their own interests in the minor roads if they are allowed to become familiar with the proposed general system, and with the theory which it represents of the interest of the district as a whole.

XI. Requirements of Detail: Planting Arrangements

It should be recognized that to carry out a natural or informal system judiciously, so that a good share of its possible advantages may be surely realized, much study of detail is required. Both for economy and for beauty local circumstances must be diligently consulted, and the treatment of the road adapted to them. Variety in this respect should be sought, not avoided. Every turn should bring something of fresh interest into view within the road as well as beyond it.

In this detail very well-considered provisions should be made for road-side planting. Ordinarily in the suburbs of rapidly growing American towns, trees are planted most injudiciously and wastefully, ill-chosen as to species for the locality, ill-placed, ill-planted, and with no suitable provision for a continuous, healthy growth. Science is yearly placing a higher estimate on the sanitary value of street trees. Paris now maintains a great nursery with a view to the systematic supply of all the city with this means of dissipating malaria and infection. London is just entering upon a similar duty. The matter of supplying New York streets with trees has been much debated by her sanitarians. The difficulty lies in the fact, that the street arrangements of the city being all designed with no reference to the purpose, the introduction of trees, with the conditions necessary to success, would be very costly and inconvenient. In laying out a new system, especially for a quarter designed to offer a beautiful and healthful relief to the more general conditions of city life, this requirement should be thoroughly well attended to.

The tracing submitted represents the outline of a general plan, the adoption of which is recommended subject to such slight adjustments, immaterial to the essential design, as may be found desirable.

A drawing is also exhibited which will serve to indicate more fully the purposes in view.

> Respectfully,
> FRED. LAW OLMSTED,
> *Landscape Architect*
> J. JAMES R. CROES,
> *Civil and Topographical Engineer*

DOCUMENT X

➤➤➤➤➤➤⫷⫷⫷⫷

Frederick Law Olmsted and J. James R. Croes

Document No. 75 of the Board of the Department of Public Parks: Report of the Landscape Architect and the Civil and Topographical Engineer, Accompanying a Plan for Local Steam Transit Routes in the Twenty-third and Twenty-fourth Wards (1877)

➤➤➤➤➤➤⫷⫷⫷⫷

March 21, 1877

Report of the Civil and Topographical Engineer and the Landscape Architect, accompanying a plan for local steam transit routes in the Twenty-third and Twenty-fourth Wards. Ordered printed as a document of the Board.

Wm. Irwin,
Secretary D. P. P.

City of New York,
Department of Public Parks,
20th March, 1877

The Hon. William R. Martin, President of the Board

Sir—In compliance with your request, the undersigned have the honor herewith to present a map, showing proposed routes for local steam transit through the Twenty-third and Twenty-fourth Wards, and connections of the same with lines, or proposed lines extending to the south end of the city.

375

I

The speed which is maintained on our railways in passing through rural districts is generally checked the moment a dense population is reached, and within our large towns the chief advantage of this great improvement upon older methods of traveling is in a great degree lost. Where, as is the case with New York, the distance between the business centre and the residence centre is great, the deprivation is a serious one, and the demand that it should be obviated has long been pressing.

The reason for the diminution of speed on entering a town lies in the fact that the long-established plan of laying out towns is not adapted to the conditions essential to rapid movement, having been devised before the necessity for it was felt, and indeed before the means of accomplishing it had been invented. Now that its accomplishment has been proved to be mechanically practicable and its necessity is recognized, it would be unpardonable, in devising plans for laying out a large territory for the accommodation of a more or less dense population, not to provide for it in advance.

II

In the existing condition of the mechanical appliances for travel at high speed it can only be accomplished by the use of heavy trains of vehicles moving on rigid lines with light gradients. For safety such lines must be so located that pedestrians and vehicles adapted to use on ordinary roads can by no possibility encounter the trains. The routes selected must, therefore, at all points of contact with common roads, be either above or below their grades. Any plan which involves adherence throughout the entire route to an invariable type of construction, whether elevated or depressed, is inconsistent with economy in any region like new wards, the topography of which is very uneven.

The conditions to be fulfilled are best found in a road running either along a hillside, in a narrow valley, or on a narrow ridge, in such a manner that intersecting streets may

376

be carried either over or under it, as local convenience may dictate, with moderate expense.

III

It has hitherto been customary in laying out routes for railways to disregard the requirements of ordinary travel and the existing and future division of property. It has, on the other hand, been usual, in dividing property by common streets, to pay no attention to the possible introduction of railway transit.

As a result of these customs, difficulty is now encountered on New York Island in arranging rapid transit routes, and in the suburban wards in obtaining safe and convenient roads adjoining and crossing existing railroads. Inasmuch as steam roads admit of less flexibility of line and grade than common roads, the determination of their location should in a plan aiming to combine the two systems satisfactorily, precede the establishment of the complete subdivision of the property, but the practicability of a proper subdivision must always be kept in view. The construction of a system devised to combine the two undoubtedly involves more expense for each, considered by itself, than if the combination could be avoided, but not so great expense or injury as the adjusting of one to the cheapest location of the other.

IV

The experience of the last twenty-five years has demonstrated that the chief obstacle to the accomplishment of speedy communication between distant points in New York City, is the difficulty of obtaining the right of way for steam roads.

There are three methods possible for acquiring the land needed:

1st. It may be purchased by the corporation which is to furnish the means of transportation.

2d. The right of way over a highway already devoted to public uses may be granted to such corporation.

3d. A new route to be used exclusively for the purpose may be provided at the public expense.

Where the transporting corporation purchases the land, the whole burden falls on the travelers, who are forced to pay in fares the interest on the purchase money, as well as on the cost of construction.

Capitalists object to this method, from a conviction that it will oblige the imposition of so high a rate of fare as to repel, rather than invite travel; or if low fares are established by legislation, that the result will be a loss to the management.

Where a street is taken which has been already acquired by the public for ordinary traffic and for access to the property fronting on it, the burden falls partly on the travelers, who pay the interest on the cost of construction, receiving an equivalent however for their money, and partly on the owners of such property as is injured, who receive no equivalent.

This method is objected to by owners of property, on the ground that it imposes the cost of the right of way on them, not indeed directly as an actual pecuniary disbursement, but indirectly, through the depreciation of the value of their property, and the diminution of their business resulting from the presence in the street of an obstruction to ordinary traffic.

Where a new route is furnished by the public, part of the burden is borne by the travelers, as in the other cases, and the rest by the property which is benefited by the facilities for travel, which includes alike the business centres and the remote residence districts.

By this method, the injury to property is reduced to a minimum, and the burden is distributed equitably among the persons who are benefited.

V

In accordance with the considerations thus presented, the plan now submitted contemplates the laying out of a system of roads on such routes and with such grades that their use can be restricted to steam travel, that they will afford moderately direct communication between the desired points, will be easily accessible from all points which they do not directly touch, will nowhere cross ordinary high ways at the same level, and will not as a rule interfere with satisfactory divisions of property.

In the arrangement of the routes the following principles have been kept in view.

(1.) The crossings of the Harlem River must be as few as possible.

(This is alike desirable whether such crossings are by bridge or by tunnel; if by the former it is important that navigation should be as unobstructed as practicable, if by the latter the expense of many crossings would be too great.)

(2.) All crossings of the river must be at such points that connection can be easily had with lines on New York Island.

(3.) Lines must be so laid out that trains passing from the city through one district may return by a loop or circuit through another.

(This not only gives to the residents of each of the districts the advantage of communication between the two, but also gives them, with the same number of trains, more frequent opportunities to reach the business centre than they would have with single lines.)

(4.) While every opportunity must be afforded to existing lines of trunk freight and passenger railroads to co-operate in the local passenger traffic, routes and river crossings must be provided which will be independent of their control.

VI

With reference to the crossing of the Harlem River, the following considerations are presented:

There are but two existing railroad crossings of the river. The New York Central & Hudson River Railroad enters on New York island by a bridge at Spuyten Duyvil, and the extension of the same road by the Spuyten Duyvil & Port Morris branch crosses at Fourth Avenue by the bridge of the Harlem Railroad, which is also used by the New Haven Railroad.

The Rapid Transit Commissioners, in 1875, authorized a crossing of the river at First Avenue, to connect with the Portchester branch of the New Haven Railroad, and another near the High Bridge, to connect with the partially constructed New York & Boston Railroad.

379

Both of these lines are so situated as to render it very unlikely that any crossing will be constructed upon them for many years to come, if at all.

As regards the first, a bridge would cause too great obstruction to navigation at a point which is now the centre of a considerable water traffic, and a tunnel is not likely to be built upon it as long as it is possible, within a mile, to construct, at one-tenth of the cost, a bridge which will not very seriously interfere with the interests of commerce.

As regards a crossing near the High Bridge, the authorized approach on the Manhattan shore passes for more than a mile along the base of a precipitous hill, which can never have a sufficient population to support a local road, and from the crossing, when made, extensions of the road can be made with advantage in only one direction.

A bridge from One hundred and forty-fifth Street, on the south side of the river, connecting with the loop line authorized by the Rapid Transit Commission, along the exterior street, and crossing to One hundred and forty-ninth Street, on the north side, will be open to neither of these objections. It will afford all the facilities for crossing which will be needed, for several years at least, and will be at such distance from any other bridge that little inconvenience will occur to navigation, even after the projected improvement of the Harlem River is made.

VII

In determining the arrangements which should be provided for steam transit after crossing the river, existing railroads must be taken into consideration.

Along the Hudson River the New York Central & Hudson River Railroad affords facilities for travel; along the Harlem River runs the Spuyten Duyvil & Port Morris Railroad; in the Mill Brook Valley the Harlem River Railroad furnishes accommodation; and further to the eastward the Portchester Branch Railroad has an opportunity for building up a large local travel as far north as West Farms Village.

Of these the Spuyten Duyvil & Port Morris branch, in

connection with the Hudson River Railroad, is the only one which at all supplies the desideratum of a circuit or loop line. It is defective, in that its termini lie on opposite sides of the city, and too far north.

The other lines mentioned must always remain pre-eminently routes of through travel, and as such their managers can not be expected to give the attention to local convenience which the interests of the city will demand.

Being, nevertheless, too important to be overlooked in any comprehensive scheme, they may be considered available as links of a system as yet incomplete, and opportunity must be given them for combining with other lines.

The three main divisions of the territory which are as yet wholly unprovided with facilities for access to old New York, are the valley lying east of the Spuyten Duyvil Promontory and extending to Yonkers, the Jerome Avenue Valley, and the Southern Boulevard district.

During most of the year, the pleasure and comfort of water travel over the route by steamboat from Harlem to the eastern lower portion of the city will always attract a large passenger traffic. It is essential, therefore, that provision should be made for the delivery of passengers from local railroads at the point now occupied by the terminus of the Portchester road, situated at the head of unobstructed navigation.

VIII

The plans submitted herewith exhibit the following main features:

(*a*.) A central crossing of the Harlem River between Fifth and Sixth avenues at a point about equidistant from the two authorized routes on New York Island, running parallel to its axis.

(*b*.) A main circuit line up the Jerome Avenue Valley to Jerome Park, thence crossing to the Harlem Railroad, by the route of the Jerome Park Branch Railroad, and following a route generally parallel to that of the Southern Boulevard to the Boston Road, thence down the Bound Brook Valley to the Westchester Road, thence to the Port Morris branch, at St. Mary's Park, and thence, crossing North New York, between One hundred and forty-fourth and One hundred and forty-fifth Streets, over the Harlem Railroad, and through Buena Ridge to the bridge at One hundred and forty-ninth Street.

(c.) A loop line, connecting with the main circuit and with the Port Morris Branch Railroad at St. Mary's Park and passing through the Notch at One hundred and forty-first Street, and southerly between St. Ann's and Brook Avenues, to a connection with the Portchester Depot, and thence, along the river, to the crossing at One hundred and forty-ninth Street.

(d.) A loop line, connecting with the main circuit at Mount Eden, and following the Valley of the Ice Pond Brook, passing under the Harlem Railroad at One hundred and fifty-fourth Street, and thence, between Morris and College Avenues, to line (c), near the Portchester Depot.

(e.) A line, connecting the main circuit and the Portchester Railroad, near Fox's Corners.

(f.) A loop line *via* the Port Morris Branch Railroad.

(g.) A line from Kingsbridge to Ludlow's Dock and Yonkers, by way of the Broadway Valley.

(h.) A route from High Bridge to Yonkers, up the valley of Tibbett's Brook, being an amendment of the route of the partly-built New York, Boston & Montreal Railroad.

All of the above described routes are so located as to be intermediate between streets intended for ordinary travel, and all such streets will cross them, either over or under the grade.

The maximum gradient will be 80 feet to a mile, and the minimum radius of curvature 521 feet. These extremes are closely approached but in a few instances.

Respectfully,
J. JAMES R. CROES,
Civil and Topographical Engineer
FREDERICK LAW OLMSTED,
Landscape Architect

PART FIVE

"THE SPOILS OF THE PARK"

T*he Spoils of the Park,* Document XI, privately printed in 1882, despite the bitter tone and critical remarks, indicates how deeply committed Olmsted remained to the improvement of New York City. The pamphlet reflects the distress felt in reviewing the innumerable conflicts and frustrations, and the personal humiliation suffered during his more than two decades of active service to the City.[1] In a sense, this is Olmsted's final statement—an effort to explain to an interested public the reasons for his failure to accomplish all that he set out to do. The pamphlet does not lend itself to easy reading. A major defect of Olmsted's style is here apparent—the tendency to mention persons and incidents without sufficient clarification. Always the reformer, he concludes with recommendations for improvement.

The pamphlet also had an immediate practical purpose: to save the original design of Central Park. Since Olmsted's dismissal, there had been set forth various proposals to alter the basic plan (see Illustration XVII). With the passing years, the changing city, and the rejection of his other plans, this park had become a symbol of his original hope for the City. Now, he learned, changes were being urged by men without any qualifications or training in landscape architecture. Since 1879 the Board had been without the services of a landscape architect. For Olmsted, who had done so much during his lifetime to establish standards for the profession, this was no different, as he put it, from managing a hospital "without [the] aid of doctors, or with that only of doctors of divinity."[2]

The problem was essentially one of politics. Appointment to the Park Board had come either from Albany or City Hall, but the caliber of the men had steadily declined, reaching a low point in 1870 under the Tweed Ring. And the Board of 1878—appointed by a so-called reform administration—was,

---

[1] Olmsted lost his stepson Owen in 1881.
[2] Frederick Law Olmsted, *The Spoils of the Park* ([?], 1882), p. 397. See Document XI.

to Olmsted's mind, no better, and in some respects worse. The primary function of the Park Commission, increasingly, was to provide employment for those who depended on the political machine for jobs. "I do not believe," Olmsted wrote, "that there has in twenty years been a time when nine-tenths of the intellectual force and nervous energy of the Board has not been given to recruiting duty."[3]

To be sure, the 1870's was a period of serious unemployment and violent labor protest throughout the nation. Touched off by the financial panic of 1874, the situation grew progressively worse. By 1878, the year of Olmsted's dismissal, "in all the great cities, from Boston to Omaha, crowds of workless and hungry men tramped the streets, hung disconsolately about the public squares, and joined in parades and mass meetings of protest."[4] In New York City during the railroad strikes of 1877, Olmsted wrote, the city was "essentially under martial law." He considered the danger of mob violence so great that he armed the Central Park headquarters. "I doubled the sentries," he wrote his wife, "and directed the armorer to load the . . . howitzers."[5] Olmsted was not at all unsympathetic to the needs of workers, but he was as opposed to mob violence as he was to making the Park Department into a social welfare agency. In the opinion of one medical expert, the Park Department had already become "an asylum for aggravated cases of hernia, varicose veins, rheumatism, partial blindness, and other infirmities compelling sedentary occupations."[6]

For this sort of stubborn integrity Olmsted paid a severe price. He was insulted publicly in print, threatened with loss of job, and physically intimidated. At times the privacy of his home was invaded by job-seekers; a candidate for political office told a gathering of people in front of Olmsted's window that a rope around his neck might make him more tractable. Despite alternating feelings of depression and anxiety, he refused to surrender the management of the Park to those who

[3] *Ibid.*, p. 417.
[4] Allan Nevins, *The Emergence of Modern America, 1865–1878* (New York, 1935), p. 384.
[5] Olmsted to Mary Olmsted, July 24, 1877, Olmsted Papers.
[6] Olmsted, *Spoils of the Park*, p. 409.

did not believe in its original purpose and meaning. "Where shall the poor man go," he asked, "when the Park has become what persistence in such management will make it?"[7]

The pamphlet concludes with Olmsted's recommendations for remedial action. He wanted to place park management above politics. But he did not mean to make it an object of the civil service reform so much in vogue in the 1880's following the assassination of President Garfield. Many readers of the pamphlet misunderstood this. "I have been very much interested in it," wrote one reader, "especially, I must confess, in its bearing on 'Civil Service Reform.' "[8] Olmsted did not trust such a solution. It lacked the personal element which he believed was needed in the administration of the Park. Instead, he advocated the selection of "an unpaid board of citizens, so large, and of such established reputation . . . that there could be some rational confidence that they would exercise conservative control."[9]

Spoils of the Park was read mainly by reformers. "I have read your pamphlet with deep and painful interest," wrote Charles Eliot Norton. "The story is worse than I knew. I am glad you have told it."[10] The President of the Park Commission, a former Republican candidate for Mayor, who considered himself a reformer, was shocked to find himself parodied as the "worthy Master Salem Wales."[11] He protested his innocence and ignorance, saying that "the serpent of politics has crawled into this paradise and evil comes of course from this blighting cause."[12] The pamphlet, however, did not elicit the kind of editorial comment which Olmsted had hoped to provoke. He had "seen but three references to it" in the New York press, "and these all turning it to some partisan account—not looking to the rescue of the park, which, of course, is a disappointment to me."[13]

[7] *Ibid.*, p. 399.
[8] J. S. Lowell to Olmsted, March 1, 1882, Olmsted Papers.
[9] Olmsted, *Spoils of the Park*, p. 438.
[10] Charles E. Norton to Olmsted, March 4, 1882, Olmsted Papers.
[11] Olmsted, *Spoils of the Park*, p. 392.
[12] Salem H. Wales to Olmsted, March 6, 1882, Olmsted Papers.
[13] Olmsted to Charles L. Brace, March 7, 1882, Olmsted Papers.

The most concrete proposal came from a young, aggressive, reform-minded politician just starting his political career in Albany, Theodore Roosevelt. Wales, out of conscience, had sent him the pamphlet, notifying Olmsted that he was taking "some steps to start your suggestions and it may be that something can be done."[14] Roosevelt responded immediately and with characteristic energy: "I have read your pamphlet with intense interest; I could check off every statement with corresponding experiences of my own."[15] He volunteered to sponsor a bill in the state legislature incorporating Olmsted's proposals and suggested a list of distinguished citizens to constitute the new Park Board, asking Olmsted for alternate names. Nothing came of it.

After his dismissal Olmsted moved his practice and family back to New England, to Brookline in the suburbs of Boston, where he resided until the final tragic years preceding his death in 1903. His reputation as landscape architect and city planner was not hurt by his experience in New York City. It thrived, culminating in his participation in the planning and design of the Chicago World's Fair of 1893. He often claimed that during this time he had cut himself off from New York City and its affairs. This was no more true than it was possible. In one way or another he had been part of the City since 1840, when as a young man of eighteen he had been apprenticed there as a clerk. For almost forty years he had invested his energies in its activities, and he was always devoted to its growth and improvement.

He still had many friends and supporters there. In 1886, with Morningside and Riverside Parks uncompleted, his services were again requested. "On behalf of this Department I desire to ask," wrote the new President of the Board, "whether you will undertake the office of examining and reporting upon the condition of these parks and preparing plans for their construction and completion, and upon what terms."[16] The

[14] Wales to Olmsted, March 6, 1882, Olmsted Papers.
[15] Theodore Roosevelt to Olmsted, March 19, 1882, Olmsted Papers.
[16] Harry Beekman to Olmsted and Vaux, June 4, 1886, Olmsted Papers.

terms were that he would work with Vaux, free from political pressures. He took occasion in the Report for Morningside, Document XII, to remind the Board that because of its failure to act in time it was no longer possible to execute the original plan for Morningside, Document VIII, which had envisaged an interrelated park system connecting it with Central Park. Immediately upon completion of the project (see Illustration XIX) in July, 1887, he resigned his position. In 1889, in conjunction with a colleague, he published a pamphlet criticizing the care and management of the landscape of Central Park.[17] In 1892 he learned through a friend of a major park expansion program, the largest since the 1850's. "More than 3,000 acres of new parks are to be laid out," he wrote to his son John, a partner in the firm, "and as for our getting the work it is a question of Tammany vs. our reputation." Although he questioned whether he had the energy and "appetite for the fight that would be inevitable," the desire to reform was still there.[18]

Parks had become a symbol of the kind of public planning and esthetics which a democratic nation needed in its cities. Olmsted understood that the failure of the American city was the failure of American civilization. "Let what the country needs of the government of its great cities," he had once written prophetically, "be compared at intervals of five years with what it finds them able to perform, and on the whole the gap will always be found ominously wider.

"If we must continue to let it widen, the occurrence of a grand catastrophe is plainly only a question of time. And it will be a catastrophe not merely for the republic but for civilization; for our great cities stretch their hands to all the world, and all the peoples of the world are provided through them."[19]

[17] Frederick Law Olmsted and J. B. Harrison, *Observations on the Treatment of Public Plantations* (Boston, 1889), *passim.*

[18] Olmsted to John C. Olmsted, Aug. 6, 1892, Olmsted Papers.

[19] Olmsted, "The Beginning of Central Park: A Fragment of Autobiography" (American Scenic and Historic Preservation Society, Nineteenth Annual Report, 1914), p. 54.

DOCUMENT XI

FREDERICK LAW OLMSTED

The Spoils of the Park: With a Few Leaves from the Deep-laden Note-books of "A Wholly Unpractical Man" (1882)

> They that have done this deed are practical;
> What private griefs they have I know not
> That made them do it; they are wise and practical,
> And will with reasons answer you.

The demand for a change in the management of the parks has taken a more distinct form, even since I left the last of this pamphlet in the printers' hands. If I had been seeking office, it would have been a most foolish thing to write it: yet it may be best to refer to the fact that the frequent appearance of my name, either as a candidate or otherwise, in the debates of the Park Board, has in every case been against my repeatedly expressed wishes; that, whenever privately consulted, I have advised the immediate employment of men who could give the assurances of *efficiency with reference to the proper ends* of park management, which are only to be found in professional standing and in arrangements for this purpose, which left my own employment out of the question. I was more immediately moved to write by the opinion of a shrewd observer that Mr. Vaux's employment was the last thing that a *majority* of the Board had ever intended, and by seeing Mr. Wales blamed for "wrangling" I had in view, at starting, only to point out good-naturedly that Mr. Wales's view of his Board's course was not that of a too contentious, so much as that of a too lenient man. Having taken up the case from this point of view, I found a more thorough treatment of it necessary. Though it is the first time I have written critically of the business of the Department, except officially and with official sanction, it must be well known to my friends that the views expressed are of very old standing. In their more important points they are not even original with me, and are as far as possible from having been developed for the occasion. Though often urged to write on the subject, I have done so now without conference with any one, and, except in closing, without reference to any plans of legislation.

F. L. O.

Detroit, Mich.,
Feb. 23, 1882

1

> *"This disorganized body has been masquerading before the public, a headless trunk, without policy, without order, without well-defined purpose."*

The words of my text were of late given to the WORLD by one of the members of the body they depict, sometime, withal, its president, worthy Master Salem Wales,—a man-of-peace, across whose shapely bows my yet more peaceful shallop could never hold her course but with the falling topsail of deferential salutation. Occasion cometh now in this wise:—

Having been kept much from home, seeing the Board and its works only through the eyes of the Press, and thus taking, if a less perspicuous, yet a more distant and therefore more comprehensive, view of its proceedings than Mr. Wales can have done, I fancy that I recognize a general drift in them of which he seems unconscious. I am the more moved to show the difference between his perspective point and mine, because I have observed, that, whereas till lately the meetings of the Board have been regarded by the Press as a sort of brawling farce, and as such, for amusement's sake, liberally reported, now for some little time back, through a growing weariness of them as it is made to appear, an entire performance often gets no other notice than a single contemptuous paragraph. Thus I see a gaining tendency to look upon the Commissioners as an incapable and harmless set of witlings, with whose doings no sensible man can be expected to much concern himself. Such an impression is clearly unjust to Mr. Wales himself, else why should he be able to do so little with them as he tells us that he is? Yet the brief characterization of the Board which I have quoted, and with which much else that he has written tallies, tends to confirm the impression that it is pursuing a heedless, aimless, and essentially a harmless course.

Comparing his accounts with those of the newspapers, and judging both in the light of my experience in affairs of the Department, I am strongly drawn to think that there is more of tragedy than of farce in what is going on; and were the integrity, frankness, and manly straight-forwardness of all his colleagues at all less assured than it is, I should be disposed to think, that so far from being without policy, order, or purpose, the Board's proceedings had been all along nicely directed by the most wary gauging of the city's patience and credulity, and with a most craftily-formed and long-ripening purpose,—a purpose, I should add, that would seem to me in direct conflict with that which the Commissioners are sworn to pursue.

Without ambition to appear as an advocate of such a view, I think it may subserve the city's interests, if, rather as a witness than an advocate, I state how it is that I can be at all tempted toward conclusions so different from those of the better-informed Mr. Wales. In the end, having on my way there shown my right to do so, I expect to testify as an expert witness. For the sake of compactness I shall confine my purpose to a review of some aspects of the Board's business with Central Park. As introductory to this, I wish to bring a few considerations to mind, upon which so much will hang of what is to follow, that I beg those in haste to get to the point, that they will not, because of the apparent self-evident character of my persuasions, leap them over. Their lack of self-evidence to many minds has cost the city millions of dollars.

1. After an investment of some fifteen millions in the Park,

now in the twenty-fourth year of its growth, what is the proper business of the Commissioners with it? It is my experience that the answer given by men, in their conduct toward and in their comments upon the business as actually conducted, varies greatly with special points of view: that, for example, of a man who visits the Park on foot only, differing from that of one who sees it habitually from a carriage; and this again from the view of riders; and this yet again from that taken by those who would, but cannot, see it from "the silent steed." There are various real-estate points of view. There is a view from behind a trotter; there is the view of an employment broker; and there is the remote view of statesmen, to whom the paltry interest of the mere local community of New York, in its vacant lots called "parks," is of consequence only as it may at a pinch be turned efficiently to account in affairs of great national and international concern.

Some more or less distorted reflections of these and of a hundred other special views may often be detected in the newspaper reports of the Commissioners' familiar discords. Putting them all aside as inadequate, and regarding the business as a trusteeship, my experience further is, that, asking what is the essence of the trust, not many business-men are to be found in Wall Street, nor yet in Water, who have ready upon it a business-like opinion. It is simpler to determine what it is not; and, by knocking off a few answers that may be suggested, we may converge toward a satisfactory conclusion.

For example: the Commissioners have elected, if I have reckoned aright, five several principal architects, one after another, to their business-staff; not one and four coadjutors, but five masters, each to a separate duty, dismissing none to make room for another. It is true that two are not appointed directly for building-duties (one being chief-of-staff, and another chief executive officer), and also that the last election was made with conditions that rendered its acceptance impossible; but as it was intended to supersede none of the previous building-strength at the Commissioners' command, sufficient, as it already was, for taking in hand all at once four great cathedrals, it strengthens the occasion for asking, at this stage,

is building the distinctive and essential business of the commission? And no man can, upon reflection, fail to see that it
is not.

The very "reason for being" of the Park is the importance
to the city's prosperity of offering to its population, as it enlarges and becomes more cramped for room, opportunity of
pleasurable and soothing relief from building, without going
too far from its future centre. What else than this purpose
justifies the reservation from commercial enterprise of more
than a hundred blocks of good building-land right in the line
of the greatest demand? Building can be brought within the
business of the Park proper only as it will aid escape from
buildings. Where building for other purposes begins, there
the Park ends. The reservoirs and the museum are not a part
of the Park proper: they are deductions from it. The sub-ways
are not deductions, because their effect, on the whole, is to
enlarge, not lessen, the opportunities of escape from buildings.
Were they placed above the general surface, and made inten-
tionally conspicuous; had they been built—as for a time it
was difficult to convince people, even intelligent critics, that
they were not—as decorative objects, it would have been in
contravention, not in furtherance, of the essential business of
the Park. Of late years they have, in the summer, almost disappeared from general view; and, by their action in facilitating
passage clear of the drives and rides, much less apparent construction serves the general public purpose of the Park. If
through ignorance and mismanagement their present seclusion
is destroyed (as the Commissioners have promised that it shall
be, as far as their means go), it must tend not to further,
but to obstruct, the proper course of the Commissioners' business. It must be concluded, then, that the Commissioners' trust
is essentially the reverse of that which the affluence of architectural force as its headquarters might be thought to imply.

If the essence of the Commissioners' business is not to be
found in building, neither is it in engineering, nor in inn-keep-
ing, nor in the decorative art of gardening, nor in a display
of nurserymen's samples, nor in forestry. All these callings
may have their place; but it is at best a subordinate and inci-

dental or auxiliary place, as calendar-printing in insurance business, as astronomy and pastry-cooking in steamship business.

2. A man may be strong for any other business commonly pursued in the city, yet unfamiliar with and inapt to acquire a sound understanding of the ends, to grasp the principles and to seize the critical points of management in the business of the Park.

3. By changes made for the purpose in the laws every few years, and by the rotation of new men into office as often as practicable, the composition of the Commission is never long the same. Its members, receiving no pay for the study they give the park business, abandon no other to take it up, and rarely make any change in their habits on account of it. Most of them deal with it, as reports of their proceedings exemplify, more in the habit of mind with which prosperous gentlemen take up their diversions, as of whist or euchre, yachting, or trotting horses, than in that with which they earn their living.

It is as unbusiness-like for the city to assume them masters of the business, in an executive or an expert sense, or to allow them to assume themselves so, as for the stock owners of a great railway to allow a constantly changing board of directors to take upon themselves the duties of its Chief Engineer.

4. The view which has been thus suggested of what the Commissioners' trust is not, and of what the business-like method of dealing with it for a board constituted as theirs is cannot be, is set forth more at length and more forcibly in a communication addressed to their predecessors in office four years ago, to which are attached such names as MORGAN, BROWN, BELMONT, STEWART, WARD, CISCO, COOPER, HAVE-MEYER, POTTER, PHELPS, DODGE, MORTON, JAY, JESSUP, SISTARE, HAMILTON, SCHUYLER, LIVINGSTON, ROOSEVELT, SHERMAN, MARSHALL, GRISWOLD, JOHNSTONE, BABCOCK, GUYON, ROBBINS, LAIDLAW, WALLACH, JAFFRAY, COLGATE, THURBER, CLAFLIN, HARPER, APPLETON, CARTER, SCRIBNER, PUTNAM, WESTERMANN, HOLT, CRAVEN, and of leading merchants, artists, physicians, and barristers, each master in his own business, ranging with

396

these on the roll of the city's worthies to the number of more than ninescore.

If Mr. Wales's name is not among them, it is probably from motives of delicacy, in view of his former connection with the Commission which the paper in question calls to account; but if otherwise, as Mr. Wales has of late been a commissioner of a public hospital as well as a commissioner of parks, he might ask himself whether, if his colleagues of the hospital trust had undertaken to manage it without aid of doctors, or with that only of doctors of divinity, he would have thought it implied but a weakness of purpose? Is it not such weakness that fills our prisons?

II

For years there was an office of the Board which at different times had different sorts of duty given it, and was designated by different titles, as the fancies of succeeding commissioners varied. It was once officially described as "the Chief Executive office by or through which all orders for the work should be executed and all employees supervised and governed"; at another and the latest period it could give no one an order—could govern nothing, only advise. But through all, one duty it held constantly, and that was to keep the Park under professional landscape-gardening supervision, with a view to the furtherance of consistency of purpose in the business of the Commissioners with it; to which end the occupant of the office had a seat with the Board, and was free to take part in its debates, though without a vote. When slighted as to this responsibility, the occupant offered his resignation, and the office was temporarily suspended.

In 1859, when it was working upon Central Park near upon four thousand men, and the records of the time say with extraordinary efficiency, the Board numbered eleven members. On the ground that it was too large for efficient *executive* management, it was gradually reduced. In January, 1879, when it was working less than two hundred men, and the records say inefficiently, it numbered four members. In

397

this month, unexpectedly to those interested in the Park otherwise than as a field of statesmanship, an element in the real-estate business, or some other specialty, the Commissioners concluded to extinguish such little (advisory) life as had till then been suffered to remain in the office. Since the day they did so, there has been no office under the Commission looking to landscape considerations; and the only man in its employment competent to advise or direct in matters of landscape-gardening has been degraded to an almost menial position, and this by methods and with manners implying a perfectly definite purpose to prevent him from exercising professional discretion, and to bring his art into contempt.

Reference is here more particularly made to occurrences imperfectly brought to public attention by reporters of the press two years ago or more; but Commissioner Wales has lately shown, to his honor expostulatingly, that the same policy is still pursued by the same methods, and with the same manners; the unfortunate representative of landscape art having been changed, and the tools of the ignoble work being new, and expressly adapted to it.

No plea will here be made that Landscape-Gardening is an art having due place side by side with the fair sisters, Poetry, Architecture, Music, Acting, Painting, and Sculpture. For nearly two centuries our greatest and our most popular teachers—as Sir Walter Scott, for example—have given it that rank; and I know not one man of accepted authority who has made bold to differ with them. Who are they that do so now? Is there an artist in any field who is with them? Is there a friend of art whose friendship is not the cloak of a hopeless snob? I am assured not one. Standing, then, for the youngest and modestest of the serene sisterhood, I know that not only every artist under every name of art, but every gentleman and every gentlewoman of New York, stands with me in challenging the Board to reconcile its course in casting out the profession of landscape art from the Park with faithfulness to its most sacred trust.

Where shall one be found more sacred?—a trust for all who, from our time onward, from generation to generation,

398

are to be debarred, except as they shall find it in the Park, from what one of old aptly styled "the greatest refreshment of man;" from what our own Lowell calls "the wine and the oil for the smarts of the mind;" what our Emerson says "yet soothes and sympathizes in all our toils and weariness;" and again our Longfellow,—

"If thou art worn and hard beset
With sorrows that thou wouldst forget;
If thou wouldst read a lesson that will keep
Thy heart from fainting, and thy soul from sleep,
Go"—

Where shall the poor man go when the Park has become what persistence in such management will make it?

III

For a few days after the determination of the Commissioners to leave the office of landscape out of their business was publicly reported, there was much interest to know their motives; and, in the absence of a satisfactory explanation, disapproval of their course was generally expressed. I had been holding the position in question, with the title, under the last shift, of Landscape Architect Advisory; and a friend had the kindness to make for me a collection of more than seventy cuttings from the journals of the time, bearing on the matter, which are now before me. Looking them over, I find, that, however differing in terms, they bear uniform testimony on a few points, which at this distance I would wish to have recalled: as, first, that to that time the people of New York had, notwithstanding some grumblings, on the whole, been proud of the Park, and especially proud of its landscape promise; second, that the business-view set forth in the previous chapter in regard to the landscape office had been generally accepted; third, that there was a general, though not generally a very definite, perception of danger involved in its abolition.

So strong was the feeling for the moment, that a Park Defence Association was organized, and at least one older organization joined with it in urging the common conviction upon the Commissioners. It may be thought strange that it should have led to no debate or remark in the Board; but is it stranger than that, against constant outcry for fifty years, New York streets should have continued till now to be the dirtiest to be found in all the large towns of Christendom?

One of the Commissioners is reported to have said, in the midst of the stir, "It will soon blow over." He appears to have been right; but, if I mistake not, a little silent breeze is even now perceptible, and if, after the revelations of the last four years, it once more gets up, it may not prove so easy to ride it gayly out.

May I refer to one thing more that appears all through these leaves?—such kind feeling toward me personally, as I have no words to acknowledge, but to which I can hardly avoid the poor response of drifting, as I write, into more personal narration than might otherwise befit my purpose.

IV

I have shown what the highest authorities in the commercial business of the city hold to be the essence of the Commissioners' business with the Park, and what is essential to their success in it. But it must be known that a strong party has always stood opposed to this view, and from the start has been incessantly laboring, and never without some measure of success, to compel a disregard for it. The counter view is commonly termed by those urging it the *practical* view; and, if this seems strange, it must be considered that a given course is called practical or otherwise, according to the object had in view at the moment by the speaker. To relieve the charity of friends of the support of a half-blind and half-witted man by employing him at the public expense as an inspector of cement may not be practical with reference to the permanent firmness of a wall, while it is perfectly so with reference to the triumph of sound doctrine at an election. It will be important, in what follows, to keep in mind this relativeness of meaning in the word.

First and last, there have been some pretty dark rams in the Park Commission; but on the whole it has been the worthiest and best intentioned body having any important responsibility under the city administration in our time, and it has, till lately, had rightly more of public respect and confidence than any other, its distinction in this respect being not always pleasing to some other constituents of the government. Yet with all the advantage their high standing might seem to give them, the Commissioners have rarely been able, when agreed among themselves, to move at all straight-forwardly upon the course, which, left to themselves, they would have marked out. Commissioner Wales has more than once, of late, referred to what he calls the "embarrassments" of the department, and has been careful to state, that, so far from these being new, he had in former years, when the public confidence in the Commissioners was much greater than at present, matched his strength with them till the breaking-point was reached, when he was compelled to resign, and go abroad to recruit his vigor in preparation for the renewed struggle in which he is now engaged.

He will excuse me for thinking that he has left the nature of these embarrassments in some obscurity, and for wishing to throw a little light upon it. I am going further on to mention circumstances connected with the dissociation of landscape-gardening from the business of the Park, which, if I had been in New York when the Commissioners' action for the purpose was taken, and had been disposed to make them public, would have added to the distrust and apprehension so generally expressed. They will even now cause surprise, even tax the credulity of many; and partly to lay a foundation for them, partly to give a clew to their significance, partly to reveal what Mr. Wales probably means by the embarrassments of the Board, I will, in this chapter, relate a few incidents of my earlier experience. My object being to throw light on methods and manners, for which we, citizens of New York, are every man responsible, and not to assail parties or persons, I shall aim to avoid names and dates.

My first narration will be of a commonplace character, and be given only to supply a starting-point.

1. The mayor once wanted to nominate me for the office of Street Commissioner. After some persuasion, perfectly aware that I was taking part in a play, though the mayor solemnly assured me otherwise, I assented, with the distinct understanding, that, if the office came to me, it should be free from political obligations; that I should be allowed to choose my own assistants, and, keeping within the law, my own method of administration. "Which," said the mayor, "is just what I want. It is because I felt sure that you would insist on that, that I sent for you." I smiled. The mayor preserved his gravity, and I took my leave. Within half an hour I received a call from a gentleman whom I had held in much esteem, to whom I had had reason to be grateful; who had once been a member of Congress,—a man of wealth and social position, but at the time holding no public office, and not conspicuous in politics. He congratulated me warmly, hoping that at last New York would be able to enjoy the luxury of clean streets. Conversation turned upon the character of the Board of Aldermen. The gentleman thought there need be no difficulty in getting their confirmation, but suggested that it might be better for me to let him give a few confidential assurances to some who did not know me as well as he did, as to my more important appointments. He soon afterwards left, regretting plaintively to have found me so "unpractical" in my ideas. It was his opinion that half a loaf of reform was better than no bread. It was mine, that a man could not rightly undertake to clean the streets of New York with his hands tied confidentially.[1]

Soon another, also not holding an office, but president of a ward club, and as such having a certain familiarity with practical politics, called to advise me that _____ wanted an understanding that I would give him fifteen per cent of my patronage. Not having it, he feared that _____ would throw his weight

[1] The word "unpractical" is not found in common dictionaries, but is so useful in our mandarin dialect, that I shall make bold for this occasion to adopt it. [1882.]

against me. I need not go on. When one of the mayor's friends in the city-hall understood that I seriously meant to be my own master, or defeated, he exclaimed, "Why, the man must be a fool!"

2. At one time, in a temporary emergency, I had the honor to be called to the quarter-deck, having been appointed a commissioner, and elected by the board of the period to be its president. In the few months that I held the position, I had some wonderful experiences, of which, for the present purpose, I will relate, because of their bearing on what follows, but five. That unpractical men may realize the wonder of them, it must be remembered that I was riding on the very crest of the glorious reform wave.

(1) A "delegation" from a great political organization called on me by appointment. After introductions and hand-shakings, a circle was formed, and a gentleman stepped before me, and said, "We know how much pressed you must be, Mr. President, and we don't want to be obtrusive, sir, nor exacting; but at your convenience our association would like to have you determine what share of your patronage we can expect, and make suitable arrangements for our using it. We will take the liberty to suggest, sir, that there could be no more convenient way than that you should send us our due quota of tickets, if you please, sir, in this form, *leaving us to fill in the name*." Here a pack of printed tickets was produced, from which I took one at random. It was a blank appointment, and bore the signature of Mr. Tweed. "That," continued the spokesman, "was the way we arranged it last year, and we don't think there can be any thing better."

(2) Four gentlemen called by appointment on "important business." Three were official servants of the city: the fourth stated that he came from and was authorized to represent a statesman of national importance. Their business was to present a request, or rather a demand, so nearly naked that it would have been decenter if there had been no pretence of clothing it, for the removal of some of the minor officers of the Park, in order to make places for new men, whose names they were ready to give me. They said nothing to

recommend their candidates, except that they were reformers. The fact that the men whose removal they called for had been long enough employed to understand their duties, and to have proved their faithfulness and unpracticalness, was a sufficient reason that they should go. They had had their "suck." After a little conversation, which I made as pleasant as I could, I said smiling, "But excuse me, gentlemen, if I ask if you consider this to be reform?" There was no responsive smile (rather the contrary), and the representative of statesmanship said sharply, "What's the use of being a reformer, if it isn't?" And seriously, to these efficient public servants, this was the high-water mark of reform.

(3) Calling at this period upon another department head, and finding his lobby packed as mine was, when, after half an hour's waiting, I was admitted to a private interview,—of which the head took advantage to eat a cold lunch that had been waiting for him,—I said, "Is it possible that you are as hard beset by these gentlemen as I am?"—"Oh! more so, I think."—"Then, when do you get time for the proper business of your office?"—"Only before and after office-hours, when they think I am gone."

(4) Among those calling on me was one official of the city, who came regularly once a week, and, having been admitted, remained sometimes two hours, saying plainly that he did not mean to go until I had given him at least one appointment. At length I remonstrated with him somewhat severely. "Well, Mr. President," he replied, "you must excuse me. You know this is my business now, and I must attend to it. If I didn't, where should I be? But I'll let you off for to-day, and go round to _____'s office, and see what I can do with him."

(5) Twice it occurred to me, after passing through a large public office with many deputies and clerks, that the Chief remarked to me, "Among them all, there is but one man who is here by my own free choice, or in whose faithfulness I have confidence."

3. It has occurred five times in succession that I have been at the headquarters of the Department of Parks on the first

visit of a new commissioner, and when, after a few passages of introductory courtesy, he has, as his first official movement in the business of the parks, asked to be furnished with a list showing the places at its disposal, the value of each, and the vacancies at the time existing. I believe that each of these gentlemen had been certified to the reporters to be entirely free from political obligations, and to owe his appointment solely to his eminent qualifications for the particular post of a park commissioner; but it will not be surprising, that, in view of my experience, I doubted the accuracy of the certificate.

4. A commissioner once said in my presence, "I don't get any salary for being here; it would be a pretty business if I couldn't oblige a friend now and then:" this being his reason for urging a most unfit appointment.

5. Writing of unfit appointments, nothing could be more ludicrous, if the anxiety they gave me had left room for a humorous view of them, than many most strenuously urged. A young man was pressed for my nomination as a topographical draughtsman. I asked to see some of his work, and, after explanations, was answered, "I don't know that he ever made any maps or drawings on paper."—"How could you think he was qualified as a draughtsman?" To which the reluctant reply was this: "The fact is, he was a little wild a few years ago, and ran away to sea on a whaler, and when he came back he brought a whale's tooth, on which he had made a picture of his ship as natural as life. Now I think that a boy who could do that, you could do most any thing with in the drawing way." The very man who said this, and, incredible as it will be thought, said it seriously, was nominated by the mayor for a park commissioner. Can the reader say, that, if the favorite remedy for the moment, and that advocated by Mr. Wales, for all the evils of the present park mismanagement, shall be adopted, this same good business-man may not next year be chosen to exemplify the efficiency of a single-headed administration?

6. I once expressed to a gentleman surprise at the accuracy of certain information of which I found him possessed. "Oh!

that's nothing," he said. "There is not a workingman living in my district, or who comes into it, or goes out of it, that I have not got him down on my books, with the name and ages of his wife and all his children, what house they are in, what rooms they occupy, what his work is, who employs him, who is to look after his vote, and so on. I have it all tabulated, and posted up. I have to make a business of it, you know. If a man means to succeed in politics, he must. It is not a business you can play with."

7. Another illustration of practical business-methods was given by a president of the Department as follows:—

"I want you to know," he said, after opening the door, looking out, closing and locking it, "of some things going on here. Yesterday a man applied for a certain position, bringing a letter dated at Albany the day before, in which the writer stated that he understood that the late holder of the position had been discharged. I told the applicant that he was mistaken; but he insisted that he was not, and I could hardly get rid of him. Here is a report coming this morning from the Park, making charges against the man in question, and advising his discharge. Information of a prospective opportunity of an appointment had gone to Albany and back, before it came to me here. You see how closely they watch us. But here is another example of it. I signed to-day an appointment which I had not determined to make five minutes before. I sent the appointee directly up to the Park, starting myself, at the same moment, for the city-hall. When I reached there, reference was made to the appointment by the first man who spoke to me, showing that not a moment had been lost in reporting it. But who made the report, and how, so quickly? I confess I hardly dare inquire. But there is something yet more inscrutable. I suspected the lock of my private drawer to have been tampered with. Last night I placed a bit of paper where it would be dislodged if the drawer was opened, and another in my memorandum-book of vacancies, applications and intended appointments. This morning I found both displaced."

8. There was an intrigue to remove a valuable officer by destroying his character, in order to make an opening for

the advancement of a subordinate strongly backed with "influence." I asked and obtained a committee of the Board to try the case. The subordinate made oath to a statement which was proved to be false; and for the perjury he was dismissed. Shortly afterwards he met me on the Park, offered me his hand, and, with much flourish, thanked me for having brought about his removal, as it had compelled his friends to make proper exertions, and he now held a position much more to his taste than any on the Park could have been.

9. At a dignified public ceremony on the Park, I saw, while listening to the oration of the day, a roughly-dressed man approach the point where the Commissioners were arrayed, all in proper black, and facing a great crowd. As the man neared their position from the rear, he reached out a walking-stick, and punched one of them. The commissioner turned; and the man threw his head back, as if to say, "Come here, I want a word with you." The commissioner fell out, and there was a whispered conversation. "Now, what does that mean?" I asked. "Don't you know? Why, that is one of our new foremen; and he and the commissioner are both members of the same district committee. He is laying in with him to make a place for some fellow whose help they need in the primaries."

10. I suspended a man because of evidence of gross disobedience of a standing rule. He told a very improbable story; and I gave him a fortnight to produce corroborative evidence of it. Instead of doing so, he set a number of his "friends" after me. His special patron was a man in office, and proprietor of a weekly newspaper. A copy of it was sent me, with a marked article containing absurd and scurrilous abuse of me, and of the Commission for employing me. As this official had shortly before called at my house, and been profuse in compliments and professions of regard, I went to see him. Referring to the article, I said, "It would have given you but the slightest trouble to ascertain that you had been imposed upon in the statements to which you have given currency." He smiled, and asked, "Would you like to see an article I intend to publish to-morrow?" handing a galley-proof to me

I read it, and said, "I have marked and numbered with my pencil seven statements in this article, which, I give you my word, can be ascertained, by any one coming to the Park, to be quite untrue." The next day a copy of the paper was sent me containing the article without the change of a word. The suspended man at last confessed, hoping to be pardoned, but was dismissed. The paper continued to be sent me every week for perhaps a year, and I was told that every number had some attack on the Park. At another period another paper pursued a similar course. One day the editor, finding the president of the Department on a railway-train going to Albany, gayly saluted him in terms of friendship. "I am surprised, sir," said the president, "that, after what you have been saying of our Board in your paper, you can offer me your hand."— "Oh!" replied the editor, "but that was business."

11. During all my park work it was a common thing to receive newspapers, addressed by unknown hands, containing matter designed to injure me; sometimes, also, anonymous threats and filthy caricatures. The object I take to have been to impress me with the insecurity of my position, and the folly of the unpractical view of its duties.

12. A foreman of laborers, discharged from the Park against strong political influence, was, at the next election, a candidate for the Legislature.

13. At one time, shortly after the police of the Park had a second time been put under my superintendence, I undertook an improvement of it. Asking the officer in charge to account for his own failure to secure the conviction and removal of some whom he described as "regular dead-beats," who had "never performed one honest tour of duty since they were taken on," he answered, "Why, damn 'em, they are every man laying wires to go to the Legislature, and they carry too many guns for me."

14. As my first step, I wrote an order to the surgeon, directing a medical survey of the force. The surgeon called on me, and said, 'I am under your orders, sir, and if you insist I shall act on them to the letter; but perhaps you do not realize, as I do, what the consequences will be to me."—

"What will they be?"—"Only that I shall have to eat my bread without butter for a while."—"I understand; but I must do my duty, and you must do yours." He did, reporting a quarter part of the entire force physically incapacitated for any active duty, and indicating that it had been used as an asylum for aggravated cases of hernia, varicose veins, rheumatism, partial blindness, and other infirmities compelling sedentary occupations. The surgeon was supported by the highest authorities of his profession, and had established on the Park an excellent character, professionally and otherwise. He had gained the affection and confidence of the force, but, in obeying orders without consulting its friends, had proved himself an unpractical man, and, as he had anticipated, was soon afterwards dismissed by order of the Board.

15. I asked an officer before me on a grave charge what he had to say. With a laugh, and a wink to his comrades, he answered, "You want to know what I have to say? Well, that's what I have to say," handing me a crumpled note which read, "If there is any thing against officer _____, please remember that he is my man, and charge it to account of Yours Truly, _____ _____." He was dismissed.

16. I set a watch upon the night-watch; and five men, receiving three dollars a night for patrol-duty on beats of which two were a mile and a half apart, were found together in the middle of their watch in a necessary building, which they had entered with false keys. They had made a fire, taken off their boots, and, using their rolled-up coats for pillows, were fast asleep; and this had doubtless been long their habit. With the sanction of the Board I changed the system, much reducing its cost, and employed mechanical detectors on the principle of those used for the night-watch of great mills. They were broken from their fastenings, and carried away. I devised a stronger and simpler apparatus. In several instances, within a week it was broken, as if by sledges, great force being necessary.

17. The eldest of the watchmen had been originally employed for several years in the Park as a land-surveyor. He had received a good education, and, after his discharge as

a surveyor, had suffered grievous domestic afflictions, and been left very poor. He was a religious man, had been active in church charities; and it was in part upon a letter from his pastor setting forth his trustworthiness that I had obtained his appointment as watchman. He had refused to join the others in their conspiracy, and was looked upon as a spy— wrongly, for he had given me no information. He was waylaid at night, murderously struck down, and left for dead. It was several weeks before he was able to leave his bed, and when he did so he was scarred for life.

18. Several other measures were adopted, all with the knowledge and sanction of the Board, and believed at the time, by the excellent gentlemen composing it, to be perfectly business-like. But they were all very unpractical in the view taken by many of the force and their friends, who consequently united in measures designed to convince the Commissioners of their mistake, and for self-protection against my cruelty. A fund was raised, and a "literary gentleman" regularly employed to write me down. At this time I received confidential warnings indirectly from high quarters outside the Commission, that I would not be allowed to succeed in what I was attempting, and had better drop it. I did not drop it, but worked on with all my might; and presently the literary gentleman got also to his work, first in some of the Sunday papers. At length, by one of those accidents that seem liable to occur in any great newspaper establishment, he managed to get a powerful article prominently displayed in a leading daily, in which, after referring to the reputation of the force with the public, gained by its alleged uniform activity, efficiency, civility; its high state of discipline and *esprit du corps,* it was represented, that, through some unaccountable freak of the Board, it had recently been placed under the orders of a silly, heartless, upstart, sophomorical theorist, through whose boyish experiments it was being driven into complete and rebellious demoralization. One of the Commissioners told me that he was asked a day or two afterwards, "Who is this young chap that you have put in charge of the police? How could you have been struck with such an unpractical fellow?"

Now it happened that I was one of the few men then in America who had made it a business to be well informed on the subject of police organization and management. I had made some examination of the French system; had when in London known Sir Richard Mayne, the organizer of the Metropolitan force, upon the model of which our New York Metropolitan force is formed; had been favored by him with a long personal discourse on the principles of its management, and been given the best opportunities for seeing them in operation, both in the park service and in all other departments. I had made a similar study of the Irish constabulary. I had originally organized, instructed, and disciplined, and under infinite difficulties secured the reputation of this same Central Park force. Finally, by a singular coincidence, I had nearly twenty years before, when my defamer was himself a schoolboy, been an occasional editorial writer for the journal which he thus turned upon my work, and had contributed to it much of the matter, which, collected in a volume, had been later twice reprinted in London, and in translations in Paris and Leipsic.

I was asked by the president of the Department to make a public reply, and was allowed by the editor to do so in the same columns. I must gratefully add that the editor afterwards made all reparation in his power consistently with the ordinary rules of newspaper business. Nevertheless, the article served its purpose, was largely circulated among practical men, and I had reason to believe that even some of my friends thought there must be something in its ridiculous falsifications. The end was, that I was relieved of responsibility for the police of the Park. My duty was mainly assumed by a committee a majority of whom were new to the business; and the only two men who, besides the surgeon, had been conspicuously resolute in carrying out my orders, and sincere and faithful in efforts to enforce them, were dismissed—neither honorably nor dishonorably discharged, but simply notified that their services were no longer required. I am sure that the commissioners whose votes frustrated my efforts had been thoroughly convinced by the advice of friends that they were acting for the best interests of the city; that my intentions were good but impractical; and that in every thing they were doing God's service. The president to the last sustained me. Because he did so, and asked it as a personal favor and act of friendship, I consented, after having resigned my office, to resume service under the Commission upon a modified arrangement, vindicating my professional standing and securing me against another similar experience.

19. Within two years the rules which the Board had been persuaded to adopt to prevent unsuitable men from being recruited, and to secure advancement by proved merit, had become a dead-letter; and the force was left to drift into the condition in which one of the Commissioners lately stated in a Board meeting that he had found it, and which led to a beautifully drawn resolution that hereafter no man who could not read and write should be taken for it. How soon to become in its turn a dead-letter, who can say? Some time after my defeat, a gentleman told me that he had walked, in a fine day, through the interior of the Park from end to end without seeing an officer. There was no lack of them on the fashionable drives; but in the most secluded and sylvan districts prostitutes were seeking their prey without hindrance, and it was no place for a decent poor woman to bring her children. I myself, since I left the Park, have seen an officer within a hundred yards of a carriage when it stopped, and when the coachman bent down an overhanging lilac-bush loaded with bloom, from which the occupants broke large branches, afterwards driving off without interruption or reproof. The officer, doubtless, thought it an unpractical thing to have lilac-bushes in the Park, as the present Commissioners think any thing like sylvan seclusion unsanitary.

At another time I met seven small boys coming from the Park, all carrying baskets. They were showing one another the contents of these as I came upon them; and I found that they were each filled with beautiful rock-moss, which they were going to sell for the decoration of hanging-baskets. The Park has always been very deficient in this lovely accompaniment of rocks, and it is difficult to secure it. I asked the boys if the police allowed them to strip it off. "No," said one: "we waits till their heads is turned." "No," said another: "they don't care; they just minds the carriages, they does." Nor are these incidents by any means the most alarming that I might report.

Do the owners of houses building near the Park fancy that its vicinity will be a more agreeable place of residence because of this practical style of management? I have seen a newspaper report that already last summer great numbers of tramps and gypsies regularly lodged in the Park. When the police was under unpractical direction, I have repeatedly walked through its entire length after midnight, finding every officer in his place, and not one straggling visitor. Hyde Park is closed at nightfall, as are all other city parks in Europe; but one surface road is kept open across Hyde Park, and the superintendent of the Metropolitan Police told me that a man's chances of being garrotted or robbed were, because of the facilities for concealment to be found in the Park, greater in passing at night along this road than anywhere else in London.

If these incidents give little idea of the number, weight, and constancy of the embarrassments with which the Park Board has to struggle, they may have made plainer the nature of them, and the soil on which they grow.

But I must add a few more, that may, in some degree, remove misapprehensions as to the responsibility for various matters which are occasionally referred to in the interest of practical park management, as if they were the result of the ignorance or perversity of which the Commissioners intended to rid the Park in abolishing the landscape office.

For several years before that event, the management of the parks had, as before stated, not been under my direction. I had only to advise about it. But even before this, there was, for some time, a standing order in force, forbidding me to have a single tree felled without a specific order, to be obtained by a majority vote of the Board. Before this order was passed, men seen cutting trees under my directions have been interrupted and indignantly rebuked by individual commissioners, and even by the "friends" of commissioners, having no more right to do so than they would for like action on a man-of-war. I have had men beg me, from fear of dismissal, to excuse them from cutting trees, and, to relieve them, have taken the axe from them, and felled the trees myself. I have been denounced to commissioners by their friends as "a Vandal" and a "public robber," because nurse-trees were cut from the plantations of the Park under my directions. It may have been noticed, that, notwithstanding much talk of the necessity of thinning plantations, Mr. Wales, in a triumphant way, announced lately that not a single live tree had been cut this winter. Why not? Nothing had been cut but bushes, the removal of which, one by one, would pass with little notice from the vigilant friends of the Commissioners. Who is there, with any authority on the Park, competent to judge what trees should and what should not be cut, with a view to the purpose for which the Park has been formed?

Rocky passages of the Park, which had been furnished under my direction with a natural growth of characteristic rocky hillside perennials, have been more than once "cleaned up," and so thoroughly that the leaf-mould, with which the crevices of the ledge had been carefully filled for the sustenance of the plants, was swept out with house-brooms in the interest of that good taste which delights in a house painted white with green blinds, whitewashed cherry-trees, plaster statuettes on stumps; and patty-cakes of bedding-plants set between rocks scraped of their dirty old lichens and mosses,— and all in the heart of an Appalachian glen. Whereupon Mr. Robinson, in that invaluable addition to the literature of landscape art, ALPINE FLOWERS, writes (I quote from a copy kindly sent me by my good friend the author, 2d London edition, p. 8),—

"In the Central Park of New York are scores of noble and picturesque breaks of rock, which have not been adorned with a single Alpine plant or rock-bush." He might have said, from which not only all such adornments, but even all the natural growth of rock-bushes, vines, perennials, and mosses, has again and again been cleaned away as exhibiting a low, depraved, and unpractical taste. The work is going on, I am assured, at this moment; and when it is finished, and August comes round again, and all the yellow turf and the dead, half-covered outcrops of smooth-faced, gray and brown ledge are fully exposed to view, God help the poor man who can find no better place of escape from the town!

20. The landscape office had been twice dispensed with for a time before its last abolition in 1879. During one of these intervals a much boasted improvement in the plan of the Park had been put through with the energy and efficiency characteristic of a bull earning his passage through a China shop. Later, something was found defective in the drainage of the adjoining region. After a tedious and costly exploration, it was ascertained that a large main drain had been cut through at a critical point, and that the tile had been so broken and deranged as to make a complete dam, after which the excavation had been filled up, and built over. This led me to look at the drainage-maps, several sheets of which proved to have been lost. I begged to have a survey made for their renewal; and a man was employed for it who had been previously engaged in the work. While he was still occupied with the duty, what passes for economy in practical park management came and dismissed him. I doubt if complete drainage-maps will be found in the Department to-day. I will undertake to satisfy a fair jury of respectable sanitarians, that, if there is reason to believe that a single case of malarial disease has originated in the Park in twenty years, it has been due to conditions which have been established or maintained against the advice of the landscape office. The reverse has been asserted or implied in scores of publications, for which no commissioner, as such, has ever been responsible.

21. The more "practical" Commissioners have often given me advice received by them from friends having no official responsibility for the parks, and which betrayed exceptional ignorance, even for city-bred men, on matters which had been my life-study; which ran also directly counter to the practice of every respectable member of my profession; the folly of which I have often seen exposed in our agricultural journals,

and the agricultural columns of our newspapers, but which they regarded, and expected me to regard, as of controlling weight. Some such advice I have, since I left the Park, seen carried out in practice.

22. The president once notified me that a friend of his was to come before the Board as spokesman for a "delegation" of citizens, to advocate the introduction of a running-course on the Park. He would ask me to explain some of the objections to the project, but hoped that I would do so in a way as little likely to provoke the gentleman as possible, as he had great weight in politics, and it would be in his power to much embarrass the Department. I followed these instructions as I best could; but it was impossible for me not to refer to the landscape considerations. At the first mention of the word the gentleman exclaimed, and by no means "aside," "Oh, damn the landscape!" then, rising, he addressed the president to this effect: "We came here, sir, as practical men, to discuss with your Board a simple, practical, common-sense question. We don't know any thing about your landscape, and we don't know what landscape has to do with the matter before us."

23. It will have been asked by many, as they have been reading, Why did you not appeal to public opinion? Why did not the Commissioners, who were superior to the courses through which your professional judgment was overruled, if they could not otherwise overcome these embarrassments, lay them frankly before us, and see what we could do? Might not a corresponding question be asked in regard to what everybody knows is going on at this moment, and has been for years going on, of the highest officer of the nation?

If the reference seems presumptuous in one respect, let me show that it hardly can be so in another; I mean in respect to the absorption of time and energy of public servants, through the pressure of "practical advice." As superintendent of the Park, I once received in six days more than seven thousand letters of advice as to appointments, nearly all from men in office, and the greater part in legislative offices upon which the Commissioners have been much dependent for the means of accomplishing anything they might wish to do,—either written by them directly, or by Commissioners at their request. I have heard a candidate for a magisterial office in the city addressing from my doorsteps a crowd of such advice-bearers, telling them that I was bound to give them employment, and suggesting plainly, that, if I was slow about it, a rope round my neck might serve to lessen my reluctance to take good counsel. I have had a dozen men force their way into my house before I had risen from bed on a Sunday morning, and some break into my drawing-room in their eagerness to deliver letters of advice. I have seen a president of the Park Board surrounded by a mob of similar bearers of advice, in Union Square, carried hither and thither by them, perfectly helpless; have seen policemen make their way in to him with clubs, drag him out, force him into a passing carriage, and lash the horses to a gallop, to secure his temporary relief from "embarrassments," the nature of which I trust that I have now sufficiently illustrated.

I do not remember ever to have seen the office of the Board without a poster, reading, "No laborers wanted;" and I do not believe that there has in twenty years been a time when nine-tenths of the intellectual force and nervous energy of the Board has not been given to recruiting duty.

V

During all of the summer before the Commissioners agreed to "damn landscape," I was aware that the practical view was getting the upper hand of them. It would take too much space to tell how I became conscious of it. There were symptoms such as this: that, while observing great ceremony of politeness with me, there were three of them whom I was never able to get to meet me on the Park (nor on any park). In the case of two, I was careful not to let a month go by without separately asking the favor of an appointment for the purpose, and in reply was always assured of a desire and intention to make it soon. Twice an appointment was actually made; and each time the commissioner failed to keep it, afterwards courteously apologizing. Thus and otherwise, there was no doubt left in my mind, that, with respect to my part of the business of the parks, these amiable gentlemen cared only how not to do it. If there had been, occurrences which have followed the abolition of my office would have removed it.

But it was not simply from observation of mere symptoms that I knew that the embarrassments affecting them were of an unusual character. I myself received from without the Board several warnings, both direct and indirect. By indirect, I mean threats made in such a manner as to leave me in no doubt that it was intended to guard against a public accountability for them. By direct, I mean not only friendly, confidential hints, but such as were given me, for example, in my own house, by a man who brought a line of introduction from a high public officer. After he had called three times (on each occasion while I was at dinner), I informed the introducer that his bearing had been such, that, if he called again, I should ask the protection of the police. I knew that my movements were being furtively dogged, and I presumed that they were so with a view to obtaining pretexts upon which to urge my removal.

Let it be understood what this meant to me,—the frustration of purposes to which I had for years given all my heart, to which I had devoted my life; the degradation of works in which my pride was centred; the breaking of promises to the future which had been to me as churchly vows. However I was able to carry myself by day, it will not be thought surprising that I should have had sleepless nights, or that at last I could not keep myself from over-wearing irritation and worry. The resulting depression, acting with an extraordinary prostration from the great heat of the summer, and the recurrence of an old malarial trouble, brought me, late in the season, to a condition comparable to that often produced by a sunstroke, perhaps of the same nature. It has taken me four years to recover the strength which I then lost within a week. In view of this loss, I was advised by three well-known physicians to seek at once a change of air, scene, and mental occupation. I knew that any prolonged absence from New York would give an opportunity to the plotters against my work that might be fatal to it; and while I hesitated an incident occurred which made my retirement for a time impossible. A newspaper was sent to my house with a marked passage stating that disgraceful charges were pending against me. The president of the Department knew nothing of them at the time; but within two days he informed me that the report was authentic.

The charter, so called, of the city, provides, that, when any one in its service stands accused of official misdoings, there shall be a form of trial open to him before his dismissal. I determined to take no notice of the charges until I had the opportunity, thus supposed to be secured to me, of looking my accusers in the face. But it never came. On the strength of the charges,—deliberate and circumstantial lies, invented, as I imagine, by spies to cover their ill success from their employers,—my name had been struck from the pay-roll. A month afterwards I found it restored; and the instalment of salary, which had been due when the charges were made, and payment of which had been stopped on account of them, was silently sent me. Thus, though no word of retraction or explanation, of vindication or apology, followed, I was left to infer that the attempt to cast me out as a culprit had been abandoned.

Of many incidents emphasizing the character of this occurrence, I will make room for but one. I have shown that the charges were given to the press before they were officially known to the Board or to me. I have to add that this which I now make more than four years afterwards is the first public mention, to my knowledge, of their falsity or abandonment.

It is not to be supposed that I was gaining ground upon my nervous disorder during this month. At its end winter was setting in, and the principal work on the parks had stopped for the season. As soon as I was released from arrest, so to speak, I presented the medical certificate I had been holding back, showing my need of temporary relief from duty; and upon it leave of absence, with suspension of salary, was given me till spring. It was while this act was fresh and operating, and I was yet on the sea, that my office was abolished.

The general mistrust of the press, that the determination

to do away with it had had other motives than those officially recorded, led to some "interviewing" of the Commissioners, under the torture of which one of them admitted that I had been suspected of having had "a pretty fat thing" in supplying the parks with trees. It happens that I had been anxious to obtain a few comparatively rare and costly trees for the Park. But I knew that the Commissioners were averse to authorizing purchases which might be taken as illustrations of extravagance. Moreover, the Park was in great need of another elephant; it actually did not possess a single rhinoceros; the gilding on the weathercocks was much tarnished; and the bronze nymph at Mount St. Vincent was almost as black as before she had, by the order of an older commissioner, been cleaned up, and painted white. Therefore I had, with the aid of friends, procured the trees I specially wanted without expense to the city. The value of the gift was, I believe, less than two hundred dollars; but that any such thing could be done from interest in the scenery of the Park had not probably occurred to the sufferer, and a confused recollection of something inexplicable about it led him, when squeezed, as I little doubt, to blunder upon the expression caught by the reporter. Still, in view of my absence from the country, to have been betrayed into such an innuendo is not characteristic of a lofty soul; and this may explain why it was also said that the Commissioners had had enough of "high tone."

But not too much importance should be given to these hasty expressions. I do not doubt that the Commissioners were quite sincere in stating that they abrogated the landscape office because they found it "of no practical use." That they really had the completest confidence in my integrity, esteem for my professional ability, and held me to have deserved well of my fellow-citizens in all official duty, they were forward to testify by placing a series of resolutions to that effect on their minutes, and also by giving me an appointment that the public has been often advised, through the published proceedings of the present Board, remains uncancelled; that, namely, of Consulting Landscape-architect (without salary).

Considering the form of this appointment,[2] it is significant, that, while I have been holding it, the Board has permitted designs prepared under its orders in my office, long discussed, laid before the public, and, after most mature deliberation, adopted by unanimous vote, to be, in some cases, strangely mutilated by men not of my profession, and of no public standing in any profession; in others, to be superseded by wholly new and radically different designs. The main object of the changes in these cases had been before most carefully considered with the aid of comparative drawings, models, and other demonstrations, and the Board satisfied that objections of a conclusive character applied to them. In the reconsideration, partly or wholly by new commissioners, no thought of these objections appears to have been had. I have been allowed no opportunity to point them out, or to defend, in any manner, the work for which I had been made publicly responsible; and they are now to be established by slow, provoking, and expensive public experience. Why was I appointed? and how is it that I still hold the office of Consulting Landscape-architect to the Board? In the four years since it was made, there has been no communication between the Board and me.

In Victor Hugo's story, the practical M. Nortier says,—

"In politics we do not kill a man: we only remove an embarrassment; that is all."

VI

When Mr. Vaux and I first put our heads together in study of the design for the Central Park, we agreed to treat nothing as of essential consequence, except with reference to results which might be looked for, at nearest, forty years ahead. And with an outlook at least that far along, all our

[2] Whereas Mr. Frederick Law Olmsted, long identified with the Central Park and its improvements, and enjoying the confidence of the community and the respect of this Department since its organization, should be placed in a position where this Department can avail itself of his large experience and intimate knowledge of the designs and objects of the work on the different parks," etc. [1882.]

work and our advice has since been given. In this has consisted a large part of its unpracticality.

If a park be got up mainly with the use of money borrowed in long loans; if the ground upon which it is formed be mortgaged as security for the ultimate payment of the loans; if the conduct of the business be placed in the hands of men who accept the trust without salary, as a consolation for the loss of a paid commissionership in a business of a very different character, or a place on a party committee, or a nomination for alderman, and who are far too knowing to accept advice except from practical men and of an instantly practical character:—if the business of these men be conducted with a view, first, to aid the cause of honest government at the next election; second, to suit the convenience of political contractors with notes coming due next month; and, lastly, to secure immediate satisfaction from one election to another of the public, it would not be surprising if even this *immediate* public satisfaction was not all they could wish.

It would be going further than is necessary to my purpose, to say that just this has occurred; but it may be well to ask if facts do not suggest methods of business which correspond nearly with what might be expected if it had. Let us see.

The Park Board, stimulated by the stings of the press and the public, and by the formal remonstrances of the leading business men of the city, has now had full four years in which to prove how well its business can be managed under the practical view, by practical men, and free from the embarrassment of professional advice and professional superintendence; and with what result?

Unless every newspaper that I have been in the way of seeing has been bearing false witness, and every thing that comes to me verbally is deceptive, no branch of the city government has ever failed so completely and humiliatingly to earn public respect and confidence. As supplying the only available pleasure-roads, the Park is yet, perhaps, with an increasing driving and riding population, increasingly resorted to in the fashionable driving and riding season; that is to say, by that part of the population who least need to have opportunities of rural recreation brought nearer to them. But spite of all that should have been gained after twenty years, by four years' growing together of trees planted with the design of securing broad, quiet, massing effects, the Park is reported to have been steadily losing attraction, and, relatively to the entire population of the city, to be made less use of, and less valuable use of, than before.

Nothwithstanding the obvious fact that the motive of the management has been favorable to what may be termed the uniformly smug and smart suburban door-yard style, in distinction from a more varied treatment admitting here and there of at least a subdued picturesqueness, the verdict appears to be, that the Park has even taken on a slovenly and neglected aspect. This is not by any means the worst of the story; but, for the present, stopping here, if an explanation is needed, may it not be given in the one word "IGNORANCE"?—not ignorance of practical politics; of the stock, cotton, or iron markets; of Greek, physics, or botany; of horticulture, floriculture, or garden decoration, but ignorance—complete, blind ignorance—of the principles, even of the motives and objects, of an art to which many men of great wisdom and venerated character have thought it right to give as long and arduous study as is often given to any other form of art, or to any learned profession,—an art to which it is no more reasonable to suppose that a man can turn at middle life, and in a few months be prepared to assume the responsibility of a great public work, than that he can, in like manner, qualify himself to take command of an army, to serve as corporation counsel, superintending physician of Bellevue Hospital; as a sculptor, chemist, or lapidary.

VII

What has just been declared impossible many have been led to believe to be just what Mr. Vaux and I attempted, and with the result of leading the city, by our unfitness for the duties we accepted, into disasters such as the present commissioners have been seeking to mitigate. I have little doubt that many commissioners before the present, have, one after another, given a certain degree, at least, of credence, to statements made with this object, and I know that not a few estimable citizens must have done so. It is a matter of some moment to the city; it is of considerable interest to my profession; and I believe it to be due to the cause not alone of my art, but of all art, that the true state of the case should be known. The delusion so common and so melancholy, that because a boy has, or thinks he has, a natural gift for sketching, or modelling, or mimicry, he may hope to mount to distinction as a painter, sculptor, or actor, without far greater labor than is required for learning a trade, has its full counterpart in respect to landscape-gardening. I cannot say with what pity I have seen young men advertising themselves as landscape-engineers, etc., on the strength of having chanced to be employed as assistant surveyors for a few months in the ruder preparatory processes of park-making. Nay, I have seen even greater effrontery than that.

Mr. Vaux had, years before he took up the work of the Park, been the chosen co-operator of the greatest master in America of landscape-gardening, and had been associated with him in the most important and best public work that had been done in the country. He was personally familiar with the most useful of European parks through having shared from childhood in their popular use. He had made, in company with other artists, long sketching-tours on foot, both in the old country and in the new; had more than ordinary amateur skill in landscape-painting, and had had thorough professional training in architecture.

I myself began my study of the art of parks in childhood. I had read, before I was fifteen, the great works upon the art,—works greater than any of the last half-century,—and had been under the instruction of older and more observant students of scenery, under the most favorable circumstances for a sound education. And there had been no year of the twenty that followed before I entered the service of the Park Board, that I had not pursued the study with ardor, affection, and industry.

I had twice travelled in Europe with that object in view;

424

had more than a hundred times visited the parks of London and Paris, and once or oftener those of Dublin, Liverpool, Brussels, The Hague, Berlin, Vienna, Florence, Rome, and other old cities. I had travelled five thousand miles on foot or in the saddle, and more than that by other private or public conveyance, in study of the natural scenery of this continent. I had been three years the pupil of a topographical engineer, and had studied in what were then the best schools, and under the best masters in the country, of agricultural science and practice. I had planted with my own hands five thousand trees, and, on my own farm and in my own groves, had practised for ten years every essential horticultural operation of a park. I had made the management of labor in rural works a special study, and had written upon it acceptably to the public. I had been for several years the honorary secretary of two organizations, and a member of four, formed for the discussion of rural themes and the advancement of rural arts. I had by invitation written for the leading journal of landscape-gardening, and had been in correspondence with and honored by the friendship of leading men in its science on both sides of the Atlantic.

And essentially what I have thus said of myself had been known to the Commissioners, if not otherwise, then through those who introduced me to them, among whom were Mr. Irving, Mr. Bryant, Professor Gray, Mr. Greel[e]y, Mr. Raymond, Mr. Godwin, General Hamilton, Peter Cooper, Russell Sturgis, Charles H. Marshall, Edmund Blunt, Cornelius Grinnell, and David Dudley Field.

It is notoriously too easy to get the use of names, one following another: therefore I add, that most of these well-known men had been either my hosts or my guests; all had met me socially, and testified of my training not without some personal knowledge.

Since then, the work of Mr. Vaux and myself speaks for itself; and judgment upon it has been given, not by New York alone, which in natural landscape art, at least, might easily for a time be misled, but by the highest authority living. On what more worthy works rests the authority of those who tell the people of New York that we were quacks and knaves, and that our designs require such recasting of competent park-makers as it is now with all possible energy receiving?

If I seem tending to their level in thus speaking for myself, let it be considered that I have yet something more to say, and that I wish it to have all the weight that my rightful good name should entitle it to; let it be considered, also, that I have twenty times seen the assertion in print, made by some of the practical hounds, to whom this is my first reply in twenty years, that Mr. Vaux and I were brought upon the Park unknown, ignorant, incompetent pretenders, to serve a knavish scheme of base politicians; and that I happen to know that inquiries have been lately making in the vain hope to find ground of support for reiteration of the stupid fabrication.

And yet, in what has been spread abroad of this sort, there is just that yarn of truth that is usually to be found in the work of practised falsifiers. It is true that I had not set up to be a landscape-gardener before I came upon the Park. I had not thought myself one, and had been surprised and delighted when I was asked if I would accept even a journeyman's position in the intended work. Why? Simply because I held the art in such reverence, that, to that time, it had never occurred to me that I might rightly take upon myself the responsibilities of a principal in its public practice. My study of it had been wholly a study of love, without a thought of its bringing me pecuniary reward or repute: in many matters of detail, therefore, it was defective (it is still very defective); and it is perfectly true, for this reason, if no other, that the task which was ultimately given me in the Central Park would have been an impossible one, had I not been so fortunate as to enjoy, for a time, the ardent and most loyal aid of men better qualified in some important respects than myself. But I am more inclined to question now than I was when I accepted my first unsought and most unexpected appointment, whether, if I had been more elaborately fitted than I happened to be, I should have been more strenuously or more intelligently bent on serving, with all such skill as I could command, the highest ends of the art, or better fitted to escape beguilements from them through the pedantries or the meretricious puerilities which hang on all its skirts. Let me illustrate my meaning.

During the last twenty years Europe has been swept by a mania for sacrificing natural scenery to coarse manufactures of brilliant and gaudy decoration under the name of specimen-gardening; bedding, carpet, embroidery, and ribbon-gardening, or other terms suitable to the house-furnishing and millinery trades. It was a far madder contagion than the tulip-mania, or the morus-multicaulis fever of our youth.

It ran into all park management, the only limit often being that fixed by annual appropriations. Long ago, for example, it seized Hyde Park, and put completely out of countenance the single charm of broad homely sylvan and pastoral simplicity which the fogs and smoke of London, and its weary miles of iron hurdles, had left to it. Why? I asked the old superintendent. "Well, you know the fashion must have its run, and it just tickles the nursery-maids." I take some credit for my schooling, then, that so far as Central Park has been under my guardianship, it has been perfectly quarantined; not a dollar having been spent, nor a rood of good turf spoiled, for garishness, under my superintendence, nor at any time, except against my protest.

Thirty years ago, before the Park was dreamed of, as a farmer, and with no more idea that I should ever be a professional landscape-designer than that I should command a fleet, I had printed these thoroughly unpractical words:—

"What artist so noble as he, who, with far-reaching conception of beauty and designing-power, sketches the outlines, writes the colors, and directs the shadows, of a picture so great that Nature shall be employed upon it for generations, before the work he has arranged for her shall realize his intentions!"

VIII

In the last chapter I observed that a loss of popular favor through slovenliness and neglect was not the worst misfortune that had befallen the Park. If it had been, I should have been still constrained to hold my peace. Neglect for considerable periods may do no serious permanent harm. Hence, while in the service of the Commission, I yielded much in that way to the practical policy. Neglect, if it continues not too long, may even have its advantages. The landscape-architect André, formerly in charge of the suburban plantations of Paris, was walking with me through the Buttes-Chaumont Park, of which he was the designer, when I said of a certain passage of it, "That, to my mind, is the best piece of artificial planting, of its age, I have ever seen." He smiled, and said, "Shall I confess that it is the result of neglect? I had planted this place most elaborately, with a view to some striking immediate effects which I had conceived, and others, to be ultimately obtained by thinnings. I had just worked out my plan, when the war came; and for two years I did not again see the ground. It was occupied as a camp; horses were pastured in it; it was cut up by artillery; fires were made in it. As a park, it was everywhere subjected to the most complete neglect. When, at length, I came back to it, expecting to begin my work over again at all points, Nature had had one summer in which, as well as she could, to repair damages; and I declare to you, that, on arriving at just this point, I threw up my hands with delight, for, spite of some yet unhealed wounds, I saw at once that in general aspect there was a better work than I had been able to imagine. That which was weak and unsuitable in my planting had, by natural selection, disappeared; and in the struggle for existence nearly all that remained had taken a wild character, such as in an art we may aim at, but can hardly hope to attain." (But see how the true artist at once bowed himself before his tutor, and recognized and seized the opportunity.)

Hence, were ignorant neglect and feeble-minded slovenliness the worst qualities of the Board's management, I should yet have had nothing to say. The reason I must now speak is, that the Park is at last, avowedly, boastfully, and with much brag of energy, managed in distinct contemptuous repudiation of the leading motives with which it was laid out.

This means, not, as Mr. Wales says, with no well-defined purpose, but with a purpose defined with perfect distinctness to undo, as far as practicable, what at least six million dollars of the city's debt have been heretofore spent to do. And of these six, two millions may be safely reckoned to be represented in structural works, which are to be found under the present policy simply obstructive to what is designed; so obstructive, that the results of this policy can at best be but botch-work. Hereafter it will always be open to say of these results, I mean, that they would have been vastly better but for the obstructions which the original purpose had placed in the way of those responsible for them.[3]

The end will be that the park to be substituted for the original Central Park, without change of name, will be one better adapted to practical management; in which, for example, every operation can be directed and performed by men who have been unable to earn living wages in sewer and pavement work, in railroad and house-building work; who have broken down from incompetency in the hat-making and in the painting and glazing lines; and the services of whose sons and grandsons in carrying torch-lights, and stocking the primaries, must in some way be suitably acknowledged. The whole story is not told in this explanation; but, if it is considered how a constant gravitation in a general direction finally operates through many thousand channels of influence, it will be found to tell a good part of it.

[3] It is to be hoped that this will be denied. I should be glad to submit the grounds of the assertion to a jury of experts; to any number, for example, of the following gentlemen, to whom the principles of landscape-gardening must have been a serious study: Adolph Strauch, Cincinnati; Henry Winthrop Sargent of Woodenethe; H. W. S. Cleveland, Chicago; H. H. Hunnewell of Wellesley; H. Hammond Hall, Sacramento, Cal.; William McMillan, Buffalo; Col. F. L. Lee, Albany; Professor Robinson, Harvard Arboretum; E. W. Bowditch, Boston; John Sturgis, Brookline, Mass.; F. J. Scott, Toledo; Professor C. E. Norton, Harvard College. There are others whom I should include, as Mr. Weidenmann, but that I happen to be informed of their views. Several of these named are personally unknown to me, and with none have I had any conversation on the subject. [1882.]

I will later testify that the pretended landscape-gardening cloak under which this proclivity is disguised is a poor, tawdry piece of motley; but for the present let it be supposed that it is what it is claimed to be,—a much better-considered, wiser, and completer design than the old one; that it represents a higher culture and a nobler art, and as such is entitled to all possible respect. Then, I want to ask, was this respect paid to it, and did it mark a high sense of the Commissioners' responsibilities, and was it studiously deferential to the intelligence of the people of New York, that it should have been adopted, and work energetically begun upon it in the manner that it has been? With, so far as can be judged from the newspaper reports, absolutely no debate in the Board upon it, even apparently upon informal orders or verbal permits of Commissioners acting individually; with no public discussion, no opportunity for asking explanations, none for hearing remonstrances; without the publication of a single drawing, map, or plan, to aid an understanding of the great undertaking? (I will soon show more fully the contrasting methods in which the first Park Commissioners proceeded, but may mention here, that, in the first four years in which their design was developing, they issued over thirty maps and drawings, several thousand of which were distributed gratuitously, and that in some cases electrotype copies of them were supplied for newspaper publication.)

How many of those who read this paper will not, for the first time, know from it that an entirely new motive of design has been lately adopted, and vigorous work in pursuing it entered upon?

It is due to the enterprise of a single newspaper reporter, moved, it would appear, rather by a sense of the ludicrous than the grave aspect of the matter, that the completest exposition of the new policy has come before the public at all. Were it a question of the refurnishing and decorating of their board-room, the Commissioners could not have observed less formality, given less evidence of deliberation, forecast, and study, or used fewer of the commonest business precautions against fool-hardy blundering, than they have in all this proceeding.

IX

The points of identity between such of the purposes and motives of the present attempt to reform the Park as have been drawn out by the reporters, and those of that which was made at the cost of a million or more in 1871, are so many and so marked, that what is deficient in our information may be fairly taken to be supplied from what is of record as to what was then in view. The difference is only in the present lack of boldness, and a disposition to generalize rather than come to definite particulars. With this additional light upon it, the character of the scheme can be made comprehensible; and it is plain, that, if there had been knowledge and skill enough at the Commissioners' command, it would have been asserted for it that a new school of landscape-gardening had arisen, adapted especially to urban parks; that it had for them great advantages; and Mr. Robinson might have been quoted, and the experience of thousands of New York visitors to Paris cited, in confirmation of this statement. It would have had the value, too, for purposes of deception, of being true; and it is apparent that a dull sense of this truth has been mixed with another dull sense of the ideal of cockney villa-gardens in determining what should be said to reconcile the public to the destruction of the original Central Park. Let us see what the new school, thus clumsily serving as a decoy, really is.

It is in fact that of which M. Barillet-Deschamps is by repute the father, and M. André the most judicious and successful practitioner. It had its origin in the revision of the small interior public grounds of Paris, undertaken by Napoleon the Third; became very popular, largely because of the striking and spectacular effects rapidly obtained by profuse use of certain novel, exotic, and sickly forms of vegetation; and was allowed to have a certain degree of influence, always unfortunate, in the detailed management of much more important works. Meaning no disrespect to it, holding it in admiration in its proper place, I should say that it bears a relation to natural landscape-gardening, like that which the Swiss

431

peasants of Mrs. Leo Hunter's costume lawn-party bear to the healthy cow-girls of Alpine pastures. As a fashion, it has had its run in Europe; and of those who have taken and carried it on as a fashion, and the results they have obtained, it is M. André himself who gives his opinion thus: "They did not see that this new art was in great part conventional." Then, after describing the misapplication of it upon works of larger scale, and in connection with genuine rural conditions, he continues, "Under the false pretext that lawns, trees, waters, and flowers are always pleasant, they have substituted for the old geometrical garden a still more artificial style. The former, at least, avowed its aim to show the hand of man, and master nature. The latter borrows the elements of nature, and, under pretence of imitating it, makes it play a ridiculous—I was going to say an effeminate—part." "It is not this—we say it emphatically—it is not this that constitutes landscape art. If art seeks means of action in nature, it is in order to turn them to account in a simple and noble way." (L'Art des Jardins, chap. V.)

The best that can be claimed for the new design of the Central Park is, that it is in part an attempt to reclothe its rocky frame with second-hand garments of the fashion thus truthfully characterized by the master to whose ability the fashion itself is a tribute of ignorant reverence.

Further, I will not attempt to characterize it, certainly not to criticise it; but I will ask any who have been induced to suppose there is a real landscape purpose in it to reflect in what respect such conception as they have been led to form of it differs in its ideals of landscape from such as might be appropriately adopted on a site like that of Union Square, and then to ask themselves whether the ends and motives suitable to the area and topography of the one city property are probably at all such as should be had in view in business with the other; whether, with no intrinsically different purpose, it is justifiable—pardonable—to close from all ordinary use, from all commercial occupation, for all the future of the city, a hundred and fifty ordinary blocks, with the avenues and streets between them, in one continuous body, and that at the point where it will cause the most inconvenience,—the very centre of the city that is to be? Could a theory of the use and value of the Park be propounded better adapted to open it continually to schemes of subdivision, intrigues of "real-estate sharps," and to all manner of official corruption?

Can Commissioner Wales be right in basing his opposition to it on the ground that this means only indecision of purpose? Is not what he calls "no definite purpose" as distinctly a default of trust as a purposeless leaving-open the vaults and the outer doors of a bank? What is "no definite purpose" under such circumstances? What would be thought of a jury that would acquit the cashier or night-porter responsible for it?

I will further ask those who may suppose that the plan of the Park needs such general revision as is now promised, in the interest of what is called "utility," if they suppose that the only utility which can be held to excuse the attempt to form a park of such dimensions, on such ground, in such a situation, has heretofore been wholly disregarded in its design?

Yet another question for these gentlemen to put to themselves. If a direct cut is to be offered between every two points where a manifest utility is to be served by permitting it, fifteen millions more may easily be spent to accomplish the result, and in the end the Park will have been obliterated. A dozen projects have already been urged for opening additional roads through the Park, and more than that for entrances and walks through parts of it. There is not one of them, which, if the process of cutting up the Park could stop with it, would not, for the time being, tell to the advantage of somebody's real estate. But how will it be in the end, if the bars are once taken down?

Are there any who suppose that those are sincere who seek to create an impression that considerations of public utility and convenience in this respect had no weight in the old design of the Park? If so, I would ask them simply to recall the fact that that design had for its starting-point the necessity of provisions for carrying the ordinary traffic of the city across it in such a manner as not to interfere with its recreative use; that it was the only one of more than thirty plans sub-

mitted by different persons and associations in which this necessity had been so much as thought of; and that the chief
opposition to the accepted design rested on the assertion that
such provision was unnecessary, and, in the manner proposed
to be used, absurdly impracticable. It has now been in use
twenty years precisely as proposed; and not one of the objections said to have been made to it by "eminent engineers"
has been heard of in all that time.

Are those who used this forecast likely to have been otherwise indifferent to motives of utility?

A very different objection to this arrangement will soon
appear, if the aims lately announced in behalf of the Park
Board are sustained, and if the work now said to be in energetic progress shall be long pursued. By a most careful disposition of plantations and underwood the sub-roads have been
so obscured (as have with equal care most of the more finished
architectural structures originally so disconcertingly conspicuous), that they make no impression upon those passing through
it. I have known visitors to make the tour of the Park several
times without being aware of their existence. How will it
be when "a free circulation of air and light" beneath every
bush and brooding conifer has been secured; when the way
of the lawn-mower has at all points been made plain, and
the face of nature shall everywhere have become as natty
as a new silk hat?

X

But one poor apology can be contrived for the course
the Commissioners have been following. That apology they
have not as yet put forward,—those responsible for recent
barbarities have not yet begun to think of apologizing,—but
attempts to supply a base for it have been often seen; and
some of the younger generation may have been led to suppose
them to have substance. They are of precisely the same character, and they have the same origin, and the same motives
and purposes, with those I have already cleared up in respect
to Mr. Vaux and myself; and to assist the truth, a slight repeti-
tion of what I believe to be the facts may be necessary.

In 1857, twenty-five years ago, eleven citizens of New York were asked to take upon themselves, as a Board of Commissioners for the purpose, the extraordinary and gravely difficult duty of preparing for the transformation of a broken, rocky, sterile, and intractable body of land, more than a mile square in extent, into a public ground, to stand in the heart of a great commercial city. The project was without precedent, and remains without parallel. There were political motives in the determination of the arrangement, and governing the choice of the Commissioners selected. Among them, most prominent, was the desire of the leaders of the Republican party to reconcile the Democratic party, largely in majority in the city, to a relinquishment of the spoils of office in the proposed work. For this purpose they provided that no one of the Commissioners should, under any pretext, be entitled to pecuniary compensation for his services. They selected for Commissioners several men unknown in politics, but of high standing in liberal, benevolent, and unpartisan patriotic movements; others, who, if known in politics, were unknown as office-seekers, or, as the term is commonly used, as politicians. In a Board of eleven the Republicans were supposed to have a majority of one; but the first President elected was a Democrat; and seldom if ever (I remember not one case) from the first, in any important matter, did a division occur on party lines. When, near the first city election after the organization, an attempt was made to obtain a party advantage on the work, under orders given by one of the Commissioners, I as superintendent at once arrested it, suspended the foreman, who had acted upon the order, and was sustained in doing so by the vote of every other Republican in the Board.

It was obvious that such a ground as has been described, of very broken topography; rocky, sterile and intractable, in the situation contemplated; to be enclosed by a compact busy city, would, under any possible treatment, entail many and great public inconveniences, and that it could only be kept in suitable order at constant great expense. Whatever its treatment, it was to be anticipated that the land would in time come to have enormous value for purposes other than those to be at first had in view, and that crafty attempts would be made to obtain advantages from it for various selfish ends. It was plain that varied and competing purposes and interests, tastes and dispositions, would be concerned in its management; and that there would always be those, who, however it might be managed, would believe that it should have been very differently treated, and that certain elements of value should have been more amply or less lavishly provided.

From considerations such as these, it followed that the foremost, paramount, and sternest duty of the Commissioners was to be cautious in determining the ends and motives with reference to which the ground should be laid out and treated; to act only upon the most thorough study, and under the most carefully digested advice attainable.

That this duty was recognized, accepted, and deliberately and laboriously met, is a matter of plain, circumstantial, and irrefutable record. This record will also show that different theories of what the circumstances would call for, different opinions, ideals, tastes, and dispositions, were given patient consideration; that views widely different from those finally adopted were ably and warmly represented in the Commission itself; and that the problem had prolonged, earnest, and elaborate discussion.

It is to be added, in view of the very different way in which the undertaking to reverse, as far as practicable, the results of this deliberation, has come to the knowledge of the public, that no body of men charged with a like public trust has ever taken more pains to invite and give opportunity for general public discussion of what it was debating, and review of what it determined; and that discussion and review were prolonged and earnest. There were great differences of opinion; but, in the judgment of those responsible, public opinion steadily moved to a more and more intelligent acceptance of the conclusions adopted in the earlier management, as wisely foresighted.

The Commissioners entered upon their duty under a cloud of jealousy and distrust, and every device of what in city politics passes for statesmanship was employed to keep them there. There were desperate men using desperate means for the purpose; there were misled honest and worthy men who labored to the same end. Nevertheless, as public discussion proceeded, the Commission steadily advanced into the sunshine of public confidence, gained the good will of the more respectable of all parties; and from that day to this no man or party has appealed fairly to public opinion against their conclusions with any degree of success.

There have been strong alliances and combinations to do so. A most energetic attempt was made, as I have before said, in 1871; but it met with decided popular reprobation, and those responsible for it retreated in very bad order, two of them going abroad to escape criminal prosecution.

Essentially, the work now being energetically pushed in the Central Park is a revival of that then defeated: it has the same avowed objects; it has the same obscured ends; it is supported by the same sophistries; it calls for a like popular rebuke.

XI

Is the honest and business-like management of the city's park business to be always "embarrassed," as it has hitherto always been, and must a dead stop and reversion of its true course be come to every ten years, in the future as in the past? If not, how is it to be avoided?

His Honor the mayor has given the more important part of the answer in his message to the aldermen on the occasion of the assassination of President Garfield.

Beyond that, possibly the time may come when the management of the parks may be overlooked, and their business audited by a body of men, among whom there shall be representatives of those to whom the wholesome charm of simple natural scenery has been, as with most of the members of the National Academy of Design, for example, a matter of business-like study, and to whom the permanent reconciliation of a certain practicable degree of such charm, with the necessary conveniences of rest and movement of a vast multitude of people of all classes of the population of a great city, would not be felt a contemptible matter, even in comparison with the immediate practical requirements, from day to day, of republican government.

I cannot see, though it is so apparent to some true friends of the Park, what is to be gained of permanent value by saying to any one man, "Go Work your sweet will there, till we find that we have had enough of you"; taking no security, making no official provision for watching, against that man's personal hobbies and freaks, ambitions and weaknesses. The concentration of executive functions in one man's hands is of too obvious advantage to ever need debate; but beyond and above this, in my judgment, it would be far better to return to something like the original arrangement, in which all questions of general administration, or of sub-legislation for the Park, and especially all determinations affecting its general design, ends, and aims, should be subject to review, discussion, and at least to veto, by an unpaid board of citizens, so large, and of such established reputation because of interest otherwise evinced in affairs allied to those of the proper business of the Park, that there could be some rational confidence that they would exercise conservative control. The labor of such a board need not be great,—a quarterly meeting would probably be sufficient for the auditing of accounts, the passing upon projects, and a review of operations upon previously prepared official reports. An annual report to the mayor would present the entire business satisfactorily to the public.

Postscript

This pamphlet had been so far written, and in part printed, before I knew that a practical proposition had been prepared—the first of the present session, and introduced in the form of a bill before the Legislature had organized—to amend the city charter in such a way as to provide for the abolition of the Park Board, and the substitution for it of a Superintendent, responsible directly to the mayor. Assuming, as I must, from the favor with which it is instantly received by friends

of the Park, that there are no private, or party, or local interests moving the proposition; that there is no understanding
as to who the superintendent is to be, whom he is to appoint,
and what work he is to prosecute,—I can only recur to what
I was just saying. If the man shall be qualified by the special
study and training required for his duty, and shall have given
proofs of it, and shall take up his duty with an earnest and
serious purpose, he cannot but desire the moral weight which
would be gained by such an arrangement as I have above
been suggesting.

Considerations against the plan as I have seen it set forth
are these:—

The results to which good management of the Park will
be directed are not to be-brought about quickly, by strokes,
but gradually, by courses extending through several years.
Good courses, consequently, require time for their vindication.
A man cannot reasonably hope to be allowed to steadily pursue
any courses looking solely to good results in the Park. He
will be constantly pressed with advice from men who are
neither competent nor disposed to give sound advice with reference to results of such limited scope,—men who will be
not at all accountable for his failure to reach vindicating results; men who will never be known to the public to have
had any thing to do with the matter; men who, nevertheless, will make a business, if he fails to be ruled by their
advice, of obstructing his way upon any desirable course,
and who, by one shameful means or another, will so accumulate embarrassments for him, that he will be fortunate if he
succeeds in escaping a mortifying and apparently disgraceful
failure.

Again: with whatever confidence we may look to the
present mayor's intentions and shrewdness, it is not to be forgotten that no arrangement for the guardianship of the park
property could be more tempting to a sly, smooth, and dou-
ble-faced schemer, than that proposed; and that such an one,
unscrupulous in making bargains for the purpose, ready to
resort to falsehood and all manner of vile intrigues, would
have unlimited advantages in contending with an honest man.

439

To come to a point, no well-matured scheme for the government of Central Park will fail to recognize that it is an essentially different form of city property,—on the one hand, from ordinary urban squares and places; on the other, from the great suburban parks of other cities,—nor will it fail to embody features nearly equivalent to the following:—

First, A definition of the trust, giving some fixed idea of what may and what may not be legally aimed at in its management.

Second, Provision for a board of directors with the ordinary duties of a commercial board of directors, in which board there will be, by some ex-officio appointment, representatives of the art of landscape-painting, of standing previously fixed by their fellow-artists.

Third, Provision for an executive office, with the executive duties of which the directors will be restrained from interfering.

Fourth, Provision for a professional adviser, qualified by study and practice in the art of landscape-gardening, with such prescribed duties and rights as will make him responsible for an intelligent and consistent pursuit of the main landscape-design of the Park; this office to be combined, or not, as may be found best by the directors, with the executive office.

Fifth, All such provision as legislators will think practicable for restraining, with reference to the park-service, that form of tyranny known as advice or influence, and that form of bribery known as patronage.

DOCUMENT XII

-》》-》》-》》《《-《《-《《

FREDERICK LAW OLMSTED AND CALVERT VAUX

General Plan for the Improvement of Morningside Park (1887)

-》》-》》-》》《《-《《-《《

New York, Oct. 1, 1887

The Honorable M. C. D. Borden,
President of the Board of Commissioners of the Department
of Public Parks of New York

SIR:
The report which we have the honor to submit will be divided under several headings, the first being a statement of—

I. The Question to Be Considered: The Manner in Which It Has Arisen, and Certain Conditions of Its Fair Discussion

Had it been determined to carry streets through the property now called Morningside Park at the usual intervals and by a continuance of the courses of those approaching it from east and west, the grades of those streets and the crossing avenues, and of all building lots opening from them for a long distance from the property on all sides, would have been so affected as to make (without any corresponding advantage) a difference of millions of dollars in the cost of preparing them in the usual manner for close permanent building.

The simplest way to avoid this was for the city to take possession of the ground, and the easiest legal way to take possession of the ground was to ordain, as a matter of form, that it should be called a park.

The city, having thus on its hands a piece of property which has come to it as an incident of an operation through which it has been saved a large profitless outlay, now asks how this property can be made useful.

To say that it can be made into a park is an insufficient answer.

Something may undoubtedly be made of it that will serve many of the purposes that are served by what are usually called parks, but it must be borne in mind at the outset that none of these have been made out of a piece of land of any-think like the character of this of Morningside, consequently, that we must set aside, not only the commonly accepted notions of what is desirable, and the routine standards of excellence, but also the ideas of "value receivable" for a given expenditure that have been formed from observation of other pieces of ground called by the name of parks.

II. The Old Plan, and Why a Revision of It Is Undertaken

Fourteen years ago a general plan was prepared by us, hereinafter to be referred to as "the Old Plan," for turning the Morningside property to use. This was provisionally adopted by your Board, record being made that it would be subject to modification should circumstances arise making this desirable.[1] You have now asked us to consider whether such circumstances have occurred, and if so, to submit a revised plan.

We respectfully report that in our opinion occasion for revision has occurred, as follows:

First.—When "the Old Plan" was proposed the elevated railroad had not been projected. It has since been built, passing along the border of the property and having a station adjoining

---

[1] See Minutes of the Board, October 16, 1873. [1887.]

it. The tracks of the road are carried over, and their supports partly obstruct, the north side walk of One Hundred and Tenth street, which was otherwise likely to be the principal approach to the Park. Consequently, passing trains, moving slowly and with considerable noise upon winding tracks and at an extraordinary height will inevitably be a very disquieting circumstance of the southern part of any pleasure ground to be formed on the premises.

Second.—The elevated road, causing the locality to be much more accessible from all distant points of the city, makes it less of a local ground than it was formerly thought likely to be, and requires a larger estimate to be adopted of the number of visitors to be provided for in its walks and other accommodations.

The topographical limitations of the property remaining the same as before, this circumstance makes necessary a more careful avoidance of nooks and passages which, with crowds entering them, are likely to be glutted, and requires that precautions should be observed against dangers that increase with the pressure of throngs.

Third.—The elevated road makes an entrance to the Park at One Hundred and Sixteenth street of more importance than any other, and a commodious route of passage from One Hundred and Sixteenth street on the east to One Hundred and Sixteenth street on the west a prime necessity.

Fourth.—The partial construction, since the plan was made, of the retaining wall of West Morningside avenue, and of outworks projecting from this wall into the Park property, on a somewhat different and more costly plan than that originally adopted, also makes adjustments necessary.

Fifth.—At the time the original plan was called for, the Park Department thought that it might become desirable to place a large Exhibition Building on Morningside Park, and with reference to such a structure, a portion of the ground was proposed in the plan to be levelled at considerable expense and a system of approaches provided for, by which it would be accessible night and day.

It is understood that it is no longer the wish of the Depart-

443

ment that such a structure should be had in view. Hence the system of approaches designed for it is no longer required.

III. Situation and Topography

Having thus shown reasons for proposing a revised plan, we shall next briefly describe the leading topographical features to which a plan should be fitted.

The map shows the precise extent and shape of the property.

Roughly described, it is a strip of land of the length of that part of Broadway below the City Hall, and eighty to one hundred yards wide. As originally assigned to your Department, it was bounded by the adjoining thoroughfares, but (as we had presumed that at some time it would be when preparing the "Old Plan") the jurisdiction of your Department has been lately extended to take those in, so that improvements can be made upon them in connection with those of the ground they enclose.

The leading circumstance of the topography of the entire property is a ledge of gneiss rock running through it from end to end.

The western part of this ledge is about sixty feet higher than the eastern part (being the height of a four-story house).

Parts are precipitous and the face of most of it too steep to be passed across except by climbing. Below it there is a strip of flat land.

There are features of decided picturesqueness, almost of grandeur, in the ledge, but nowhere any trees or other vegetation of consequence, or any water. The general character of the ground is that of a rugged waste.

IV. The Heights

We assume that any value the property can be made to have will be proportionate to the degree in which those resorting to it will find refreshing relief from the confined scenery of streets and buildings, and that the plan required

444

must be adapted to furnish such relief and make it conveniently available with no costly disturbance of the natural features.

The best opportunity of furnishing it in large measure, without excessive outlay, does not lie within the territory originally taken for a park, but in the thoroughfare called Morningside Avenue West, to carry which a causeway supported by a retaining wall resting on the upper part of the ledge, has already been constructed. This wall is generally from twenty to thirty feet high, so that the surface of the avenue for a distance of more than half a mile is essentially a hanging terrace of the height of a six-storied house above the eastern side of the property.

When the city shall have been built up on the Harlem Plain, there will be no outlook from any point within the park, but all along this high terrace walk a great expanse will be open to the eastward, the eye ranging over the ledge and over the roofs of houses to stand on the other side of the park.

Beyond the latter will be seen, first, the waters of the East River, with the shipping upon them, from Hell Gate to the Sound; next, the suburban region of Long Island, and back of this, wooded hills, to a great distance. Provided it is seen under circumstances favorable to its enjoyment, it is not to be supposed that anything that can be provided by improvements within the park will be more refreshing than this broad prospect, reaching far out of town, and including much that is bright and rurally cheerful. All that is wanted for the full enjoyment of it is, *first,* a safe and convenient shady place from which the visitor, while strolling easily, may take it in; *second,* a more congenial foreground.

The plan provides for the first in a Mall, to be shaded by two rows of trees, with a number of bays which will serve as resting places and invite contemplation at the best points of view. We shall hereafter refer to this arrangement as "The Heights."

It was the intention of the "Old Plan," that the wall supporting the walk on the Heights, the tourelles carrying the bays, the stairways leading from them, and the parapet required for the safety of visitors, should be built of stone in a rustic and inexpensive manner, dependence being placed on a garniture of vines and rock plants to make them beautiful.

A variation from this plan has since been adopted, following the same leading lines, but providing some additional bays and staircases, and requiring a much more massive, elegant, and obviously costly form of construction.

The greater part of this plan has been executed, and as there is nothing in what has been done that mars the general design of the work as a whole, it is accepted and incorporated in the present plan.

The intention has been, however, in addition to what we have stated, to break the wall along the Heights into several level sections, to be connected by short stairways, the flanks of these stairways being decorated with piers, ramps, and vases of polished granite, and with flower beds.

However elegant, we think that such an arrangement would be seriously inconvenient, would lead to accidents, and would be difficult to maintain in good order. No part of it having been executed, we therefore advise a return to the original plan of an uninterrupted walk.

As to strengthening the effect of the distant prospect from the Heights by a more emphatic foreground, as much as possible is intended by the plan, to be accomplished by plantations on the park immediately below, care being taken that the choice and disposition of trees is such that those nearest shall in time form simple broad masses of foliage, pleasing to look down upon, and that, except at occasional points, none shall grow to a height at which they will hide the horizon.

The result of what shall be done in this way will be to put apparently further away, break up and make less strenuous upon the attention, the rows of buildings which will come into the view next beyond the park, and, by giving prominence, close at hand, to sylvan elements, secure unity between the nearer and distant parts of the landscape.

The value of the broad outlook from the high, breezy and conspicuous terrace walk that we have described will be so great that whatever may be offered in the park below it must be of minor importance. Consequently nothing should be aimed at which will at all detract from the value of what is to be provided on "the Heights."

This consideration rules out all artificial objects that would be so prominent as to engage particular attention when seen from above.

V. The Lower Ground

What is next to be desired in this pleasure ground is a form of refreshment from the ordinary city scenery of streets and buildings which shall so differ from that to be obtained on the Heights that one shall be an agreeable contrast to the other, and each give a zest to the enjoyment of the other; the principle to be pursued corresponding to that which governs the order of courses in a refreshing repast. To this end the plan provides another broad walk of equal length with that on the Heights, but of a sheltered character, and carrying the visitor through sequestered rural scenery. The attention of those passing through this walk will be chiefly directed to features comparatively near at hand, and the pleasure to be had from resort to it will come in a greater degree from a sense of retirement and seclusion, and of immediately surrounding sylvan quietude.

The second walk thus proposed will be seen in the drawing between the foot of the ledge and the eastern boundary of the park, running near the base of the declivity in the middle part; and, in the northern and southern quarter, diverging so far from it as to allow spaces of turf to be introduced between it and the rocks which, in these quarters, are bolder than elsewhere, and will be seen in landscape composition with larger bodies of foliage.

The course of the walk, determined by regard for natural circumstances, is moderately winding and so ordered as to avoid steep grades or the necessity of stairs. An invalid will be able to move through it on a wheel chair.

Where it passes that part of the ledge, nearly a quarter of a mile in length, in which the rock, though less bold and

447

salient, is most unbroken, and therefore affords the least opportunity for trees to grow upon it, the walk is to follow near its base, at a grade below that of the original surface, and sloping banks are to rise on each side, which are to be planted with low spreading trees and underwood, so that the effect of a natural bowery passage will be had.

There are, however, to be frequent lateral depressions of the sloping banks, and openings of the foliage through these, looking upon grassy spaces, among trees on one side, and upon the rocky declivity and wall above it, on the other. Trees at a little distance on the east will everywhere obscure, not only the buildings but the rows of trees on the avenue, so that the latter will but give density to the general umbrage.

The present aspect of the declivity, as it may be looked up to from the line of this walk, is comparatively hard, bleak, barren and gloomy; where it is most so, however, it is practicable to induce it to adopt a sufficient proportion of certain forms of vegetation to take on a cheerful and even a gay character.

There would, for example, be that of various vines and creepers, especially of the smaller woody sorts; that of prostrate and low-headed conifers, dwarf brambles, myrica, comptonia, rock ferns, genistas, bearberry, the smaller sumachs and other bushes that flourish in dry ground, and that of certain yuccas, of Indian figs, sedums, semper vivum, of golden rods, asters and other low perennials.

Where seen through openings of the bowery walls of the walk at the base of the declivity, an interesting and refreshing effect will be produced by these modest forms of vegetation, their outer parts observed in perspective, as they will be in looking upward, fold upon fold of them mingling with projections of the gray ledge, and the undraped parts of the crowning wall with the spray of trees on the Mall hanging over it.

Between the southern part of this lower walk, and the base of the declivity we proposed in "the Old Plan" that there should be a body of water. This will be a most desirable feature of the park, because its banks, being on all sides deep and sheltering, the water would generally have a still surface, reflecting masses of rock rising vertically from its western verge with foliage hanging over them, in entire consistency with the sequestered character which is to be aimed at in all these parts of the ground.

Nevertheless, we omit the feature from the drawing of the revised plan, not because we have come to think it undesirable or permanently impracticable, but because an adequate supply of water is not likely to be obtained for some years to come, unless your Board should conclude to make some special and, as yet, uncontemplated provision for it.

A space of turf will supply an element of scenery having a similar, though less attractive relation with that of the rocks and the Heights beyond them. Whenever water can be provided, as, sooner or later, in our opinion, it must be, in connection with the requirements of the Central Park, it can be made to take the place represented in the present drawing to be occupied by turf, by an excavation which will then cost but little more than it would now.

When this shall be done, the bodies of foliage designed to be planted on the borders of the turf will remain and will overhang the water.

VI. The Southern Hill Side

Between the base of the western retaining wall and the brow of the rocks, which have just been under consideration in connection with the water question, there is a space less rocky and less steeply inclined than any other part of the declivity. For this reason, in "the Old Plan," it was taken as the site of the proposed Exhibition Building. In the present plan the main purpose to be accomplished on this ground is to present bodies of foliage, so disposed as to add to the freshness and beauty of the view downward from the Mall on the Heights, and of the view upward from the lower walk.

It is compatible with the purpose, however, to make a pleasant rambling ground upon it. The intention of which is indicated in the drawing by a walk making a circuit about

449

a small glade among the trees and by a structure (The Rest-awhile) intended to serve the purpose of a general shelter in case of showers and also of a retiring cottage.

It is to be low-walled, and, when trees shall have been grown, is to be visible neither from above nor below. It is to be entered, in a manner to be explained later, from the Mall on the Heights.

VII. The Central Hill Side

North of One Hundred and Sixteenth street, the face of the ledge, between the base of the retaining wall and the flat land is narrow and more inclined, its lower parts being generally precipitous, and much of its upper parts too steep for safe footing. From these upper parts there will be no out-look; on one side close at hand, will be the high retaining wall, as of a fortress, on the other, eighty yards away, blocks of buildings. There is so little soil and so little opportunity for forming artificial stores of soil upon it, that no continuous walk along the brow of the declivity would be well bordered either by trees or turf, nor could a convenient broad walk be constructed without violence to nature. No attempt, there-fore, is proposed to make this district, like the last, pleasant for rambling and rest. The designed treatment of it has been explained in describing the intended character of the view upward and westward from the long, lower walk; but, to facilitate the movements of laborers and police engaged in the care of the park, as well as to provide a passage for visitors between the foot of the stairs on the north, and the rambling ground last described, on the south, a path is shown, carried as near the base of the retaining wall as will leave planting space to be prepared for creepers to be grown upon the wall, and shrubbery to obscure what would otherwise be a harsh line at its base.

VIII. The Northern Hill Side

The northern part of the property is a mass of rock, and the walks carried through it, as shown in the drawing, are designed with reference to little else than convenience of passage across it to other parts, the purpose being to accomplish what is necessary to the result with no more blasting or building than is indispensable to the purpose. The heaviest part of the work has been already done.

The walls of a construction in this quarter, said to have been made as a part of a line of fortifications, and thus having a historical interest, are preserved and made accessible. It is intended that soil shall be banked up against the inside of these walls, being retained by a rough additional wall, the latter forming the backing of a seat, as shown, and that in the soil, vines shall be planted to droop over the rude masonry of the exterior.

IX. The Outer Promenades and the Cross-Ways of the Park

One of the earliest determinations to be made, in forming a plan for a city park, is that of the question whether it shall be adapted to use at night. As a rule, a park for night use should be of a simple character; its foliage should be in the form of open groves with little underwood; its walks broad, of easy grade, and it should be free from stairs, which would be stumbling blocks, and from all conditions that would give ruffians special opportunities for sudden acts of violence and for escaping observation; it should be well lighted at all points and be free from dark shadowy places. To make it so it would be necessary to sacrifice much of the attractiveness which it might have, if fitted exclusively for use by daylight.

The topography of the Morningside property is all against an intention to adapt it to night use; to do this would add greatly to its original cost and compel a much more expensive system of maintenance. Out of the conclusion that it should not be prepared for night use grow two features of the plan that remain to be spoken of. The first is that of a continuous broad promenade all around the park, easily well lighted and in all respects suitable for night use, this to be separated from the interior park by a wall, not sufficient to prevent a determined man from making his way in, but sufficient to make it clear that no one who shall have made his way in has done so without an intention to break the law.

SECOND.—It would be seriously inconvenient to the public not to be able to get across the park at night. Hence, two passages are proposed, one connecting the two parts of 116th street, the other, the two parts of 120th street. They are to be made as nearly direct as they can be without becoming unbroken flights of stairs, but so far indirect as to keep close to the natural surface, and to play smoothly in with the walks, the general direction of which is across their course. They are designed as shown on the drawing to be bordered with iron fences in which there will be gates where other walks lead out of them, these gates to be closed at night.

One Hundred and Sixteenth street being of greater width than 120th, and having the railroad station upon it, the crossing between its two points is likely to be much the more used of the two; it is therefore made of ampler dimensions and at a point between the two principal flights of stairs at the foot of the tourelle, a broad open landing is introduced giving opportunity for a resting place. This, together with the entire line of the passage, will be brightly illuminated by electric lights on the tourelles, and on the gateways upon the avenue.

X. Sheltered Conveniences

As in the summer nights, great numbers of women and children must be expected to resort to the Heights for enjoyment of the brilliant spectacle which will there be presented, and of the breeze from the sea, it has been thought necessary that access should be allowed them to the cottage before spoken of, at which there would be a female attendant. This cottage (being situated so far below the level of the mall that the eye will range over it) is to be approached by a short flight of steps which in the daytime will also be an entrance to the park, while at night a fence and gates will restrict its use to those needing to enter the cottage, through which there will then be no passage. Another smaller shelter is proposed to be centrally situated in the northern section of the park, and the base of each of the tourelles is intended to be utilized, either as a shelter, or a place of retirement for the public or as a tool-room, storage-room or sub-station for the Parkkeepers. Such use of them has not apparently been contemplated heretofore, and, that it may be had, doors and windows will have to be made in some of them.

XI. Approach from Central Park

In "the old plan" it had been assumed that visitors approaching Morningside from Central Park would nearly all take the northern sidewalk of 110th street. The change made by the railroad destroys this approach. It has occurred too, since the old plan was prepared, that 110th street, from the Central Park to the corner diagonally opposite the south-east corner of the Morningside property, has been widened on the south side. It seems advisable that this widening should be continued opposite Morningside Park, and if this can be done the arrangement shown on the drawing will, we think, be the best that can be made for a foot approach from the Central to the Morningside Park, and for an entrance to the latter at the nearest point at which it can be reached.

XII. Note on the Order of Operations

It is not our present duty to counsel you as to details of the general plan we submit, nor as to proceedings to follow should your Board see fit to adopt it. But we propose to offer one suggestion in this latter respect, because, if the course we indicate is not taken, it is probable that a very different result will follow from that which we have had in view in the preparation of the drawing now laid before you. We cannot, however, venture to make this suggestion without connecting it with some general observations more or less applicable to all considerable park undertakings.

The drawing submitted, and this report in which we aim to supplement the drawing, cannot possibly represent more than a dry and imperfect frame-work of what Morningside Park is designed to be. Endless drawings, and volumes of written explanations of matters of detail would not present the life and soul of the design, which can never be realized, except through a broad comprehension of, and sympathy with, its leading motives in *the direction* of the required operations, and this not simply for two or three years, but constantly and permanently thereafter.

It is easily possible that something which might be called a park should be formed on this ground, in which every line on the drawing would be closely followed, and yet with a result egregiously different from that intended. It is easily possible that everything that is necessary to a realization of the design, shall be done, so far as this is practicable within a certain period, at the end of which period the construction of the park would be called complete, and yet, a few years afterward, that the park should have a character wholly different from that designed, and with a view to which all previous work had been planned. And the waste of such earlier work may occur with no definite intention but simply from ignorance, or irresponsible omission to do what is continuously necessary to the purpose.

Waste, through failure to follow up with due continuous operations the primary constructional work of a park, is apt to be (in a degree very difficult to realize) the result of self-seeking influences in its management, or of fallacious popular assumptions of what is necessary to produce desired results. Of such assumptions none are more common than those that relate to park plantations; and of these the most common, and influential on park management is the assumption that the planting of trees is in the nature of a final operation; that trees once well planted may shift for themselves.

In the examination upon which this report is based, we have come upon so striking an illustration of the manner in which this fallacy works wastefully that we wish to call your attention to it.

At some distance on all sides about the Morningside property, much building is in progress, population is moving in and land coming into use and tax-paying productiveness. Immediately about the property, there is no building. The chance that a park will be formed upon it, which will make it a particularly desirable place of residence prevents building about it for any other purpose than that of a superior class of residences; the ground is of a character so different from that upon which any satisfactory city park has ever been formed, that there is, unavoidably, a vague distrust of the possibility that anything satisfactory in the way of a park can be made of it. No one going upon the ground can avoid seeing that if residences of any description were to be built about it while it remains in its present condition, the so-called park would be an intolerable nuisance.

Under these circumstances, the city has been much urged to begin improvements, and has, during the last ten years, at different times, entered upon several pieces of work, which it has been led to believe would have the effect of improvements, in giving assurance that the present state of things at least, was not to last.

One of these pieces of work has been the planting of two rows, each nearly a mile long, of Oriental Plane trees on the north and east margin of the park property. These were well planted, large pits having been prepared for them with three feet in depth of mould, the trees were of suitable size, thrifty, well set, and each was duly provided with an iron hurdle as a protection.

It is common, all over the country, to assume that, by such an operation an improvement is accomplished, so far at least that nature may be left to complete it. The result in this case is that, so far from helping forward a park-like character, in the neighborhood, the operation has simply made the place look much more squalid than before, the chief result being a broken series of stumps standing among dusty weeds, and a lot of rusty and dilapidated iron guards, guarding nothing. More than ninety per cent. of the trees are dead. Of another series of trees planted a few years earlier on the south border of the property but five, we believe, remain. (We do not understand that your Department has been responsible for the wastefulness of either of these operations.)

The point to which these observations tend is this, that, in any well-conceived park design, the most important hostile

455

influences to guard against are procrastination, incompleteness and inefficiency, in respect to matters of vegetation.

There is so much rock exposed and so much more close below the surface of the Morningside Park ground, that a desirably fresh, luxuriant and cheerful character can only be had in it by what would elsewhere be a more than liberal—a profuse—use of a variety of plants such as we have already mentioned; plants adapted to grow in dry shallow soils or to hang or creep over rocks from pockets of soil outside of them. If what we have advised in this respect shall be done, the result, in a few years, will be a park of a very distinguished character, and which in this special description of vegetation will have a unique interest.

The plants we speak of are nearly all American and natural to the circumstances—such as are not so are fully naturalized. With suitable arrangements they will be inexpensive to establish on this ground, and once established, will, better than most plants, take care of themselves.

The plants cannot be obtained in the necessary quantity ready grown from the commercial nurseries, and the demand for most of them, in ordinary gardening, is so little that, when grown, they are sold only at many times what their cost would be if a larger market for them could be calculated on. If, therefore, your Board should adopt the plan now submitted, and it is determined to do anything toward carrying it out during the next three years, we advise that large quantities of the desired plants be at once propagated in the nurseries of the Department, and that the business of furnishing the ground with suitable vegetation take precedence, as far as possible at all times hereafter, of other business. The outlay required for all that is to be desired in this respect will be a small item in the general cost of the park.

We have ventured to urge at length this special preparation of a suitable vegetation because it is the essence of our design that Morningside Park should, in a certain artistic sense, be considered a reservation for the illustration of a subtle and delicate though dormant landscape possibility, and not an opportunity for mere miscellaneous park treatment.

XIII. The Question of Cost

Much the larger part of the cost of executing this plan will be that of operations of preparing walks, stairs of rough stone, and other constructional work similar to what has been done on the rocky ground of the Central, East River and Mount Morris Parks. We do not offer estimates of cost, understanding that it will be more satisfactory to the Board to receive such information as it may desire in this respect from its executive agents who have been engaged in the operations referred to.

We may point out, however, that (for reasons that have been given) certain costly items of the original plan are omitted from the revised plan; those, for instance, of the terrace for the Exhibition Building and the approaches to it, and the extensive structure in connection with the southwest entrance. Also that much of the work required both by the original and the present plan has been executed.

Supposing that some part of the work must be delayed until further appropriations for it are authorized, we advise that no money shall be spent on any of the permanent outworks of the park, but that such inexpensive, temporary and provisional fences as are necessary to guard against accidents, shall be used in connection with the outer streets, until these shall be fully put in good order.

If this policy is adopted the fund that has been authorized to be appropriated would be available for the preparation of the ground to be dressed and planted, and for walks and other constructional work, which must be completed before the interior of the park will be in a condition to be conveniently, safely and enjoyably used by the public.

Careful calculation will, we think, show that the cost of accomplishing this would be within the amount authorized to be appropriated, provided the work is vigorously, steadily and systematically prosecuted.

Respectfully,
FREDERICK LAW OLMSTED,
CALVERT VAUX,
Landscape Architects

457

ACKNOWLEDGMENTS

DURING the course of my research into the work of Frederick Law Olmsted, my obligation to institutions, librarians, and scholars has been very great indeed. Since my contribution to this publication represents only a part of my work both in England and America, the list which follows is hardly indicative of the debt incurred.

The most important single Olmsted manuscript collection is housed at the Library of Congress, and I am particularly indebted to Mr. David C. Mearns and Dr. C. P. Powell of the manuscript division of that institution for the use of this material. I am grateful as well to the late Mr. William Jackson and Miss Carolyn Jakeman of the Houghton Library, Harvard University; to Mr. Stephen T. Riley, Mr. Warren G. Wheeler, and Miss Winifred V. Collins of the Massachusetts Historical Society; to Mr. Robert W. Hill, Mr. Paul R. Rugan, and Miss Jean McNeice of the New York Public Library; to Dr. James J. Heslin, Mr. James Gregory, Miss Shirley Beresford, Miss Nancy Hale, Mr. Wilmer R. Leech, Mr. Arthur J. Breton, and Miss A. Rachel Minick of the New-York Historical Society; to Mrs. Mary L. Wilkins of the Garden Library, Dumbarton Oaks; to Miss Caroline Shillaber, Librarian of the Graduate School of Design, Harvard University; to Mr. George O. Pratt, Jr., Director of The Staten Island Institute of Arts and Sciences, and to its Librarian, Mrs. Gail K. Schneider; to Mr. James A. Kelly, Historian of the Borough of Brooklyn of the City of New York; to Mr. James F. Waters, Supervisor, Historical Division, Kings County Clerk's Office, New York State; to Mr. Arthur Konop, Jr., Archivist, Brooklyn Historical Studies Institute, St. Francis College, Brooklyn, New York; and to the staff of the Long Island Historical Society. Without the cooperation of these librarians

459

and the institutions they represent this anthology could not have been presented to the public.

During my research and writing I have been fortunate in having the help and advice of experts in the fields of city planning and landscape architecture. Professor James M. Fitch of Columbia University has made many valuable suggestions. Professor Christopher Tunnard of Yale University has provided assistance at several points during the course of my work. I also had the advantage of acting as consultant to the Centennial Exhibition of Frederick Law Olmsted's contribution to the profession of landscape architecture. This exhibition, a student project, was cosponsored by the Department of Landscape Architecture of Harvard University and the American Society of Landscape Architects, and I learned much from working with the students engaged in the project and from discussions with members of the faculty: Professors Hideo Sasaki, Charles W. Harris, Donald Olsen, Norman Newton, and Peter Hornbeck.

I am grateful for the support I have received from the Dumbarton Oaks Library, where I have been a Harvard Junior Fellow in Landscape Architecture for the past two years. The reproduction of illustrative materials is due in part to the publication fund of that institution. I especially appreciate the help of Mr. John Thacher, Director of Dumbarton Oaks, and the encouragement of the Garden Advisory Committee. The late Mr. Leon Zach, who was Chairman of the Committee and a former associate of the Olmsted Office, was particularly kind and helpful. Conversations with my colleague at Dumbarton Oaks, Mr. David B. Chase, enriched my knowledge of the history of landscape architecture. Special acknowledgment must go to Mrs. Robert W. Bliss, whose generosity and interest have made both the library and the gardens of Dumbarton Oaks into vital parts of what that distinguished institution is today.

Dean Milton M. Klein of Fredonia College has never failed to give generously of his time and knowledge on matters pertaining to my work. In addition, I have profited from the suggestions of Professor Milton W. Brown of Brooklyn College,

ACKNOWLEDGMENTS

Professor Mair J. Benardete of Brooklyn College, Professor Elliott Gatner of Long Island University, and Mr. Victor Backus, formerly Director of Publications for Long Island University. Professor Barclay G. Jones of Cornell University has always been helpful in discussing matters concerning the publication of this book, as has the staff of Cornell University Press. Other Olmsted scholars who have kindly offered assistance based on their own work are Dr. Charles McLaughlin of American University and Mr. Jon Peterson of Harvard University.

I am most indebted to three people: Professor Richard Hofstadter of Columbia University, who has always encouraged me in the direction of my research and whose seminal contributions to the fields of political, social, and intellectual history have played an important part in the development of my own thinking; Mrs. Laura W. Roper, the principal Olmsted scholar, through whose many kindnesses the present publication has been made possible, and not least in that she made available for duplication her own valued Olmsted Reports, given to her by Frederick Law Olmsted, Jr.; and, finally, my wife, whose superb editorial ability and careful eye caused every word in my text to be questioned.

For any misinterpretations or errors of fact I alone, of course, am responsible.

ALBERT FEIN

The Dumbarton Oaks Library
Washington, D.C.
September 1, 1966

GENERAL INDEX

INDEX OF PERSONAL NAMES

Adams, Henry, 47
Anderson, Dr. William C., on malaria, 209, 280
André, M. Edouard:
  landscape architect of Paris parks, 428, 431
  L'Art des Jardins, 432
Andrews, Dr., 279
Appleton, [D.?], 396
Attrill, H. Y., 301

Babcock, [Samuel D.?], 396
Bancroft, George, 47
Banker, Mrs., 231
Barillet-Deschamps, M., 431
Bellows, Rev. Henry W., 26, 28, 32
Belmont, [August?], 396
Bestor, Arthur E., Jr., *Backwoods Utopias: The Sectarian and Owenite Phases of Communitarian Socialism in America*, 10n
Blunt, Edmund, 425
Bogart, Dr., 280
Bogart, John, 40n, 130
Bolestra, M. P., on malaria, 210–211
Borden, M. C. D., 441
Bowditch, E. W., 429n
Bowditch, Dr. H. I., 279
Brace, Charles L., 26, 30
Brooks, David, 5
Brooks, Preston, 16
Brown, Addison, 396
Bryant, William C., 6–7, 425
Bushnell, Horace, 8

Carlyle, Thomas, *Sartor Resartus*, 7–8, 8n
Carter, [James C.?], 396

Chadwick, Sir Edwin, 32
Chadwick, George F., *The Works of Sir Joseph Paxton (1803–1865)*, 14n
Chandler, Prof. Charles F., 279
  analyzes drinking water of Staten Island, 285–288
Cisco, [John C.?], 396
Claflin, [Horace B.?], 396
Clark, Dr., 280
Clark, Dr. Ephraim, 280
Claude, Lorraine, 185
Cleveland, H. W. S., 429n
Colgate, [James B.?], 396
Collins, George R. and Christiane C., *Camillo Sitte and the Birth of Modern City Planning*, 33n
Cooper, James F., *Home As Found*, 12n
Cooper, Peter, 396, 425
Cortelyou, Peter L., 231, 279
Cotes, Dr. J. B., on malaria, 215
Craven, John J., 396
Crawford, Thomas, 22n
Croes, J. James R., 349, 375
Crooke, Mr., 231, 279
Curtis, George W., 40n

Davis, J. P., 129
De Bow, James D. B., 17, 20, 21
Dickens, Charles, on living conditions of East London, 197
Dodge, [William E.?], 396
Dongan, Gov. Thomas, Staten Island manor of, 245
Donn, Capt., 308
Downing, Andrew J., 43n
  Horticulturist, 29
  urges public parks in New York City, 51–52
Drake, Dr. Daniel, on malaria, 211

INDEX OF PLACE NAMES
(Including Buildings and Monuments)

The Greater City of New York, consisting of the five boroughs of Manhattan, Brooklyn, Staten Island, Queens, and The Bronx, did not come into being until 1898. Until 1874 the political boundaries of New York City were contained within Manhattan Island (with part of what is now The Bronx annexed). Hence, places, buildings, and monuments which are today most precisely designated as being in Manhattan are located here in "New York City," as they were in Olmsted's day. Also, some of the places identified here as parts of Brooklyn, Queens, and The Bronx were not, at the time they were discussed in the documents, within the boundaries of these boroughs as we know them today; they were gradually annexed preceding the final amalgamation. It should be noted that the Index includes names of places for which plans were not executed; most of these pertain to Staten Island.

INDEX

Isle of Wight (Eng.), healthfulness of, 223–224

Jamaica (West Indies), 141
Jamaica Bay (Queens), 308
  lagoons of, 308, 309
James River, 24
Jardin des Tuileries (Paris, Fr.), 67
Jefferson Market Court (New York City), 43n
Jerome Avenue Valley (Bronx), 381
Jerome Park (Bronx), 381
Jerome Park Branch Railroad (Bronx), 381
Jersey City (N.J.), 251
Jersey Street (Staten Island), 257

Kansas, 16, 54
Kennebeck River, 5
Kent (Eng.), 214
"Kentucky grasslands," 18
Ketchum's Dam (Staten Island), 246
Ketchum's Grist Mill (Staten Island), 245, 255
Ketchum's Millpond (Staten Island), 285
Kew Gardens (Eng.), 86
Kills (Staten Island), 252n, 278
Kingsbridge (Bronx), 382
Kings County, 179, 217

Leamington (Eng.), 363
Lemon Creek (Staten Island), 278, 279, 283
Lincolnshire (Eng.), 214
Linden Avenue (Berlin, Ger.), 158
Little Clove Valley (Staten Island), 246
Liverpool (Eng.), 13, 14n, 32, 33, 356, 425
  Irish immigration, 148
  mortality rate, 148
  population density, 147–148
  "urban renewal," 184n
London (Eng.), 14n, 32, 33, 40, 67, 149, 181, 183, 227n, 273, 352, 356, 413, 425

condition of streets in eighteenth century, 142–143
East End:
  development of, 194
  improvements in, 198
  intolerable conditions of, 197
  fire of, 139–140
  green fields in, 139
  growth of suburbs, 141, 364
  life expectancy, 32
  mortality rate, 148
  old part of, 364
  Olmsted on parks of, 56
  Parliament authorizes improvement of street plan, 142
  periodic epidemics, 139
  population density, 147–148, 190
  population growth, 1–2
  restrictions placed on commercial traffic, 152
  Thames River, 139
  trees used for health purposes, 373
  "urban renewal," 184
  use of open spaces, 139
  villas, 194–195
  widening of streets in fire, 139–140
Long Branch (N.J.), 310, 311, 318
  hotels at, 319
Long Island (N.Y.), 180, 180n, 220, 245
  census of towns (1865–1870), 284
  future commercial area of, 154
  topography of, 154
Long Neck (Staten Island), 220
Long Neck Road (Staten Island), 257
Louisville (Ky.), 22
Lynn Beach (Mass.), 310

Madeline, La (Paris, Fr.), 353
Madison Square (New York City), 365
Manhattan Beach (Brooklyn), 318
  hotel at, 306
  pavilion at, 315

482

Staten Island (New York City)
(*cont.*)
unhealthiness, most serious planning problem, 205
villa plots, 261
waters, analysis of, 285–288
watershed, 266
water supply, future, 272–273
water supply, pure, need of,
244–246
water transportation, 289
water-works system, 283
western water preserve and public common, 279, 283
*see also specific locations, and
see* Drainage *in* General
Index
Stirlingshire (Scot.), 214
Sussex (Eng.), 214
Syracuse (N.Y.), 5

Tannochside (Scot.), 294
Tarpeian Hills (It.), 214
Tarrytown, *see* Greenburgh
Taylor's Brook (Staten Island),
225
Terrace Road (Staten Island), 257
Thames River (London, Eng.),
139
Third Street (Brooklyn), 123
Tibbett's (Tippett's) Brook
(Bronx), 382
Tiber River (Rome, It.), 214
Tompkins Landing (Staten Is-
land), 173, 194, 254, 255
Tottenville (Staten Island), 252,
254, 255, 259, 264, 280, 281
Trevi Fountain (Rome, It.), 79
Trinity churchyard (New York
City), 66
Tuileries, Jardin des (Paris, Fr.),
67
Twenty-first Ward (New York
City), 276
Twenty-third and Twenty-fourth
Wards (Bronx):
conflict over plans, 359
cost of development to be pri-
marily private, 363–364

grid system, unsuitability for
adaptation to, 361
institutions, future, 362
plan for by-roads, 372
plan for major roads, 371
rapid transit routes, 378–381
topography, 360–361

Union Pacific Railroad, 28, 134
new towns planned along, 134
Union Square (New York City),
276
mob gathering at, 417

Vanderbilt Avenue (Brooklyn),
121
Verrazano Bridge (Staten Island),
169
Vienna (Austria), 40, 352, 425
Villa Borghese (Rome, It.), 63
Villa d'Este (Tivoli, It.), 63
Virginia, 51, 141

Walcheren (Neth.), 218
Wall Street (New York City),
179, 181, 394
commuting to, 201–203
Ward's Point (Staten Island), 209,
259
Warren Street (Brooklyn), 97
Washington Avenue (Brooklyn),
97, 122
Water Glade (Staten Island), 274,
276, 277
Water Street (New York City),
394
West Brighton (Staten Island),
280
Westchester, "Westchester
County" census of 1865–1870,
284
Westchester County (New York),
39, 43, 179, 180, 180n, 217, 220
annexation of part of, by New
York City, 330
census of towns (1865–1870), 284
see also specific locations